MEANINGS BENEATH SKIN

MEANINGS BENEATH SKIN

The Evolution of African-Americans

Sherle L. Boone

ROWMAN & LITTLEFIELD PUBLISHERS, INC.
Lanham • Boulder • New York • Toronto • Plymouth, UK

Published by Rowman & Littlefield Publishers, Inc.
A wholly owned subsidiary of The Rowman & Littlefield Publishing Group,
Inc.
4501 Forbes Boulevard, Suite 200, Lanham, Maryland 20706
http://www.rowmanlittlefield.com

Estover Road, Plymouth PL6 7PY, United Kingdom

British Library Cataloguing in Publication Information Available

Library of Congress Cataloging-in-Publication Data

Boone, Sherle L., 1946-
  Meanings beneath the skin : the evolution of African-Americans / Sherle
L. Boone.
      p. cm.
  "Published in partnership with the American Educational Research
Association."
  Includes bibliographical references.
  ISBN 978-1-4422-1310-4 (cloth : alk. paper)—ISBN 978-1-4422-1312-8
(electronic)
  1. African Americans—Race identity—History. 2. United States—Race
relations—Psychological aspects. I. Title.
  E185.625.B66 2012
  305.896'073—dc23   2011021359

©™ The paper used in this publication meets the minimum requirements of
American National Standard for Information Sciences—Permanence of Paper
for Printed Library Materials, ANSI/NISO Z39.48-1992.

Printed in the United States of America

CONTENTS

ACKNOWLEDGMENTS

Since beginning this work more than 15 years ago, I have received blessings, editorial suggestions, critical reviews, and encouragement from many friends, colleagues, and family members. Although it would be impossible to note everyone that helped me as this work evolved, I must thank Howard McGary and Barry Silverstein for constantly noting the value of the work. They provided suggestions that strengthened some important points discussed in this book. I am grateful for the thoughtful observations provided by Larry Duncan, Christopher Harris, Alberto Montare, Mark Seglin, Donald Vardiman, and Jeff Hitchcock during early phases of this work. Larry Duncan was very helpful as a sounding board for several ideas presented in this book. I am especially grateful for the editorial assistance provided by Rakia Clark and Carl Winfield in the final preparation phase of this work. I also appreciate the clerical support services provided by Elizabeth Siders. The research and analyses on critical race theory provided by Matthew Birkhold were invaluable.

I am deeply grateful to William Paterson University for providing the release time, research facilities, research resources, and other supportive services necessary for the completion of this work from its inception to completion. The university provided resources as well as a community that inspired my work and enriched my scholarship.

The observations provided by students enrolled in my Psychology of African American Life classes at the university were very helpful in the preparation of this book.

I am especially grateful for the unwavering support and encouragement on many different levels provided by my wife, Peggy, and my children, JaSaun, Derrick, and Sheree. Undoubtedly, this work would not have been possible without their support. They were a tremendous source of motivation and inspiration for me throughout this work. The editorial comments provided by Peggy were always on target.

INTRODUCTION

Questions about the identity of American-born people of African descents have been debated for decades across multiple disciplines. From the humanities to the social sciences to mathematics, these debates, rightfully, were guided by an assumption that the process of moving from slavery to the nation we have today required an intense adaptability on the part of the African American community at large. From the end of slavery to Jim Crow to election of the first black president of the United States, that says much about the strength of a people and the strength of a nation. However, that truth only addresses a small part of the much larger question about the significance of the concept of race. Over the years, I have pondered even more questions about the cultural and psychological distinctions that these experiences have revealed.

At the university where I teach a course on the psychology of African American life, each year I stand at the front of the class and ask my students for a self-description of their ethnicities and nationalities. It is usually a combination of African American, Caribbean, Latino, and white students, but African American students almost always make up the majority. One of my early assignments for everyone is to write an essay that describes the cultural practices and psychological characteristics of African Americans. I discourage students from using any physical or socioeconomic descriptions. They also are instructed to provide a clear rationale for everything that they write.

After reviewing over 300 essays in six years, I noticed a pattern. Black students *raised in America* described experiences that are the direct result of the country's racially divisive history. They described the remnants of racial slavery and how that has led to disproportionate housing, education, and employment issues among African Americans today. They mentioned successful struggles to overcome these problems, but they also described personal experiences with racism. However, the effects of these racially motivated experiences on African Americans' behavior, emotions, and ways of thinking were noticeably absent in the essays. Conversely, both nonblack students and black students *raised abroad* concentrated on cultural contributions (i.e., jazz and soul music) and perceived personality traits (i.e., hostilities, athletic prowess, strong religious faith), and they largely ignored the deep hole from which these qualities sprang.

The vast differences in the responses from my students compelled me to examine closely the psychological significance of race for African Americans. Unlike indigenous Africans, African Americans have evolved from a society separated largely by race alone. Geneticists and other scientists conclusively debunked the concept of racial superiority in the early 1990s.[1] And in the 21st century, socioeconomic factors seem to play a bigger part in our nation's cultural conflicts. Still, old ideas die hard, and race continues to be a great divider.

Historically, racial categories provide unspoken guidelines for daily interactions among people. Even though the use of racial categories is inherently flawed and provides a support system for racism, they still play a fundamental role in the organization and structure of our world.[2] But the pattern I noticed in my students' essays should not have been as surprising to me as it was. Over one hundred years ago in *The Souls of Black Folk*, W. E. B. Du Bois argued that the process of adapting to racially oppressive conditions forced African Americans to develop a unique way of defining themselves. In an article from just a few years ago by Howard Dodson, director of the Schomberg Center for Research in Black Culture of the New York Public Library, called "'What's at Stake?' Re-defining African-American," Dodson strongly suggests that the unique racial history of African Americans makes them highly distinctive from other ethnic groups.[3]

On the other hand, several African American scholars, including Na'im Akbar, Daudia Jani Ya Azibo, Kobi K. Kambon, M. K. Asante, and Wade Nobles share an Afrocentric theoretical worldview about people of African descents in general.[4] This worldview maintains that people of African heritage share a core of values, beliefs, and behaviors that set them apart from white Europeans. Thus, Afrocentric theorists view people of African descents as a collective community with similar psychological and cultural roots.[5] However, this theoretical perspective has been called into question for several reasons. Numerous differences in the historical experiences have been documented between people of African descents from country to country as well as differences among blacks within the same country. This observation is noteworthy because human values, beliefs, and behaviors are primarily reflections of the historical experiences of people. Unlike most indigenous Africans, African Americans have evolved for several centuries in a racially stratified society dominated by European teachings, philosophies, and customs. In earlier years, few African Americans had opportunities to learn about their African past. Thus, services provided by churches, schools, families, government, and media in many African American communities have been insufficient to teach, maintain, and reinforce universal beliefs and values. Very few empirical studies comparing and contrasting values and belief systems of African Americans and indigenous Africans have been conducted. The research presented in this book casts doubt on the validity of the Afrocentric worldview because, surprisingly, even when compared against groups of people of African descents raised outside of the United States and Africa, the distinctions among African Americans still hold up. But why?

I think it all comes down to how the concept of race is interpreted. The racially stratified landscape that has dogged African Americans for centuries has forced them to evolve a concept of race that is different from other ethnic groups. In particular, findings suggest that African Americans attribute more significance to the concept of race in self-construction than do indigenous Africans. However, the significance attributed to the concept of race by African Americans has evolved in a manner that reflects changes in racial practices, policies, and racist thinking in the United States. Since the early 1950s, numerous measures were implemented at the municipal, state, and federal government levels to eliminate racial discrimination in almost every sector of American society. Despite legal measures and actions taken to bring about racial equality, remnants from the legacy of racial inequality and racial oppression created and sustained by centuries of racial slavery and white supremacy still exist. A basic tenet of critical race theory is that racism remains deeply entrenched in the structural fibers of American society as well as social and political thought in this country—so much so that it often goes unnoticed and is viewed by many people as an ordinary way of life. For these reasons, meanings attributed to the concept of race continue to play significant roles in shaping the behavior and thinking of African Americans. Although blatant racist practices that most people would acknowledge and condemn have declined sharply since the end of the civil rights era, an overwhelming majority of African Americans still believe that racism is alive and well today in the United States. However, most African Americans would agree that considerable progress has been made toward deconstructing racial divides and hierarchies in this country. Therefore, African Americans born after or near the end of the civil rights era may be inclined to attribute less significance to the concept of race and more significance to their nationality than African Americans born before or during the early and middle phases of the civil rights era. Nevertheless, the concept of race continues to play significant roles in shaping the behavior and thinking of African Americans born before, during, and after the civil rights era.

Even though there is a lack of clarity regarding the meaning of race, it always has been a primary defining feature of African Americans' social identity in the United States. African Americans base their racial identity on the perception of a shared racial heritage with other people of African descents.[6] A study by Sherle L. Boone and Steven Buyske notes that, unlike indigenous African respondents, the concept of race for African Americans implies a collective racial consciousness or a sense of "we-ness" that connects them to other people of African descents globally.[7] This collective racial consciousness provides the impetus for African Americans to search for and embrace historical and cultural continuities between themselves and other people of African descents. Historically, African American leaders have been staunch advocates for economic aid and other assistance for black African nations. Further, in light of this racially conscious mindset, African Americans can sometimes lose sight of what makes them unique culturally, even among people who look like them. These psychological distinctions influence how African Americans perceive their relationships among themselves and toward other groups. And it begs several questions: Are African Americans really all that different from other people of African descents around the world? How does race affect these differences psychologically? How large an influence has centuries of exposure to European American values and cultural practices been? What kind of cultural imprint did slavery leave on African Americans, and how is that different, psychologically, from the wars that have occurred in Sub-Saharan African countries between Africans? And finally, are African Americans a "new people" because they have psychological and cultural traits that distinguish them from other ethnic groups?

In short, *Meanings Beneath the Skin* examines how the history of race in America has affected American-born blacks psychologically. By tracing the cultural and psychological transformations among black people in America from the 17th century through today, it examines the concept of race as a psychological construct. This is important because race is the prism through which African Americans view the world. Of course, this is not a hard and fast rule. But generally, the influence of race is so central to shaping the way African Americans see themselves and the world that it often is overlooked and/or underestimated. There are countless historical events and experiences, many of them discussed within this text, that shed light on why this evolved and how this group gradually transformed from African people in America into a "new people" with different personal and global worldviews.

To explore these claims, I have divided the book into eight chapters. While deeply rooted in psychology, in order to fully explore the questions I posed, I turned to history and critical race theory (CRT). This theory suggests that because of racism, the psychological development of American-born blacks cannot be separated from the psychological development of American whites.

Emerging as a critique of the aspect of the civil rights movement that utilized a legal strategy to gain victories, CRT assumes that, at best, courts may be an undependable ally in the struggle for racial equality because the law is not neutral. Accordingly, critical race theorists (CRTs) assume that the protection of white advantage or privilege is a central operating principle in the United States. Therefore, for CRTs, the assumption that the law is neutral serves only to mask the way in which the law is active in producing and maintaining white domination in the United States. Because the law actively produces and maintains white dominance, using it as a means to end white dominance is equivalent to expecting a master to grant his slave freedom on moral grounds. Following this through to its logical conclusion, CRTs argue that legal changes in race and legislation toward racial equality are never only morally motivated but instead occur when the interests of an oppressed group and the interests of whites converge.

Given this insight into the process of interest conversion and the centrality of whiteness, it is important to understand that African Americans have never existed in complete isolation from white Americans. Consequently, it is crucial to explore how changes in United States laws and practices pertaining to racial equality and inequality affected both blacks and whites. Thus, while it is quite obvious that the end of slavery would have changed the way in which race was experienced as a psychological category for blacks, this book provides insights on how the end of slavery also changed race for whites.

Chapter 2 discusses the precursors that contributed to the emergence of racist thinking. This chapter also explores the conditions that led to the expansion of racial slavery along with the emergence of the concept of race as a psychological phenomenon. Chapter 2 examines the impact of slavery and racial oppression on the psychological makeup of American-born blacks. This chapter discusses the use of science to justify the maintenance and expansion of racial slavery. This chapter also explores how the centrality of whiteness informed what I call "folk racism" and played a role in shaping the ways the study of black people was approached and thought about. In this chapter, I use what Du Bois referred to as the "public and psychological wage" of white people—or what many scholars call "white privilege"—as an important force in shaping what I call a "racist worldview."[8] Chapter 3 utilizes the theoretical concepts of the first two chapters and illustrates how they played out historically up until the end of the American Civil War. In chapter 4, I introduce the idea that with the end of chattel slavery there evolved a conflicting psychological dilemma for African Americans that forced them to choose among or try to balance their self-interests, loyalties to their ethnic/racial group, and loyalties to their country.

Chapter 4 marks a turning point in the book because in this chapter it becomes clear that identity formation in American-born blacks has never been fixed. Instead, it has changed in a manner that reflects the ways that the racially driven practices and policies have changed in American society. While not a strictly historical study, the practice of periodization has been quite helpful here. While I do not rigidly categorize the process of psychological racial identity development in African Americans, I do argue that four distinct periods emerge historically. During the first period, from 1619 through 1865, slave communities were transformed from an overwhelming majority of African-born to American-born slaves. Chapters 1, 2, and 3 trace the transformation of Africans brought to America into a "new people" and examine the psychological and cultural implications of this transformation among blacks. Chapter 4 explores identity development in African Americans from the post–Civil War era up to the United States Supreme Court's 1896 decision in the *Plessy v. Ferguson* case. Chapters 5 and 6 cover the third and fourth periods, from the era of post-Reconstruction and Jim Crow laws up to the United States Supreme Court's 1954 decision in the *Brown v. Board of Education* case. Chapter 6 examines the impact of mass protests against Jim Crow laws during the era of the civil rights movement, and beyond, on the identity formation in African Americans. Chapter 7 is a case study exploring the different ways in which American-born blacks view race as compared to other members of the African diaspora. Chapter 8 attempts to take all of the previous arguments and use them to demonstrate how African Americans are a distinct people. A brief epilogue closes the book.

①

DIFFERENT PERSPECTIVES ON THE SIGNIFICANCE OF RACE FOR BLACK PEOPLE

It is not what you call me.
It is what I answer to.

—African Proverb

The history of the racially motivated experiences of blacks in mainland North America is well known and documented. Clearly, the circumstances surrounding the process of adapting to a racially stratified society for blacks in America were unique. The processes involved in their adaptation were dynamic, often reflecting a combination of ongoing changes in racial policies and practices as well as "the spirit of the times." The uniqueness of these experiences fueled the significance and meanings they attributed to the concept of race. Unlike blacks residing in both African and Caribbean nations, blacks residing in America have been identified or referred to primarily by their racial group membership. Historically, they often were lumped together by white Americans with other people of African descents without regard for the unique experiences that served to distinguish them psychologically and culturally. Thus, unsurprisingly, the concept of race has been of paramount importance for self-identification and group identification among them. All in all, when the history of American racial slavery is viewed in combination with racial discrimination, it should be relatively easy to see how the concept of race acquired unique meanings for African Americans.

On the other hand, for people who reside in countries like Ghana or Sierra Leone where the so-called racial makeup is mostly homogenous, characteristics apart from race are used to differentiate people (i.e., religion, tribe, language, etc.). Africans and non-Africans commonly refer to indigenous blacks residing in African nations by their nationalities and ethnicities. Therefore, the significance and meanings associated with the concept of race between African Americans and indigenous Africans are likely to be different. Although the racist history of African Americans and the racist experiences of Africans under colonialism share some similarities, they were not the same. The historical differences between practices of racism in our country and colonialism in Africa cannot be ignored. These differences in practices of racism provided seeds for differences in racial conceptualizations between these groups.

With a focus on racial slavery during the colonial period and colonialism in Africa, this chapter provides a glimpse of conditions and experiences that seemingly contributed to different perspectives on the significance and meaning of race between blacks in America and indigenous Africans. The roles played by leading scholars and members of the scientific community in the growth and maintenance of racist thinking are explored also in this chapter.

THE EMERGENCE OF RACE AS A PRIMARY SOURCE FOR HUMAN GROUP CLASSIFICATION

Originating in the seventeenth century as a group classification, initially race had multiple meanings and was used interchangeably with terms like "nation," "kind," "type," "stock," and so on. But starting as a folk idea in mainland North America and in the British Island plantations, by the late 1600s, race became a popular way of grouping people into separate, discrete, and exclusive populations.[1] It lacked any scientific merit or objective research at the time, but it stuck. And the physical traits that distinguished human groups from each other were arbitrarily linked to behavioral, temperamental, and intellectual qualities that would later become fixed in the mindsets of colonists and used to justify the enslavement of Africans.

Eventually, the science tried to catch up to the folklore. During the second half of the 1700s, the theory that physical traits were somehow linked to psychological traits was challenged by some egalitarians and other antislavery proponents. Yet, in spite of contentions by many anti-slavery proponents that human experiences and not physical traits were of central importance in shaping psychological characteristics, the popu-larity of this belief persisted and grew even stronger into the nineteenth century. Scientists were never able to link the two conclusively, and today's scientists would find the very idea preposterous. But it speaks to the idea that if enough people share a belief, it becomes affirmed, with or without proof. Moreover, if it endures for several generations, the be-lief is accepted as truth. It is widely acknowledged today that folk ideas about race were created to support the expansion and maintenance of slavery in America.[2] And there is growing evidence that the growth of racism and folklore about race were accelerated in response to Bacon's Rebellion in 1676.[3]

Bacon's Rebellion began as a heated debate within the ranks of the Virginia Colony's elite about its Indian policy and profit-making op-portunities. The debate degenerated into an open rebellion that pitted the lower classes, European American bond-laborers, propertyless free people, and black slaves against colonial government leaders and the plantation-owning ruling upper class. Nathaniel Bacon, an influential member of the Colony Council, organized and led the rebellion against the plantation bourgeoisies.

In his book, *The Invention of the White Race*, published in 1997, historian Theodore W. Allen notes that historians have debated about the cause and aim of the uprising for approximately three centuries.[4] Allen contends that some historians have viewed Bacon's Rebellion as an ill-fated attempt to eliminate English domination and establish an independent republic. It also has been viewed as a self-serving vendetta orchestrated by Nathaniel Bacon against William Berkeley, the Virginia governor.[5] Nevertheless, the show of solidarity between the enslaved blacks and laboring-class whites suggests that they collectively resented the oppressive and exploitive conditions imposed on them by the white ruling elites. However, this work is concerned with the significance of that event's aftermath in shaping racial slavery during the seventeenth, eighteenth, and nineteenth centuries.

Although the rebellion was unsuccessful in achieving its desired goals, its popularity led to a temporary breakdown in the governance and social control exercised by colonial leaders. In the aftermath of Bacon's Rebellion, colonial leaders devised ways to strengthen social control over the laboring classes of people as well as other elements of society that threatened their leadership and authority. An issue of importance for them was "how was laboring-class solidarity to be undone?" The preservation of chattel bond-servitude was the primary concern at the highest levels of government in Virginia and in England.[6] A controllable, cost-efficient labor force, as well as social mechanisms for preventing similar class rebellions in the future, was one of the ruling elite's highest priorities. Having already imposed lifetime, hereditary bond-servitude on the black population, colonial leaders recognized that African bond-laborers provided them with a permanent labor force capable of yielding steady profits under difficult economic conditions. The colonial leaders were unyielding in efforts to prevent circumstances that showed potential of jeopardizing the chattel bond-servitude status of African laborers. Therefore, colonial leaders viewed acts of solidarity between African bond-laborers and the laboring, poor European American population as a serious threat. In response to this perceived threat, they enacted laws, policies, and other plans of action that accentuated the significance of race and de-emphasized the significance of class as classification modes of human group differentiation in colonial America. These acts collectively represented a clear sign of racial oppression.[7]

In writings on slave societies, Ira Berlin, a notable historian on American slavery, points out that enslaved blacks were consigned to childhood and savage status. With rare exceptions, free blacks did not fare much better than enslaved blacks. Most free blacks in the Lower and Upper South spent their lives working and living alongside slaves. Unlike white laborers, free blacks were treated often in the same manner as enslaved blacks by the white, ruling elite planters. Although free blacks could hire out their labor, they often were denied rights guaranteed to white laborers.

Colonial leaders promoted racial pride as the major symbol of social distinction among all European Americans, regardless of backgrounds.

Unlike the African bond-laborers and free black population, the colonial leaders knew that a large proportion of the white laboring-class population had criminal backgrounds. The desire to maintain chattel bond-servitude by focusing on race differences outweighed issues of fairness and justice toward people of African descents, regardless of their free or bondage status.

Colonial leaders also created a class division aimed to strengthen social control and reduce laboring-class solidarity. Using an adaptation of the British social class system, the ruling elite planters and public officials created an intermediate (yeoman) category of people to operate as a buffer between themselves and the larger population comprised of all people of African descents along with masses of working people of European descents. Members of the yeoman or middle-class strata were European Americans who received access to some forms of wealth and status as well as privileges and opportunities that were denied to blacks, regardless of their free or bondage status.

In his work on *The Invention of the White Race*, Allen asserts that the banning of free black people from the intermediate stratum was a corollary of the establishment of "white" identity as a mark of social status and race as the major symbol of human group differentiation in the Virginia Colony.[8]

In keeping with efforts to increase the significance of race as a mode of human group differentiation, the Virginia General Assembly passed a series of racial discriminatory laws between 1690 and 1723 that fostered white contempt for blacks and Native Americans. For example, blacks and Native Americans were forbidden to marry whites. The banning of interracial marriage was another way of reinforcing the inferior status imposed on black people in colonial America.[9] It was a way of declaring legally that even if free and prosperous, a black person was not the equal of any white person.

Importantly, average working whites—not just colonial elites—experienced material gains in life because of the ways race changed after the rebellion. By 1660, the terms *black* and *slave* were used often interchangeably in the United States, and between 1680 and 1682, the slave codes became law. With the passage of the slave codes, blacks were not allowed to travel without passes, publicly assemble, testify in court, own property, or participate in general civil liberties or experience any civil rights. In addition to the slave codes, labor also added importance to the way in which race was thought about and experienced by both blacks and whites at this time. Taking into account the awful conditions experienced by industrial white laborers in the North, W. E. B. Du Bois would argue that despite the fact that enslaved black workers were guaranteed housing and food that wage laborers risked going without, "no matter how degraded the factory hand, he is not real estate. The tragedy of the black slave's position was precisely this; his absolute subjection to the individual will of an owner and to 'the cruelty and injustice which are the invariable consequences of the exercise of irresponsible power, especially where authority must be sometimes delegated by the planter to agents of inferior education and coarser feelings.'"[10] Importantly, the reality that black people were real estate meant that white workers were given a degree of freedom only because they were white. Consequently, whites had a different psychological experience than blacks.

With the end of white indentured servitude, blackness became synonymous with being enslaved, and whiteness became synonymous with being free. As noted in the writings of Cheryl L. Harris, "The ideological and rhetorical move from 'slave' and 'free' to 'Black' and 'white' as polar constructs marked an important step in the social construction of race."[11] According to Harris, "because the 'presumption of freedom [arose] from color [white]' and the 'black color of the race [raised] the presumption of slavery,' whiteness became a shield from slavery, a highly volatile and unstable form of property."[12] Thus, due to their possession of white skin, white people experienced the world as free human beings exempt from the threat of becoming real estate. In relation to black enslavement, whiteness became a source of privilege and protection because without white skin, the threat of becoming real estate was very real. Hence, for Harris, "Slavery as a system of property facilitated the merger of white identity and property. Because the system of slavery was contingent on and conflated with racial identity, it became crucial to be 'white,' to be identified as white, to have the property of being white. Whiteness was the characteristic, the attribute, the property of free human beings."[13]

The psychological consequences of this are explicit. No matter how poor white workers in the North were, they were free to sell their labor at their own liberty. In fact, to make this relative privilege explicit, white apprentices ceased to use the word "master" and instead began using the word "boss" to describe a master tradesman in an attempt to distance themselves from black laborers.[14] To maintain this distance, Northern whites would often riot and burn worksites where whites worked with free blacks.[15] In the South, there existed among poor whites an animosity toward the planter class rooted in traditions of class struggle that was undermined by hatred for blacks for two primary psychological reasons. First, poor whites "constituted the police patrol who could ride with planters and now and then exercise unlimited force upon recalcitrant or runaway slaves; and then, too, there was always a chance that they themselves might also become planters by saving money, by investment, by the power of good luck; and the only heaven that attracted them was the life of the great Southern planter."[16] All of these dreams required the possession of white skin. Among whites, the idea that whiteness guaranteed their right to have access to jobs without competition from black workers became a form of common sense that undeniably shaped the way in which they viewed the world, black people, and themselves.

Blacks were denied the ownership of certain types of property, they were denied voting rights and forbidden to hold any office of public trust, and they were denied rights to bear arms to protect their property. Any free black was subject to thirty lashes at the public whipping post for lifting his or her hand against any European American. Edmund S. Morgan was forthright in his contention that race initially gained popularity as a major classification scheme of human group differentiation because of the ruling elites desire to prevent class rebellions involving masses of working people. Solidarity between dangerous free whites and dangerous enslaved blacks was a major source of concern among the ruling elite European Americans. The Virginia General Assembly deliberately adopted policies that galvanized racial solidarity among all classes of European Americans. Racial preference policies adopted by the Virginia Assembly ensured that race would supersede class as a determinant of people's social position in colonial America, regardless of their economic status, because it gave poor whites a stake in being different from blacks.

The adoption and implementation of racial preference policies effectively united all classes of European Americans against the laboring class of blacks in America. In so doing, racial group membership became more significant than social class membership in shaping the social, political, and economic system in colonial America. Although the ruling elite colonists understood that opportunities for making the transition to the yeomen stratum were limited and only a few poor and propertyless European Americans could ever achieve it, they succeeded in using race to forge a consensus among upper- and lower-class European Americans. In colonial America, race became a primary symbol of status in the late seventeenth century. The significance of the social control system established in the Virginia Colony rested on the fact that it served as the model of social order for plantation settlements in other colonies that subsequently evolved.

Racial discrimination laws, myths, stereotypes, and the need to justify racial slavery were pivotal in shaping the early ideas of race. However, the myths and stereotypes that became associated with race thinking were not all new inventions. In an essay entitled, "Antecedents of the Racial Worldview," Audrey Smedley shows that several substantive aspects of race's referential meaning were already well established among the English before they began to use race to denote human group differences.[17]

The concept of "savages," which was introduced by the English during the Middle Ages (and thus long before Europeans had contact with Indians and Africans), contained ideologies in line with the same inequalities racial differentiations supported. The writings of Smedley and Leonard Liggio suggest that the preexistence of the English attitudes and beliefs about the nature of "savagery" were precursors of the elements contained in the meaning of the classificatory term of "race."[18] In the aftermath of conflicts with the Irish, the English introduced the notion of savagery to describe their perceptions of them. In a synthesis of the evolution of the concept of savagery, Smedley suggested that for English people, it reflected a worldview of Irish people. She defined worldviews as highly conditioned mindsets that constitute systematic ways of perceiving and interpreting various world realities through a culturally constructed lens.

The English believed that "savagery" was the most extreme form of the uncivilized human conditions. Their attitude of contempt for Irish lifestyles evolved from a longstanding feud between these two peoples that started with the English invasion of Ireland under the leadership of Henry

II in 1169 and 1171. For the English, savages represented an inherently inferior cohort of human beings who were incapable of civilization and not receptive to redemption or conversion. In a critique of English thoughts and beliefs about the idea of savagery, Smedley put it this way:

> Savages were heathens, having no knowledge of proper government or religion; they were nomadic in their habits, naked, rude, irrational, violent, evil, superstitious, and given to treachery, stealing, and other forms of immoral behavior. . . . In the English collective consciousness, "the savage" was thus a kind of composite of these streams of negative ideas and images that flourished during a period of much social disorder, change, and unrest.[19]

Smedley's own writings not only show a cavalier dismissal of anything that deviated too sharply from the English cultural norms, but they also support the idea that the English are inherently superior to all other groups. Given the longevity of the cultural image of savagery in England and the fact that even the Irish were thought of as inferior, it is not surprising that the colonists viewed Africans and Indians as the most barbarous and uncivilized creatures on Earth.

In the absence of any scientific data or semblance of objective criteria, alleged racial group characteristics as conceived by European Americans were conceptualized as genetically programmed, inheritable, and unalterable for its members. Therefore, unlike the other human group classification terms mentioned earlier, this folk concept of race emphasized presumed innate traits that were created and governed by the rules of nature. The European Americans' folk concept of race assumed that distinct cultural behavior observed in Africans and other non-Europeans was innate or endowed by God. Thus, for many Europeans, the folk idea of race entailed a belief in unalterable propensities that underlay distinct behavioral characteristics associated with different groups. The subjective judgments about distinct physical and behavioral characteristics attributed to different racial groups led to intergroup comparisons and social ranking. Although it contained faulty evaluative judgments that dehumanized people of African descents, by 1723, the folk concept of race was the primary classification category European Americans employed in human group differentiation. They used race to promote the belief that social, political, and economic inequality were in keeping with God's world order.

The first attempt in science to investigate the idea of race occurred in 1735, when Carolus Linnaeus, a professor of botany, grouped human beings into white European, red American, dark Asiatic, and black negro. Using an adaptation of an ancient model of the great chain of being, a hierarchical structure of all living things, Linnaeus ranked these groups in a hierarchical manner. Although physical features provided the primary basis for this racial grouping, Linnaeus also distinguished each racial group by behavioral and other psychological characteristics that confirmed preconceived ideas about race. The rankings favored white Europeans over all non-European groups and placed people of African descents at the bottom of the hierarchical structure. Thus, rather than challenge the validity of the folk notion about race, Linneaus, and subsequently other learned men, engaged in efforts to find support to confirm the European racial worldview. As can be seen here, science is not culturally free; it is influenced by existing knowledge, values, and presuppositions.[20] In an in egalitarian society already characterized by divisions along social class and gender lines, the status elevation of race as a social ranking category provided another mode of human group differentiation to justify social discrimination as well as unequal access to society's resources and rewards.

During the early decades of the eighteenth century, race became *the* major mode of social differentiation in colonial America. As a social principal that influenced the way society allocated resources and status, race superseded all other modes of human group differentiation. In a synthesis of the concept of race, Smedley points out that the use of race for human group differentiation was so pervasive during the eighteenth century that by the early decades of the nineteenth century the concept of race represented a worldview.[21]

Smedley identified several ideological elements contained in the race concept in North America during the eighteenth and nineteenth centuries that clearly provide links to the savage concept. It was the synthesis of these elements that gave meaning to the race concept. Smedley described these elements as:

1. "A universal classification of human groups as exclusive and discrete biological entities. The classifications were" based on

categories that included "superficial assessments and value judgments of phenotypic and behavioral variations."

2. "The imposition of an inegalitarian ethos that required the ranking of these groups vis-à-vis one another." The ranking reflected a re-adaptation of the great chain of being.

3. "The cognitive linking of physical features with behavioral, intellectual, temperamental, moral, and other qualities."

4. The belief that all of the previously referenced qualities were inheritable;

5. "The belief that each exclusive [racial] group. . . so differentiated, was created unique and distinct by nature or by God, so that imputed differences" were innate "and unalterable." Race group differences "could never be bridged or transcended."[22]

When viewed as parts of a whole, these elements created or at the very least reinforced race as a hierarchical concept. This, of course, drew lines of demarcation between racial groups, and anyone who did not abide by this new social paradigm faced dire consequences.

This tactic spread widely during the eighteenth and nineteenth centuries. And this culturally constructed race concept became a racial worldview in the United States, England, France, and other countries in which it mattered.[23] The continued use of the race concept from the twentieth century through present times has served to maintain key elements of the earlier racial worldview in the original forms.

SCIENCE DEBUNKS RACIAL SUPERIORITY THEORIES

Meanwhile, scientific reports continued to disprove theories about racial superiority. Under the auspices of the United Nations Educational, Scientific and Cultural Organization (UNESCO), in 1950, a group of scientists convened to present facts to combat racism. The group concluded that no reliable scientific evidence existed to make biological distinctions for racial group membership. They reported, "For all practical social purposes, race is not so much a biological phenomenon as a social myth . . . [that] has created an enormous amount of human and social damage." Scientific inquiries by groups of experts convened under the auspices of UNESCO in 1951, 1964, and 1967 reached the same conclusion. In recent years, geneticists and other biological scientists who studied physical and genetic factors associated with racial group membership were not successful in efforts to identify genes or physical traits shared by every member of any of the main racial groups. Physical characteristics associated with racial group membership, such as skin color, hair texture, and bone structure, tend to differ more within each racial group than they do between any two racial groups.[24] Moreover, because of racial interbreeding, there are no pure distinct races in a strict biological sense.[25]

Although the scientific merits of racial group membership have never been confirmed, a racial worldview that includes the folk sense of fundamental differences and inequality between human groups classified as separate races is still alive and well in the first decade of the twenty-first century. Folk beliefs about psychological differences based on race remain deeply embedded in the social reality of American life. William I. Thomas captures the essence of it, stating, "If people define situations as real, they are real in their consequences."[26] In an essay on the status of the concept of race, Howard Winant elaborates on the significance of race in the present era. In criticisms of race as ideology, Winant highlights the social reality of race today:

> The longevity of the race concept and the enormous number of effects race thinking (and race acting) has produced guarantee that race will remain a feature of social reality across the globe, and *a fortiori* in the United States, despite its lack of intrinsic or scientific merit. . . . At the level of experience, of everyday life, race is a relatively impermeable part of our identity. U.S. society is so thoroughly racialized that to be without racial identity is to be in danger of having no identity. To be raceless is akin to being genderless.[27]

Observations over many decades clearly show that for most individuals in American society, perceptions of race differences become conditioned early in their lives and bonded to emotions nurtured in childhood. According to Joyce E. King, for whites, these perceptions take the form of "dysconscious" racism. After performing extensive qualitative analysis on the work of her undergraduate teacher-education students, King concluded that white students were dysconsciously racist, regardless of their conscious intentions. They explained the persistence of racial inequality by using white norms and privilege as universal and unquestioned. According to King:

> Dysconscious racism is a form of racism that tacitly accepts dominant White norms and privileges. It is not the *absence* of consciousness (that is, not unconsciousness) but an *impaired* consciousness or distorted way of thinking about race as compared to, for example, critical consciousness. Uncritical ways of thinking about racial inequality accept certain culturally sanctioned assumptions, myths, and beliefs that justify the social and economic advantages White people have as a result of subordinating diverse others.[28]

For King, these tacitly accepted assumptions, myths, and beliefs play a major role in constituting the self-image of many white people. Hence, "any serious challenge to the status quo that calls this racial privilege into question inevitably challenges the self-identity of White people who have internalized these ideological justifications."[29]

Because race plays such a central role in configuring the worldview of whites, many African Americans perceive racial oppression as a relatively permanent condition for them in a society dominated by white Americans. It is a way of thinking that can be hard to break away from. And, it is widely acknowledged. In fact, while addressing approximately 1,400 people during the 2009 Major League Baseball's Beacon Awards program, former President Bill Clinton pointed out that despite such racial progress as the election of Barack Obama as president, the struggle to overcome problems stemming from racism and racial inequality is "nowhere near over."[30] But how does the significance of race for African Americans set them apart from other people of African descents?

Because beliefs about inherent psychological differences associated with racial group membership have been pivotal in shaping African Americans attitudes, feelings, and actions, race is an important socially constructed concept in the larger American society. The meaning of race in this work is guided by the peculiar socially-culturally motivated conditions and treatment imposed by white Americans on African Americans. This work is not concerned with whether race is a meaningful category in terms of biology but rather the prolonged effects of the socially constructed concept of race in the United States on the thinking, emotions, and behavior of African Americans.

THE MEANING AND SIGNIFICANCE OF
RACE FOR BLACK AFRICANS

The idea that race refers not only to people who share physiological traits as descendants of Africa but also cultural and human bonds that reinforce racial solidarity has been embraced by several prominent African American leaders throughout the nineteenth, twentieth, and now the twenty-first centuries, including Alexander Crummell, Edward Blyden, Henry Highland Garnet, and the first president of Senegal, Leopold Senghor. They all believed that the shared struggle among people of African descents was cause for a global coalition, which could be harnessed to fight racial exploitation by whites in any country around the world.[31] After all, the histories and cultural practices of African Americans and people of several African nations parallel in many, many ways. But it is the distinctions unique to each group that make it quite different.

For centuries in precolonial Africa, ethnicity or tribal group membership was the primary source of identification, as it was assigned at birth. Members of an ethnic group shared the same humor, ancestral memories, cuisine, responsibilities, religion folk beliefs, language, myths, heroes, dances, music, dress patterns, language, religion, and family arrangements that distinguished their culture from the culture of others.

People of the same ethnicity shared common ancestry and a common cultural heritage. They considered themselves connected by blood family. In writing in "Language and Ethnicity," Joshua A. Fishman suggests that ethnic identification played an important role in shaping belief systems and cultural practices among the indigenous people in African societies. Commenting on the importance of kinship to ethnic group membership, Fishman states that kinship

> is the basis of one's felt bond to one's own kind. It is the basis of one's solidarity with them in times of stress. It is the basis of one's right to presume upon them in times of need. It is the basis of one's dependency, sociability and intimacy with them as a matter of course. . . . Ethnicity may be the maximal case of societally organized intimacy and kinship experience.[32]

Additionally, in precolonial Africa, ethnic group membership involved a deep, lifetime, emotional bond that required its members to put the group's interest above any individual. Led by kings, chiefs, or queen mothers, ethnic groups defined the ways their members organized and expressed their thoughts, behaviors, and feelings. They also provided religious teachings and practices for their members. Religion was the central cultural component in all ethnic groups. Participation in the practices of traditional African religions among fellow ethnics was a mainstay in all ethnic groups. As can be seen, ethnic identifications reflect the complex interplay of many psychological, social, and cultural variables. Therefore, changes in variables such as race and religion may not negate the ethnic-cultural commonalities that form the core for ethnic identification. Therefore, a person can have strong identification bonds with a racial group, a country, as well as an ethnic group.

Drawing from writings about the Atlantic slave trade, it seems safe to infer that race was conceptualized by Africans only in terms of physical criteria. They did not attribute psychological, cultural, or social significance to the concept of race. The *Atlantic Slave Trade* involved the purchasing and transporting of masses of Africans to the Americas and West Indies as slaves. The cooperation of African kings and traders with European traders was a necessary condition for the mass enslavement of Africans. In the book *Topics in West African History*, Adu Boahen makes these observations about the Atlantic slave trade:

> African scholars and politicians today must be honest and admit that the enslavement and sale of the Africans from the seventeenth century onward were done by Africans themselves, especially the coastal kings and their elders, and that very few Europeans actually ever marched inland and captured slaves themselves. . . . All these slaves were bartered for European merchandise such as guns, gunpowder, calico, rum, and iron and copper bars.[33]

Under the direction of European slave traders, slave dungeons were built on the coastline in West Africa and served as holding posts for enslaved Africans before transporting them across the Atlantic Ocean. The duration of their stay in these dungeons was from three to six months. The treatment of enslaved Africans in these dungeons was so brutal that many of them died there. The conditions in the dungeons could not have gone unnoticed by Africans residing on the coastline. Bearing this in mind, it seems as though very few, if any, of these Africans perceived the European slave traders' actions as racist.

It was renowned African American scholar W. E. B. Du Bois who provided the intellectual framework that first raised the idea of racial consciousness among Africans. In his essay "The Conservation of Races," published in 1897, he writes that it is the duty of people of African descents to conserve "our physical powers, our intellectual endowments, our spiritual ideals; as a race we must strive by race organization, by race solidarity, by race unity to the realization of that broader humanity which freely recognizes differences in men."[34] Du Bois assigned social and psychological significance to the meaning of race. His writings on the significance of race, however, do not include references to cultural commonalities among people of African descents. In light of differences in the geography as well as historical experiences between people of African descents globally, it is hardly surprising that significant cultural differences existed between them then and now. Perhaps as an unintentional result, the absence of common cultural content connecting the indigenous black people in Africa to African Americans and other people of African descents may have decreased the effectiveness of race as a unifying force among people of African descents.

Du Bois also provided the philosophical and practical underpinnings for the Pan-African movement whose aim was to promote racial solidarity among people of African descents all over the world. The decolonization of Africa was one of its top priorities. In the 1997 publication *W. E. B. Du Bois and American Political Thought*, Adolph L. Reed, professor of political science at the New School for Social Research, suggested that Pan-Africanism was a part of a strategy used by Du Bois for African unity, decolonization, and self-governance. At the core of Pan-Africanism was Du Bois's belief in the existence of spiritual ties that bound all people of African descents together. Guided by his vision, the first of five Pan-African congresses was held in 1919. Subsequently, Du Bois became recognized worldwide as the intellectual leader and visionary scholar of the Pan-African movement.[35]

Kwame Nkrumah, the first president of Ghana and a close friend of Du Bois, was the chief proponent of the Pan-African movement in West Africa. Nkrumah supported Du Bois's ideas and worked toward one united, independent West Africa. Before then, for most West Africans, race only signaled biological distinctions. But Nkrumah's (and by extension Du Bois's) use of the term "race" poked at the scabs the exploitation of colonized Africans by Europeans had left years prior.

Nkrumah rarely included the racial problems and struggles of African Americans in his protests. He concerned himself virtually exclusively with the plight of the indigenous people of Africa. Nkrumah was able to use race as an organizing principle politically.[36] While Nkrumah's use of race may have facilitated revolts against colonization in West Africa, it was lacking in cultural content. Thus, it fell short of its original goal to create a united and independent West Africa.

Leading scholars on racism in postcolonial Africa share the belief that remnants of colonialism remain alive and well in Africa today. Although the former European colonies in Africa have been sovereign countries for several decades, in writings published in 2003 and 2008 about the politics of racism in postcolonial Africa, Paul Tiyambe Zeleza, a historian, argues that many postcolonial conflicts in Africa are rooted in the political and cultural economies of former colonial powers. Since achieving independence, African countries have remained economically dependent on former colonial powers. Consequently, many African heads of state may have limited control and influence over resources needed to address pressing economic problems in their countries. These remnants of colonialism have served to keep African countries integrated into the world in subordinate positions. In his book, *The Great Lakes of Africa: Two Thousand Years of History*, published in 2003, French historian Jean-Pierre Chretien notes that racist practices and identities, which were crucial to colonialism, continue to structure African lives. For example, after invading Rwanda, the Belgians placed the Tutsi people in leadership positions over the Hutu people.[37] Starting in 1928, the Belgians established segregated schools for Tutsi children that were superior to schools for Hutu children. Chretien notes that in creating racist education and economic systems that favored the Tutsi, the Belgians share responsibility for the genocide that occurred in Rwanda in1994. In light of the indirect rule that guided colonialism, it is unlikely that the Hutus and Tutsi people perceived the Belgian practices and policies as racist.

Thus, it is not surprising that Du Bois's idea of bringing people of African descents together as one people to resist racist practices and racist policies has not occurred. Kwame Anthony Appiah clearly asserts that what race meant to Africans in postcolonial Africa was not consistent with what it meant to blacks in America. Differences in racial conceptualization between African Americans and indigenous Africans may account, in part, for the failure of attempts by some Pan-Africanists to unite people of African descents for action against racist policies and practices globally. In Appiah's *In My Father's House*, he points out that following decolonization many Africans, including his father, married European women and maintained close ties with Europeans. They did not harbor racial hatred toward Europeans. However, there is no evidence supporting that Appiah's father's personal experience was a trend or response to the Pan-African movement. For example, it is widely recognized that the vast majority of indigenous West Africans had then, and have now, few opportunities for direct contact with Europeans and other white people. Less than 10 percent of West Africans can either afford or obtain a visa to travel abroad to countries in the Western Hemisphere. With a few exceptions, most Africans who travel abroad are students, educated and skilled professionals, or affluent entrepreneurs in their native countries. Members of these groups represent a relatively small proportion of the overall population in their countries. Therefore, to generalize observations about racial attitudes of Africans from these groups to the masses of indigenous people in West Africa is neither conceptually nor scientifically healthy. An idea supported by anecdotal observations and propounded as truth by a scholar that goes unchallenged potentially has enormous consequences, especially on a topic as emotional as race.

Nevertheless, there are several other reasons why Appiah's claim may be true. First, since racism often was manifested by European colonizers through indirect rule, it was not apparent among the indigenous people. Second, many of the indigenous moral and cognitive conceptions remained intact during the colonial and postcolonial periods. Europeans always constituted a tiny proportion of the population in Africa, and as such, most native Africans had minimal contact with white people. Therefore, racial tensions and racial attitudes were not as emotionally driven in West Africa as they were in the United States, South Africa, and Zimbabwe. However, to avoid the pitfalls of being guided by untested beliefs on the social and psychological significance of race among the indigenous people in West Africans, empirical studies of their beliefs are essential.

If race plays a significant role in their psychological makeup, then, what factors or events contributed to it, and what is the nature of the interplay between race, ethnicity, and nationalism among them? Results derived from studies I conducted to assess the significance of the concept of race in the psychological makeup of indigenous Ghanaians and African Americans that are discussed in chapter 7 may help to answer these questions. Unlike African Americans, the results indicate that Ghanaians did not perceive racial group membership as a significant factor in self-construction. Moreover, Ghanaians viewed nationality, cultural kinships, and economic factors as more significant than racial group membership in shaping their relationships with various groups represented in these studies. Therefore, the psychological and social significance of the concept of race for them does not appear to be the same as it is for African Americans.

THE SIGNIFICANCE OF RACE IN THE DIASPORA

People of African descents in the diaspora share many past and present encounters with white people that link them together as a racial group. For example, European slave traders and settlers displaced various groups among them in foreign lands involuntarily; members of these groups were enslaved, humiliated, physically abused, economically exploited, and racially degraded by Europeans, and they were globally oppressed and often culturally uprooted by Europeans. These longstanding practices globally by white people against people of African descents have contributed to the belief among many African Americans that the psychological profiles and perceptions about the social and psychological significance of race are very similar among all people in the diaspora. A careful examination of this assumption reveals a dearth or lacking of definitive evidence to support it.

The practices used in economic exploitation and maintenance of slavery systems globally were not the same. It seems reasonable to conclude from these observations that significant differences in behaviors, attitudes, and beliefs evolved in various slavery societies. In a comparison of slavery in capitalist and noncapitalist societies, Stanley M. Elkins points out many distinctive characteristics of the American slavery system. Elkins indicates that the American slavery system was more self-contained than in most slavery societies, especially noncapitalist societies. In the American slavery system, all avenues of recourse and all channels of communication to the open society for slaves began and ended with the slave master. In his writings on *Slave and Citizen*, Frank Tannenbaum observed that in southern Europe and Latin America, the slave was never cut off from the rest of society.[38] In contrast to the American slavery system, slavery in southern Europe and Latin America was embedded in a legal, ethical, moral, and religious matrix that combined to preserve the slave's individual integrity as the possessor of an immortal human soul. While in America, a slave was a slave for the duration of his or her life, with very little, if any, hope for reversal of perpetual servitude. In Latin American countries, there were a variety of ways that a slave could be emancipated.

Since marriages between slaves in the American slavery system were not legally sanctioned, it was common for husbands, wives, and children to be auctioned and sold to different slaveholders. In Latin America, slaves' marriages were legally sanctioned, and they could not be separated by slave sales after marriage. Elkins notes that slave masters in the American slavery system exercised more disciplinary authority over the enslaved population than in any slave society in the Western Hemisphere. Elkins describes it this way: "The master's disciplinary authority never had the completeness that it had in the United States, and nowhere did he enjoy powers of life and death over the slave's body."[39]

At the core of the American slavery system, there was the assumption that people of African descents were inherently inferior to all other racial groups. This assumption permitted white Americans to denigrate slaves to the status of property and ignore their humanity. Since this race theory was used to justify the American slavery system, free black folks were also viewed in ways similar to enslaved black folks by European Americans. The assumption that slaves were property and subhuman beings was not shared in all systems of slavery in the Western Hemisphere. According to Tannenbaum, Spanish and Portuguese slave laws preserved the human identity of slaves. He describes it this way: "The distinction between slavery and freedom is a product of accident and misfortune, and the free man might have been a slave. As can be seen here, the theory of racial inferiority was not used to justify the enslavement of Africans in the Spanish and Portuguese slave systems."[40]

Since the assumption concerning the racial inferiority of Africans became so deeply embedded in American society, the psychological significance of race for people of African descents in America cannot be ignored. In his best-selling book, *Race Matters*, Cornell West highlights the critical role that race plays in the lives of all African Americans. He notes that all African Americans in the United States were potential victims of white supremacist abuse. Even if they are motivated solely by self-interest and have no interest in concerns of the larger African American community, West contends that they must have concerns about resisting racism. Unlike societies in which the vast majority of its population consists of people of African descents, combating racism is a constant factor in shaping intra-group and intergroup relationships among African Americans. Orlando Patterson argues that the peculiar racist practices in the American slavery system and its aftermath, the neo-slavery of Jim Crow, fundamentally transformed African Americans in ways that make them dissimilar to other people of African descendants in the diaspora. In his book *Rituals of Blood: Consequences of Slavery in Two American Centuries*, Patterson makes the claim that immigrants from Africa are considerably more culturally different from African Americans than are African Americans from any group of white Americans.[41]

The distinctiveness of the American slavery system, coupled with the racial policies and practices that survived it, begs questions concerning its impact on the psychological profiles of African Americans. Did it make African Americans a marginal version of white Americans with a blending of African physical features? Or did it make African Americans a distinctive ethnic group in their own right? Are African Americans a new group of people? Just who are African Americans? This book presents research and analyses that shed light on answers to these questions. Because of the psychological and social significance attributed to race in the United States, it is essential that this factor be considered in any attempt to delineate the distinctive characteristics of African Americans.

In chapter 2, historical events and conditions that most likely were pivotal in shaping the meanings black people attributed to the concept of race during the emergence of African slavery in mainland North

America are examined. Several factors that may be significant in self-identification between both African Americans and other people of African descents, including race, ethnicity, nation, religion, occupation, and the communities in which they live, are examined. But the primary focus of this work is on the social and psychological significance of race in the identities of African Americans as well as its implications for relationships between African Americans and other descendants of Africa.

2

CHANGING FROM AFRICANS TO AFRICAN AMERICANS AND CONCEPTS OF RACE

Ask yourself what would happen to your own personality if you heard it said over and over again that you were lazy, a simple child of nature, expected to steal, and had inferior blood. Suppose this opinion were forced on you by the majority of your fellow-citizens. And suppose nothing that you could do would change this opinion— because you happen to have black skin.

—Gordon W. Allport, 1954

THE EMERGENCE OF RACIAL SLAVERY

Because of the psychological and social significance attributed to race by the larger white American community along with its dominant political, economic, and social positions over African Americans from the eighteenth century to present, the concept of race as a primary source of both self-identification and group identification has been deeply woven into the psyches of African Americans and whites. As a result of slavery and racial discriminatory policies and practices in America, by the turn of the nineteenth century, the concept of race had become a well-entrenched psychological phenomenon for all people in the United States. Audrey Smedley contends that by the end of the eighteenth century, the concept of race had become a worldview, reflecting several beliefs about human differences fused together in a manner that served the political and economic interests of members of the European and American aristocracy.[1] Racial practices and policies undoubtedly helped to shape African American perceptions of themselves and others.

Race, as a folk idea embodied with ethnocentric values, became the centerpiece for shaping the distinctiveness of the psychological makeup of African Americans, which still lasts today. The lasting ramifications of racial discrimination and the strong need some African Americans have to adapt physically to European American physical standards strongly suggests that, for African Americans, race as a psychological phenomenon distinguishes them from other ethnic groups more than anything else.

In 1619, the first cohort of African slaves arrived in Jamestown, Virginia. While this group of twenty new arrivals included some individuals directly from Africa, most of them were Atlantic Creoles, or slaves of African descents who had mixed European ancestry as well. Atlantic Creoles were originally from the western, coastal region of Africa, but because of their parentage, they understood the European languages spoken by colonists and had knowledge about Christianity and other aspects of European culture.[2] They, of course, retained their familiarity with the languages and cultural practices of native Africans who resided in the interior parts of West Africa. This allowed them to have unique, complicated access to both communities, and as Ira Berlin suggests, it helped them function well as brokers in trade negotiations between European traders and leaders of various nations in the coastal region of West Africa. Europeans traders regarded these Africans as shrewd traders with keen knowledge of the intricacies involved in intercultural negotiations. In stark contrast to the full-blooded African slaves who would later be enslaved, the Atlantic Creoles' ability to adopt English cultural practices and to assimilate to colonial society made them seem more of European than African descents.

The slavery practices and policies imposed on the Atlantic Creoles varied from region to region. On one hand, some slave-owners used physical force and other fear-inducing practices to enhance the work performance levels of servants and slaves. On the other hand, some slaveholders provided generous incentives, such as opportunities to hire out their labor, to maintain both favorable working conditions and production levels. This disparity was determined mostly by differences in economic and agricultural conditions that generated wealth and shaped lifestyles in each region.[3] The production of tobacco shaped the economy in the Chesapeake region, which included colonies in Virginia and Maryland. Rice and indigo production shaped the economy in the South Carolina low country. And slave labor in the North and the Chesapeake region supplemented that of family members and European indentured servants. The course of slavery development in each region was influenced primarily by the organization of its economy.

Representing less than 5 percent of the population in mainland North America, early slaves like the Atlantic Creoles were marginal to the central productive processes or economic backbones of colonies in mainland North America. The bulk of the labor force was comprised of laborers transported from Europe—mostly Ireland—as indentured servants. During their terms of service, the working conditions for indentured servants were very similar to the working conditions imposed on the Atlantic Creole slaves. Indentured servants worked without wages from their masters for a term of seven years. Upon the completion of their term of service, they were free to leave, but without any resources to build their own lives, they were unable to become economically independent of the ruling class. The English laws and customs that ruled the New World provided some protection against physical abuse and labor exploitation. Indentured servants, in general, were not required to work on Sundays or holidays, they worked only half the day on Saturdays, and they often took advantage of midday rest periods during the workday. Although English laws did not provide protection for the Atlantic Creole slaves, they received the benefits extended to white indentured servants into the mid-1800s. And though there were sure to be property owners who occasionally treated their indentured servants with extreme cruelty, the courts could get involved to resolve matters of discipline. This is one of the major characteristics that would distinguish *societies with slaves* (like those described here) from *slave societies* (which later changed the face of the new nation and became the new normal).

In slave societies, slavery was the centerpiece of economic production, and large slaveholdings were commonplace. In general, there was minimal contact between slave masters and slave field hands. In societies with slaves, by contrast, slaveholdings were generally small, and slaves were not the primary source of labor. In addition, slave labor was not essential to the central productive processes and was only one of several forms of labor.

Many slaveholders provided independent labor opportunities for slaves and indentured servants. Slaves used the pay derived from their independent labor partially to support themselves and to buy their way out of bondage. Manumission was a widely accepted practice in societies with slaves. While earning reputations as clever bargainers, many black slaves brought to mainland North America before the middle of the seventeenth century gained their freedom. However, since the overall slave population was less than 5 percent of the total population, the free black population during the seventeenth century was too small and too dispersed to constitute a community.

Before the Atlantic Creoles arrived in mainland North America, it was widely acknowledged that people of African descents were enslaved throughout the Atlantic world. They already were debased in the eyes of whites before discriminatory laws were enacted. Early writings suggest that colonists viewed the first African arrivals in mainland North America as inherently inferior to whites from the very beginning.[4] As race was not a common mode of human group differentiation until the last decades of the seventeenth century,[5] social class standing was a significant factor in shaping relationships between Africans and Europeans in the New World. Because of their polygamy traditions back in their homeland, the mostly Irish indentured servants were viewed as uncivil. But the social class differences did not keep slaves, masters, and indentured servants alike from working shoulder-to-shoulder in the fields. Close contact with European Americans on a regular basis enabled slaves in the early years of the seventeenth century to learn firsthand about English cultural practices. Consequently, they were able to make relatively smooth transitions into colonial society when granted freedom.

Even though race may not have been an important determinant of the conditions imposed on people of African descents in America's charter generations, it was a common practice for the English elite to show contempt for any poor and powerless group, especially if they were not English. Ethnocentrism was deeply embedded in the mindsets of English colonists long before they settled in mainland North America. That is to say, the English generally believed that the traditions, customs, values, and beliefs they shared were inherently superior to cultural practices of other groups. Even though they were not too proud to work alongside the Irish or the Atlantic Creoles, the English perceived them with contempt.

As the English colonists continued to establish settlements in mainland North America, they displayed contempt toward Native Americans in a manner reminiscent of their attitudes and behavior toward the Irish. The Native Americans resisted the Christian religious teachings of the English colonists and were consequently labeled evil, sinful, devilish savages. Smedley observed that this belief was pivotal in shaping the English colonists' attitudes toward not just the Native Americans, but the Atlantic Creoles, as well.[6] This misguided belief that non-English, darker-skinned ethnic groups were ungodly made it easier for the English to excuse mistreating them. However, their attempts to impose their attitudes and cultural practices on Native Americans were not successful. In fact, the English dependency on Native Americans' knowledge about the landscape contributed to the English's more restrained efforts to change Native American cultural practices.

THE RISE OF RACIAL SLAVERY AND RACISM

During the second half of the seventeenth century, plantations with large labor forces grew steadily. The growth of plantations in the Chesapeake region and, subsequently, in the Lower South regions, increased the demand for large slave-labor forces. With the expansion of plantations, elite slaveholders and other members of the ruling class transformed societies with slaves into slave societies in the Chesapeake. The transformation usually involved the development of commodities like sugar, rice, tobacco, and indigo, that could command a good price on the international market. The potential for economic growth led to slave societies, which in turn led to an expansion of the Atlantic slave trade. Transported like livestock, human captives were enslaved for lifetime servitude. Unlike the Atlantic Creoles who came from the coastal region of West Africa a century earlier, slaves from the Atlantic slave trade were brought from the interior parts of Africa in the 1700s. The native Africans had experienced little contact with Europeans before they were boarded on ships and transported across the Atlantic Ocean. Ira Berlin observed that slaves from the interior of Africa were provincial with deep roots in the village, ethnic group or nation, and households.[7] European customs, attitudes, and cultural practices were unknown to them.

Back in their homeland, the native Africans identified with their ethnic group or nation but not the continent of Africa. They came from societies in which ethnicity was the principle identifier. Although the institution of slavery was commonplace in West African societies during the same period in history, race did not play any role in it. Therefore, for the first time, Africans brought to America had to view themselves through the eyes of race. Black people brought to mainland North America came from many different nations, but by the time they arrived, the process by which they came to share a common identity was already firmly established.[8] Adapting to conditions of enslavement in a culturally different society that was undergoing rapid transformations forced them to develop behavioral strategies and psychological frames of reference for understanding and coping with the new circumstances they faced.

In contrast to the Atlantic Creoles who had already adapted many European American cultural practices, the new, native African slaves did not readily assimilate. The slaves wanted to preserve their African cultural practices, so they resisted European authority and ignored European cultural practices to the extent that they could. They had to reconcile the gap between their African past and the new, foreign communities that were springing up in the New World, which was changing too rapidly to get a firm grip on it in the first place. There were the white members of the ruling and slaveholders' class, members of the white laboring class, and the Native American population. The new identities among African slaves were also influenced by the land they farmed, the types of crops grown there, as well as the number and origin of slaves imported to work the land. Additionally, their identities were shaped by the nationalities and beliefs of the slave-owning class and the white, non-slave-holding population alike.[9] For these reasons, identity formation in the African slave population followed different paths in the Chesapeake region, the low country, the North, and the Lower Mississippi Valley.

As elite slaveholders and public officials transformed societies with slaves into slave societies, the Virginia Assembly and the Maryland Assembly imposed lifetime service on new arrivals from Africa with laws passed in 1661. Slaves and their offspring became bound to their owners for the duration of their lives, with slave owners assuming almost complete sovereignty over the domain of the plantations. These laws accelerated and reinforced the process of institutionalizing African slavery in mainland North America. Following the lead set forth by the Virginia Assembly and Maryland Assembly, colonies in the Southern region imposed lifetime servitude on enslaved Africans and their offspring. The laws also denied recognition of slaves' humanity, which further facilitated the expansion of slave societies.

The social order of the plantations conceded almost everything to the slave owner and very little to the slave.[10] In view of the authority masters exercised over slaves, paternalism played an important role in shaping all relationships. Slave owners granted themselves the right to enter into the slaves' most intimate affairs, demanded the complete obedience due fathers, and consigned slaves to a permanent childhood. Further, plantation owners treated slaves as though they were too savage to ever rise above the subhuman status imposed on them. Even the death of a slave at the hand by his or her owner no longer constituted a felony in Virginia, and black slaves could not appeal their cases to a court of law. The combined effect of these demeaning practices became a major force in shaping slave life and further perpetuated negative ideas about race. Greed and an unwavering desire for economic growth along with the dishonored status imposed on the slave populations contributed to a callous indifference toward their suffering.

In 1668, white indentured servants still represented the bulk of the labor force. European conquest and disease contributed to a steady decline in the Native American population, and white indentured servants outnumbered black slaves more than five to one in the Chesapeake region. But the rapid growth of plantations required more help. This led to an increase in the number of black indentured servants. And the more black indentured servants and black slaves there were, the fewer white indentured servants were needed. By 1680, plantation slavery became synonymous with African slavery. Although there were some free blacks in colonial America, it was assumed that if you were black, you were a slave. By the end of the seventeenth century, there were considerably more black slaves than white servants. Before the end of the seventeenth century, the permanence of the low social status of black people in mainland North America was established, along with the rise in racial stereotypes and negative attitudes about black people in general.

Blacks that arrived after 1661 worked harder and died earlier. Within a year after their arrival, approximately a quarter of them died. There were no gender distinctions when tasks were assigned. Female slaves were forced to perform the same field tasks as male slaves. And as part of the dehumanizing process, black slaves rarely had surnames, and their first names were commonly shared with barnyard animals.

Systematic and relentless violence occurred frequently. Violence on the part of members of the enslaved population as well as the enslavers was inherent in the management process of forced labor in slave societies. Since slave owners controlled the weapons of coercion, slaves were forced often to behave in accordance to the desires of slave masters and overseers. Slaves strongly resisted the brutality and harsh conditions of enslavement. When violent forms of discipline increased, the level of slave resistance increased. The slaves' resistance occurred in a variety of forms including, but not limited to, suicide, escape, truancy, and insurrections.

Even though slaveholders exercised considerable control over the lives of the enslaved population, slaves were cognizant of the value of their labor. They contested the organization, pace, and intensity of labor on plantations. Slaves became masters of devising strategies to challenge slave owners' demands and expand control over their own labor and lives. The master-slave relationship required a coexistence that fostered cooperation and contestation. With knowledge of their economic value to slave owners, slaves often used this as leverage very effectively to improve their circumstances. Withdrawal of labor or threatening to withdraw labor at critical junctures in the productive process were effective measures taken by slaves to counter slave owners' excessive demands.[11] Slaves were not passive respondents to the demand imposed by slave owners or white overseers. They often took the initiative to operate as change agents in the struggle to control the events that shaped their lives. The behavioral repertoire used by slaves to control their lives and lessen the burdens of enslavement included both proactive behavior patterns (i.e., flattery, cajolery, and appeasement) and reactive behavior patterns of behavior (i.e., truancy, insurrections, stealing, etc.). In his description of the power struggle between slave owners and slaves, Berlin sums it up in this way, "The contest of master and slave was a never-ending war in which the terrain changed frequently but the combatants remained the same."[12] Berlin's observations show that slaves exercised some control over the slave owners as well as themselves.

It was not uncommon for slaves to negotiate better working conditions on plantations, especially in the low country of South Carolina. In the book *Rice and Slaves: Ethnicity and the Slave Trade in Colonial South Carolina*, historian Daniel C. Littlefield notes that unlike most white planters and white laborers, Africans brought to South Carolina were already familiar with the cultivation of rice and other staple crops. Rice was being cultivated in West Africa long before the arrival of Europeans. Slave owners in South Carolina were dependent often on the knowledge of the enslaved population. These slaves used this knowledge to negotiate better working conditions. On many plantations, slaves were permitted to hire out their services on weekends, raise gardens, and sell and trade goods in open market places. These activities provided them with opportunities to become independent and control their personal lives. Financial resources derived by slaves from hiring out their services permitted them to establish a black economy that grew steadily throughout the eighteenth, nineteenth, and twentieth centuries. Knowledge of their influence in shaping their personal lives and lifestyles on the plantations undoubtedly helped the enslaved population maintain their human dignity under conditions aimed to rob them of it.

During the last decades of the seventeenth century, skin color and other physical traits increasingly were used to downgrade the human worth of black people. While focusing on physical and cultural differences, influential slave-owners promoted the idea that Africans were heathens endowed with distinctive physical attributes that made them naturally well equipped for subservient roles as slaves. The application of the term *heathens* to characterize any group of humans implies that the members of such groups tend to display uncivil behavior and intellectual immaturity. Therefore, the colonists began linking together psychological and physical characteristics to justify the treatment of enslaved Africans during the early emergence of plantations.

Winthrop D. Jordan notes that, in response to pressure to justify the slave trade during the eighteenth century, some Englishmen found a way to depict Africans as beasts by comparing them with apes.[13] They made the claim that people of African descents shared closer resemblance to apes than other human beings. Since apes and Africans shared the same homeland, the appeal of this claim was enhanced. This claim allowed them to advance and solidify folk ideas about the savage nature of Africans. Many white folks believed that the use of excessive physical force was in accord with their Christian duty to control the beast in unruly Africans as perceived by them.

The psychological significance colonists attributed to the concept of race evolved from a desire to justify the maintenance and expansion of slavery. From its inception, this idea regarding the natural inferiority of Africans went unchallenged and arguably gave rise to the popularity of the folk idea of race. The degraded status of slaves and meanings associated with the folk concept of race became closely connected. The authority and control exercised by slave owners permitted them to suppress the intellectual, social, and cultural development of enslaved blacks. They altered conditions in ways that reinforced their negative perceptions about people of African descents.

The degradation of the black slave populations was accompanied also by the degradation of free persons of African descents in mainland North America. For example, laws were passed that denied free blacks from employing the services of white indentured servants. Laws were enacted that reduced opportunities for interracial mixing among black and white people. Article XI contained in the 1705 Virginia slave code adopted by the General Assembly shows the rise of racism in mainland North America:

> And for a further christian care and usage of all christian servants, Be it also enacted, by the authority aforesaid, and it is hereby enacted, That no negros, mulattos, or Indians, although christians, or Jews, Moors, Mahometans, or other infidels, shall, at any time, purchase any christian servant, nor any other, except of their own complexion, or such as are declared slaves by this act: . . . shall, notwithstanding, purchase any christian

white servant, the said servant shall, ipso facto, become free and acquit from any service then due, and shall be so held, deemed, and taken: And if any person, having such christian servant, shall intermarry with any such negro, mulatto, or Indian, Jew, Moor, Mahometan, or other infidel, every christian white servant of every such person so intermarrying, shall, ipso facto, become free and acquit from any service then due to such master or mistress so intermarrying, as aforesaid.[14]

Dialectically, this gave rise to the importance of whiteness as a social category and even as a form of property.

Quoting Jeremy Bentham, legal scholar Cheryl Harris argues, "Property is nothing but the basis of expectation . . . consist[ing] in an established expectation, in the persuasion of being able to draw such and such advantage from the thing possessed."[15] Thus, as the slave codes became law, whiteness became a form of property because it carried with it the expectation that one would remain a free laborer. Bearing this in mind, as the number of imported Africans increased and the number of indentured white servants decreased, the slave codes gave formerly indentured white servants the reasonable expectation that they would not again have to return to a life of servitude. Harris contends that this development is crucial because:

> In a society structured on racial subordination, white privilege became an expectation and . . . white-ness became the quintessential property for personhood. The law constructed "whiteness" as an objective fact, although in reality it is an ideological proposition imposed through subordination. This move is the central feature of "reification": "Its basis is that a relation between people takes on the character of a thing and thus requires a 'phantom objectivity,' an autonomy that seems so strictly rational and all-embracing as to conceal every trace of its fundamental nature: the relation between people."[16]

For Harris, what was in all reality a human relation became a fixed object, and this object resulted in one group of people being seen as human with another group of people seen as property themselves.

The growth of black indentured servants and the degradation of free black people were indications that race as the primary criterion of human group differentiation was increasingly becoming more prevalent. Racism consequently became a burden for all people of African descents, no matter their social status (if they were free) or their ancestry (if they were an Atlantic Creole). The laws adopted by the Virginia General Assembly affirmed the inferior social status assigned to all people of African descents and also provided the legal framework for three separate and unequal nations, comprised of white people, black people, and Native Americans.

Economic and political circumstances in the second half of the seventeenth century were pivotal in the creation of race as a major mode of social division. Plantation owners' concerns about the stability of chattel bond-servitude were heightened after Bacon's Rebellion of 1676. Owners believed that slave labor was necessary for the critical commerce on which the colonies depended. Slavery was a profitable enterprise for slave traders, slave owners, and the English government. The dependence on black bond-labor coupled with fear of coalitions between the black and white bond-labor classes compelled white plantation owners to accentuate the racial differences to maintain social order and economic prosperity. Although racial discrimination laws had been enacted during the 1660s, it was not until the late seventeenth century when major writers began to use race as an organizing idea and as a way of describing human groupings.[17] Many key ideological ingredients contained in the folk concept of race that shaped a racial worldview in the nineteenth century already existed in the late years of the seventeenth century before educated, elite Europeans considered it as a way of interpreting human group differences.

RACIAL OPPRESSION, THE CONCEPT OF RACE, AND IDENTITY IN THE 1700S

It was early in the eighteenth century that racial slavery became fully intertwined into the social, cultural, economic, religious, education, and government underpinnings in mainland North America. With race and slavery already closely linked together, race became the major mechanism employed by Europeans to deal with human group differences. Race took priority over social class, gender, religious, and cultural considerations as ways of interpreting human group differences in Europe and mainland North America. From its inception, the folk idea of race denoted non-transcendent differences between human groups. While promoting the idea that different physical characteristics account for differences in cultural behavior, European American colonists used race to make social, political, and economic inequality a condition governed by the rules of nature. Even in the absence of scientific merits, the folk idea of race went unchallenged by learned men of that era.

In the 1700s, many European scholars were members of the privileged class with vested interests in international trading markets. Self-interest and ethnocentrism raise serious doubts about the willingness of these scholars to be open minded in their judgments of Africans. The popularity of using the folk idea of race to justify the enslavement of blacks grew steadily. As slave societies grew during the 1700s, European Americans' beliefs in the inherent inferiority of people of African descents hardened. Violence and dehumanizing conditions imposed on enslaved blacks escalated steadily. These conditions were countered often by violent expressions of resistance among the enslaved population. In 1712, a slave revolt occurred in New York City, which involved approximately twenty-five blacks. In 1739, a revolt involving between fifty and one hundred slaves took place in Stono, South Carolina.[18]

Although opportunities for slaves to control their fates were sharply curtailed by slaveholders, the slave revolts indicate that the struggle to control their own destinies was an ongoing process. This ongoing power struggle between slaveholders and the enslaved population indicates that slavery always was an unstable institution. The instability of slavery served to keep hope alive among the enslaved population. Berlin notes that almost all agreements that evolved in the master-slave relationship were tentative.[19] Most agreements were short lived because as power shifted "from master to slave and back to master, the terms of slavery would again be renegotiated."[20] Slaves' knowledge about the economic value of their labor precluded slave owners from ignoring their concerns.

Increasingly, the property value of enslaved blacks overshadowed their personhood in the eyes of whites. The ownership of property was highly prized in English culture. Historically, in England an individual's human value was assessed primarily in terms of the property that one possessed.[21] A person without property lacked respect and was viewed as a social nonentity in English society. This cultural mindset of European Americans facilitated the psychological transformation of people of African descents into slave property characterized by an existence as things or nonhuman forms of beings. When viewed as property or things rather than persons, gross brutality can be inflicted on such persons without feelings of guilt.

Lacking economic and political clout to effectively challenge racism, free blacks could no longer take refuge in the laws established for free white people. As previously reported, in the early 1700s, laws were enacted in the Chesapeake region that denied free people of African descents the right to vote and participate in any role of public trust. Legislation was enacted that barred them from serving as witnesses in any case against a white person under any circumstances. Laws also forbid free blacks from possessing guns and any weapon of self-defense. They were subject to thirty lashes at the public whipping post for acts of self-defense against a white person. Free blacks in slave societies, like enslaved blacks, had no legal recourse if their rights were violated by a white person, including the sexual abuse of black females. In a word, the actions taken by legislators and public officeholders in slave societies cemented the low social status of both free and enslaved people of African descents. The laws enacted denied all people of African descents opportunities to advance their social status by reducing all of them to the same low social status in the eyes of whites.

In this spirit of the times, lawmakers in the Chesapeake region enacted legislation that racially discriminated against people of African descents, ranking their social status below criminals. The emergence of race as the dominant mode of social stratification forced both free and enslaved black people to pay close attention to how whites thought about race. They had to understand all the social, political, and economic consequences if they were ever going to have a chance of defining themselves individually or gaining their own freedom. Moreover, they had to understand that, as CRTs have advocated, the historical existence of racism and white privilege desensitized many white Americans to racism. Racism became so deeply entrenched in their thinking as well as actions that it often was non-contemplative and an ordinary way of life.[22] As a result, the meanings white people attributed to the concept of race served as psychological frames of reference for blacks, which included guidelines for their thinking, behavior, and emotions in the presence of whites. Because the white way of seeing and doing things was the dominant way of doing things, CRTs have called white descriptions of social realities "stories" or "dominant narratives." On the other hand, the meanings black people attributed to the concept of race provided different frames of reference, which governed their thinking, behavior, and emotions in the presence of other blacks. CRTs have called these "counter-stories" or "counter-narratives." The survival needs created by circumstances surrounding the lives of black people may have precluded most of them from openly expressing candid viewpoints about the significance of race, yet many blacks shared a common understanding of how to survive.

Africans brought to America spoke many different languages when they arrived. But the language barriers between them were short lived. In his writings about racial slavery in the United States, Eugene D. Genovese suggested that even during the voyage to America, enslaved Africans began breaking down language barriers among themselves.[23] The nature of the harsh conditions imposed on enslaved Africans made communication among themselves more important than with whites. Africans brought from the interior parts of Africa had very limited or no knowledge of the English language. They had problems comprehending and expressing ideas to English-speaking persons. The communication barriers encountered by these Africans made it easier for their enslavers and other English speakers to formulate negative perceptions about them. Limited English linguistic skills made enslaved Africans easier targets for scorn and racist epithets.

As the hostility between slaves and masters became more intense, African slaves had little opportunity to seriously contemplate the meanings behind race or why and how it progressed. But there is evidence that some enslaved Africans did. During the first quarter of the eighteenth century in the Chesapeake region, in fact, numerous conspiracies and insurrectional plots against slavery occurred.[24] Given the unpleasant circumstances in which black people struggled with white people to control their destinies, it raises the possibility that most blacks may have placed more psychological significance on the idea of race in defining white people than in defining themselves.

Going into the eighteenth century, racial discrimination and slavery exacerbated cultural-behavioral differences between slaves and masters. Native-born Africans laid the foundation for the cultural life that evolved in slave communities.[25] They defined the codes of conduct, morality, and interpersonal relationships within the slave quarters. Native Africans defined the conduct of religious services, family life, entertainment, and communication practices. The cultural life in slave communities was rooted in African tradition. Shortly after African slaves arrived in America, they began merging their cultural commonalities together to form a mutual support community for the preservation of their human dignity and collective survival. The oppressive and brutal conditions of enslavement forged a sense of community and family among them. African beliefs and values provided the psychological and social underpinnings for the slave communities that evolved.[26] It was in this sense that Du Bois would insist in 1935 that, "in origin, the slaves" in the United States "represented everything African."[27]

In view of slaveholders' plans of action to wipe out African cultural practices among enslaved Africans, enslaved Africans had to change many native cultural practices in order to adapt to conditions of enslavement. The process of adapting to the institution of racial slavery and racial oppression required native Africans to assimilate and accommodate their African cultural practices to the dominant European culture in America. The maintenance and nurture of select African customs, beliefs, and values, coupled with accommodation to European customs, beliefs, and values among native Africans in America, provided seeds for the evolution of a new distinctive ethnic group consisting of people of African descents born in America.

The cultural-behavioral gap between blacks and whites widened even more on plantations where slaves were forced to survive under brutish and primitive conditions. When forced to live under inhumane conditions, slaves invented and practiced unique emotional and behavioral responses that helped them cope or survive as they searched for ways to improve or escape from these conditions. Therefore, it is hardly surprising that as living conditions for blacks worsened, the cultural-behavioral gap between them and whites grew. It was a longstanding practice among elite members of English society to use so-called natural laws to account for behavioral differences associated with social class and cultural variations. The expansion of the cultural-behavioral gap between blacks and whites reinforced the belief among whites that physical and behavioral traits were inherently connected.

GROWTH AND DIVERSITY IN THE BLACK POPULATION

Throughout the eighteenth century, the black population grew steadily and became more diverse. The slave population was 6,971 in 1680; 28,958 in 1700; 70,043 in 1720; 246,648 in 1750; 469,867 in 1770; and 717,021 in 1790. These groups consisted of native-born enslaved Africans, American-born enslaved Africans, and other people of African descents with partial Indian and/or white European bloodlines. Race was the primary factor used by whites to determine worth and/or social status. But more drastic physical differences exacerbated the harsh treatment many slaves were already receiving. The more African a black person's features, the more likely he or she was to be enslaved. Blacks with more European features (due to interracial mating) were treated more humanely.

In the early decades of the eighteenth century, native-born Africans represented an overwhelming majority of the black population in mainland North America. But, American-born people of African descents were the faster-growing enslaved population. These American blacks constituted the emergence of a "new people" characterized by a phenomenology or view of the world that was different from their enslavers and their ancestors. Before the end of the 1740s, the American-born enslaved population had outgrown the native-born enslaved African population. This population shift contributed to cultural changes in slave communities as well as changes in the conduct of the power struggles between the enslaved population and the enslavers. The new generation of American black people was healthier and lived longer than the new arrivals from Africa. Unlike non-English-speaking Africans, American blacks spoke English and more easily accepted Western culture. This transformation in the worldview of American blacks signaled the beginning of the evolution of a new people characterized by a worldview and frames of references that were different from their African ancestors. They had, at best, very limited second-hand information about African history and cultural practices. The meanings and historical significance of cultural practices that were retained on plantations were unknown to most American blacks. Given this condition combined with the lowered status and restrictions imposed on African cultural practices by white Americans, it would seem that American blacks would have readily adopted European cultural practices. However, this did not occur because native Africans had already established, in slave quarters, ways of thinking and acting that had survived the Middle Passage. Therefore, the American blacks performed African rituals and other cultural practices, which were retained in slave communities, without knowing the meaning or historical significance of them. Many African cultural links were either lost or changed in ways noticeably different from their original forms.

The rapid growth of American blacks had a pronounced impact on the culture that evolved in slave communities as well as cultural life among free blacks in America. With English as their first language, American blacks were able to adjust their sacred and secular worlds to the requirements of the European culture. With the emergence of the new culture, African Americans were equipped with the knowledge to challenge their owners from a newfound position of strength.[28] There was considerable congruence between the cultural practices of American blacks and Anglo American culture. However, American blacks adjusted and maintained many African cultural practices in the ways that they understood them.

The provincial nature of enslaved native Africans, as well as their limited communication skills in English, prevented them from fully understanding the worldview of their white masters. Though language and some other cultural differences existed between native enslaved African and enslaved American blacks, they were able to bridge communication and cultural gaps to permit a sense of community to evolve among them. The process of adapting to racial slavery forged a sense of community among them with African beliefs and values providing the psychological and cultural underpinnings for it. Building community and emotional bonds helped Africans in America survive and retain their human dignity.

The collective suffering and yearning for freedom from the burdens of enslavement shared among native Africans and American blacks apparently promoted group solidarity and provided them with a basis for group membership identification. Group solidarity in slave communities made it easier for them to overcome the language and cultural barriers that existed in the slave quarters. Ideas about the meaning of race probably carried greater psychological significance for American blacks than it did for displaced native Africans in America. Unlike American blacks, ethnic identification provided most Africans brought to America with a coherent sense of self before they were captured. Native-born Africans were less likely than American blacks to assimilate European American ideas about race into their psychological makeup. Folk ideas about the significance of race were pivotal in shaping the psychological makeup and cultural lifestyles of American blacks.

The living and working conditions for slaves varied from plantation to plantation and was based largely on the whim of the slave owner. But different regions had their own trends. Slaves were denigrated to the base of civilization as savages.[29] In the Chesapeake area, chattel slavery connected the slave to his master as personal property, transferable at will to another person. In colonial South Carolina in the early decades of the eighteenth century, the master was entitled to the slave's service but not to his person. Though its usage developed earlier, it was not until 1740 that lawmakers in South Carolina enacted legislation to legalize chattel slavery.[30]

During the last decade of the seventeenth century in low country South Carolina, rice became the dominant staple crop. Wealth derived from rice exports led to the rapid growth of plantations in this region. Thousands of slaves were imported from Gambia, Angola, and other rice-growing regions in Africa. By the 1720s, the slave population more than doubled the white population in low country South Carolina. European colonists in South Carolina showed a preference for importing Africans who were familiar with rice cultivation. In his work on slavery in South Carolina, Peter Wood indicates that many Africans from rice-growing regions probably knew more about rice cultivation than their masters.[31] Rice was cultivated in West Africa long before the arrival of Europeans.[32] Knowledge about rice cultivation that Africans brought with them to South Carolina placed them in strategic positions to negotiate working conditions. This knowledge provided them with some control over shaping their lives in their ongoing power struggle with slave masters.

Unlike in the Chesapeake region, where ethnic groups were broken up, the slavery trade practices in South Carolina allowed for enslaved ethnics to remain in close proximity with each other and to retain many African cultural practices on plantations. There were plantations in this region comprised of several hundreds of slaves living in large units and working under the supervision of black drivers with rarely a white person in residence.[33] Elite slave-owners in South Carolina often resided on estates in nearby urban areas and employed propertyless white men from the laboring class as overseers of the plantations. Employing poor white persons as overseers was just one of several ways that ruling elite colonists gave social significance to the meaning of race. A message conveyed through this practice was "Every white man, no matter how degraded, could now find pride in his race."[34] Although these elite slave-owners in South Carolina periodically visited the plantations, slaves who worked in the fields had very little or no contact with them. These slaves learned very little about their owners or European cultural practices. Consequently, the imported African population was able to retain many African cultural practices, including linguistic expressions, on plantations in low country South Carolina with minimal interference from whites. It was not unusual for slave owners in this region to support reproduction and stability in slave families. The practice of keeping slave families intact usually reflected slave owners' desires to bolster wealth rather than humanitarian reasons. The maintenance of stability in slave families was aimed to increase the reproduction of prospective bond-laborers and curb threats of runaways.

The slaves' demography and economy in South Carolina were different from the same in other colonies in a variety of ways. Demographic and economic conditions helped to shape the distinctiveness of cultural life in slave communities as well as the power relationship between masters and slaves in this region. Many slaves, who resided in the cities of Charleston and Savannah, were granted opportunities to hire out their labor and trade at market places. The lifestyles of free blacks and many slaves who resided in these Southern cities were often quite similar.[35] Founded as a non-slave colony in the 1730s, with exconvicts and other poor whites as laborers, by 1750, the colony of Georgia followed the lead of South Carolina and also became a slave society.

Even as the lower states abandoned societies with slaves, colonies in the North held firm to it. Slave labor in the Northern colonies played a vital role in generating wealth, but slaves there performed their tasks side by side with white indentured servants and free blacks. The high demand for slave labor led to a steady growth of the enslaved black population in the North during the eighteenth century. By midcentury, slaves represented approximately one-third of the labor force in southern New England.[36] Historians have not reported any significant antislavery sentiment in the European American population during the first half of the eighteenth century.

The living conditions for blacks in societies with slaves in the North were not better than slaves elsewhere. And, as time wore on, their privileges became more and more limited.[37] During the early 1700s, for example, slaves in New York lost the right to hold property as well as the choice of living with family members. And slave owners often separated family members and restricted visitation opportunities for them. Laws were enacted in Northern colonies that both expanded the power of slave owners over slaves and made manumission more difficult by imposing penalties on slave owners for the conduct of former slaves.[38] In many Northern colonies, free blacks were denied the right to vote, testify in court, serve on juries, bear arms for protection, and own property. Free blacks could be punished like slaves for certain offenses. In a word, they were treated like "slaves without master." Unsurprisingly, the free black population declined steadily during the early decades of the eighteenth century.

In light of differences in the geography, demography, economy, and history of each region, variations in cultural practices in the slave communities were inevitable. That is to say, while there were probably many similarities in lifestyles of slaves in general, there were some differences in slaves' lifestyles that reflected some of the unique features in each region.

Practices of racial oppression and racial discrimination directed toward people of African descents were just as widespread in the Northern colonies as in other colonies in mainland North America. By the early years of the eighteenth century, European Americans viewed slavery as a natural condition befitting people of African descents across the colonies throughout mainland North America. This attitude among white people was so pervasive that most of them viewed free blacks as misfits in the larger society. Before the Revolutionary era, the free black population was small and possessed limited resources. They lacked the political and economic clout needed to get favorable consideration for their concerns. It was a common practice for white people to lump together free blacks and the enslaved black population and to view them with the same manner of contempt. This practice contributed to a complex interplay between slavery, social class status, and racial group membership. That is, for people of African descents, race was likened to slavery and low social class status. In the eyes of white people, if you were black, presumably you were a slave relegated to permanent low social standing. If you were among the small cohort of free blacks, your social standing in the larger society was no better. You still were considered subhuman with social standing below even white criminals, beggars, and convicts. To liken blacks to slaves was to denote the inherent inferiority of their personhood and deny them the natural rights granted to white people.

THE REINFORCEMENT AND MAINTENANCE OF FOLK IDEAS ABOUT RACE

The imbalances that characterized the development of slavery were not evident in the evolution of folk ideas about race. Unchallenged by clergymen, political leaders, or members of learned societies, popular folk ideas about race strengthened throughout the eighteenth century. Historians have not provided evidence that shows that the evolution of ideas about race followed the same pattern. The practices of lawmakers and slave owners in each region show that the evolution of the folk idea of race remained intact. Beginning in the 1730s and continuing through the twentieth century, members of learned societies conducted studies to confirm the presumed inferior nature of Africans and their descendants.[39]

The assumption of African inferiority was derived primarily from descriptions, commentaries, speculations, and opinions of white slave-owners, travelers, missionaries, explorers, and slave traders.[40] It is widely acknowledged that when self-interest is at stake, such as in the situation of the European colonists, people's perceptions and interpretation of events are often biased by their preconceived beliefs and expectations. They tend to see what they want to see and remember those things that fit preconceived beliefs and expectations. Events that do not confirm or refute people's preconceived beliefs are often ignored, misperceived, or forgotten. Psychologists suggest that this confirmatory bias or selectivity in both perception and memory is an unconscious process that may be triggered to help sustain a person's desired self-image.[41] It concludes that reports about Africans from slaveholders, slave traders, and others were full of subjective prejudiced confirmatory biases. Given the insights of Cheryl Harris and David Roediger, what must also be inferred from this is the idea that white scientists were actively confirming their own whiteness by ignoring, misperceiving, and forgetting events that did not support their view of black people and conversely of themselves. For the duration of the eighteenth century, leading European scholars and writers relied heavily on information obtained from these sources to inform the public about the nature of black people. Viewed as highly credible sources, the writings of these scholars reinforced the belief in the natural inferiority of people of African descents in the minds of the vast majority of Europeans and Americans during the eighteenth century and also confirmed the image white people had of their own whiteness. It was in the latter years of the eighteenth century when the physiologist and founder of modern anthropology, Johann Fredrick Blumenbach, published anatomical research to investigate the relationship between primates and humans, and this work led to an increase in naturalistic studies on race differences. Nevertheless, the earlier nonscientific reports prevailed as primary sources for information about Africans and other racial groups.

Before scientists began to study racial group differences during the eighteenth century, the assumption that Africans and their descendents were inferior to whites was a shared foregone conclusion. The observations of the Scottish philosopher David Hume illustrate the role that ethnocentrism played in the formulation of Europeans' negative perceptions of Africans. Hume said:

> I am apt to suspect, the negroes, and in general all the other species of men (for there are four or five different kinds) to be naturally inferior to the whites. There never was a civilized nation of any other complexion

than white, nor even any individual eminent either in action or specula-
tion. No ingenious manufactures amongst them, no arts, no sciences.
On the other hand, the most rude and barbarous of the whites, such as
the ancient GERMANS, the present TARTARS, have still something
eminent about them, in their valour, form of government, or some other
particular. Such a uniform and constant difference could not happen, in
so many countries and ages, if nature had not made an original distinction
betwixt these breeds of men.[42]

Like the writings of Linnaeus and other contemporary scholars in Europe, Hume's writings were widely read by educated and influential
people in mainland North America and Europe. Leading scientists,
philosophers, and people of letters throughout the mainland shared
ideas about the nature of people of African descents. They reached a
consensus that Africans were naturally inferior to white people.[43] By
the mid-1700s, this belief about people of African descents had become
so widespread that even free blacks with impressive credentials were
viewed with contempt by the least respected members of the white
population. This observation suggests that an overwhelming majority
of white Americans believed that there were innate psychological differences between the races that favored them. Thus, when whiteness
became a form of property and science began to protect that relationship as legitimate scientific knowledge, slaveholders no longer harbored
fears of white indentured servants and blacks uniting in servile rebellion, such as Bacon's Rebellion of 1676, because they no longer had to.[44]
The belief of black inherent inferiority to other human groups was so
widespread and deeply embedded in the psyches of white people that
it would have taken several generations to change this mindset. Given
that the poorest white people also benefitted from this belief, there was
no compelling reason for them to change this mindset.

Deeply grounded in ethnocentrism, the folk idea of race, which
linked together physical traits, psychological traits, and cultural practices as natural givens, had become widely accepted throughout Western Europe and North America by the mid-eighteenth century. As a
way of interpreting what was already viewed as an inherently unequal
hierarchy of human groups, race clearly took priority over social class,
gender, age, religion, ethnicity, nationality, and any other sources used
to interpret human group differences during the mid- and late-1700s.[45]

Even though white people, in general, apparently viewed blacks as ugly, treacherous, uncouth, childlike, stupid, and ignorant, Winthrop Jordan reported that miscegenation was widespread in all English colonies.[46] The mulatto population grew steadily during the eighteenth century. While acknowledging the incompleteness of information about interracial sexual unions, Jordan suggested that miscegenation probably occurred more during the eighteenth century than any time since. The miscegenation that involved white women and black men occurred occasionally, but interracial sexual unions involving white men of every social rank and enslaved black women occurred so often that colonists as well as European travelers in the colonies acknowledged it as another facet of American life. Throughout colonies in the mainland, English settlers frowned on miscegenation and used the legislative process to pass laws that prohibited it. Nevertheless, interracial sexual unions between white men and enslaved black women persisted for the duration of the eighteenth century. The interracial sexual practices during the eighteenth century cast doubt on the firmness of white men's conviction about the so-called subhuman and savage characteristics of Africans. It would seem that the perceived negative characteristics that they associated with Africans would have served for them as an aversion for sexual unions with women of African descents. On the contrary, the widespread miscegenation raises the possibility that white men of the eighteenth century perceived black people as being more similar to them than they were willing to acknowledge. Some white men who had sexual intercourse with enslaved black women could have been acting out lustful fantasies of power and control related to negative images about race, gender, class, or fear of personal inadequacy. On the other hand, some white men showed genuine compassion for black concubines and offspring born from such sexual unions but were unwilling to publicly acknowledge the contradictions in their behavior, attitudes, and beliefs about race.

THE RISE OF OPPOSITION TO THE AMERICAN SLAVERY SYSTEM IN THE 1700S

From the beginning, the power struggle between slaves and their owners played a pivotal role in shaping the relationships between black and white Americans. Black people learned to mask feelings of resentment, mistrust, and hostility, as they did what they had to do to survive, all the while surreptitiously plotting strategies to gain freedom. After all, human oppression breeds resistance. Rumors about slave revolts were widespread after slavery was legalized. Winthrop Jordan points out that from the last quarter of the 1600s through the eighteenth century, many white settlers were consumed with fears of African slave rebellions on plantations in slave societies and in some areas of the North.[47] Fear of slave rebellions compelled planters to adopt slave codes for the prevention and deterrence of them.

Although rumors of slave rebellions were common, actual rebellions were not common.[48] However, slave rebellions occurred often enough to leave long-lasting horrific impressions that left no doubt about slaves desire for freedom. The following excerpt from a report on the slave insurrection in South Carolina in 1739 provides a glimpse of the intensity of the hostility, hatred, resentment, and violence that slavery fostered:

On the 9th day of September last [1739] being Sunday which is the day the Planters allow them to work for themselves, Some Angola Negroes assembled, to the number of Twenty; and one who was called Jemmy was their Captain, they surprised a Warehouse belonging to Mr. Hutchenson at a place called Stonehow; they there killed Mr. Robert Bathurst, and Mr. Gibbs, plundered the House and took a pretty many small Arms and Powder, which were there for Sale. Next they plundered and burnt Mr. Godfrey's house, and killed him, his Daughter and Son. They then turned back and marched Southward along Pons Pons, which is the Road through Georgia to Augustine, they passed Mr. Wallace's Taxern towards day break, and said they would not hurt him, for he was a good Man and Kind to his Slaves, but they broke open and plundered Mr. Lemy's House, and killed him, his wife and Child. They marched on towards Mr. Rose's resolving to kill him; but he was saved by a Negroe, who having hid him went out and pacified the others. . . . They burnt Colonel Hext's house and killed his Overseer and his wife. They then burnt Mr. Sprye's house, then Mr. Sacheverell's, and Mr. Nash's house, all lying upon the Pons Pons Road, and killed all the white people they found in them. . . . They increased every minute by new Negroes coming to them, so that they were above Sixty, some say a hundred, on which they halted in a field, and set to dancing, Singing and beating Drums, to draw more Negroes to them, thinking they were now victorious over the whole Province, having marched ten miles & burnt all before them without Opposition, but the Militia being raised, the Planters with great briskness pursued them and when they came up, dismounting; charged them on foot. . . . In the whole action about 40 Negroes and 20 whites were killed.[49]

The 1739 slave insurrection in South Carolina is just one indication that the level of tension between slaves and their owners was intensifying. Violence was becoming more and more common.

Still, some slaves employed a variety of nonviolent strategies to cope with the oppressive conditions. The egalitarianism sentiments contained in sermons of white clergymen during the revivalism of the Great Awakening in the 1740s provided a source of hope and relief for many slaves. Egalitarianism was guided by the assumption of equality among humankind regardless of race, class, ethnicity, or gender. Egalitarians believed that human beings were members of the same family or species created by God. They maintained that the laws of nature entitled black people to the same natural rights that other human beings share. A theme that permeated evangelical egalitarianism was: *We were created in the image of God, and we are all God's children.* During the Great Awakening, historians reported that many slaves became Christians and attended churches regularly.[50] Slaves' participation in the church reinforced their sense of personhood as well as the belief that they were equal to whites in the eyes of God. As Christians, slaves also shared brotherhood and sisterhood with other Christians. The absence of information about the number of slaves who became Christians or attended these religious services, including a breakdown of native Africans versus American-born blacks, precludes us from knowing how the Great Awakening experience was perceived by the larger black population.

Even though evangelism of the Great Awakening did not call for the abolition of slavery outright, the advocacy of egalitarianism by white clergymen had antislavery overtones. The conversion of slaves to Christianity posed slave owners with a troublesome question: How can you justify the enslavement of your Christian brothers and sisters? In 1740, the remarks of George Whitefield, a prominent evangelist, provide a glimpse of the egalitarian implications in Protestant Christianity:

"Think you" that your children "are any way better by Nature than the poor Negroes? No, in no wise. Blacks are just as much, and no more, conceived and born in Sin, as White Men are. Both, if born and bred up here, I am persuaded, are naturally capable of the same [religious] improvement."[51]

The religious egalitarianism suggested that people of African descents possessed immortal souls and were the equals of white men in the eyes of God.

The Great Awakening provided an impetus for the antislavery movement that evolved during the early 1740s and grew steadily for the duration of the 1700s. Although resistance to slavery by the enslaved population always was ongoing, a relatively small minority of white people strongly denounced it. John Woolman, a Quaker, who viewed slavery as morally wrong and incongruent with the teachings of Christianity, founded the antislavery movement in 1743. In a statement grounded in egalitarianism, Woolman observes:

Placing on Men the ignominious Title, SLAVE, dressing them in un-comely Garments, keeping them to servile Labour, in which they are often dirty, tends gradually to fix a Notion in the Mind, that they are Sort of People below us in Nature, and leads us to consider them as such in all our Conclusions about them.[52]

He maintained that the perceived negative traits of enslaved blacks were byproducts of the oppressive conditions of enslavement. Woolman called for an end to slavery as a necessary condition to reverse these negative traits. Support for Woolman's position grew steadily as the nation moved toward the American War of Independence.

GLIMMERS OF HOPE AND DESPAIR DURING THE REVOLUTIONARY ERA: 1750–1800

After spending more than a century in mainland North America, white Americans increasingly became cognizant of ideas and other things that set them apart from the English. They recognized how the experiences involved in shaping a new nation had transformed their ideas about liberty, property, and equality. By the second half of the eighteenth century, environmentalism had become a popular way of interpreting human group differences. Guided by an assumption that differences among humans were circumstantial, environmentalism suggested that human minds were primarily shaped by living conditions and other experiences humans encountered. In a word, the environmentalists argued that people's habits, behavior, and psychological characteristics were molded by living conditions and other experiences. The primary intellectual support for environmentalism was provided in the writings of John Locke. Locke denied the existence of innate ideas and contended that the mind is like a blank slate at birth. He noted that the mind is shaped from experience. Locke's philosophy suggests that the mind reflects the sum product of a person's experiences. The focus on environmental conditions to account for human differences was one of the major historical developments of the second half of the eighteenth century.

Similarities between the logic of American colonist's desire for independence of English rule and slaves' desire for freedom galvanized the antislavery movement. During the third quarter of the eighteenth century, Winthrop D. Jordan notes, many white Americans recognized that the institution of slavery was not only deeply woven into the economic structure of the country but also into the minds of white Americans.[53] As they pondered ideas of equality about themselves in light of the American Revolution, white Americans were compelled to confront contradictions in the assessments of themselves and the status of enslaved black people. The idea of human equality that was used by American settlers to justify the American independence movement served as a potent weapon for black people and white abolitionists to call for the abolition of slavery and to champion egalitarianism. They repeatedly used the poor environmental conditions to account for the debased status of black people. Abolitionists argued that ignorance and other negative characteristics attributed to black people were caused by the oppressive conditions of enslavement.[54] After 1760, clergymen focused less attention on converting blacks into Christians and began preaching about the sinfulness of enslaving them.

With a focus on egalitarianism and environmentalism, Anthony Benezet, a respected writer, points out in 1762 that on the basis of his experience with children in Negro schools, he could "with Truth and Sincerity declare . . . that the notion entertained by some, that the Blacks are inferior to the Whites in their capacities, is vulgar prejudice, founded on the Pride or Ignorance of their lordly Masters, who have kept their Slaves at such a distance, as to be unable to form a right judgment of them."[55]

In his observations about the relationship between vice and slavery, Dr. Benjamin Rush, an outspoken critic of slavery, made the following statement in 1774:

> Slavery is so foreign to the human mind, that the moral faculties, as well as those of the understanding are debased, and rendered torpid by it. All the vices which are charged upon the Negroes in the southern colonies and West-Indies, such as Idleness, Treachery, Theft, and the like, are genuine offspring of slavery, and serve as an argument to prove that they were not intended, by Providence for it.[56]

Abigail Adams, wife of President John Adams, also opposed slavery and expressed her disenchantment about the inconsistency between the idea of human equality and slavery. In a letter to her husband, Abigail Adams stated, "It has always seemed a most iniquitous scheme to me to fight ourselves for what we are daily robbing and plundering from those who have as good a right to freedom as we have."[57] Encouraged by these antislavery declarations, slaves in many parts of the country pressed for freedom and rights that they had been denied. Slaves in New England, for example, petitioned state governments for freedom in the name of human and natural rights. In Massachusetts, blacks staged a successful campaign for the right to vote.[58]

The antislavery arguments used by abolitionists were very similar to the arguments colonists used to support the Revolution. Using the Declaration of Independence in 1775 to denounce slavery, the Quaker David Cooper notes:

> If these solemn truths, uttered at such an awful crisis, are self-evident: unless we can show that the African race are not men, words can hardly express the amazement which naturally arises on reflecting, that the very people who make these pompous declarations are slave-holders, and, by their legislative conduct, tell us, that these blessings were only meant to be the rights of white men not of all men; and would seem to verify the observation of an eminent writer; "When men talk of liberty, they mean

their own liberty, and seldom suffer their thoughts on that point to stray to their neighbours."[59]

While the antislavery movement spearheaded by the religious groups forced white Americans to recognize discrepancies between their self-serving motives, political desires, and religious beliefs, the movement also enhanced political awareness and political action among black people. Black people took advantage of the egalitarianism that spearheaded the American Revolution. Many slaves demanded freedom, and free black people demanded equality.[60]

The American War of Independence weakened the control that slaveholders exercised over the enslaved population. It pitted slaveholders against each other, with some of them fighting for independence from England and others fighting as loyalists for the English. The war created opportunities for slaves to challenge the institution of slavery and white supremacy. Thomas Paine in 1775 exposed the hypocrisy of the struggle for political independence and the institution of American slavery. He raised the question, how can Americans "complain so loudly of attempts to enslave them, while they hold so many hundreds of thousands in slavery?"[61] After pondering the logic of Paine's observation, some slaveholders granted freedom to their slaves, especially in some Northern areas where slaves were numerically few and economically marginal.[62] The antislavery movement gained momentum steadily during the Revolutionary era, as can be seen in the following excerpt from a Methodist resolution of 1784, which called for an end to slavery:

> Every member of our society who has slaves is his possession, shall, within twelve months after notice given to him by the Assistant, (which notice the Assistants are required immediately and without delay to give in their respective circuits,) legally execute and record an instrument, whereby he emancipates and sets free, every slave in his possession—those between the ages of 25 and 45 immediately, or in five years; if between 20 and 25, within ten years; if under 20, at the age of 25 at farthest; and every infant born in slavery after the above mentioned rules are complied with, immediately on its birth.[63]

The efforts put forth by abolitionists and religious groups paved the way for freedom for many enslaved blacks. However, freedom was rarely granted without them actively pressing their owners for permission to buy freedom and threatening to run away or threatening a rebellion if refused.

The Patriots and Loyalists were compelled to use their slaves in ways that weakened the authority that some masters exercised over slaves. Many slaves were offered freedom in return for military service. As a result of military service, runaways, self-purchase, manumission, and state-sponsored manumission, the free black population grew at an unprecedented pace during the Revolutionary era, especially in the North and the Chesapeake and Upper South regions. Just as the institution of slavery and the status of black life varied from region to region before the Revolution, it also varied from region to region during and after the Revolutionary era. While the free black population witnessed manifold growth in all regions, the enslaved population decreased in some regions and increased in other regions. During the late 1700s and early 1800s, the enslaved black population grew faster than the free black population. The revival of the Atlantic slave trade from the late 1700s through the early years of the 1800s contributed to the growth of the enslaved population. The enslaved black population was larger at the end of the Revolutionary age than it was at the beginning of it.[64] The Revolutionary era paved the way for the emergence of a black leadership class with clergymen in the vanguard. The growth of the free black population increased the diversity among them in areas such as occupation, place of residence, and property ownership. Thus, a social class structure evolved among blacks with freedom, skin color, property ownership, and rural or urban residence providing the social strata. Light-skinned free blacks who possessed employable skills and owned property held high social standing in black society.

THE NORTH: FREEDOM AND SLAVERY IN THE REVOLUTIONARY ERA

Slavery and black life were radically altered in the Northern region during the Revolutionary age. After rooting out the few remaining remnants of a slave society and then restoring a society with slaves, the Northern region was gradually transformed from a society with slaves to a society without slaves. The process was slow and uneven with emancipation taking place sooner in New England states where slaves were numerically few and economically marginal as opposed to New York and New Jersey, the largest slaveholding states in the North. Many slaves in New York and New Jersey remained in bondage until the mid-nineteenth century and longer.

Ignoring the objections of slave owners, thousands of enslaved blacks escaped to freedom. Throughout the 1790s, slaves in the North escaped from slavery with help from newly freed slaves and abolitionists. Incidents involving arson, which slave owners attributed to slave revolts, occurred frequently. These events, along with other antislavery activities, weakened even more the institution of slavery in the North. Since slave labor was not essential for the growth of economies in the North, the institution of slavery did not have as much stability and support there as in the South. Recognizing that slavery demise was inevitable in the North, many Northern slave-owners who were driven by economic considerations refused to yield to antislavery pressure and sold their slaves to Southern planters.

In response to pleas from egalitarians that all humans were equal in the eyes of God, some slave-owners in the North granted slaves freedom and denounced slavery. Some blacks relentlessly challenged the unequal application of notions of universal human equality that justified the American Revolution. During a meeting in 1781, a group of blacks in Philadelphia strongly condemned the double standards that provided credence for white Americans to fight for their own freedom while they denied it to blacks. White abolitionists formed antislavery societies, such as the Pennsylvania Society in 1775 and the New York Manumission Society in 1787, which worked to abolish slavery and the slave trade as well as educate and protect free blacks from the dangers of re-enslavement.[65]

Despite antislavery agitation, in 1780, the government of Pennsylvania passed a law that called for the gradual emancipation of slaves. The law guaranteed that the demise of slavery would be a slow and deliberate process. Other states north of the Chesapeake followed the lead of the government of Pennsylvania and enacted a similar plan for emancipation during the last years of the 1700s and the beginning of the 1800s.[66] In 1799, for example, the New York state assembly passed a bill that declared "a female born of a slave mother would be free after twenty-five years of service, and a male of a slave mother could be free after twenty-eight years."[67] By requiring slaves to accept long-term periods of indenture as a condition for their freedom, the enacted gradual emancipation laws prolonged slavery in the North. Consequently, many blacks in the North remained enslaved well into the 1800s. The black population in the North in 1790 included 27,054 free blacks and 40,420 slaves; in 1810, the black population included 75,156 free blacks and 27,054 slaves. In 1820, the population in the North included 19,108 enslaved black people, with 10,088 in New York and 7,557 in New Jersey. As late as 1860, there were 64 enslaved blacks in the North, including 18 in New Jersey.

Unlike free blacks in the Lower South, free blacks in the North were committed to ridding themselves of all remnants of the slave experience. They collectively took action to affirm their personhood and control their fates. They dropped their slave names and replaced them with biblical and common Anglo American names. Taking on new names also symbolized their desire to rid themselves of the stigma of slavery and psychological bruises associated with it. As acts of racial pride, self-determination, and political defiance, free blacks in the North proclaimed their African identity and supported the designation of the term "African" in the naming of black institutions and organizations during the eighteenth and nineteenth centuries. The names of newly founded black institutions tended to reflect connections between the American and African identities of black people. These identity connections observed by blacks suggest an awareness of some distinctions between themselves and other people of African descents. Observing the use of African in the names adopted for black institutions/organizations and European first names for individuals, Horton concluded that it showed the existence of the double consciousness in blacks that W. E. B. Du Bois discussed in his essay "Of Our Spiritual Strivings."[68] These observations lend support to the idea that American-born blacks were cognizant of differences between themselves and native Africans in terms of the way they conceptualized the world and its surroundings.

Unlike free blacks in the South, who were denied the right to assemble in groups without a white person present, free blacks in the North took advantage of the right to assemble in groups without a white person present. During these meetings, they formed black institutions and organizations to serve the needs of black people. These meetings also created opportunities for them to develop and cultivate leadership talent in black communities. In Philadelphia and Newport, Rhode Island, the Free African Society, founded in 1780, was among the first black institutions to designate the term "African" as expression of pride in the African past and self-determination.

Freedom provided blacks with more leverage in their ongoing power struggle with whites for the right of self-determination. In renaming themselves and proclaiming African identity, free blacks conveyed that they were destined to define their personhood and permanently remove the remnants of slavery. However, the granting of freedom to blacks in the North during the Revolutionary era did not change the social order in this region. The actions and attitudes of white people made it very clear that freedom from enslavement would not reduce the racial oppression of blacks. They continued to lump together free blacks and enslaved blacks at the bottom of the social ladder, beneath the social status of any white person. In many ways, white domination relegated the granting of freedom to blacks as barely more than a symbolic gesture. White people held onto as much power over blacks as the laws permitted. The power struggle continued because whites continued to exercise considerable control over conditions that influenced the lives of all black people in the United States. In light of the continual power struggle, the resentment, distrust, and hostility inherent in the relationship between black and white people in the North persisted.

After granting freedom to their slaves, many former slave-owners showed very little or no concern for their well-being. Although many of the newly freed blacks were skilled tradesmen, they faced racial discrimination in the workforce. Whites tended to employ the newly freed blacks as unskilled laborers and in the service trades that had been associated with slavery.[69] The maritime industry served as the largest employer of black men. Lawmakers and other public officials made sure that blacks did not equate freedom with equality. Free blacks could hire out their services and own property; however, in many Northern areas, they were denied the right to vote, testify in court, and sit on juries, and they were subjected to curfews and restricted in their travel. Economic hardships forced many free blacks to continue working for and living in the households of their former owners. This practice reinforced the idea that they were no more than slaves without a master. In many ways, white domination relegated the granting of freedom to blacks as simply a symbolic gesture with superficial features of self-determination. Clearly, white leaders aimed to deny or delegitimate any attempt by free blacks to change their long-standing low social status that had been relegated to them because of their racial group membership.

THE CHESAPEAKE: FREEDOM AND SLAVERY IN THE REVOLUTIONARY ERA

In the Chesapeake region and Upper South, the Revolutionary era brought about changes in the economy and the institution of slavery. With many blacks gaining freedom through manumission, self-purchase, successful escape, or rendering their services in the military in exchange for freedom during the Revolutionary era, there was considerable growth in the free black population in the Chesapeake and Upper South. The free black population was 30,258 in 1790 and 94,085 in 1810. In contrast to the trend in the North, the slave population in the Chesapeake and Upper South grew steadily from the beginning to the end of the Revolutionary era. The slave population was 171,846 in 1750; 322,854 in 1770; 520,969 in 1790; and 810,423 in 1810. The abolitionists' movement and evangelical egalitarianism did not avert the growth of slavery in the Chesapeake and Upper South region.

The instability of slavery heightened by the Revolutionary War led to continuous shifts in the power struggle between slaves and slave owners over the terms of labor and other conditions that shaped slave communities.[70] Berlin reported that the slave economy grew during the Revolutionary era because many slaves spent more time working for themselves than in their owners' fields.[71] The growth of the slaves' economy enabled slaves to market and keep profits from an increase in goods they produced on their own time, and slaveholders were prime customers of these goods. The marketing of the goods they produced created opportunities for slaves to assert their personhood in dealings with slave owners.

Although thousands of blacks escaped from bondage during this era in the Chesapeake and Upper South region, slaveholders kept their slavery operation on track by providing refuge to some slaves, disciplining others, and renegotiating labor conditions with others. The economy in this region expanded during the Revolutionary era and became more diverse and less dependent on tobacco production. Mixed farming that included dairying and the production of corn, wheat, and other vegetables became major resources that shaped the economy in the Chesapeake and Upper South region. The transition to a more diverse and complex economy in this region changed the working conditions and way of life for both enslaved and free blacks. The plantations and farms required more skilled workers and fewer field workers.[72] Given that most slaves lacked many specialties needed in the new economy, they often worked in a racially mixed labor force in various places in the region over the course of each year to fill the demands of a diverse economy.[73] This movement from place to place provided opportunities for slaves to interact with a larger variety of people and gain a better understanding about conditions that shaped their lives.

The knowledge slaves gained from hiring out their services, marketing goods they produced, and working in a variety of settings often made them more effective in negotiations with slave owners. Through negotiations with slave owners, slaves gained more control over their domestic lives. They gained more control over the time spent with their spouse and offspring. Many slaves moved freely from place to place in local townships. Berlin noted that slaves viewed towns as "great emporiums in which everything was for sale," including opportunities for them to purchase freedom.[74] To curb disruptive behavior and maintain work performance at satisfactory levels, many slave-owners in the Chesapeake region and Upper South promised slaves freedom contingent on good behavior. Since the slave population increased by natural means each year, granting freedom to slaves for good behavior did not affect the economy in the region. This program worked well for slave owners as well as slaves. Many slaves took advantage of it and gained freedom through this route.

The steady growth of the slave population created a larger bond-labor workforce than was needed in this region. It allowed for many non-slaveholders to become slaveholders, and it also bolstered the interstate trade between Chesapeake planters and Lower South planters. Planters in the Chesapeake region and Upper South derived considerable wealth from selling slaves to planters in the Lower South where the demand for slaves was higher than ever before. Between 1790 and 1810, approximately 115,000 slaves in the Chesapeake region and Upper South were sold to planters in the Lower South. This forced migration of slaves to the Lower South broke up families and destroyed the domestic lives of many slaves.

The growth of the free black population made it more difficult for planters and other slaveholders in the Chesapeake region and Upper South to maintain stability in the slavery system. Slaves refused to believe that they were destined to be slaves for the duration of their lives. Seeing friends and relatives living as free people, many slaves designed as well as implemented plans of action to overcome enslavement. The relatively large free black population made it more difficult for white people to distinguish between them and enslaved blacks. The presence of a large free black population increased slaves' likelihood of success in attempts to escape from slavery. Many free blacks in the Chesapeake region and Upper South aided and abetted escape efforts undertaken by fugitive slaves, especially when close kinship or friendship ties existed between them.[75] To curb this practice, the Virginia Assembly, in 1798, enacted a law that called for thirty-nine lashes for free blacks convicted of harboring fugitive slaves.[76] Lawmakers in the Chesapeake region and Upper South enacted laws aimed to reduce contact and bonding between free blacks and enslaved blacks. In 1795, the North Carolina Assembly enacted legislation that restricted conditions of contact between free blacks and slaves. Jordan noted that free blacks had to get permission from slave owners and two justices of the peace to marry or cohabit with slaves. In 1808, the Maryland Assembly passed a law that permitted slaves to testify in court against free blacks on any matter. Despite these laws, free blacks and slaves often worked, lived, and worshiped together. They leaned on each other for support to withstand unjust treatment from white persons. A greater sense of community between free blacks and enslaved blacks existed in the Chesapeake region and Upper South than in the North.

Similar to free blacks in the North, many free blacks in the Chesapeake region and Upper South continued to live with their former masters because their children and spouses were still enslaved by them. In 1810, approximately one-third of the Baltimore free blacks lived with slave owners. By constructing a sort of counter-narrative, many free blacks in this region renamed themselves, severed ties with their former masters, left and never returned to the site of their enslavement, reunited their families, and hired out their services. Newly freed slaves were faced with many problems, including unemployment, poverty, and racial discrimination, which forced them to accept employment from whites on terms that bore close semblance to slavery. Some free blacks entered into sharecropping agreements, which locked them into tenantries that kept them indebted to the property owner. Similar to the enslaved black population, many of them were treated as property by the ruling white elites.

As slaves gained their freedom and reconstructed their lives, they still were faced with the ongoing struggle of defining their personhood and controlling their fates. Whites did not relinquish the control they exercised over defining the personhood and controlling the fates of ex-slaves. White lawmakers instituted laws that reinforced racial oppression and clearly conveyed the message that freedom would not remove the stigmatized racial status of black people. They adopted policies and practices that made free blacks powerless and nonthreatening to the institution of slavery and the social order that existed. These practices and policies created, on the surface, an appearance of freedom for free blacks while keeping them in a state of slavery without any requirements for whites to assume responsibility for their upkeep.

Led by Baptist and Methodist evangelical preachers and attracting an unprecedented number of enslaved black people, the Great Awakening movement was reignited during the latter part of the eighteenth century. They represented a substantial minority of Baptist and Methodist congregations. With a focus on the sinfulness of slavery, evangelical ministers preached that all human beings were God's creation and imbued by the creator with natural rights that should not be denied by other human beings. In keeping with the biblical interpretation, they maintained that all human beings had the natural right to be free. Armed with hope inspired by the teachings of Christianity, enslaved blacks embraced the creed that all humans were created equal in the eyes of God and used it to redress their owners' authority.[77] The religious awakening brought the free black and enslaved black populations together in settings that reinforced a sense of community among them. It provided them with opportunities to collectively experience emotional relief from the burdens of racial oppression. The experiences of the Great Awakening also contributed to the growth of black preachers, who helped to pave the way for the development of the black church.

THE LOWER SOUTH: FREEDOM AND SLAVERY IN THE REVOLUTIONARY ERA

The Revolutionary War weakened the authority of slaveholders and created chaos on many plantations in South Carolina and Georgia. With leadership in disarray, slaves escaped for freedom from plantations in huge numbers. Between 1775 and 1783, in South Carolina, the slave population declined by approximately 25,000 or 25 percent of the prewar slave population. During the same period, in Georgia, the slave population declined from 15,000 to 5,000.[78] Many slaveholders were forced to concede to slaves' demands for more control over their labor during the Revolutionary War. During the postwar years, lawmakers and slaveholders expressed strong convictions to repair and expand the institution of slavery. Slaveholders and lawmakers in the Lower South were not swayed by the antislavery arguments put forth by egalitarians and abolitionists. They stayed united in their resolve to protect the institution of slavery in the South. In 1787, at the Constitutional Convention in Philadelphia, representatives from South Carolina and Georgia stated firmly that their economies could not survive without slavery and threatened to leave the Union if representatives at the convention voted to abolish it. A majority of the representatives at the convention, including Thomas Jefferson, supported the recommendation from South Carolina and Georgia representatives to preserve slavery. Jefferson's support may have been based, in part, on his knowing that over 80 percent of the United States' international trade was in products produced by slaves, and as such, the new nation's wealth depended on it.[79]

The invention of the cotton gin by Eli Whitney in the 1790s eventually made cotton the leading staple crop in the Lower South. The cotton gin could separate the green seed from the shorter fiber and allowed for cotton production at an unprecedented level. The record growth of cotton production along with the resumption of prewar staple crops increased the demand for slaves in South Carolina and Georgia. Between 1787 and 1808, approximately 90,000 slaves from Africa were imported into South Carolina, and by 1810, one slave in five was born in Africa. They were assimilated into a slave culture already dominated by American-born slaves. Slaveholders also purchased slaves from the North and Upper South.

As in the Upper South, in the Lower South, the free black population and the slave population grew many folds during the Revolutionary era. The slave population in the Lower South was 39,900 in 1750; 92,178 in 1770; 136,932 in 1790; and 303,234 in 1810. Faced by a power struggle during the postwar years with slaves who refused to relinquish the independence they exercised during the Revolutionary War, slaveholders effectively used force to reestablish their control on the plantations, restore staple production at a profitable level, and expand the plantation system. Berlin observed that the level of violence on plantations in the Lower South escalated during the early postwar years.[80]

Selective paternal manumission, self-purchase, and the immigration of several hundred free refugees from Saint Dominique between 1790 and 1810 contributed to a steady increase in the free black population in the Lower South. The free black population in the Lower South was 2,199 in 1790 and 6,355 in 1810. Women who were house servants and artisans composed the majority of manumitted adults. Many of free blacks in the Lower South were fathered by slaveholders and retained close relationships with them after they were granted freedom. Light-skinned color complexions were an important source of status in the Lower South's free black community, especially in Charleston, where mulattoes made up a large proportion of the free black population. Unlike ex-slaves in the North and the Upper South, free blacks in the Lower South did not rid themselves of the names of their former owners, and they continued to live nearby their former owners. The sense of community among free and enslaved blacks that existed in the Upper South rarely occurred in South Carolina. In his writings about blacks in Savannah from 1788 through 1864, Whittington B. Johnson notes that little distinction was made between free blacks and slaves.[81] Founded in 1788 in Savannah, with Andrew Bryan as its minister, the First African Baptist Church was the place of worship for slaves and free persons of color. Establishing this church represented the combined efforts of slaves and free blacks. Johnson points out that by being an agency of inclusion, rather than of exclusion, the First African Baptist Church played a major role in shaping a sense of community between slaves and free persons of color in Savannah. Unlike in Charleston, free persons of color in Savannah, including mulattoes, were not likely to bargain with whites to promote themselves at the expense of slaves. Free persons of color in South Carolina showed very little or no interest in the conditions that shaped the lives of enslaved black people.

While drawing as much distance as they could between themselves and the enslaved black population, free blacks in South Carolina took advantage of opportunities to maintain close identification with the slaveholding class. It provided them with economic security, social status, and protection from vigilantes and the abuse of poor, lowlife white men. The relationship between free blacks and their former owners precluded them from openly expressing opposition to slavery or expressing aspirations for equality. In fact, following the lead of white slaveholders, many free blacks in South Carolina also became slaveholders. Loyalty to their former owners did not erase feelings of fear and apprehension that white Southerners shared about free persons of color. Reflecting on white Southerners' views about free blacks, Ulrich Bonnell Phillips states: "Many men of the South thought of themselves and their neighbors as living above a loaded mine, in which the negro slaves were the powder, the abolitionists the spark, and the free negroes the fuse."[82] According to Phillips, laws were enacted in the Lower South to reduce slaves' access to freedom and restrict the mobility of free blacks.[83]

Denied voting rights and other citizenship rights that white Americans had, like free blacks in other regions of the new nation, free blacks in the Lower South also experienced racial oppression. Even though some free blacks in South Carolina attained considerable wealth, they still had no right that any white person was bound to respect. Nonetheless, the absence of these rights did not weaken the aspirations of mulattoes, especially in Charleston, for acceptance by members of the white aristocracy. They apparently suppressed their negative feelings about racial oppression and overtly projected racial and social class attitudes that reinforced their feelings of superiority over other blacks and poor whites. Because of their biological kinship, whites tended to view mulattoes less negatively than blacks of the darkest hue. This attitude reinforced status distinction on the basis of skin color in black communities.[84]

As previously observed, the economies, working conditions, and cultural practices that helped to shape the lives of black people in mainland North America varied from region to region. Nevertheless, the stigmatized racial group status imposed on them was pervasive in the new nation. Throughout the United States, all people of African descents were lumped together by most whites as one undifferentiated stigmatized status group and treated as inherently unequal human beings or subhuman. They generally were denied opportunities to improve their economic status because of their racial group.

The belief that Caucasians were naturally superior to members of other racial groups, in terms of their intellectual, moral, and behavioral traits, was entrenched in the minds of Europeans and white American of all classes. Many of them, including Thomas Jefferson, who opposed slavery on humanitarian grounds, believed that Africans were inherently inferior to white people, and as such, should not be assimilated into the mainstream of American society on equal terms with them. Describing Jefferson's central dilemma, Winthrop D. Jordan states, "He hated slavery but thought Negroes inferior to white men."[85] Jefferson's comments on the rebellion in Saint Dominique, which was also known as Haiti, provide a glimpse of his antislavery feelings. In 1793, he notes:

> I become daily more and more convinced . . . that all the West India Islands will remain in the hands of the people of colour, and a total expulsion of the whites sooner or later take place. . . . It is high time we should foresee the bloody scenes which our children certainly, and possibly ourselves . . . have to wade through, and try to avert them.[86]

In reflections on the intellect of black people, Jefferson wrote:

> Comparing them by their faculties of memory, reason, and imagination, it appears to me, that in memory they are equal to the whites; in reason much inferior, as I think one could scarcely be found capable of tracing and comprehending the investigations of Euclid; and that in imagination they are dull, tasteless, and anomalous. It would be unfair to follow them to Africa for this investigation. We will consider them here, on the same stage with the whites, and where the facts are not apocryphal on which

a judgment is to be formed. It will be right to make great allowances for the difference of condition of education, of conversation, of the sphere in which they move. Many millions of them have been brought to, and born in America. Most of them indeed have been confined to tillage, to their own homes, and their own society: yet many have been so situated, they might have availed themselves of the conversation of their masters; many have been brought up to the handicraft arts, and from that circumstance have always been associated with the whites. Some have been liberally educated, and all have lived in countries where the arts and sciences are cultivated to a considerable degree, and have had before their eyes samples of the best works from abroad. . . . But never yet could I find that a black had uttered a thought above the level of plain narration; never see even an elementary trait of painting or sculpture.[87]

Jefferson's observations reveal how some whites could have been anti-slavery but firmly believed in the innate inequality of race groupings. The deep-seated nature of racism and ethnocentrism reflected in Jefferson's writings provided a signal to newly freed ex-slaves that they were less likely to have support from whites in their struggle for the attainment of racial equality than in their struggle for freedom. Like Jefferson, most white opponents of slavery also believed that the perceived social-cultural gap between white Americans and black people could be understood best in terms of the natural inferior racial status of the latter group.[88]

Given the significance that white Americans attributed to race, the process of adapting to conditions that stemmed from racial oppression was, most likely, the most potent force in shaping the psychological makeup of all black people in the United States. Racial oppression contributed to a caste system that locked black people into servitude roles and deprived them of opportunities to advance socially and economically while simultaneously giving whites a form of property, which allowed them to construct a self-image using enslaved blacks as a negation. Black people had to always stay on guard and not "cross the color line" in the presence of any white person while whites frolicked freely. Negative sentiments about racial oppression shared among black people overshadowed their concerns about cultural and economic differences that existed between them. Racial oppression helped to maintain the shackles of slavery in the minds of ex-slaves. It helped whites maintain considerable control over the personhood and fates of ex-slaves and the personhood and self-image of themselves.

THE LOWER MISSISSIPPI VALLEY: FREEDOM AND SLAVERY

During the Revolutionary War, settlements in the Lower Mississippi Valley region, including Louisiana, were controlled by Spain but eventually France took control of Louisiana. In 1805, the United States purchased Louisiana from France, and with the emergence of sugar as a major staple crop in Louisiana during the early years after the Revolutionary War, it became a slave society. Cotton production was expanded in the Lower Mississippi Valley, and the slave population grew steadily. Slaveholders and other influential whites in this region showed no sympathy for antislavery arguments posed by egalitarians and abolitionists. Slaveholders sponsored manumission, but the number of slaves who purchased their freedom dropped sharply with the expansion of sugar and cotton production in this region. Slaves were brought into this region from all parts of the United States as well as from Angola in Africa. The slave population in Mississippi was 4,730 in 1750; 7,100 in 1770; 18,700 in 1790; and 51,748 in 1810. In the Mississippi Valley, there were no free blacks in 1790 and 7,825 in 1810.[89] As in other slave societies, the threat of violent confrontations between masters and slaves was always present in the region. In 1791, 1795, 1804, and 1805, slave masters uncovered major slave conspiracies.

When the United States took control of the Lower Mississippi Valley region, approximately 1,800 free persons of color lived in the region, with the largest concentration in New Orleans. By 1810, this population had grown to 7,825. As in the North, Upper South, and Lower South, many persons of color attained freedom through escape, manumission, and self-purchase. It was common for slave masters to grant freedom to their mistresses and racially mixed offspring. During the period of Spanish rule, Ira Berlin reported that approximately two-thirds of the slaves who were granted freedom in New Orleans were women, and more than half of volunteer manumissions after 1769 were for paternal reasons.[90]

Many of the free people of color were former overseers on plantations in Haiti who fled to New Orleans for refuge during slave rebellions in Haiti. Forced out of Cuba by Spanish officials, approximately 3,000 Haitian mulatto refugees relocated in New Orleans in 1809. In 1810, free people of color represented approximately 30 percent of New Orleans population.[91] Given that these Haitian refugees came from a nation that separated racially mixed people from enslaved Africans, they did not identify themselves with black slaves. Bearing this in mind, Haitian refugees exploited opportunities to align themselves with whites and maintained as much distance as possible from the enslaved population in the Lower Mississippi Valley region. Not surprisingly, some of them eventually became slaveholders, and like many white slaveholders, they displayed insensitivity to the humanity of slaves.[92]

Like free people of color in South Carolina, native free people of color in the Lower Mississippi Valley region nurtured ties with influential whites who had helped them gain freedom. They kept their old surnames that linked them with slaveholding families. While displaying no concern for the plight of enslaved blacks, they often kept their distance from slaves in a manner similar to the free blacks in South Carolina. To derive wealth, social status, and make their case for voting rights and equality, some free persons of color became slaveholders. As slaveholders, free blacks believed they demonstrated their allegiance to the ideals of white society and affirmed their loyalty to influential whites who served as their patrons and protectors. When the Lower Mississippi Valley region was under Spanish and French rule, free people of color in this area had privileges that were not extended to free persons of color in the United States. They served in the military and frequently socialized with whites in social settings. Courtships involving white men and black females were common occurrences in social clubs.

After the Lower Mississippi Valley region came under the rule of the United States, many of the restrictions on privileges of free blacks that existed in the Upper South and Lower South were imposed on free blacks in the Lower Mississippi Valley region. Legislation was passed that banned free blacks from carrying guns and serving in the military. Slaves were permitted to testify against free blacks but not whites. A law was enacted that stated that, "free people of color ought never to insult or strike white people, nor presume to conceive themselves equal to whites."[93] By informing mulattoes and other free blacks that their status was below the status of any white person, this law put a stamp on racial oppression in the Lower Mississippi Valley. It forced Haitian refugees and their descendants as well as other mulattoes in this region to acknowledge their African roots that many of them would have preferred to ignore or deny.

By the end of the eighteenth century, the combined efforts of scholars, political leaders, slave owners, and others who derived economic benefits from African slavery, had succeeded in instilling in American and European social thought the idea of blacks' natural inferiority to other human groups and the rules of nature that allowed for the evolution of a social order that placed them in subservient roles to whites. Hence, for an overwhelming majority of Europeans and Americans at the end of the eighteenth century, race signified a fixed or permanent ranking order created by nature that ranked Caucasians at the top and people of African descents at the bottom of the hierarchy.[94]

The belief in natural inequality of racial groups was so widespread that it would have been impossible for any black person, including mulattoes, living anywhere in the United States to escape problems stemming from racism and racial oppression. Learning to cope with these problems was a burden that they had to master to survive. For people of African descents living in the United States during this era, this belief in the natural inequality of racial groups would have played a key role in formulating assumptions they made about race and in shaping commonalities in their attitudes and behavior toward Caucasians. Commentaries from black leaders along with slave narratives and interviews from writings about American slavery during the nineteenth century, which shed light on blacks attitudes and behavior toward whites, are presented in the next chapter.

THE EMERGENCE OF A RACIAL WORLDVIEW

The psychological and social significance attributed to the meaning of race from the latter part of the seventeenth century through the twentieth century has been used as leverage, by many people, to influence the ongoing debate and power struggle about issues concerning the personhood and fates of black people in mainland North America. As blacks engaged actions to establish and affirm the personhood that they had been denied, whites engaged actions to strengthen and maintain the economic, social, and political benefits they derived from slavery and racial oppression.

The institutionalization of slavery in the 1700s combined with writings and research by scientists and other scholars to support the belief of blacks' natural inferiority to other human groups and the humanity of white people were pivotal in the development of a racial worldview that debased the status of people of African descents while idealizing the status of whites in many ways that far outlived the abolition of slavery.

As statesmen with enormous respect and influence, James Madison and Thomas Jefferson did more to sustain racial inequality and the negative image of blacks than any of their contemporaries. During a period in history characterized by considerable debates about the humanity of blacks, in a speech to the Continental Congress at the Constitutional Convention in 1787, James Madison effectively argued slaves were both persons and property:

> That they partake of both these qualities; being considered by our laws, in some respects, as person and in other respects, as property. In being compelled to labor not for himself, but for a master; in being vendible by one master to another master; and in being subject at all times to be restrained in his liberty, and chastised in his body, by the capricious will of another, the slave may appear to be degraded from the human rank, and classed with those irrational animals, which fall under the legal denomination of property. In being protected on the other hand in his life and in his limbs, against the violence of all others, even the master of his labor and his liberty; and in being punishable himself for all violence committed against others; the slave is no less evidently regarded by the law as a member of society; not as a part of the irrational creation; as a moral person, not as a mere article of property. The Federal Constitution therefore, decides with great propriety on the case of our slaves, when it views them in the mixt character of persons and of property. This is in fact their true character. . . . Let the compromising expedient of the Constitution be mutually adopted, which regards them as inhabitants . . . which regards the *slave* as divested of two fifths of the *man*.[95]

Following deliberations, the convention adopted a resolution to count the slave as three-fifths of a person for apportionment of political representatives and taxes. Although it has been suggested that Madison's re-

marks were intended as a political definition of blacks and not as a judgment of their human worth, for many whites, it clearly gave credence
to the idea that people of African descents were subhuman. Madison's
remarks along with actions subsequently taken in this regard by the convention had ramifications that influenced white attitudes toward blacks
well into the nineteenth century.

As a national figure and preeminent statesman, Thomas Jefferson's
commentaries and observations had a tremendous impact upon American public opinion.[96] As noted earlier, Jefferson believed that blacks were
inherently inferior to whites in both body and mind. Jefferson was not
unlike many antislavery proponents during the late eighteenth and early
nineteenth centuries. Graham Richards observed in his book 'Race,' Racism and Psychology that during the eighteenth and nineteenth centuries,
many white antislavery advocates shared the prevailing view that blacks
and whites were unequal.[97] But Jefferson's call for the use of science to
provide evidence to show or prove it was a major setback for advocates
of racial equality. In calling for scientists to provide evidence to support
his belief in the innate inferiority of blacks, Jefferson states:

> The opinion, that they are inferior in the faculties of reason and imagina-
> tion, must be hazarded with great diffidence. To justify a general conclu-
> sion, requires many observations, even where the subject may be submit-
> ted to the Anatomical knife, to Optical glasses, to analysis by fire, or by
> solvents. How much more then where it is a faculty, not a substance, we
> are examining; where it eludes the research of all the senses; where the
> conditions of its existence are various and variously combined; where the
> effects of those which are present or absent bid defiance to calculation.[98]

As can be seen here, Jefferson called for the use of science in the resolution
of a political question about race in ways that would compromise scientific
objectivity. Heedful of Jefferson's challenge, numerous studies yielding
results that confirmed the inferior nature of people of African descents
were conducted. The racially biased research, writings, and attitudes of
European and American scholars during the 1800s ensured that two separate warring nations, namely, black people and white people, which had
been pitted against each other since the beginning of the formation of this
new society, would continue through the twentieth century to maintain an
often strained and volatile but also cooperative relationship.

Spurred often with support from pro-slavery activists and white supremacists, racial research gained considerable popularity in the nineteenth and twentieth centuries. In his book, *The Science and Politics of Racial Research*, William H. Tucker provides critiques of a large body of racial research conducted in the nineteenth and twentieth centuries that show the linkage between science and politics. Scientists' beliefs and other preconceived ideas strongly influenced how they conducted the research and interpreted the findings. Tucker suggests that the belief that the operation of science was objective, unbiased, and free from politics provided these researchers with a powerful strategy for influencing public policy. During the early 1900s, there were white Americans, with racist views, who believed that blacks would have endured immeasurable mistreatment in the absence of scientific proof to support their views.[99] For many white Americans, the role of science included conducting research to preserve social stability and maintain the status quo in the society. Researchers were expected to provide findings that confirmed that the policies and practices directed toward black people were just. With findings derived from racial studies in the nineteenth and twentieth centuries, white Americans obtained empirical underpinnings to justify their treatment of black people in America.[100] These studies also provided planters, politicians, and other influential whites who opposed freedom and equality for blacks with more ammunition to determine the rules and parameters for negotiations dealing with the personhood and fates of blacks. Bearing this in mind, the hostility, resentment, hatred, and distrust that characterized the relationship between an overwhelming majority of blacks in America and white Americans progressively worsened, with members of both groups living daily in fear of intergroup violence.

With the insight into the importance of whiteness to race in the United States provided by Du Bois and CRTs, the argument that the historical existence of racism and white privilege have served to desensitize many white Americans to racism takes on new importance and legitimacy in light of 18th-century developments in scientific racism. This research was performed solely by whites in a world in which whiteness was invisible for them. Yet, because it functions invisibly for them, often they may tend to think that their life experience is a universal norm. Dreama Moon has called this phenomenon "white solipsism."[101] Consequently, the existence of racism can be explained by what James Scheurich and Michelle Young call "civilizational racism." According to Scheurich and Young, four levels of racism exist: individual, institutional, societal, and civilizational. White solipsism is a product of civilizational racism and produces what Scheurich and Young call "epistemological racism."

Quite important to an understanding of both modern and historical racism in the United States, and our academic understanding of it, is the reality pointed out by James Scheurich and Michelle Young that almost all of the major influential theorists of the humanities, social sciences, natural sciences, politicians, and educational leaders have all been white. This is important because, according to them, "It is they who have constructed the world we live in—named it, discussed it, explained it. It is they who have developed the ontological and axiological categories or concepts like individuality, truth, education, free enterprise, good conduct, social welfare, etc. that we use to think . . . and that we use to socialize and educate children."[102] Because these theorists have constructed our ways of being in the world as well as our theories of values, it is only natural that our ways of knowing or epistemologies are influenced by their writings. Importantly, these theorists were all recipients of what Du Bois calls the "public and psychological wage." They established what some educators consider official knowledge within the realm of racism. Because the ways of knowing developed by these theorists were done within the confines of white supremacy, the presumptions that flow from these epistemologies have shaped the research agenda of scholars and the policy decisions of politicians and are all tainted by the epistemological limits of white supremacy. Consequently, from a CRT perspective, what is typically called "folk racism" or "scientific racism" is, in fact, an unavoidable consequence of using ways of knowing developed under the guise of protecting white dominance and the psychological needs of white people.

THE EVOLVING OF A RACIST WORLDVIEW AND PSYCHES OF AFRICAN AMERICANS

Because of the way in which whiteness and blackness developed in relation to one another, the American-born slave population grew at a rapid rate from the early 1800s through the pre–Civil War years. According to United States Census data, there were approximately 697,897 enslaved people of African descents in 1790; 893,041 in 1800; 1,191,345 in 1810; 1,538,125 in 1820; 2,000,043 in 1830; 2,487,455 in 1840; 3,204,313 in 1850; and, 3,953,760 in 1860. With the abolition of the Atlantic slave trade in 1807, the discrepancy between the size of the American-born slave population and the African slaves brought to America accelerated. Given the duration of this growth trend, by 1860, native Africans were less than 10 percent of the slave population. By the beginning of the nineteenth century, second- and third-generation American-born people of African descents had replaced native Africans as cultural trendsetters in American society. Although American-born blacks, or African Americans, shared many things in common with their African counterparts, they possessed psychological and cultural characteristics that set them apart from other people of African descents.[1]

Importantly, the psychological and cultural characteristics that set enslaved American-born blacks—distinct from mulattoes and free blacks—apart from other people of African descents also set them apart from white people. In this chapter, I explore various ways that this setting apart from whites took the form of counter-narratives and, in fact, made the marginalization of black people in the United States not just a site of despair but provided simultaneously a space of resistance. During this period, African Americans constructed a series of counter-narratives that enabled them to survive in white-dominated America.

PSYCHOLOGICAL AND CULTURAL CHARACTERISTICS IN AMERICAN-BORN BLACKS

Being neither Africans nor European Americans in terms of their worldview and orientation toward surroundings, American-born blacks were a group with both psychological and cultural characteristics that reflected the fusion of African and European values and beliefs under peculiar circumstances in which they suffered and endured heightened emotional turmoil. The peculiar characteristics of racial oppression and the American slavery system, in which the cultural fusion occurred, shaped the psychological and cultural distinctiveness of American blacks. That is, for them, this fusion did not merely involve the assimilation and accommodation of African and European cultural practices. The fusion took place in a rapidly changing society characterized by European Americans imposing racial slavery along with a variety of untested practices or conditions on people of African descents. American blacks shaped their cultural practices in ways that permitted them to adapt to the unique living conditions they faced.

Racial slavery and racial oppression in mainland North America seemingly contributed to a host of psychological traits and cultural practices that set American blacks apart from other people of African descents. One legacy of the institution of slavery in America was community bonding among both enslaved and free people of African descents in America. In response to the oppressive and brutal conditions of enslavement along with racial discrimination and oppression in the open society, most African Americans developed an oppressed communal orientation toward their surroundings. For example, during illness, injury, and death, they took care of each other. When death or sale took the parents of young children, the children were raised and cared for by other enslaved black people, irrespective of blood linkage. Although color differences threatened racial solidarity, it was not uncommon for enslaved blacks to display empathy and group solidarity or strong allegiance toward other members of their slave community.[2] African Americans linked conditions for the survival and uplift of their racial/ethnic group to conditions for individual survival and uplift within the group.

Enslaved native Africans came to America with a communal orientation toward their surroundings. They had been socialized to put their own god first in their lives and then to take on the needs of their respective ethnic groups. For displaced native Africans, self-interests were closely tied to the concerns and needs of one's ethnic group. However, practices in the American slavery system effectively destroyed ethnic group identities and membership among Africans in America. For many enslaved Africans brought to America, their ethnic ties had been severed before they arrived. In response to the harsh conditions of enslavement and racial oppression, the communal orientation previously adopted by enslaved native Africans was replaced by an *oppressed communal orientation*. The oppressed communal orientation was characterized by deep feelings of concern among them about each other and other people of African descents who resided in their region. They perceived it as their duty to help and protect members of their racial group. This oppressed communal orientation became entrenched in America's slave communities. In an essay on slave culture, John W. Blassingame put it this way:

> They united to protect themselves from the oppressive features of slavery and to preserve their self-esteem. . . . They found some protection in the group from their masters. . . . A communalism born of oppression led to an emphasis on mutual cooperation, joyful camaraderie, humor, respect for elders, and an undisguised zest for life.[3]

The oppressed communal orientation displayed by enslaved black folks was readily apparent in slave families. Blassingame contends that the slave family provided an invaluable survival support institution from the hardships of racial slavery.[4]

American-born blacks linked conditions for the survival and uplift of their racial group to conditions for individual survival and uplift within the group. For most people of African descents who were born in America, a communal orientation was essential for survival during the nineteenth century, especially before the Civil War, and this created the conditions for the creation of counter-narratives among blacks. The oppressed communal orientation that influenced the thinking, emotions, and behaviors of American-born blacks was in sharp contrast to the individualistic worldview that was shared by most white Americans. With relatively few exceptions, American free blacks also were denied opportunities outside of their immediate households to adopt an individualistic orientation toward their surroundings. In her book *Yearning: Race, Gender, and Cultural Politics*, bell hooks theoretically places this development in community that contrasts white individualism by claiming that black "living depends on our ability to conceptualize alternatives, often improvised."[5]

By the beginning of the nineteenth century, American-born slaves were guiding the evolving culture in slave communities in accordance with their orientation to America that was different from their native African counterparts. While the rudiments of select African values, beliefs, and cultural practices were preserved, the cultural practices that evolved in slave communities both during and after this period were shaped primarily by American-born slaves' reactions to enslavement and racial oppression.

The American slavery system provided a particular environment for the evolution of an African American cultural system. As a result, distinctive qualities in some cultural expressions of American blacks appeared. For example, the story of the creation of the Negro spiritual titled "Swing Low, Sweet Chariot" shows how the American slavery system contributed to the distinctiveness of African American slave culture. In the spiritual, the chariot referred to a small, sled-like truck that was used by enslaved blacks to transport tobacco on the plantations. Following Nat Turner's revolt, in 1831, enslaved blacks increasingly felt pressure from the enforcement of stricter slave codes. Accordingly, a legend evolved whereby they visualized a huge chariot swinging from heaven to carry their souls over the Jordan River. "Swing Low, Sweet Chariot" was created in 1847 by Sarah Hannah Sheppard, a slave in Tennessee, through the heartfelt pain of being forced to give up her baby. Sheppard had been sold as a slave to a slaveholder in Mississippi, and the day of separation from her baby was rapidly approaching. She vowed to throw herself and her baby into the Cumberland River rather than be a slave in Mississippi. As she stumbled in desperation along the high river road, a prophetic old black woman, realizing what she was up to, approached Sarah, and she cried out, "Don't you do it, honey." Then, she tenderly said, "Wait! Let the chariot of the Lord swing low. Listen! I will read one of the Lord's scrolls to you." Reading in pantomime, she continued, "There's a great work for this baby to do here on earth. She's going to stand before kings and queens. Now don't you do it honey. . . just don't you do it." Sarah was startled but deeply moved. She returned home and allowed herself to be taken to Mississippi. The idea of "God's chariot swinging low" stayed with her continually until she finally gave expression by creating "Swing Low, Sweet Chariot." Some twenty-five years later, the old black woman's prophecy came true. Sarah's baby, Ella Sheppard Moore, enrolled in Fisk University and joined the original Fisk University Jubilee Singers. As their pianist, she went on concert tours beginning in 1871.[6]

As can be seen in the creation of "Swing Low, Sweet Chariot," to endure the conditions of enslavement, African Americans developed ways to release the frustrations, anxieties, resentments, and sorrows that human bondage caused. Music, dance, and folklore became venues that permitted psychic release for their emotional turmoil. These cultural arts were expressed with openness in feelings that blended together incompatible emotions such as suffering, frustration, sadness, sorrows with spiritual yearnings, hope, and joy in a manner that produced creative expressions and deeply moved the performer and audience. The emotions and spiritual yearnings of American-born slaves were blended into the African and European cultural practices they adapted; their distinctive expressive qualities can be defined as *soul*. Thus, the interplay of soul with the fusion of African and European cultural practices produced cultural forms that were distinctive in their own right. This dynamic fusion provided the foundation for African Americans to evolve as a new ethnic group in America.

Born and socialized in a racially stratified society, American blacks learned at an early age that skin color combined with other racial physical characteristics were critical determinants of the social roles and behavioral requirements for them in the larger society. They also learned that white people viewed blacks as inferior people with very limited potential for self-advancement. In his writings about the slave family, John W. Blassingame observes that in roles as playmates for slaveholders' young children, some black children did not fully grasp their assigned inferior status as early as most of them did.[7] Lunsford Lane comments on his childhood as a young slave in North Carolina, stating, "I knew no difference between myself and the white children, nor did they seem to know any in turn. Sometime my master would come out and give a biscuit to me and another to one of his white boys; but I did not perceive the difference between us."[8] However, in watching the physical punishment and violent abuse of older blacks, including parents, on the plantations, young black children undoubtedly learned early about the significance of the link between race, privilege, and slave status. Blassingame suggests that the "shock" of observing their parents being unmercifully whipped was a potent reminder to black children of the significance of race and slavery in their lives.[9] Although parents tried hard to protect and shield their children from the violence and abuse inflicted on enslaved blacks, Blassingame notes, "One of the most important lessons for the child was learning to hold his tongue around white folks."[10] As can be seen here, during the critical years of self-development, young black children had many opportunities to learn lessons about the significance of skin color while growing up in the United States. Learning to control one's emotions when a family member or a close friend was being brutally flogged or abused in other ways was one of the most difficult lessons for black children to grasp.[11] In writings about the slave family, Blassingame cites revelations from several former slaves about the painfulness of early lessons they learned about race and slavery. Austin Steward, a former slave in Virginia and New York, provides this chilling account of how he felt during childhood when he watched a white man whipping his sister:

> The God of heaven only knows the conflict of feeling I then endured; He alone witnessed the tumult of my heart, at this outrage of manhood and kindred affection. God knows that my will was good enough to have wrung his neck; or to have drained from his heartless system its last drop of blood! And yet I was obliged to turn a deaf ear to her cries for assistance, which to this day ring in my ears. Strong and athletic as I was, no hand of mine could be raised in her defense, but a peril of both our lives.[12]

Steward's testimony suggests that for many black children the early lessons about race and slavery were so painful that the negative effects lingered throughout their adult years. Learning to deal with the humiliation and brutal beatings inflicted on parents, siblings, and friends during the early and mid-1800s, forced slave children to acknowledge the significance attributed to the idea of race in the larger society. Excerpts from a slave narrative by James Curry provide another glimpse of how racist behavior observed by slave children seemingly contributed to long-lasting negative effects on their attitudes about race and slavery. Curry's story illustrates the agony, pain, and emotional turmoil many slave children endured as they adapted to slavery in a racially stratified society.

> I was born in Person County, North Carolina. . . . My mother was the daughter of a white man and a slave woman. She, with her brother, were given, when little children, to master's mother, soon after her marriage, by her father. From my childhood until I was sixteen years old, I was brought up a domestic servant. . . .While I worked in the house and waited upon my mistress, she always treated me kindly, but to other slaves, who were as faithful as I was, she was very cruel. At one time, there was a comb found broken in a cupboard, which was worth about twenty-five or thirty-seven and a half cents. She suspected a little girl, 9 or 10 years old, who served in the house, of having broken it. She took her in the morning, before sunrise, into a room and calling me to wait upon her, had all the doors shut. She tied her hands, and then took her frock up over her head, and gathered it up in her left hand, and with her right commenced beating her naked body with bunches of willow twigs. She would beat her until her arm was tired, and then thrash her on the floor, and stamp on her with her foot, and kick her, and choke her to stop her screams. Oh! It was awful! And I was obliged to stand there and see it, and to go and bring her the sticks. She continued this torture until ten o'clock, the family waiting breakfast meanwhile. She then left whipping her; and that night, she herself was so lame that one of her daughters was obliged to undress her. The poor child never recovered. A white swelling came from the bruises on one of her legs, of which she died in two or three years.
>
> My mother was cook in the house for about twenty-two years. . . . After my mistress's death, my mother was the only woman kept in the house. She took care of my master's children, some of whom were then quite small, and brought them up. One of the most trying scenes I ever

passed through, when I would have laid down my life to protect her if I had dared, was this: after she had raised my master's children, one of his daughters, a young girl, come into the kitchen one day, and for some trifle about the dinner, she struck my mother, who pushed her away, and she fell on the floor. Her father was not at home. When he came, which was while the slaves were eating in the kitchen, she told him about it. He came down, called my mother out, and, with a hickory rod, he beat her fifteen or twenty strokes, and then called his daughter and told her to take her satisfaction of her, and she did beat her until she was satisfied. Oh! It was dreadful, to see the girl whom my poor mother had taken care of from her childhood, thus beating her, and I must stand there, and did not dare to crook my finger in her defense.[13]

As can be seen from the testimonies provided here by ex-slaves, black children had to learn at an early age how to mask their true feelings in the presence of white people and behave in an obedient and non-threatening manner toward white peoples' perceived superiority over them. The racist behavior observed and experienced by black children during the 1800s, especially slave children, supports the claim that the idea of race became a powerful frame of reference for most of them at an early age. In light of the centrality of race in the structure of the larger society during the nineteenth century, a concept of race most likely became a relatively stable frame of reference in the psychological makeup of American-born black children. The nature of American society made it impossible for black people living here to ignore the social and psychological significance of race in their lives. On the other hand, most native Africans brought to mainland North America had a coherent sense of self through ethnic identification before they arrived. While the process of adapting to racial slavery over time compelled them to develop a concept of race as a frame of reference, it might not have operated with as much stability in native Africans as in American-born blacks. Previous learning experiences prior to their arrival in the United States may have lessened native Africans' susceptibility to internalizing ideas about race.

Although the folk idea about race that evolved during the seventeenth century lacked scientific merits, it remained as the primary determinant of relationships between American blacks and white Americans. Numerous letters, speeches, interviews, and biographies of former slaves quoted in John N. Blassingame's works provide irrefutable evidence that they were deeply concerned, and rightfully so, about ideas on race differences that were being shared among whites. In writings about the entrenchment of a racial worldview, Audrey Smedley maintained that during the nineteenth century, the idea of race differences became more dominant than ever before as the principal mechanism of social division and stratification in mainland North America.[14] It increasingly became a more central component in the American social structure, shaping values and lifestyles.[15]

In light of the critical role the idea of race played in shaping American society, it most likely had a strong association with experiences that shaped its meaning for American blacks and also native Africans in America. Aristotle contended that the more two things occur together in experience, the more the association between them becomes stronger.[16] It follows from this observation that as the strength of an association between two things increases, the greater the likelihood that the recall of one thing will increase the recall of the second. It appears that the concept of race acquired meaning for black people in America from the things that became associated with it in their experiences. The nature of American society afforded numerous daily opportunities for blacks to establish associations between the idea of race and other things in their experiences. Recognizing that blacks could not ignore nor always escape from racially motivated actions of whites, the following questions warrant consideration: How did the idea of race acquire associative value or meaning for black people in the United States during the nineteenth century? And, what associations or meanings did they connect to it?

The idea of race acquired meaning for blacks through their understanding and interpretation of the racially motivated things they saw, heard, read, or any combination of these learning activities. Blacks' interactions and relationships with whites, Native American Indians, as well as other blacks were critical forces in shaping the things they associated with race. Given perceived group differences in the interaction patterns and relationships between blacks and whites, as well as blacks among themselves, the things they most likely associated with the meaning of race in the presence of whites were likely to be different from the things they associated with the meaning of it in the presence of other blacks and Native Americans. As noted earlier, throughout the eighteenth and nineteenth centuries, the relationship between black and white people in the United States involved an intense power struggle characterized by violence, hostility, distrust, and hatred. Therefore, in the presence of whites, blacks learned to connect their perceived racial group membership with a variety of negative things, such as the lack of protection of the laws, involuntary servitude, the absence of beauty or physically attractive characteristics, the absence of abstract logical reasoning skills, the absence of respect as people of worth in the human family, objects of charity, the absence of opportunities for self-advancement, and skin color predestination to subordinate roles.

On the other hand, the oppressed communal orientation adopted by many blacks helped them to perceive themselves in a favorable light in the presence of other black people. In this context, they learned to connect their racial group membership with more positive things and fewer negative ones, such as family and community, love and emotional support, respect as people of worth, and so on. Faced with the burden of racial slavery as well as other problems stemming from racial oppression, blacks in America learned to attribute some meanings to the concept of race in ways that affirmed their humanity and ensured their survival.

In light of the fact that interaction patterns and relationships between blacks and whites as well as free blacks and enslaved blacks varied to some degree from one region to another and within each region, blacks' perceptions about things associated with the meaning of race were not necessarily the same from one place to another. However, it appears that the significance attributed to the relationship between skin color and race was the same throughout the United States. The stigma that became associated with black or dark skin was a major source of concern among American-born blacks.[17] For example, the Brown Fellowship Society, an organization founded in 1790 by free blacks in Charleston, South Carolina, used skin color as a criterion for membership. In an essay titled "Identity and Ideology: The Names Controversy," Sterling Stuckey indicates that only light-complexioned people who paid an admission fee of fifty dollars were admitted. He also noted that during a meeting of the Negro convention movement in 1835, there was a great deal of discussion about the stigma associated with blackness between William Whipper, a wealthy black lumberman from Pennsylvania, and Samuel Cornish, a black editor of *Freedom's Journal* in New York. The racial stratification of American society forced black people to view skin color as a primary basis for both self-identity and group identity.

Notwithstanding that the meanings black people in America attributed to race remain an open question, it became for most of them an organizing and unifying principle to adapt to and combat problems caused by racial oppression. Guided by the belief that the fates of American blacks were tied together, race denoted a shared sense of group solidarity for most of them, including free blacks. Excerpts from a statement prepared by William Whipper and others for the 1835 Negro convention movement illustrate links between the plights of enslaved and free blacks as perceived by some black leaders during the first half of the nineteenth century:

> That we find ourselves, after the lapse of three centuries, on the American continent, the remnants of a nation amounting to three million people, whose country has been pillaged, parents stolen, nine generations of which have been wasted by the oppressive cruelty of this nation, standing in the presence of the Supreme Ruler of the Universe, and the civilized world, appealing to God of Nations for deliverance.[18]

For many free blacks of mixed racial ancestry or mulattoes, especially those who resided in the South, race was not a desired source for self-identity and group identity. It appears that with some exceptions, many mulattoes, especially Southerners, accepted some of the European American beliefs about the inferior nature of African people. The genotypes and phenotypes of mulattoes often made them more similar in appearance to their European ancestors than their African ancestors. Consequently, mulattoes most likely were baffled by the logic of their racial group classification as well as the psychological significance attributed to it. In an essay, "The Mulatto in Three Antebellum Communities," James Oliver Horton suggests that many mulattoes viewed themselves as inherently superior to darker people of African ancestry.[19] They viewed their European American ancestry to be a source of elevation above the black masses. On the other hand, they viewed their African ancestry with shame and contempt. In light of the negative connotations associated with blackness as well as a lack of knowledge about their African heritage, many mulattoes in the South sought to identify with their

European ancestry by displaying strong identification with the values, attitudes, and practices of European Americans, especially with members of the white aristocracy. The incongruence in mulatto's physical characteristics and racial classification, which lacked sound scientific merit, most likely contributed to ambivalent feelings and confusion for many of them concerning their perceptions of racial identity. However, recognizing that racial laws and policies lumped free mulattoes together with other blacks, they could not deny the racial problems they shared in common with other American blacks.

THE GROWING SIGNIFICANCE OF
FOLK IDEAS ABOUT RACE

By the beginning of the nineteenth century, folk beliefs about race had become intimately woven into almost every aspect of American society. As a result, opportunities for blacks to make progress toward freedom from slavery and the attainment of racial equality more than ever before became bleak prospects. The most salient feature of the folk beliefs about race in America was the presumption of the inherent racial inferiority of people of African descents and the inherent superiority of Anglo Saxons. More than anything else, this presumption defined the treatment and attitudes toward blacks.[20] The idea of the natural superiority of whites over blacks was a central component of racial ideologies that evolved in North America during the late 1700s through the 1800s.[21] As previously observed, racial oppression and racial slavery rested on the presumption of the natural superiority of Anglo Saxons over black people. It became an important part of the justification of laws enacted to keep the races separated and protect the privileged status afforded planters and other members of the aristocracy.

In his writings on the social construction of race from an anthropological perspective, Lee D. Baker indicates that the institutionalization of racial slavery along with the writings of scientists and other scholars about the racial inferiority of black people were pivotal "in the evolution of the formation of a radicalized worldview."[22] During the early years of the nineteenth century, racial ideologies became crystallized and deeply embedded in American social and scientific thought. In her observations about the significance of the race as a folk system of thought, Audrey Smedley states:

> By the end of the eighteenth century, . . . a variety of beliefs about human differences had emerged and now became fused together, both in the popular mind and in scientific thinking, to form an internally consistent cosmological system. . . . Race, thus became a potentially comprehensive worldview.[23]

Therefore, all blacks, free and slave, were subjected to treatment that set them apart from other racial groups in ways that indicated that they were the lowest-ranked group in a racial scale of being.

Given the high degree of integration of racial ideologies into Western social thought and practices, it seems reasonable to postulate that the idea of race became a central component in the identity development of American-born blacks. No black person in the United States could ignore the social, political, economic, and psychological significance of race in daily life. Support for this assertion can be found in the writings of Reverend H. Easton, a black clergyman of Hartford, Connecticut. In his work *A Treatise on the Intellectual Character, and the Civil and Political Condition of the Colored People of the United States, and the Prejudice towards Them,* Easton sheds light on the pervasiveness of race as a folk system of thought in the United States during the first half of the nineteenth century:

> I have no language wherewith to give slavery, and its auxiliaries, an adequate description, as an efficient cause of the miseries it is capable of producing. It seems to possess a kind of omnipresence. It follows its victims in every avenue of life. The principle assumes still another feature equally destructive. It makes the colored people subserve almost every foul purpose imaginable. Negro or nigger, is an opprobrious term, employed to impose contempt upon them as an inferior race, and also to express their deformity of person. Nigger lips, nigger shins, and nigger heels, are phrases universally common among the juvenile class of society, and full well understood by them; they are early learned to think of these expressions, as they are intended to apply to colored people, and as being expressive or descriptive of the odious qualities of their mind and body. These impressions received by the young, grow with their

growth, and strengthen with their strength. The term in itself, would be perfectly harmless, were it used only to distinguish one class of society from another; but it is not used with that intent; the practical definition is quite different in England to what it is here, for here, it flows from the fountain of purpose to injure. It is a baneful seed which is sown in the tender soil of youthful minds, and there cultivated by the hand of a corrupt immoral policy.

The universality of this kind of education is well known to the observing. Children in infancy receive oral instruction from the nurse. The first lessons given are, Johnny, Billy, Mary, Sally, (or whatever the name may be,) go to sleep, if you don't the old *nigger* will care you off; don't you cry—Hark; the old *niggers'* coming—how ugly you are, you are worse than a little *nigger*. This is a specimen of the first lessons given.

The second is generally given in the domestic circle; in some families it is almost the only method of correcting their children. To inspire their half grown misses and masters to improvement, they are told that if they do this or that, or if they do thus and so, they will be poor or ignorant as a *nigger*; or that they will be black as a *nigger*; or have no more credit than a *nigger*; that they will have hair, lips, feet, or something of the kind, like a *nigger*. If doubt is entertained by any, as to the truth of what I write, let them travel twenty miles in any direction in this country, especially in the free States, and his own sense of hearing will convince him of its reality.

See nigger's thick lips—see his flat nose—nigger eye shine—that slick looking nigger—nigger, where you get so much coat?—that's a nigger priest—are sounds emanating from little urchins of Christian villagers, which continually infest the feelings of colored travellers, like the pestiferous breath of young devils; and full grown persons, and sometimes professors of religion, are not unfrequently heard to join in the concert.

A third mode of this kind of instruction is not altogether oral. Higher classes are frequently instructed in school rooms by refering them to the nigger-seat, and are sometimes threatened with being made to sit with the niggers, if they do not behave.[24]

As can be seen in the previously referenced excerpts taken from Reverend Easton's comments, along with the slave remarks presented earlier, the connotations blacks associated with race gave it meaning while strongly influencing their behavior, feelings, attitudes, and beliefs. The content of the slave narratives and the writings of black leaders, such as Reverend Easton, suggest that the experiences of slavery and oppression provided the core for meanings attributed to the concept of race by blacks in America. While policies and practices of racial discrimination varied from time to time and place to place, no blacks, including black slaveholders, could avoid it.

During the first half of the nineteenth century, studies on race differences expanded well beyond levels of previous years. Perhaps they were inspired by Thomas Jefferson's call for more research to confirm the inferior nature of people of African descents, but scientists and other scholars during this era showed a greater interest in shaping social thought about race differences than ever before. Many of them seemed destined to prove that blacks were subhuman and not members of the same species as other human groups. Antislavery opponents used findings derived from these studies to strengthen racial ideology and make the claim that blacks were not full humans.[25] The use of science to promote the idea that blacks were subhuman during the first half of the nineteenth century encouraged the domination and exploitation of blacks by whites to remain unchecked in all segments of American society.[26]

The Aristotelian presumption that human inequality was the foundation of natural order shaped studies on race differences conducted by scientists and other scholars during the nineteenth century.[27] In writings on racial research in the nineteenth century, Tucker reviews several studies on race that show that the assumptions of the great chain of being and ranking of the races were entrenched in scientific thought in Europe and the United States. He notes that researchers who conducted these studies searched for physical or biological traits that "would distinguish higher animals from lower ones and noble races from savages."[28] Therefore, these researchers were predisposed to search for race differences and interpret the findings in a biased manner that favored the natural superiority of Caucasians over other racial groups.

Focusing on anatomical structure, Charles White, an English surgeon and member of the Royal Society, published a study in 1799 on race differences that portrayed blacks as subhuman, an intermediate group between white Europeans and apes. White claimed that the anatomical evidence showed that blacks were closely akin to "brute creation" and not truly humans in the same way as Europeans.[29] In making the claim that blacks were subhuman, White states, "Orang-outangs," later known as chimpanzees, "have been known to carry off negro-boys, girls, and even women, with a view of making them subservient to their wants as slaves, or as objects of brutal passion: and it has been asserted by some, that women have had offspring from such connections."[30] Although he later admitted it was hearsay, White's observations reveal how extreme ethnocentrism could have biased his research. Commenting on Europeans, White revealed his ethnocentric biases, noting: "Ascending the line of gradation, we come at last to the white European; who being most removed from the brute creation, may, on that account, be considered as the most beautiful of the human race. No one will doubt his superiority in intellectual powers."[31] Challenging the idea of the unity of the species, White contended that each race was the product of a separate species and separate creation, a polygenic view of the species.

Although White's 1799 book was not widely read by the general public, it received serious attention in academic societies.[32] The wealth of the anatomical data contained in White's publication heightened interest among his scientific contemporaries concerning the question of race. Were blacks members of a different species from Europeans as suggested by White? Noting that White's publication added scientific legitimacy to folk beliefs about the inferior status of blacks, Smedley wrote, "It took the question of the Negro's place in the natural scheme so widely held by Europeans and placed it unambiguously in the realm of science."[33] White's publication was widely cited from the 1840s through the 1860s by prominent scientists who believed that, unlike white Europeans, people of African descents were products of a distinctly inferior species.[34] However, the monogenic notion that races were products of the same creation and same species was widely shared among white Americans and Europeans. Nevertheless, in Europe and the United States during the eighteenth century and through the first half of the nineteenth century, there was widespread support for the idea of the hierarchical organization of the races. In general, white Europeans believed that "humanity . . . comprised a hierarchy ranging from inferior to superior individuals," and blacks were destined by nature to be more highly represented among the inferior group.[35]

Polygenism, or the idea that the races represented separate species, was advocated by several highly regarded scientists of the nineteenth century, such as Dr. Samuel G. Morton, a Philadelphia physician well known for his research on human skulls. In Morton's first major publication, in 1839, *Crania Americana*, a racist perspective was evident before he presented the findings. He proclaims, "the Caucasians had given the earth 'its fairest inhabitants' and were distinguished for the 'highest intellectual endowments,' whereas American Indians were 'averse to cultivation,' and blacks were 'the lowest grade of humanity.'"[36] Comparing the features of different human skulls, Morton reports that the skulls of each race of humans have distinctive skull shapes and sizes. Before his death in 1851, Morton had convinced most of the scientific community that human races represented different species. Professor Louis Agassiz, an internationally acclaimed Swiss naturalist at Harvard University, also provided support for the claim that blacks were an inherently inferior racial group and of a different species from other human groups. Stephen J. Gould suggests that Agassiz's observations, seemingly, were primarily products of ethnocentrism rather than scientific inquires.[37] Following his initial contact with blacks, Agassiz writes:

> I experienced pity at the sight of this degraded and degenerated race, and their lot inspired compassion in me in thinking that they are really men. . . . In seeing their black faces with their thick lips and grimacing teeth, the wool on their head, their bent knees, their elongated hands, their large curved nails, and especially the livid color of the palm of their hands, I could not take my eyes off their faces in order to tell them to stay far away. . . . What unhappiness for the white race—to have tied their existence so closely with that of negroes in certain countries![38]

The popularity of the concept of polygenism grew in the United States when the slavery debate peaked during the 1850s and 1860s. Even in the South, Graham Richards notes, polygenism only gained popularity in the final years of slavery as a ploy to preserve it.[39] Thomas Gossett maintains that polygenism offered pro-slavery advocates "an excellent rationale for the defense of slavery" as well as powerful partners in the scientific community.[40] However, in 1859, Dr. Theodore Waiz discredited polygenism by convincing the scientific community that human races were more similar than previously observed. But his observations did not change the belief that race relegated blacks to the lowest ranking group in a chain of human beings. The debate about race differences between the monogenists and polygenists had already damaged the image of blacks so badly that the damage still lingered on into the twentieth century.

REGIONAL DIFFERENCES IN THE LIFE EXPERIENCES OF BLACK PEOPLE

Regardless of slave or free status, wealth, employment status, accomplishments, or even where black people lived in the United States during the early and middle years of the nineteenth century, racial slavery had tainted them as an inferior people with social standing below all other racial groups. Indeed, the racial stigma imposed on people of African descents in the United States retarded their life chances for education, economic, social, and political advancement then and now. For black people living in the United States during the 1800s, an escape haven from racial oppression did not exist. The oppressive racial policies, practices, and racist beliefs helped sustain the struggle for control over the labor and fates of blacks, a long-standing problem that characterized the relationship between them and the white ruling class.

The beliefs and hostile attitudes that blacks and whites shared toward each other before the Revolutionary era still existed after it. After the Revolutionary era, whites, in general, continued to treat blacks as unequal members of the human family. In every region of the United States, blacks had experiences with whites that conveyed to them that African ancestry tainted them and their color was a badge of degradation. Blacks recognized that although they were born in and lived in America, they were not accepted as Americans. They were viewed as property of white Americans with "no rights which the white man was bound to respect."[41] White Americans viewed free and enslaved people of African descents in every region of the United States with contempt. All blacks experienced humiliations, degradation, and other acts of cruelty associated with the debased racial group status imposed on them. Racial prejudice was so widespread and accepted among white Americans that they openly expressed racist attitudes in the presence of African Americans in the North as well as the South.

To deal with the humiliation that stemmed from these racist attitudes and racist behavior, African Americans had to make relatively permanent cognitive and emotional adjustments to retain their human dignity. As mentioned before, they had to become masters at concealing their true feelings in the presence of white Americans because their survival necessitated it. Comments on observations of enslaved African Americans at Port Royal in South Carolina in 1862 by A. M. French, a white woman and a "dedicated humanitarian," illustrate this point.

> The slave, too, conceals. He is never off guard. He is perfectly skilled in hiding all emotions. The downcast eye, dull when he wills it, conceals his opinions, the hearty laugh his grief. His master knows him not, except, possibly, as to what brute force will best subdue him. Nothing is more apparent now that the mask is thrown off, than that owners never understood their slaves. . . . Of course, no sensible slave would be so out of love with life, as to say to his master, "I desire freedom." And the more he was plotting for it, the more loving and contented he would appear. So, in everything, long habit has inured them to deception. Often, they act the opposite of what they feel, as it seems almost involuntarily.[42]

Along with slaves not usually displaying unhappiness with their slave status before their masters, French's observations also reveal how accommodating to conditions of enslavement helped to shape distinctive psychological characteristics in African Americans. Fear of punishment, sexual abuse, and other undesirable experiences that slaveholders, slave overseers, and other white people imposed on enslaved African Americans forced them to conceal a variety of their thoughts, feelings, and behavior. As a result, distinctive psychological patterns for engaging thoughts, feelings, and behavior evolved in enslaved African Americans. They developed unique compensatory ways of making life livable. For example, behind their humor was a very complex pattern of emotions and a complicated social history. Their humor often served to mask sorrow and resentment, both during and after enslavement. It served as a psychological weapon of appeal and appeasement, out of perceived powerlessness. In a word, humor was not only a source of entertainment for some blacks, but also it served as a survival mechanism employed by them to influence the behavior and attitudes of whites toward them. As French observed, these psychological patterns were understood well among blacks but only rarely understood among white people. Black people also had to console and provide emotional support for each other. They had to find venues for expressing their feelings that were acceptable to white people. Lacking individual liberties and opportunities afforded white Americans, many free and enslaved black people gravitated toward community bonding with each other. The loss of hope and fear of the unmitigated power of whites over them characterized the attitudes of many blacks, enslaved and free.

The conditions that shaped their life styles and the relationships between slaves and free blacks varied within and between different regions in the larger society.[43] Comparing blacks in Charleston and New Orleans with blacks in Savannah during the early and middle years of the 1800s, noticeable differences in lifestyles as well as the relationships between slaves and free blacks become evident. In Charleston and New Orleans, mulattoes represented an overwhelming majority of the free black population. Joel Williamson and James Oliver Horton have both reported that many English settlers who migrated to Charleston from Barbados shared the belief that mulattoes, because of their European ancestry, were inherently superior to darker blacks.[44] During times of racial unrest in slave communities, many whites among the ruling elites believed mulattoes would side with them. It is widely held that free mulattoes in Charleston and New Orleans segregated themselves as much as possible from the slave populations.

A substantial proportion of the free mulatto population in New Orleans consisted of wealthy migrants who fled there during the revolution in Santo Domingo. As former overseers of plantations in the West Indies, they brought with them mindsets that predisposed them to feel superior to darker black people.[45] Some of these mulattoes became slave owners and attained the status of planters. Black slaveholding became so widespread in Charleston that, between 1820 and 1840, a majority of free black house-heads owned slaves.[46] Berlin noted that some free blacks in Louisiana worked as slave catchers to demonstrate loyalty to the white elite ruling class.[47] Indeed, free blacks in the South avoided situations that whites could have construed as a threat to the institution of slavery. Faced with very few or no allies in the free black population, slaves living on plantations in the rural areas outside of Charleston and New Orleans worked under conditions that reduced opportunities for them to establish gardens and provisions for themselves. The death rate outnumbered the birth rate on many plantations, especially on the sugar plantations in Louisiana.[48] Although the experiences of free blacks in Charleston and New Orleans were similar, free blacks in New Orleans were permitted to testify in court against whites, but in Charleston, free blacks were denied this right.

The relationship between free blacks and slaves in Savannah differed from that of blacks in Charleston and New Orleans. In describing the black community of Savannah between 1788 and 1864, Whittington B. Johnson notes, "Although a color bias existed in Savannah that favored mulattoes, the social line between free African Americans and slaves was blurred."[49] The free black population in Savannah lived under conditions that imposed more significant constraints on their economic development than free blacks in Charleston and New Orleans. Free blacks in Charleston and New Orleans were permitted to own real estate and often had support from wealthy white planters. Thus, they had the most prosperous free black population in the Southern tier.[50] On the other hand, free blacks in Savannah were prohibited by law from owning real estate and rarely had the support of wealthy whites. They also had more restrictions imposed on the occupations they could pursue than most slaves. For example, free blacks were prohibited from piloting vessels on the Savannah River but were allowed to own and operate vessels.[51] They had more restrictions imposed on the occupations they could pursue than most slaves in Savannah. Unlike most free blacks in the South, free blacks between the ages of fifteen and sixty who lived in Savannah during the early and middle 1800s, were required by law to perform public work up to twenty days in any calendar year without compensation. This requirement showed free blacks how similar their circumstances were to the slave population.

Slaves who resided in Savannah exercised more control over their lives than slaves in the Charleston and New Orleans regions. In his essay on slaves in Savannah, Johnson states, "The mechanism of social control was less confining. They were persons more than they were property; they managed their lives instead of having others manage them."[52] Labor demands and other restrictions imposed on slaves in other parts of the Deep South did not permit the slaves' human value to overshadow their property value. The slave population in Savannah included many slaves who hired out their own time and lived in their own households away from the supervision of their owners and slaves who lived with their owners and performed various jobs for them on the premises. As might be expected, Savannah became a popular city for runaway slaves. In Savannah, slaves and free blacks openly mingled together, attending the same social functions and churches, living in the same homes, performing the same jobs in workplaces, and intermarrying.[53] These observations suggest that there might have been more racial solidarity and cultural connectedness between slaves and free blacks in Savannah than elsewhere in the Lower South.

However, since laws had been passed to abolish slavery in the North during the American Revolutionary era, combined with the scarcity of the black population there, black people in the North had more freedom for self-expression than free black people in the South. Nevertheless, because of the gradual-emancipation laws enacted by many Northern state governments and with the lack of adequate protection from the daily threat of being kidnapped and sold into slavery to Southern slaveholders, the free status of Northern blacks was fragile. Therefore, free blacks in the North had to be concerned about protecting their freedom when speaking out against slavery and racial injustices. In the Upper South and Northern regions, free blacks often guarded their behavior and emotional reactions toward whites, but they also showed compassion for the plights of enslaved blacks and often worked with them under the supervision of white overseers.[54]

Most free blacks in the Lower South and Mississippi Valley regions did not dare make public gestures of pride about their African roots. They tended to show more interest in maintaining favorable relationships with influential white slaveholders than open concern about the plights of enslaved blacks. Eugene Genovese notes that free blacks in the South lived in constant fear of repercussions from the hostility and resentment many white Southerners felt toward them.[55] White slaveowners, in general, believed that enslaved blacks could not be content with their slave status with free blacks in their presence. Free blacks served to keep hope for freedom alive among enslaved blacks. With thousands of runaway slaves or fugitives reported every year, attempts by enslaved blacks to escape from slavery occurred frequently.[56] Viewed as threats to the institution of slavery, Southern states adopted laws to restrict the mobility of free Southern blacks.

While it was the desire of whites to maintain lines of demarcation between free and enslaved blacks, racial oppression tended to strengthen
group solidarity along racial lines among free black people and their
enslaved counterparts. The intimate link between racial slavery and
racial oppression created a dependency between enslaved and free
blacks that could not be ignored by either group.[57] A desire to escape
from the despicable conditions associated with racial oppression made it
easier for free black people to work toward helping enslaved blacks and
eliminating slavery. However, as previously observed, the writings of Ira
Berlin clearly show some local and regional variations in the relationship
between free and enslaved blacks.[58]

During the early decades of the nineteenth century, race bonding and
race consciousness grew among blacks who resided in the Upper South
and Northern regions of the United States. Excerpts from a speech
made on January 1, 1808, by Peter Williams, a minister in New York
City and also the son of a cofounder of the African Methodist Episcopal
Zion Church, shed light on the significance race played in community
bonding among blacks. In a speech delivered at the African Church in
New York, Williams states:

> But to us, Africans and descendants of Africans, this period is deeply inter-
> esting. We have felt, sensibly felt, the sad effects of this abominable traffic.
> It has made, if not ourselves, our forefathers and kinsmen its unhappy vic-
> tims and pronounced on them and their posterity, the sentence of perpetual
> slavery. . . . But you, beloved Africans, who had passed the days of infancy
> when you left your country, you can tell the aggravated sufferings of unfor-
> tunate race; your memories can bring to view these scenes of bitter grief.[59]

His remarks suggest that race may have been a potent unifying force
for some African Americans. Although the extent that Williams's views
were shared by other free blacks cannot be determined, his remarks reflect empathy for enslaved African Americans and a strong sense of duty
on the part of black leaders to get slavery abolished in the United States.
Williams's observations suggest that racial slavery had become a potent
force in shaping the behaviors, attitudes, and emotions of many African
Americans. On the other hand, there were social class, skin color, and
gender, cultural, ideological, and political differences that threatened
racial solidarity in black communities. The potential threat these factors

may have posed for racial solidarity among blacks almost certainly varied from region to region and from time to time as well as in the value they attributed to these factors.

As previously observed, during American slavery in the nineteenth century, blacks were forced to deal with the reality that whites viewed them as inherently inferior. Based on this reality, one is inclined to reason that daily encounters with the manifestations of these (racist) views would have forged, among blacks, a common sense of people-hood based upon race as the common denominator. Nonetheless, there were differences among blacks related to skin color, class considerations (skilled workers vs. unskilled laborers or free vs. slave), and regions of residence. As such, we must ask: Did these differences create differentiation within racial identities of blacks? If so, how did these differences impact upon the ways in which blacks related to one another?

While a given population or racial/ethnic group may endure a common oppression, it does not automatically follow that all the members of the oppressed population identify with each other. The experiences of Jews in the concentration camp presented in the 1984 publication of *Man's Search for Meaning* by Viktor E. Frankl show that some prisoners, namely the Capos, identified with the oppressor. Frankl states, "Often they were harder on the prisoners than were the guards, and beat them more cruelly than the SS men did."[60] As can be seen, common oppression may lead some members of the oppressed group to identify with the oppressor. Some members may exploit their own people as in the case of some black slave-owners, some members may compete for favor with whites at the expense of other blacks, and some members may take out their frustrations on other blacks in the form of direct violence-prone aggression. In a word, there existed several forces creating division and competition within both the slave and free black population that worked against a common racial identity and sense of racial solidarity, even when a black person was opposed to whites.

THE LOWER SOUTHERN REGIONS

The rapid and steady growth in the production of staple crops in cotton, sugar, and hemp during the early and middle 1800s increased the demand for slave labor in South Carolina, Georgia, Alabama, Mississippi, and Louisiana.[61] Triggered by high demands for cotton in England, Trotter indicates that cotton became the center of Southern and United States economic growth during the early and mid-1800s. A steadily rising demand for laborers accelerated the price of slaves in the Southern interior and the internal slave trade. The internal slave trade, or second Middle Passage, involved selling and transporting slaves from states in the Upper South and North to states located in the Southern interior region.

Beginning early in the 1800s and continuing through the 1850s, the internal slave trade became a major economic enterprise. Commenting on the high demand for slave labor, Trotter writes, "The rising demand for black labor stimulated a thriving domestic trade in human beings. Numerous small traders entered the field and worked aggressively to build up their stock."[62] During the second decade of the nineteenth century, Ira Berlin observed that traders and slaveholders sent approximately 120,000 slaves from the Upper South to the Southern interior, with Georgia, Tennessee, Alabama, and Louisiana being the largest recipients, and approximately 300,000 during the 1830s.[63] By 1860, approximately one million slaves, who represented nearly a third of the slave population, were sent for slave labor from the Upper to the Lower South.[64]

The increase in the price and demand for slaves increased threats of re-enslavement among free blacks in the Upper South and Northern regions. Kidnapping and re-enslaving free blacks as well as abducting and selling slaves who had been promised freedom occurred so often during the first decade of the nineteenth century that blacks viewed re-enslavement as a serious problem in Northern cities and states located in the Upper South.[65] These illegal practices often involved collaborations between corrupt law officials, slaveholders, and slave traders. The hatred and distrust that had evolved over time between black and white people in the United States most likely was made more intense by these illegal and immoral practices.

As noted earlier, local and regional differences existed in the economic, political, and social environments in which both free and enslaved blacks lived. Horton observed that distinctive cultural practices and race relations within the black communities were significantly influenced by differences in several demographic and local structural factors, such as size and proportion of free blacks and slaves in the region, the nature of the economies in the region, and so on.[66] The transporting of slaves from the Northern and Upper South regions to the Lower South created more fluidity in the cultural exchanges among slaves from different regions. Accordingly, blacks living in different regions were likely to share many similarities in their cultural practices, beliefs, and attitudes about race.

A great deal of the writings about American slavery, especially in the Lower South, focus on the way regional differences impacted upon the practices and policies of slavery. Consequently, slave owners and overseers have been lumped together in a manner that obscures individual differences between them—that is, the different ways they managed slaves in their separate slave facilities. On large plantations, where the bulk of the slave population could be found, slave owners delegated responsibilities for daily operational matters to others and rarely had direct contact with the general slave population. Most slave-owners had fewer than ten slaves, and they often worked together with them on the production of different crops. Thus, significant differences were likely to have existed in the interaction patterns between slaves and small slave-owners versus slaves and large slave-owners.

Generalizing slave owners' management of slaves in different regions may yield skewed and distorted descriptions about it. On the other hand, there is a dearth of information concerning differences in slavery practices that most likely occurred within the various regions. In each slave living quarter, the temperaments and management practices of slave masters and overseers were different. Slave masters, in general, placed profits derived from bond labor above the human value of slaves, but some slave masters seemed to show a preference for the use of positive reinforcement as the primary management strategy of slaves, directing overseers to show some compassion toward slaves. Conversely, the actions of many slave masters indicated a preference for the use or threat of punishment as the dominant management strategy of slaves. Undoubtedly, the attitudes and behavior of slaves were significantly influenced by the labor management strategies adopted by slave masters and overseers. Excerpts taken from Washington's instructions to his overseers illustrate how some slave masters adopted management practices that showed concern for the humanity of slaves.

> The health of the negroes under your charge is an important matter. Much of the usual sickness among them is the result of carelessness and mismanagement. Overwork, or unnecessary exposure to rain, insufficient clothing, improper or badly cooked food, and night rambles, are all fruitful causes of disease. . . . Whenever you find that the case is one you do not understand, send for a physician, if such is the general order of your employer. By exerting yourself to have their clothing ready in good season; to arrange profitable in-door employment in wet weather; to see that an abundant supply of wholesome, well-cooked food, including plenty of vegetables, be supplied to them at regular hours; that the sick be cheered and encouraged, and some extra comforts allowed them, and the convalescent not exposed to the chances of a relapse; that pregnant women be particularly cared for, and in a great measure exempted from labor, and certainly from exposure and undue exertion, for some time before confinement. . . . By using such means for their comfort as every judicious, humane man will readily think of, you will find the amount of sickness greatly lessened.
>
> It is indispensable that you exercise judgment and consideration in the management of the Negroes under your charge. Be firm, and at the same time gentle in your control. Never display yourself before them in a passion. . . . When you find it necessary to use the whip . . . apply it slowly and deliberately, and to the extent you are determined, in your own mind, to be needful before you began. The indiscriminate, constant and excessive use of the whip, is altogether unnecessary and inexcusable. . . . Whenever an opportunity is afforded you for rewarding continued good behavior, do not let it pass—occasional rewards have a much better effect than frequent punishments.[67]

The slave narratives presented earlier provide glimpses of the physical and psychological abuse exercised by some slaveholders and overseers as a way of managing slaves. It seems reasonable to conclude that the treatment of slaves and the behavioral norms in slaves' living quarters most likely varied from one living quarter to another and from one situation to another within the same living quarter. Therefore, the experiences that shaped slaves attitudes and behavior should significantly vary within the same regions. Living under these circumstances would have required them to adapt their attitudes and behavioral practices in accordance to the uniqueness of the norms that most likely operated in the various slave quarters. Nevertheless, historians have noted striking similarities across regions in blacks' cultural practices and perceptions about race during the nineteenth century.

For blacks, it appears that the tension and other negative emotions associated with their ongoing power struggle with the ruling white elites for control of work and other living conditions that shaped the fates of blacks superseded local and regional variations in their attitudes toward whites. Resentment of racial oppression and the racial stigma imposed on them was shared among all blacks, including black slave-owners. For most blacks, this resentment heightened race consciousness and racial solidarity to levels that superseded the humane gestures exercised by some slave masters. It is widely known that black skilled workers and domestic slaves were treated more humanely than field workers. Even though skilled and domestic slaves may have experienced a better quality of life than the field workers, runaway slaves were often skilled workers and domestic workers who serviced the household needs of slaveholders. Often, it was very difficult, if not impossible, to distinguish runaway slaves who were skilled workers and household specialists from other free blacks. Through their close contact with members of the slaveholders' families as well as friends and guests of the slaveholders, these slaves became well adept to European cultural practices and verbal communication. Their knowledge of European culture and practices helped them to be effective at disguising their identities as free blacks and escape bondage. These observations provide support for the notion that, regardless of work and living conditions, a yearning for control of their fates was a common desire among all blacks.

GOVERNANCE ON PLANTATIONS

A majority of blacks in the Lower South lived on plantations consisting of twenty or more slaves. Plantations operated relatively free of legal restrictions or governmental overseers to ensure that slave owners adopt humane practices in managing the bond-labor workforce. As slavery expanded in the Southern interior, slave owners strengthened control over government offices. They controlled the legislative, judicial, and executive branches of government at the state, county, and local levels.[68] By tightening the grip on government, any form of treatment imposed by slave owners on the enslaved population could go easily without being questioned by law officials.

The organization of the workforce on plantations created a slave class structure that fostered division and distrust within the enslaved population. While focusing on matters that maximized profits, planters or large slave-owners assigned the daily management of the plantation labor force to hired white overseers who often were at odds with the enslaved population. Overseers were required to keep daily records and make reports periodically to the owner.[69] Leaving the direct supervision of field hand slaves to blacks assigned by slave owners as "head driver," slave owners and overseers rarely spent time with enslaved field hand workers. Patrolling on a horse with a whip nearby, the head driver was required to establish the work pace for workers that ensured adequate production levels and to enforce discipline. If the overall levels of production dropped below owners' expectations, drivers placed themselves at high risk of getting beaten and demoted into the ranks of field hands.

As can be seen by plan and design, the division of labor on plantations pitted drivers against the field hands and created conditions that had high potential for breaking down trust within slave communities. In writings on the slave labor hierarchy, Joe William Trotter suggests that drivers and forewomen were ranked at the top tier of the labor hierarchy followed closely by artisans and craftsmen.[70] Artisans and craftsmen were followed by household specialists, which included cooks, butlers, valets, coachmen, seamstresses, nurses, and manufacturers of household items. The bottom of the labor hierarchy, Trotter notes, consisted of field hands, household laborers, and personal servants. However, slaves in high standing with slave owners or overseers frequently were not perceived in a favorable light by other slaves. Within slave communities, slaves earned the respect of fellow slaves by displaying a willingness to challenge directives of slave owners and overseers rather than seeking to befriend them.[71]

The division of labor on the plantation was an easy source for creating dissension within local slave quarters. Seemingly, the slaves' quest for freedom and recognition as members of the human family, with the same entitlement to natural rights as whites, were priorities that reduced the significance of differences between them that may have been rooted in the labor pecking order. That is to say, there has been considerably more historical documentation of collaborative efforts among blacks to combat racial oppression than confrontation reflecting class differences between blacks, especially in slave populations. Eugene D. Genovese suggests that field hands generally maintained close friendship ties with house servants and other slaves on the plantations.[72] Marriages between field hands and house servants were common occurrences on most plantations. Friendships slaves established during childhood frequently were sustained through the adult years after work assignments in the fields or the slave masters' living quarters. Genovese notes that racial solidarity between house servants and field hands was the norm on most plantations. Well-treated house servants showed sympathy and compassion for field slaves when they observed them being beaten by overseers. House slaves and field slaves collaborated on plots to escape to freedom.

It appears that the long-standing power struggle that characterized the relationship between enslaved blacks and white slave-owners overshadowed or defused conflicts among slaves that may have been rooted in the slave-labor pecking order. The meanings blacks associated with the idea of race and their slave status seemed to have played a greater role than either differences in skin complexions or labor class rankings in shaping blacks' relationships with whites as well as blacks' relationships with each other. The slave insurrection planned over several years by Denmark Vesey, before it was uncovered in 1822, suggests that the idea of race had become a powerful frame of reference for shaping black thought and a force for galvanizing support for solidarity among blacks.[73] It also showed how fear and self-interest led to the betrayal of blacks involved in the plot by two other slaves.[74]

Inspired by the successful slave revolt in Santo Domingo, during the period from 1818 to 1822, Denmark Vesey developed a comprehensive plan to free the slaves and destroy slave-owning inhabitants in Charleston, South Carolina. Vesey, a free mulatto of wealth, recruited several hundreds of loyal black folk, including mulattoes, to carry out the rebellion. Vesey's character personified unquestionable black pride and courage. Commenting on his conspiracy, Vesey said, "If we did not put our work and deliver ourselves, we should never come out of slavery." When he observed a slave bow to a white man, he would say to the slave that all men were born equal and that he was surprised that anyone would degrade himself by such conduct, that he would never cringe to the whites.[75] Following an unsuccessful attempt by a Vesey loyalist to recruit him, Peter Desverneys, a well-treated, skilled mulatto slave, revealed the plot to the wife of his master. Employed by Charleston authorities to attend a meeting of the slave rebels, the slave George Wilson confirmed Desverneys's story.[76] Peter Desverneys subsequently was granted freedom along with economic incentives for his loyalty to his white master. And his disclosure of the conspiracy revealed the lack of racial solidarity some Southern mulattoes shared with other black people in America. The actions of Denmark Vesey and his coconspirators, on the other hand, provide a primary example of the communal bonding in response to racial oppression during the pre–Civil War years. A careful review of slave narratives also shows that many mulattoes, who were ex-slaves, joined the abolitionist movement and spoke out against slavery as well as other racial inequities in the United States.

SLAVE LABOR SYSTEMS

The expansion of cotton production led to changes in the mode of organizing work assignments. The "gang" system became the mode of organizing work on cotton plantations. This system forced large numbers of slaves to work at the master's pace under close supervision of an overseer. Before the rapid growth of the cotton enterprise during the 1800s, the task system was a widely used mode of organizing work on plantations. Under the task system, enslaved workers were required to complete a specific number of "daily tasks." After overseers and drivers approved the completed tasks, the slaves could use the remaining hours in the workday to do as they chose.[77] Historians tend to agree that most slaves, used this "free time" in a variety of ways, including, but not limited to, raising their own gardens and marketing the products, selling their labor, and doing other things that improved the quality of their lives. This "free time" may have had strong reinforcement value for the enslaved population because it provided them with opportunities to exercise some control over their fates.

Introduced to increase cotton production, the gang labor regiments sharply reduced free time for the enslaved population. Ira Berlin suggests that the introduction of gang labor led to the demise of black foremen and drivers.[78] Using the lash of the whip to enforce work performance at the master's pace, white overseers supervised field hands and kept them working at a steady pace. Blacks viewed overseers as ruthless, low-life people, with a reputation for brutality. Describing work on the Louisiana plantation where he lived after being kidnapped in New York and sold into slavery, the ex-slave Solomon Northup shares these memories:

> The hands are required to be in the cotton field as soon as it is light in the morning, and, with the exception of ten or fifteen minutes, which is given them at noon to swallow their allowance of cold bacon, they are not permitted to be a moment idle until it is too dark to see, and when the moon is full, they often times labor till the middle of the night.[79]

Obviously, the sunrise-to-sunset labor demands curtailed, even more than before the American Revolutionary War, opportunities for field hand slaves to experience some control over their lives. Forced to become field hands during the expansion of the cotton enterprise, many enslaved skilled tradesmen, craftsmen, and artisans were denied opportunities to use or hone their skills and subsequently pass them on to their offspring. The tension, hostility, and animosity, which were always present in conflicts between the slaves and slave owners, became more intense, with slaves regularly sabotaging property. Slaves expressed their discontent in a variety of ways, such as refusing to work, breaking or destroying tools and other valuable equipment, setting fires to barns, maiming animals, and so on.[80] The relationships that evolved between masters and slaves on cotton plantations during the early decades of the 1800s were highly volatile, characterized by a constant spread of rumors about slave insurrections. In 1812, a Mississippi territorial governor remarked, "Scarcely a day passes without my receiving some information relative to the designs of those people to insurrect."[81]

Bearing in mind that the United States was racially divided by Europeans to derive profits from the exploitation of black slave labor, the struggle of blacks to exercise more control over their labor and personal lives against the objections of whites may have predisposed many blacks to perceive themselves as underdogs or victims rather than accept a racial worldview of themselves as inherently inferior people. It would have been relatively easy for blacks who may have adopted an underdog or victim mindset to perceive the relationship as "us against them," and whites would have been viewed as the common enemy. Viewing white people as the common enemy could have reinforced racial solidarity and racial group identification among free and enslaved blacks. However, as noted earlier, members of an oppressed population may not respond to common oppression in the same manner. On the one hand, many blacks developed feelings of inferiority to whites and negative associations to blackness. On the other hand, many noted blacks of the nineteenth century exhorted racial pride and refuted ideas of black inferiority. For example, David Walker, Denmark Vesey, Nat Turner, Edward W. Blyden, Alexander Crummell, Henry Highland Garnet, and Fredrick Douglass vehemently denounced slavery and exhorted the importance of racial pride and equality. By the same token, many blacks might not have consciously internalized stereotyped ideas of black inferiority imposed on them by a group perceived as their oppressor or common enemy. However, there remains the possibility that they internalized such negative feelings and perceptions concerning blackness on an unconscious level.

The increased tension between slaves and white slave-owners may have exacerbated negative racial attitudes and racial stereotypes that blacks may have shared among them about whites. It also may have increased the probability of race becoming an organizing and unifying principle for blacks to cope with conditions imposed on them. The sense of group solidarity that blacks seemed to have shared was reinforced by whites' racially motivated behavior. The masses of black people in the United States believed that, because of their race, their fate was intimately tied together. In a word, the dehumanizing characteristics of racial slavery appeared to serve as a potent reminder of the significance of race for individual and group identification among enslaved black people.

FREE BLACKS IN THE LOWER SOUTHERN REGIONS

From the beginning of the nineteenth century through the early 1860s, with the exception of Louisiana, states located in the lower Southern tier, including South Carolina, Georgia, Mississippi, Alabama, and Arkansas, had very small free black populations. The combined free black population in South Carolina and Georgia was never higher than 2 percent of the total black population in this region from 1810 through 1860. As in other lower Southern regions, the slave population in South Carolina grew at an unprecedented pace during the first 60 years of the nineteenth century, with 196,365 in 1810; 258,475 in 1820; 327,038 in 1840; and 402,406 in 1860.[82] On the other hand, the already tiny free black population, in proportion to the total black population, only grew slightly during this same period, with 4,554 in 1810; 6,826 in 1820; 8,276 in 1840; and 9,914 in 1860. An even smaller number of free blacks, less than 1 percent of the total black population, lived in Mississippi, Alabama, and Arkansas during this period. In 1810, shortly after the Louisiana Purchase, there were approximately 7,585 free blacks and 34,660 enslaved blacks in Louisiana. From 1810 through 1840, in Louisiana, the free black population grew at a very slow rate while the slave population grew at a very rapid pace. In 1840, there were 25,502 free blacks and 168,452 slaves in Louisiana. From 1840 through 1860, the free black population dropped to 18,647, and the slave population almost doubled to 331,726.[83]

The passage of bills by state assemblies in the South, which made manumissions more difficult to attain, contributed to the slow growth of the Southern free black population. In writings about black slaveowners in South Carolina, Larry Koger notes that, after 1820 in South Carolina, free blacks who purchased family members or friends were denied approval by the state assembly to grant them freedom.[84] An overwhelming majority of the slave population living quarters were located in rural country surroundings, isolated from the towns and cities. On the other hand, a large proportion of the Southern free blacks lived in the towns, industrial villages, and cities, such as Charleston, New Orleans, and Savannah, but Genovese observes that the majority of them lived in rural areas.[85]

The scarcity of free blacks and the heavy concentration of them in cities and towns sharply reduced opportunities for contact between free blacks and slaves in the lower Southern tier, even if they desired it. As previously observed, living with no rights that whites had to respect, free blacks had to learn to cope with the constant fear of being humiliated, harassed by law officials, or kidnapped and sold into slavery.[86] Having either seen or perhaps heard about the consequences of the Denmark Vesey slave plot, some free blacks may have felt too powerless and afraid to speak out against the racial injustice they witnessed. Some free blacks sought permanent refuge to Northern cities to escape from racial oppression in the South.[87] Some free blacks in the South accepted invitations from the American Colonization Society to resettle in Liberia.[88] Founded in 1816, by whites, including several influential slave-owners, the American Colonization Society aimed to help blacks resettle in Africa and other black nations. Black leaders such as David Walker and Henry Highland Garnet denounced the organization, contending that its primary objective was to ensure the growth and stability of the American slavery system.

Skin complexion was a primary characteristic used in racial group classification, and as such, it significantly influenced blacks' attitudes about themselves and their relationships toward each other. It also influenced the attitudes and behavior of black and white people toward each other. The writings on race differences during the seventeenth and eighteenth centuries by notable European scholars, such as Comte de Buffon, Baron de Montesquieu, Carolus Linnaeus, Johann Friedrich Blumenbach, and others, suggest they associated unattractiveness or ugliness with dark complexion and the purity and natural beauty with whiteness. On one hand, they tended to associate dark complexion with stupidity, uncivil behavior, and heathenism, but on the other hand, whiteness was associated with civility, intelligence, and beauty.[89] Skin complexion, especially blackness, seemed to be of central importance in the assessment of non-Europeans by learned people of Europe. Winthrop Jordan contends that the concept of blackness carried negative connotations for English people even before they had contact with Africans.[90] The idea of blackness, Jordan notes, represented for English-speaking people "a way of expressing some of their most ingrained values."[91] Perceiving the complexion of black people as a physical defect, Jordan suggests that, during the seventeenth and eighteenth centuries, learned people of Europe were consumed with trying to account for its cause and origin, and its significance.[92] Commenting on black folks' skin pigmentation and other so-called racial characteristics, Montesquieu writes:

> It is hardly to be believed that God, who is a wise Being, should place a soul, especially a good soul, in such a black ugly body. It is so natural to look upon colour as the criterion of human nature, that the Asiatics, among whom eunuchs are employed, always deprive the blacks of their resemblance to us by a more opprobrious distinction. . . . It is impossible for us to suppose these creatures to be men, because, allowing them to be men, a suspicion would follow that we ourselves are not Christians.[93]

Given that white Americans also attributed negative connotations to the concept of blackness, it seemed to have influenced the subjective judgments about human beauty and self-worth of most American-born black people. Many blacks experienced feelings of ugliness, shame, and a sense of inferiority because of their dark complexion. Conversely, many light-complexion blacks or mulattoes displayed attitudes and feelings of superiority toward dark-complexion blacks during the nineteenth century. Although there was no legal distinction between the living conditions of mulattoes and darker blacks, numerous writings on American slavery suggest that many light-skinned people with blood linkage to Africans ascribed to the notion that the physical differences between them and darker people of African descents denoted inherent psychological and behavioral differences between them. Mulattoes frequently segregated themselves from other darker people of African descents. During the antebellum period, they formed associations, schools, and churches that discriminated against darker people of African descents. The Brown Fellowship Society provides an example of an association comprised of mulattoes that discriminated against the darker black masses.[94]

The Brown Fellowship Society had as its foundation stone "charity" and "benevolence" and its capstone, "social purity." Only free mulattoes and their descendants were granted membership in the Brown Fellowship Society. The society's membership certificate stipulates these are to certify that only a property-holding free brown man of Charleston was regularly admitted as a member of the Brown Fellowship Society. Some of its members were black slaveholders. In addition to monthly dues, the initiation fee into the organization was fifty dollars. If certified by one of the society's officers, any member who suffered a serious ailment could claim a sick benefit of one dollar and fifty cents per week while incapacitated. The group also provided burial financial assistance for any deceased member expenses that needed it. If the deceased left children without adequate provisions for their education, the group was obligated to maintain and to educate the children until age fourteen, at which time they would be apprenticed for a trade. The association provided loans to its members. Its preamble also included a clause for relief to any poor, free, colored orphan or adult deemed worthy by the membership.

Most free mulattoes in Charleston attended Saint Mark's Episcopal Church. Although the congregation did not have a formal policy that denied dark-skinned black people membership, there is no evidence that any dark-skinned black belonged to the church. In a paper titled "Charleston's Free and Afro-American Elite," Robert L. Harris Jr. suggests that social class, rather than color consciousness, was the primary determinant in social relations among Charleston's free black population. Harris notes that, in general, mulattoes were more financially secure than the darker-hued African Americans.[95] But he also acknowledged that Thomas Small, a prosperous dark-complexioned Charlestonian, was denied membership in the Brown Fellowship Society because of his skin color. Although there was social class distinction in the free black community in Charleston, most scholars agree, in some cases, skin color and not social class provided the primary reason for discrimination among free blacks. Mulattoes were very sensitive about skin color because of the psychological significance attributed to race in the larger society as well as their precarious social relations with upper-class Southern whites.

The idea that blacks with European blood linkage were inherently superior to blacks with no white blood was widely touted and reinforced by whites. White slave-owners generally extended preferential treatment to mulattoes over darker blacks because they believed that the infusion of white blood enhanced their intellectual and social potential. Rarely used as field hands on plantations, mulattoes were more likely than darker blacks to be free, skilled workers, literate, and considered intelligent by whites.[96] Enslaved mulattoes were employed more often as domestics in the household of slaveholders rather than as field hands. Shortly after the American Revolution, many Southern slaveholders freed their enslaved mulattoes. In his book *Free People of Color*, James Oliver Horton suggests that slaves freed in the lower Southern tier tended to be the children of slave masters and their slave concubines.[97] Granting freedom to slave concubines and their mulatto offspring was a common practice of white slaveholders. It was not uncommon for slaveholders to provide schooling privileges, freedom with economic support, and slaves to mulattoes with blood linkage to them.[98] By 1860, mulattoes constituted approximately 75 percent of the free black population and less than 10 percent of the slave population in the lower Southern tier of the United States. In Charleston, New Orleans, and many other Southern cities, lighter skin was a mark of upper-class status among blacks.[99]

In the Lower South, it was commonplace for white people to openly express their preference for mulattoes over darker blacks. In Charleston, for example, where mulattoes were 75 percent of the free black population, Alfred Huger, postmaster of Charleston, describes free blacks, in 1858, best as "an intermediate class in the world because they provided an insurmountable barrier between the slaves and slave holders."[100] He also notes that because of their mechanical skills, mulattoes could help keep the white working class in check. The preferential treatment practices displayed by white Americans toward mulattoes, over blacks of darker hues, reinforced many mulattoes' belief that their Caucasian ancestry made them inherently superior to the darker masses. Accordingly, in many communities, relationships were strained between light-skinned and dark-skinned black people.

Undoubtedly, being of mixed racial ancestry and living in a racially stratified society heightened mulattoes' anxiety and confusion about their racial group identity. Their African ancestry did not permit them to escape the racial stigma associated with blackness, despite their desires to do so. They yearned for the day that whites would judge them primarily on the basis of their achievements rather than their race, but they lacked the economic leverage that was needed to keep this hope alive. In a story entitled "A Matter of Principle," Charles Chesnutt, a free mulatto proclaims, "If we are not accepted as white, we can at any rate make it clear that we object to being called black."[101]

The mixture of European and African ancestry in a racist society posed highly complex psychological and social dilemmas for mulattoes. They endured considerable emotional turmoil and ambivalence about it. In light of obvious genetic evidence to the contrary, to be classified as a black people and denigrated to slave status by their Caucasian fathers must have been terrifying realizations for most mulattoes. Horton describes the mulatto's dilemma in this way: "The tragic mulatto was one torn in identity, yearning toward the elevation that genetically and socially was beyond the grasp, forced to settle for a lower place in the social order."[102] Bearing this in mind, mulattoes were predisposed to be more sensitive than either dark-skinned blacks or Caucasians to the psychological significance attributed in America to skin complexion and other racially distinctive physical characteristics. Faced with this dilemma during the nineteenth century, many light-skinned people of African descents gravitated to the middle-class and upper-class white people (to the extent that they were permitted to do so by whites) and, when possible, distanced themselves from the black masses.

Being rejected, scorned, and viewed with scrutinizing eyes by white Americans on one hand and distrusted, envied, and sometimes resented by the darker masses of blacks in America on the other, mulattoes were divided in their allegiance to darker-skinned black people. However, as noted in the actions of Denmark Vesey, there were mulattoes in the antebellum South who viewed themselves as equal members of the larger black society and sacrificed their lives and personal well-being for the black masses. The practice of segregating themselves from dark-complexioned blacks was especially evident among free mulattoes in New Orleans. Many free mulattoes in New Orleans were refugees who fled during the successful slave revolt in Saint Dominique. As slave overseers before the revolution, they were familiar with the three-tier model of racial stratification consisting of white, mulatto, and black that existed in Saint Dominique. Therefore, many mulatto refugees in New Orleans practiced caste discrimination against dark-complexion blacks in ways that closely resembled the racial practices of white Americans.[103]

Free blacks in the South often became targets of racial hostility and racial injustice. Therefore, paternalistic relationships with influential white people provided free blacks with protection against racial violence and other forms of racial mistreatment by other white people. It was

easier for mulattoes than other blacks to establish paternalistic relationships with influential white people. Commenting on the benefits derived from these relationships, James H. Holloway, a free mulatto who
belonged to the Brown Fellowship Society, put it this way:

> On the one hand we have the dominant race, on the other we have the
> backward race. The first looked with scrutinizing eyes on our every move-
> ment, so as to charge us with being a disturbing element in conditions
> that existed . . . but fortunately there were the classes in society, and as
> our fathers allied themselves with them, as a consequence, they had their
> influence and protection and so they had to be in accord with them and
> stand for what they stood for.[104]

As can be seen here, many mulattoes felt trapped in the middle of racial
hostility. Moreover, their economic survival depended on the patronage
of influential white citizens. Therefore, free mulattoes often believed it
was in their self-interest to distance themselves from darker blacks and
befriend the Southern gentry.

4

DEHUMANIZED AND STIGMATIZED IN A RACIALLY STRATIFIED SOCIETY: PSYCHOLOGICAL IMPLICATIONS FOR AFRICAN AMERICANS

Given the eighteenth-century reality that mulattoes, in general, clearly did not perceive themselves as either black or as white, it makes sense to assume that racial group membership became a more complex lived phenomenon among African Americans than science conducted in the realm of epistemological racism could see or describe. This chapter is devoted to exploring this complexity. Underlying this chapter is the assumption that we cannot view American black identity as an unchanging thing but must instead see American black identities as significantly influenced by particular historical events. As such, black identities are subject to change within the lifetimes of individuals and generations in response to personally and historically significant cultural events. Accordingly, this chapter argues that, before the end of the Civil War, there emerged a dualistic psychological tendency among African Americans that tore them between their own individual interests and those of the race at large, brought about in relation to the end of chattel slavery. This chapter traces this tendency from the early 1800s until the early 1900s and concludes by arguing that by the beginning of the twentieth century, the concept of race, as a frame of reference, functioned as a psychological filter for all African Americans.

BLACK SLAVEHOLDERS IN THE ANTEBELLUM SOUTH

Given the predominance of an individualistic orientation in the larger American society and the economic benefits derived from individual property ownership, such as enjoyed by members of the white aristocracy, many free Southern mulattoes adopted an individualistic outlook rather than the oppressed communal orientation, which seemed to be more characteristic of the black masses. Although they lacked the individual rights guaranteed to citizens under the United States Constitution, they were as strongly committed as European Americans were to individualistic and capitalistic pursuits. They enthusiastically adopted the philosophy of self-help as the strategy for individual and group advancement. The similarities between these groups were evident especially in Charleston and New Orleans. In these cities, elite mulattoes bought and sold slaves, intermarried, made marriage settlements, owned church pews, and organized exclusive associations for only mulattoes. They exploited opportunities to make themselves useful and respectable citizens, hoping that they could convince whites that their prejudices were unfounded. They wanted to be accepted as Americans in an integrated society and have the same legal rights as European Americans.[1] This was especially the case among some free blacks that were fathered by white slaveholding planters. In his work *Black Slave Owners*, Koger notes that there were black slaveholders in every Southern state that championed slavery.[2] According to the United States Census of 1830, black slaveholders in Louisiana, Maryland, South Carolina, and Virginia owned more than 10,000 slaves. The vast majority of black slaveholders did not have firsthand knowledge of the dehumanizing nature of slavery because they had never been enslaved.

In Charleston, South Carolina, there were 407 free black slaveholders. The majority of black slaveholders were females because the population of free black women was considerably larger than the same for black men. Since black females could not refuse sexual advances by white slaveholders, some obtained their freedom when they birthed the child of their masters. Regrettably, most enslaved females who were impregnated by their slave masters remained enslaved along with their mulatto children. In 1820, free black women accounted for approximately 68 percent of the heads of family and 71 percent of black slaveholders. Most black slaveholders were mulattoes, and many of them were provided with slaves by their white slaveholding fathers. Mulattoes accounted for 83.1 percent of the black slaveholders in South Carolina, in 1850.

In his writings in *Free Negro Owners of Slaves in the United States in 1830*, Carter G. Woodson indicates that most black slaveholders were benevolent or philanthropic. He notes that the majority of black slave-holders purchased relatives and friends who were enslaved by white slaveholders and then treated them as equals.[3] However, it appears that the so-called benevolent black slaveholders in Woodson's observations also included some black slave-owners who freed one slave and then sold another for profit.[4] After 1820, free blacks who purchased spouses, family members, or friends had to obtain approval from the state to grant them freedom from bondage. The state legislative bodies rarely granted manumissions because white slaveholders resented the presence of free blacks. As a plan of action to curtail growth of the free black population, laws that required blacks to leave upon being granted freedom were passed in many states in the Upper and Lower South.[5] Although Woodson's benevolent interpretation for black slaveholders has merits, there was a relatively small group of black slaveholders who were motivated to enslave other black people for greed, profits, and other self-serving purposes. Woodson notes that after some husbands purchased their wives, they kept them as slaves to ensure their loyalty and acceptable behavior.[6] James Pendarvis, the offspring of a white slaveholding father and a black mother, inherited more than 100 slaves from his father and became the largest slaveholder in South Carolina. Prior to his death in 1798, he owned 155 slaves, including 21 slave children. He used the labor of slaves to cultivate rice crops, and they did not receive any monetary compensation for services provided. In his will, Pendarvis gave the slaves to his son and grandchildren.

After obtaining his freedom for disclosing Vesey's conspiracy, Peter Desverneys, a mulatto, became a slaveholder. In 1840, he was head of a household that included six slaves. In 1849, Desverneys sold the nine-year-old son of a married slave couple he owned. In his will, he states to his executors to "sell the said Slave [Lavinia Cole Sanders] with the issue and increase at public auction and execute [a] good and sufficient Bill of Sale."[7] The apathy, exploitation, and betrayal of the black masses in the South, especially in Charleston and New Orleans, by mulattoes like Desverneys, were pivotal in shaping the image of mulattoes among the black masses. Sentiments of distrust and hostility toward light-skinned African Americans harbored by their darker-skinned counterparts continued after the abolition of slavery and into the twentieth century.

In his book *Slaves without Masters*, Ira Berlin reports that some slaveholding free black planters shared views about slaves that were similar to white slaveholders.[8] For example, Andrew Dunford, a slaveholding free black person, owned a Louisiana plantation that he worked with seventy-five slaves. Berlin states that Dunford took pride in his role as their protector and owner and never displayed any desire to grant them freedom. In contrast to white slaveholders who used racial theories to justify the enslavement of black people, black slaveholders, like James Pendarvis and Andrew Dunford, did not apply race theories to justify their practices. They seemed to have been driven solely by economic benefits derived from the slavery system in America. Berlin put it this way: "They saw themselves not merely as men the equal of others but as men better than most."[9] He notes that they despised poor whites and found their way of life as alien and distasteful. These slaveholders also distrusted the congeniality between lower-class whites and slaves. The vast majority of black slaveholders were mulattoes who resided in Charleston and New Orleans. In many cases, their wealthy white fathers provided them with slaves and land. Consequently, they benefited from the networks established by their fathers with other white planters.[10]

Enslavement practices among free black slaveholders raise several questions: How did they treat their slaves? Did they show compassion and respect for the humanity of their slaves? What were the slaves' attitudes toward their black masters? Did black slaveholders with large plantations use white or black slave overseers? Koger suggests that life for slaves on rice plantations owned by black slaveholders was not significantly different from the life of slaves held by white planters.[11] However, his descriptions of the working conditions for slaves held by black planters do not include the dehumanizing physical beatings, sexual abuses, and racially oppressive conditions that were commonplace on many plantations owned by white slaveholders. Because of the scarcity of black slaveholders, slave narratives, letters, and interviews are not available to provide clues about black planters' treatment of their slaves.

As previously stated, black slaveholders always constituted a statistically insignificant percentage of the African American population, and they did not wish to be identified with other people of African descents. Free black slaveholders personified what sociologists have called the "marginal man." The marginal man concept refers to people who stand on the borders or margins of two cultural worlds but are not fully members of either.[12] Most black slaveholders strived to identify with and be accepted by the elite white slaveholders. They acquired material possessions, formed elite associations, made legal contracts, and filed lawsuits to protect their property, including slaves. They adopted white planters' values and were ambivalent in their attitudes toward their African ancestry. While black slaveholders felt superior to poor whites as well as all free and enslaved people of African descents, they felt inferior to upper-class white Americans. However, because the racial status of black planters precluded them from sharing the individual liberties of even the lowest whites, they could not ignore the psychological significance of race. It was a significant source of identity for them.

The dilemma that black planters might have faced was one of reconciling discrepancies in the psychological and social significance of race in one's personal identity and one's racial group identity. Differences in the historical contexts of race relations between American blacks and whites during the nineteenth through twenty-first centuries may render contemporary interpretations of nineteenth-century American black identity, based upon twentieth-century psychological theories, flawed by the limitations of presentism. In view of the enduring psychological significance of race, we cannot view American black identity as an ahistorical phenomenon; American black identities are significantly influenced by the events of the particular historical matrix within which they develop, and, they are subject to change within the lifetime of individuals and generations in response to personally and historically significant cultural events. Findings derived from research on black identity during the late 1960s and early 1970s suggest that dramatic cultural changes during that period may have produced significant changes in the racial identities of black children and adults. In addition, findings indicated that the more a black person aspired to be accepted as an equal by whites, the more that person was likely to have a negative racial identity.[13] This observation raises the hypothesis that black planters who sought the acceptance of upper-class and influential whites may have attempted, on one hand, to increase the significance of social class identification and, on the other, diminish the significance of racial group identification.

THE CHANGING WORLD OF BLACKS IN THE UPPER SOUTH / CHESAPEAKE REGION

During the nineteenth century, the transformation of local economies in states located in the Upper South and Chesapeake region contributed to changes in the labor force and the growth of the black population throughout the region. The region included Delaware, Maryland, Virginia, North Carolina, Kentucky, Missouri, Tennessee, and the District of Columbia. Small-scale manufacturing and mixed farming (i.e., small grain production, tobacco production, cattle raising, dairying, and truck farming) shaped local economies in the upper Southern tier and Chesapeake region.[14] These economic enterprises relied on small work units as opposed to the large work units employed on cotton, rice, and sugar plantations. The expansion of mixed farming and small-scale manufacturing contributed to a steady decline in the dependency of slave owners on slave labor. Small, racially mixed labor forces, which included slaves working side by side with their owner, and other black and white free people became the working norms in most states in the Upper South.[15] Increasingly, as the centrality of slavery in economic production diminished, the internal slave trade gained momentum. The sale and exporting of male slaves between fourteen and twenty-five years of age from the Upper South to the Lower South occurred at an alarmingly high rate, creating a disproportionate larger population of older slaves and females in the Upper South. Consequently, in 1800, approximately 75 percent of the American slave population was concentrated in the Upper South and Chesapeake region, but the proportion declined to less than 65 percent by 1820 and to approximately 50 percent by 1840.[16] By the same token, the total slave population in the Upper South and Chesapeake region grew steadily during the nineteenth century with 810,423 in 1810 and 1,530,229 in 1860. From the early 1800s through the late 1850s, the internal slave trade accounted for the routine up-rooting of slave families in the Upper South and Chesapeake region. Ira Berlin notes that the internal slave trade contributed to the breakup of one slave marriage out of three and separated 20 percent of all slave children under fourteen years of age from one or both of their parents.[17]

The story told by Josiah Henson about the agonies of family separa-tion as he stood on an auction block in Montgomery County, Maryland, shows the emotional turmoil caused during the sale of slaves for depor-tation to the Lower South. Although it may seem unconscionable, Hen-son's narrative shows that slaveholders expected allegiance to them from enslaved black mothers to supersede the mothers' moral and maternal obligations to their biological offspring. Henson escaped from slavery and went to Canada in September 1830. The following experience Henson describes occurred when he was a young child and many years before his escape from slavery.

Common as are slave-auctions in the southern states, and naturally as a slave may look forward to the time when he will be put up on the block, still the full misery of the event—of the scenes which precede and suc-ceed it—is never understood till the actual experience comes. The first sad announcement that the sale is to be; the knowledge that all ties of the past are to be sundered; the frantic terror at the idea of being sent "down south"; the almost certainty that one member of a family will be torn from another; the anxious scanning of purchasers' faces; the agony at parting, often forever, with husband, wife, child—these must be seen and felt to be fully understood. Young as I was then, the iron entered into my soul. The remembrance of the breaking up of McPherson's estate is photo-graphed in its minutest features in my mind. The crowd collected round the stand, the huddling group of Negroes, the examination of muscle, teeth, the exhibition of agility, the look of the auctioneer, the agony of my mother—I can shut my eyes and see them all.

My brothers and sisters were bid off first, and one by one, while my mother, paralyzed by grief, held me by the hand. Her turn came, and she was bought by Isaac Riley of Montgomery County. Then I was offered to the assembled purchasers. My mother, half distracted with the thought of parting forever from all her children, pushed through the crowd, while the bidding for me was going on, to the spot where Riley was standing. She fell at his feet, and clung to his knees, entreating him in tones that a mother only could command, to buy her baby as well as herself, and spare to her one, at least, of her little ones. Will it, can it be believed that this man, thus appealed to, was capable not merely of turning a deaf ear to her supplication, but of disengaging himself from her with such violent blows and kicks, as to reduce her to the necessity of creeping out of his reach, and mingling the groan of bodily suffering with the sob of a breaking heart? As she crawled away from the brutal man I heard her sob out, Oh, Lord Jesus, how long, how long shall I suffer this way! I must have been then between five and six years old. I seem to see and hear my poor weeping mother now. This was one of my earliest observations of men; and experience which I only shared with thousands of my race, the bitterness of which to any individual who suffers it cannot be diminished by the frequency of its recurrence, while it is dark enough to overshadow the whole after-life with something blacker than a funeral pall.[18]

Slaves in the Upper South viewed deportation to the Lower South, especially to Louisiana, as one of their worst nightmares. Although they deeply feared deportation to the Lower South, they lived with the expectation that it would happen, especially where slave owners perceived a surplus in the labor force. Sales of slaves involving the separation of families often occurred suddenly without the slaves having prior knowledge about it. Slave owners in the Upper South and Chesapeake region knew very well that slaves dreaded deportation to the Lower South and viewed it as the worst condition that could be imposed on them, so slave owners often used it to their advantage.

As noted in the writings of Berlin and Trotter, slaveholders in the Upper South and Chesapeake region played on the fears of their slaves by using the threat of sale for deportation to the lower Southern tier as a weapon to control them.[19] Promises of faithful service and pledges of loyalty were elicited from slaves by slaveholders routinely. Berlin suggests that the sale and threat of sale also served as measures to remove effective leaders from slave quarters and induce fear in those slaves who remained. An observation provided by Fredrick Douglass in his autobiography sheds light on the capricious manner that some slaveholders employed in the sale of slaves for deportation to the Lower South. Describing the sale of a Maryland man to a Georgia slave trader, Douglass notes that "after the man expressed concerns to his master about 'mistreatment' and 'hardwork,' he was immediately chained and handcuffed. Without a moment's warning, he was snatched away, and forever sundered, from his family and friends, by a hand more unrelenting than death."[20]

Even free blacks in the Upper South and Chesapeake region could not avoid the fear tactics employed by slaveholders to extract maximum profits from the American slavery system. Unlike in the Lower South, a significant proportion of free blacks in the Upper South and Chesapeake region had enslaved family members and friends, including their children and spouses. Fear of sale and deportation of loved ones forced some free blacks to make working concessions, which almost always served the self-interest of slaveholders. For example, it was not uncommon for slaveholders to require the free spouse to apprentice themselves as a condition for visitation rights or the promise of future freedom.[21] It seems that these fear tactics employed by white slaveholders might have stirred up a lot of emotional turmoil in blacks and intensified their distrust and hostile racial attitudes toward whites. The often-referenced armed slave rebellion led by Nat Turner in Virginia during the summer of 1831, in which fifty-nine white people were killed indiscriminately, showed the high level of racial hostility toward whites, in general, that was shared among some enslaved blacks. Turner, a slave preacher, assembled a group of approximately seventy enslaved blacks, and within twenty-four hours, they killed ten men, fourteen women, and thirty-five children.[22]

The threat of sale also heightened race bonding and race consciousness among blacks in the Upper South. It was common for slaves on one plantation to help those on other plantations by protecting runaways, providing foodstuff to each other, celebrating special events together, and worshipping together.[23] In the Upper South, black family ties extended beyond biological family members. The uncertainty created by the threat of sale forced black families to share domestic responsibilities with a larger kin group that extended beyond the individual farm or plantation. A former Tennessee slave mother summed it in these words, "The night before the sale they would all pray in their cabins."[24] News of a sale drew hundreds of slaves to say a final goodbye to those who departed. Given the trauma of losing loved ones and the dehumanizing nature of the process, the sale of slaves could have reinforced negative associations blacks already might have linked to the meaning of race.

SLAVES AND LABOR ARRANGEMENTS

In contrast to the harsh demanding labor conditions that field-hand slaves worked under in the Lower South during the early through middle 1800s, many enslaved blacks in the Upper South were afforded more opportunities to make and save money, negotiate working and living, and travel across the countryside and urban landscape. Since slavery was no longer central to economic production, Upper South slaveholders rented slaves or let slaves hire themselves out during slack periods in the work cycles. By the middle of the nineteenth century, the hiring-out system had become prominent in the Upper South.[25] Notwithstanding their ultimate yearning for freedom, unsurprisingly, slaves in the Upper South expressed a preference for the hiring-out system because it provided them with more independence and control over their daily activities.

Generally, the hiring-out system allowed slaves to have free time after they completed the work assignments. The hiring-out system expanded opportunities for slaves to travel freely, interact openly with free people, and get a glimpse of life outside of slavery.[26] By the middle of the nineteenth century, an overwhelming majority of slaves in the Upper South had work experience in the hiring-out system.[27] Many of them, especially skilled workers, saved enough money earned through self-hiring to purchase their freedom.[28]

Working frequently in mixed labor units—which included property owners, free blacks, and white workers—created the opportunity for hired-out slaves to learn some of the intricacies of European American thoughts, behaviors, and cultural practices. It also created opportunities for them to develop and reinforce relationships with free blacks. It appears that many slaves in the Upper South became adept to the thinking, behavior, and lifestyles of free people, thereby making it more problematic for them to be distinguished from free blacks in the Upper South. This contributed to higher incidences of successful runaways in the Upper South than in the Lower South. The presence of free black people helped keep hope for freedom alive among enslaved blacks. With thousands of fugitives reported every year, Eugene D. Genovese suggests that attempts by enslaved blacks to escape from slavery occurred frequently.[29]

Recognizing the threat to slavery posed by the presence of free black people, Southern lawmakers passed laws that reduced their rights and opportunities almost to the same status as slaves. They were required to carry a certificate of freedom at all times. Any white person could demand to see their certificate of freedom anytime, and they were obliged to show it. Free black people were not permitted to testify in court against a white person. Because runaway slaves constituted a significant number of the hired workers in the Upper South, distinguishing between runaways as hired slaves and hired slaves as runaways posed problems for Upper South slave masters.[30] The most notable runaways in the Upper South were Fredrick Douglass and Harriet Tubman. Douglass made a successful escape from a Baltimore shipyard to New Bedford, Massachusetts, and Tubman escaped from the eastern shore of Maryland to Pennsylvania.

UPPER SOUTH FREE BLACKS IN THE 1800S

Beginning in the second half of the eighteenth century and lasting until the onset of the Civil War, the free black population in the Upper South grew at a considerably faster rate than it did in the Lower South. The free black population in the Upper South grew from 30,158 in 1790 to 224,963 by 1860, but in the Lower South, the free black population was merely 14,346 in 1860. The largest growth spurt in the free black population occurred between 1790 and 1820, and then the growth rate continued at a slower pace. While a substantial proportion of free blacks in the Upper South lived and worked in cities, many of them were farmhands and unskilled laborers who lived on the plantations and small farms of whites.[31]

During the early through the middle years of the nineteenth century, an overwhelming majority of the free black population were ex-slaves and descendants of slaves. As previously noted, since many free blacks in the Upper South had family members and close friends who were enslaved in the Upper South and Lower South, they were intimately connected to the struggle for freedom. Therefore, to the extent that they could, free blacks in the Upper South tended to display more empathy and concern than free blacks in the Lower South for the plights of

enslaved blacks. Some free blacks in the Upper South became spokes-
men and spokeswomen on behalf of the enslaved population on a wide
range of issues, including the threat of sale to the Lower South, the
terms of hire, and the conditions of freedom.[32] Some free blacks committed their lives to buying freedom for others and helping newly freed
slaves get settled.[33]

NORTHERN FREE BLACKS' STRUGGLE FOR EQUALITY DURING PRE–CIVIL WAR PERIOD

Unlike their counterparts in the South, free blacks in the North confronted considerable racial discrimination in the workforce during the
pre–Civil War years. The steady influx of white immigrants increased
job discrimination against Northern black workers, especially skilled
black workers.[34] White craftsman would not provide apprenticeship
opportunities for them. They also were denied membership in trade
unions. Consequently, African Americans were confined to menial jobs
as domestic workers and common laborers. Being denied apprenticeship opportunities from trades they practiced as slaves weakened the
economic foundation in Northern black communities. White Northerners were no less steadfast than white Southerners in their efforts to deny
black people the same rights guaranteed to white Americans.[35] Blacks
were permitted to vote in only a few states. In New York, for example, a
black person could vote only if he or she owned real estate worth at least
$250.00. In five states, a black person was barred from testifying against
a white person. Massachusetts was the only state that permitted black
people to serve on juries.[36] They were discriminated against in almost all
public and private facilities. Church groups that were among the leaders
of the abolitionist movement, such as the Quakers, also discriminated
against black people in their meetings.

Many Northern legally free blacks and fugitives lived in fear of being
recaptured or kidnapped and sold into slavery. The free black population in the North included a substantial number of Southern-born
former slaves and runaways who had been assisted in escaping from the
South by the Underground Railroad.[37] Founded by abolitionists in the
eighteenth century, the Underground Railroad helped slaves escape

from the South and relocate in the North as free people. By 1850, nearly 30 percent of the free black population in Pennsylvania and 20 percent of the black population in New York consisted of Southern migrants, and nearly 70 percent of Cincinnati's black population was from the South.[38] The Fugitive Slave Law of 1850 increased Northern free blacks' fears of being recaptured or kidnapped because it made the legal defense against kidnappers more difficult by denying suspected fugitives the right to testify on their own behalf.[39]

While Northern free blacks had to contend with many of the same racial problems as free blacks in the South, there were significant differences. First, the restrictions against Northern free blacks were not as severe. Second, they could protest against restrictions and the denial of rights often without fear of deportation or re-enslavement. However, Northern free blacks expressed fear of kidnappers selling them into slavery. They had more opportunities for self-expression through independent black churches, newspapers, conventions, the abolitionists' movement, and other reform movements.[40] Thus, the most prominent black critics of racial slavery and racial oppression, including Southern black migrants, such as Fredrick Douglass and David Walker, resided in the North during their years of leadership in blacks struggle for freedom and equality.

Daily activities that brought Northern blacks in direct contact with whites provided many firsthand experiences for them to observe the significance whites attributed to the idea of race. Although slavery was unpopular in the North by 1830, Benjamin Quarles contends that blacks "still bore the indelible mark of a degraded inferior."[41] As noted earlier, during the early and middle 1800s, the writings of American and European scholars reinforced the long-standing, widespread belief that blacks were inherently inferior individuals and unequal members of the human family. Therefore, Northern blacks and Southern blacks most likely shared much in common in terms of their perceptions of events and experiences that influenced the significance they attributed to the idea of race when in the presence of white people.

Although white abolitionists championed the antislavery movement, they did not subscribe to the idea that all men, regardless of race, creed, or color, were created equal in the eyes of God.[42] During the pre–Civil War years, only a few white people, such as Benjamin Rush and Samuel S. Smith, called into question the assumption that people of African descents were inherently inferior to Caucasians. By 1850, racial determinism had become the most popular explanatory model to account for differences in human achievements and cultural behavior.[43] Therefore, the dominant position white Americans held over African Americans, combined with their racist attitudes and racist practices, seemingly, predisposed all American blacks to keep things and events they associated with the meaningfulness of race in the forefront of their thinking. The idea of race for American blacks may have influenced almost every aspect of their thinking, even during the intimate moments in family life.

Speeches made in 1837, by Theodore S. Wright, pastor of the First Presbyterian Church in New York City, and in 1858, by John S. Rock, a schoolteacher, dentist, physician, lawyer, and graduate of the American Medical College in Philadelphia, show the social and psychological significance of race for African Americans in self-identification and group identification, as well as group solidarity. The speeches show that racial oppression was consistently a potent force in shaping the behaviors, attitudes, and emotions of African Americans. While speaking about prejudice against black people in the United States at the convention of the New York State Anti-Slavery Society, September 20, 1837, the Reverend Theodore S. Wright noted social and psychological consequences of being free people of African descents living in the United States. Excerpts from his speech reveal hardships caused by racial oppression and the denial of individual liberties to African Americans residing in New York state more than two decades before the Civil War.

> The prejudice that exists against the colored man, the freeman, is like the atmosphere, everywhere felt by him. It is true that in these United States and in this state, there are men like myself, colored with the skin like my own, who are not subjected to the lash, who are not liable to have their wives and their infants torn from them, from whose hand the Bible is not taken. It is true that we may walk abroad; we may enjoy our domestic comforts, our families; retire to the closet; visit the sanctuary, and may be permitted to urge on our children and our neighbors in well doing. But sir, still we are slaves. Everywhere we feel the chain galling us. It is by that prejudice which the resolution condemns, the spirit of slavery, and the law which has been enacted here, by a corrupt public sentiment, through the

influence of slavery which treats moral agents different from the rule of God, which treats them irrespective of their morals or intellectual cultivation. This spirit is withering all our hopes, and ofttimes causes the colored parent as he looks upon his child to wish he had never been born. Often is the heart of the colored mother, as she presses her child to her bosom, filled with sorrow to think that, by reason of this prejudice, it is cut off from all hopes of usefulness in this land. Sir, this prejudice is wicked.

If the nation and Church understood this matter, I would not speak a word about that killing influence that destroys the colored man's reputation. This influence cuts us off from everything; it follows us up from childhood to manhood; it excludes us from all stations of profit, usefulness and honor; takes away from us all motive for pressing forward in enterprises, useful and important to the world and to ourselves. In the first place, it cuts us off from the advantages of the mechanic arts almost entirely. A colored man can hardly learn a trade, and if he does it is difficult for him to find any one who will employ him to work at the trade, in any part of the state. In most of our large cities there are associations of mechanics who legislate out of their society colored men. And in many cases where our young men have learned trades, they have had to come to low employments for want of encouragement in those trades.[44]

In his speech "I Will Sink or Swim with My Race," delivered March 5, 1858, at a meeting commemorating the Boston Massacre in Boston, Massachusetts, Dr. John S. Rock shows that the presumption of the inherent racial inferiority of people of African descents was widely held by white Americans. As previously noted, Rock attained impeccable credentials. In 1850, he began practicing dentistry in Philadelphia, and in 1851, he received a silver medal for the creation of artificial teeth and another silver medal for a prize essay on temperance. In 1852, he graduated from the American Medical College in Philadelphia and, the following year, began the practice of medicine and dentistry in Boston. He was admitted to practice law in Massachusetts in 1861, and in 1865, he was accredited as a Supreme Court lawyer. Although Rock's achievements, like many other free black people, provided strong empirical evidence against the presumption of the inherent racial inferiority of black people, the legal and social status of black people worsened during the pre–Civil War years. His remarks show how this presumption reinforced racial hostility and racial group identification among African Americans.

The prejudice which some white men have, or affect to have, against my color gives me no pain. If any man does not fancy my color, that is his business, and I shall not meddle with it. I shall give myself no trouble because he lacks good taste. If he judges my intellectual capacity by my color, he certainly cannot expect much profundity, for it is only skin deep, and is really of no very great importance to anyone but myself. I will not deny that I admire the talents and noble characters of many men. But I cannot say that I am particularly pleased with their physical appearance. If old Mother Nature had held out as well as she commenced, we should, probably, have had fewer varieties in the races. When I contrast the fine tough muscular system, the beautiful, rich color, the full broad features and the gracefully frizzled hair of the Negro with the delicate physical organization, wan color, sharp features and lank hair of the Caucasian, I am inclined to believe that when the white man was created, nature was pretty well exhausted. But, determined to keep up appearances, she pinched up his features and did the best she could under the circumstances.

I would have you understand that I not only love my race, but am pleased with my color; and while many colored persons may feel degraded by being called Negroes and wish to be classed among other races more favored, I shall feel it my duty, my pleasure and my pride to concentrate my feeble efforts in elevating to a fair position a race to which I am especially identified by feelings and by blood.[45]

Observations reflected in the remarks of Dr. Rock and Reverend Wright suggest that the experiences of American blacks that gave meaningfulness to the concept of race had become potent forces in shaping distinctiveness in ways in which they related to whites and expressed their thinking, feelings, and behavior in the presence of whites. Blacks, in general, had become conditioned to embrace race as a unifying theme in response to the racial oppression. Since skin complexion and other physical differences were central components of race categorization (as can be seen in the remarks of Rock as well as the attitudes of light-skinned Southern blacks), they heavily influenced blacks perceptions of themselves and others. While race might have been the major determinant of group identification among blacks, skin complexion became the most divisive force among them in the Lower South, Upper South, and North. As slave owners in the Upper South and North granted freedom to slaves without regard to color differences and blood ties, skin color became a major source for conflict within free black communities.[46] As previously observed, the Brown Fellowship Society denied membership to dark-skinned people regardless of their wealth and achievements.

THE CRISIS OF SKIN COMPLEXION IN FREE BLACK COMMUNITIES

Historical accounts suggest that perceptions about the significance of skin color created social division within free black communities before the beginning of the nineteenth century. The Brown Fellowship Society provided institutional support for social division among free blacks based on skin color. However, with the influx of light-skinned immigrants from Saint-Domingue, color divisions already had become evident in the Mississippi Valley region as early as the 1770s.[47] During the first half of the nineteenth century, color consciousness appears to have become a crystallized phenomenon in free black communities throughout the United States. Since light-skinned blacks were more likely than darker-skinned blacks to be property owners, literate, and skilled workers, color consciousness became intertwined with class consciousness in free black communities. The nature of the relationship between color consciousness and class consciousness among free blacks permitted these phenomena to reinforce each other.

As noted earlier, color divisions among blacks were aided and abetted by whites in a variety of ways. In the antebellum North and South, evidence suggests that European Americans showed favor toward the employment of free mulattoes over dark-skinned blacks in the workforce. In an essay on the status of the mulatto in antebellum South, Robert Toplin noted that Southern whites displayed favor toward mulattoes and provided them with better opportunities than darker people of African ancestry in slavery and freedom.[48] A similar pattern showing better employment opportunities for free mulattoes over other blacks was observed in Northern cities. In his writings on mulattoes in three antebellum Northern communities, James Oliver Horton notes that mulattoes in Buffalo, Boston, and Cincinnati were occupationally better off than darker blacks.[49] The occupational advantage mulattoes had over darker blacks was due, in part, to the fact that they usually were better educated and more highly skilled than darker blacks as a consequence of more opportunities for schooling and learning trades. Unsurprisingly, many whites contended that the achievements of lighter-skinned blacks resulted from their having more white blood, which gave them greater intelligence and abilities than blacks with little or no white blood. By the same token, some light-skinned blacks could have agreed with them in light of the gaps between their achievements and the achievements of the darker masses of black people. Even near the end of the nineteenth century, it appears that it was widely assumed that white blood increased intelligence and African blood decreased intelligence. In Fredrick Douglass's obituary in 1895, the *New York Times* made the following observations:

> It might not be unreasonable, perhaps, to intimate that his white blood may have had something to do with the remarkable energy he displayed and the superior intelligence he manifested. Indeed, it might not be altogether unreasonable to ask whether, with more white blood, he would not have been an even better and greater man than he was, and whether the fact that he had any black blood at all may not have cost the world a genius, and be, in consequence, a cause for lamentation instead of a source of lyrical enthusiasm over African possibilities. It is always more or less foolish to credit or discredit a race with the doings, good or bad, of a particular member of that race, but if it must be done, plain justice should see to it that the race gets the glory or the humiliation.[50]

Even though segregation and discrimination based on skin color was practiced openly among free blacks in the South, it was by no means limited to this region. Using census data in 1850 and 1860, Horton reports that, in the North, many mulattoes lived in neighborhoods that separated them from the dark masses of the larger community.[51] In general, mulattoes lived in more affluent neighborhoods than darker-hued blacks. In Cincinnati, for example, residential clustering along skin color lines showed that there was as much residential separation between darker blacks and light-skinned blacks in Cincinnati as there was between blacks and whites in Brooklyn or San Francisco. To a lesser degree than in Cincinnati, residential separation between darker blacks and light-skinned blacks was found in predominantly black neighborhood in Boston and Buffalo. It should be noted that, in 1860, approximately 70 percent of the free black population in Cincinnati consisted of Southern migrants with mulattoes representing a substantial majority of it.[52] As previously noted, lighter-skinned blacks usually were better off than darker blacks economically. Therefore, social class distinctions may have been more significant than skin color in the residential separation between darker blacks and mulattoes, but the reverse may have been true also. Another factor that may have contributed to the residential separation among free blacks was fear among light-skinned blacks of being too closely identified by whites with the darker masses of blacks. Some light-skinned blacks may have feared the loss of the advantages they received from whites over darker blacks in the workforce, schools, and so forth or that their loyalty to elite whites could have been called into question by them, and, in turn, they could have jeopardized their privileged status with them.

Perhaps the most revealing evidence that shows the psychological and social significance mulattoes attributed to skin color can be observed in their choice of marriage partners. Mulattoes were more likely to inter-marry among themselves, and they encouraged their offspring and other family members to do the same. This marriage pattern was apparent in antebellum Northern cities and Southern cities. The census data pre-sented in the writings of Horton show that 92 percent of the mulatto men in Cincinnati, 73 percent of the mulatto men in Buffalo, and 72 percent of the mulatto men in Boston married mulatto women.[53] Less than 8 percent of the mulatto men in these cities married darker black women.

While perceived intra-group racial superiority may have contributed to the intra-color marriage pattern among light-skinned blacks, the influence of economic factors cannot be ignored. Light-skinned black women also married dark-skinned men who were skilled and financially secure. In Cincinnati, 90 percent of the darker men who married light-complexion women met these criteria. Although the percentages were lower in other Northern cities, the same marriage pattern emerged.[54] The economic and social advantages provided by white Americans for light-complexion over dark-complexion blacks, undoubtedly, influenced light-skinned and darker-skinned men's choice of light-skinned black women as marriage partners. They also may have been guided by the assumption that their children would be light-skinned and, as such, improve their life chances for economic and social success.

The high percentage of similar-complexion marriages among light-skinned blacks may have been due to a variety of interrelated factors. Some factors that almost certainly contributed to the intra-color marriage pattern among them include their perceived inherent superiority over darker blacks, physical attractiveness of partners, compatible lifestyles, economic advantages, and enhanced opportunities and life chances for their children or a combination of these factors. There is no empirical evidence to determine which among these factors they perceived, either individually or collectively, to be most significant in choosing their marriage partners. In the absence of clarity about the causes of the high percentage of similar-complexion marriages among light-skinned blacks, the reasons remain open to debate. Given the degradation of blackness and the superiority attributed to whiteness in the larger society, a majority of darker blacks might have assumed that light-skinned blacks tended to marry each other because they perceived themselves to be intellectually and socially superior to, and more physically attractive than, darker black people. If these assumptions are valid, then it follows that the intra-color marriage pattern among mulattoes expanded the communication gap between mulattoes and other blacks in America.

While there was tension between mulattoes and other blacks in Northern cities, it was not as strong as the tension between Southern mulattoes and other blacks residing in the South.[55] A significant proportion of the Southern black immigrants in the North were light-skinned, skilled, literate, economically successful, and politically active. In the North, dark-skinned blacks expressed feelings of hostility toward mulattoes for any one or combinations of the following reasons: in response to perceived arrogance displayed by mulattoes; jealousy of mulattoes' more privileged social status; envy of mulattoes' physical appearance; distrust of mulattoes' relationships with white people; and displaced aggression caused by frustration from racial oppression, discrimination, and rejection. However, as previously mentioned, intra-group racial tension between mulattoes and darker-hued black people in the North did not infuse as much open hostility as it did in the South. Many conditions affecting race relations in the North were different from those in the South. There were fewer blacks, including mulattoes, in the North than in the South. In light of the fact that slavery had been dying in the North since the beginning of the Revolutionary era, there was an absence of paternalism of the type that was commonplace in the South.

In a society that assigns psychological and social significance to the meaning of race, it stands to reason that individuals with mixed racial bloodlines and noticeable Caucasian physical features would have ambivalent feelings about the meaning and significance of race, especially during a period in history when very little was known about it and when scholars, seemingly, were unable or unwilling to conduct unbiased research on the topic. In the absence of knowledge about their heritage and proper guidance, they were predisposed to suffer from a great deal of identity confusion, especially if the racial group that they yearned to belong to denied them acceptance. This dilemma characterized the fate of many mulattoes in the antebellum North and South. Viewed with pity and contempt by elite and influential white Americans, on one hand, and distrusted, envied, and sometimes resented by the darker masses of blacks in America, on the other hand, mulattoes were divided in their allegiance to darker-skinned black people.[56] Like Denmark Vesey, there were mulattoes in the antebellum South who viewed themselves as equal members of the larger black society and sacrificed their lives and personal well-being for the black masses. In the North, mulattoes constituted a substantial proportion of participants in the state and national conventions that shaped social and political thought in black communities.[57]

Although the skin complexions of most black leaders in the antebellum North cannot be easily discerned from available records, several mulattoes assumed key leadership roles in the movement against slavery. Robert Purvis, a wealthy and educated mulatto who resided in Philadelphia, donated money in 1831 to Henry Lloyd Garrison to help him publish *The Liberator*, an antislavery publication for the abolitionist movement. Purvis was founder of the Pennsylvania Anti-Slavery Society, president of the Pennsylvania Underground Railroad, and a leading critic until his death, in 1898, of the United States government for its treatment of black people. In 1816, Daniel Coker, a mulatto, was elected the first bishop of the newly formed African Methodist Episcopal Church Conference. Subsequently, he conceded the position to Richard Allen, a dark-skinned black theologian. Since threat of enslavement did not exist in the North after 1807, there was no need for

Southern-style paternalism, and blacks were afforded more latitude to protest racial maltreatment. These conditions provided Northern mulattoes with more opportunities than were available to Southern mulattoes to develop bonds with other blacks without fear of economic or physical repercussions from white people.

Southern mulattoes were divided in their support for the freedom of enslaved black people. In general, they were divided in their attitudes about being grouped with other people of African descents. As previously noted, in their efforts to be accepted by European Americans and become participants in the American economic enterprise, some mulattoes displayed an individualistic orientation toward their surroundings that often precluded them from bonding with the masses of darker-skinned black folks. However, as noted earlier, the conditions of enslavement and racial oppression often forced free and enslaved dark-skinned folks to put aside internal differences for the safety and well-being of each other.

In debates among free blacks concerning strategies and priorities to achieve freedom and equality, social class differences were noted. The laboring poor appeared to be more concerned about economic issues related to supporting themselves, while the more affluent blacks showed greater interest in equality and attaining American citizenship, but they also showed interest in the economic issues of the laboring poor.[58] Though social division along the lines of skin color and class consciousness within the free black population augmented distrust, envy, and resentment among them, they were united in their aspirations for equality. They invested a lot of personal as well as collective energy and other resources into achieving privileges and rights as a part of the human family.

The fight for freedom and equality was dealt a serious setback by the United States Supreme Court's historical decision of 1857 in the case of Dred Scott, a fugitive slave who sued in the courts for his freedom. The Supreme Court adopted a position that appeared to be guided by a belief in the perceived subhuman nature of black people, an idea that had been touted during that era by several notable scholars, including S. G. Morton and Louis Agassiz. In taking action that reinforced the widespread belief in white supremacy, the Supreme Court declared that the property rights of American whites took precedence over the human rights of American blacks. The ruling also suggested that American blacks, in general, were not and could not become citizens in either state or federal jurisdictions. The court's decision stated that: *the Negro had no rights that the white man was bound to respect.* The Dred Scott decision, Smedley contends, lumped together all people of African descents, including mulattoes, as a stigmatized and inferior group in the larger racial scheme of things.[59]

It appears that the United States Supreme Court justices believed, as did an overwhelming majority of their contemporaries, that racial group differences were innate and they justified a natural unequal ranking order of the racial groups. Smedley put it this way: "Going beyond slavery or the concept of property rights, it captured the essence of the American perspective on race differences between blacks and whites. . . . The Dred Scott case . . . made 'race' the specific arbiter of human, legal, and property status, overshadowing the status of slave."[60] This decision weakened the possibilities of blacks to control their own destiny and most likely intensified tension in the ongoing power struggle between black laborers and white bosses. Negative associations that might have given meaning to the idea of race for blacks in the presence of whites could have been reinforced and exacerbated by deep-seated feelings of resentment of blacks toward whites.

SOCIAL DARWINISM AND EUGENICS IN THE SOCIAL CONSTRUCTION OF RACE: 1860–1900

As can be seen in the writings of Carolus Linnaeus and his contemporaries, from the beginning of European scientists' interest in the concept of race, more attention was devoted to the study of racial group differences in physical, mental, and moral traits than to similarities in these traits between racial groups. Although notable scientists and learned persons of the eighteenth century did not always agree about the nature of race differences, they shared the belief that physical race differences were naturally linked to psychological phenomena in ways that ranked Europeans at the top and Africans at the bottom of a presumed natural order of human groups. The writings of eighteenth-century European and American scholars on race differences provided legitimacy for

Aristotle's contention that some people are born to be free and others are born to be slaves.[61] By suggesting that slavery maintained a state of equilibrium or harmony between natural law and social organization, Aristotle, inadvertently, may have helped white people maintain and sustain the belief that people of African descents possessed nothing of worth but their potential as laborers.

By focusing on racial differences while using physical and cultural traits of Europeans as the ideal norms and then interpreting these differences as products of the natural order of human development, scholars of the eighteenth century helped justify racial slavery and maintain the status quo or social order in American society. Their writings on race differences also could have caused negative images and perceptions of blacks that already existed to become even more entrenched in Western social and political thought. Ethnocentric thinking, characterized by feelings of natural superiority among Europeans as well as white Americans, might have been strengthened by these writings on race differences. It seems reasonable to conclude that the preoccupation with race differences by notable scholars during the eighteenth and nineteenth centuries might have gradually conditioned all people living in the American society to focus primarily on differences rather than similarities among members of the human family. If race research of the eighteenth and nineteenth centuries had emphasized commonalities in the psychological makeup of human beings, then white people might have experienced more cognitive dissonance and moral emotional turmoil in reconciling the discrepancies between their Christian religious teachings and the practice of both racial slavery and racial oppression, but the idea that whiteness functions as a form of property allows us to understand why this would not have happened.

During the nineteenth century, writings on race differences were expanded and, seemingly, the research became more contaminated or biased by ethnocentrism and European values. Before the nineteenth century, an overwhelming majority of white Americans and Europeans viewed blacks as inherently inferior members of the larger human family but not subhuman.[62] During the nineteenth century, most prominent scientists and intellectuals in Europe and the United States shared the belief that the human family consisted of inherently unequal racial groups with superior individuals more highly represented among Europeans and inferior individuals highly represented among non-Europeans, especially among Africans. The major concern in the scientific community was seemingly the magnitude of the perceived racial differences and providing scientific explanations to account for these differences.[63] While the idea of the innate inferiority of blacks persisted through the nineteenth century, the scientific community devoted very little attention to the roles that slavery as well as racial oppression played in shaping the intellectual, social, and cultural gaps between black and white people in the United States. As a result of the way in which these lessons were taught and handed down, whiteness became invisible and black inferiority as an explanation for the gaps became a plausible explanation.

In what may have been, in part, politically motivated to prolong slavery and weaken the abolitionist movement, some leading scientists of polygeny during the nineteenth century, which included Samuel G. Morton and Louis Agassiz, argued that blacks were subhuman and belonged to different and inferior species from other members of the human family.[64] As the idea that blacks were subhuman from a separate species increased in popularity in the United States during the 1850s, the hope for attaining some semblance of racial equality that was shared among free blacks became an even more farfetched possibility. In declaring that black people had no rights as citizens under the United States Constitution, the United States Supreme Court's decision in the Dred Scott case of 1857 suggested that Chief Justice Roger B. Taney shared the view that blacks were subhuman or at the bottom in the scale of created beings.[65] Proponents of polygeny, or the idea that black people were descendants from a different species than their European counterparts, provided information and ideas which helped to strengthen white Southerners' resistance to antislavery pressure and it also contributed to the entrenchment of a racial worldview concerning the innate inferiority of black people.[66] By making the claim that blacks were subhuman, the racially motivated negative experiences and events that blacks might have associated already with the idea of race could have become hardened and more resistant to extinction.

The publication of Charles Darwin's *On the Origins of Species by Means of Natural Selection*, in 1859, shifted the focus of the perceived inferiority of blacks from a supernatural force responsible for the creation of the universe and all living things in it to the evolution of human beings and animal life. Although Darwin's theory became a dominant force in shaping race thinking in Europe and the United States, proponents of polygeny continued to influence social and political thought in the United States during the latter part of the nineteenth century.[67] Darwin suggested that all living species evolved from a single original life form through a long gradual process of natural selection. Variations within species occurred by chance, and the survival of an organism is determined by that organism's ability to adapt to its environment. Moreover, the survival advantages of some organisms over others were more likely to be preserved and transmitted to offspring.[68]

Darwin's work became viewed as of such importance that many prominent people in government and corporate America, such as President Theodore Roosevelt, Andrew Carnegie, James J. Hill, and John D. Rockefeller, firmly believed that evolution was applicable to political and economic life.[69] Convinced of this, James J. Hill, who had acquired considerable wealth in the railroad business, made the following remarks, "The fortunes of railroad companies are determined by the law of the survival of the fittest."[70] Herbert Spencer and Francis Galton, both world-renowned British scientists, were most influential in making the link between Darwin's theory and race. It was Spencer, the chief proponent of social Darwinism, who coined the well-known phrases "survival of the fittest" and "the struggle for existence."

Herbert Spencer contended that, unlike black people, Europeans possessed sophisticated neurological organization in their brains that enabled them to handle the complex associations needed for "civilized" life.[71] According to Spencer, "The dominant races overrun the inferior races mainly in virtue of the greater quantity of energy in which [the] greater mental mass shows itself."[72] Viewed as descendants of a weak or inferior race, Spencer suggested that, if left alone, black people would become extinct because their natural and irreversible racial inferiority predisposed them to failure or self-destruction and extermination.[73] Proponents of social Darwinism viewed black people as a worthless burden who could have weakened the white race through amalgamation. While social Darwinists showed no moral concern for the plight of black people in the United States, they were against slavery because they believed that it had prolonged life for blacks by "artificially shielding them from nature's struggle" or open competition with white people.[74] Given the superior position whites had over blacks, social Darwinists argued that inevitably, the race struggle would lead to the extermination of black people. Therefore, proponents of social Darwinism opposed governmental programs that could improve the quality of life for black people in the United States. The widespread popularity of social Darwinism expanded the role of science in shaping the nation's social and political agendas on race in America. During its peak years in the late nineteenth century, social Darwinist theory had considerable influence in the shaping the American nation's social, political, and education agendas on race in the United States.[75] As can be seen here, social Darwinist thinking contributed to a racial climate or national sentiment that made it acceptable for whites to lynch blacks or commit other heinous acts against them. The rise of social Darwinist thinking made the prospect for racial equality almost unthinkable for blacks born during the second half of the nineteenth century.

Charles Darwin's work *On the Origin of Species* inspired Francis Galton, Darwin's first cousin, to become a proponent of improving the human race in a scientific guise by regulating the evolutionary process. Galton used the term "eugenics" in reference to his idea of improving the genetic pool of the human race. By using a method of selective breeding similar to the principles of animal husbandry, Galton believed a highly gifted human race would evolve.[76] Galton expressed racially biased attitudes long before the publication of *On the Origin of Species*. During expeditions to Syria and Egypt in 1845 and 1846, as well as to South-West Africa in 1850 through 1852, Galton described the customs of the people in these societies as savage superstitions beneath Anglo Saxon contempt.[77] Though Galton's observation were based on anecdotal evidence, William H. Tucker notes in an essay on eugenics that Galton referred to Africans as childish, stupid, and simpleton-like in ways that made him ashamed of his own species.[78] In his 2005 writings on scientific racism, Thomas L. Graves, professor of biological sciences at North Carolina A and T University, states that Galton's preconceived racist beliefs precluded him from understanding that the survival and well-being of blacks in America often depended on them behaving like buffoons and giving the appearance of intellectual inferiority. In light of this observation, some scholars have suggested that since Galton's eugenic convictions were fully formed before he began collecting data, he used science in the service of his social prejudice.[79]

In *Hereditary Genius*, Galton argued that geniuses often come from superior human stock represented by a relatively small number of families who tend to be related to one another.[80] Thomas F. Gossett notes that Galton downplayed the effects of social and economic conditions, proclaiming, "The men who achieve eminence, and those who are naturally capable, are, to a large extent, identical."[81] Firmly convinced that heredity was of central importance in the development of certain qualities like intellect and moral fortitude, Galton cautioned people not to become sidetracked by moral considerations and make use of science to develop programs for the improvement of the race.[82] While acknowledging that some blacks were considerably above the average of whites, Galton argued that the intelligence of blacks, in general, was considerably below their white counterparts. Using the normal distribution curve of ability he had devised, Galton concluded that the distribution of ability for blacks was significantly below that for whites.

Although Galton expressed many of his racial views on the relationship between heredity and intelligence before he coined the term "eugenics" in 1883, the popularity of his work surged during the first quarter of the twentieth century in the aftermath of the historic 1896 United States Supreme Court decision in the case of *Plessy v. Ferguson*. In 1901, Galton gained international acclaim for his presentation "The Possible Improvement of the Human Breed under Existing Conditions of Law and Sentiment," as the Huxley lecturer at the British Anthropological Institute. Subsequently, the presentation was published in both *Nature* and *Popular Science Monthly*.

Galton's presentation of his work sparked considerable public interest in eugenics in the United States among a large range of professionals, including educators, biologists, animal breeders, psychologists, and other social scientists, and prominent political leaders. The upsurge in eugenics popularity in the United States occurred during an era in which the nation had become legally racially segregated and polarized and when many white Americans feared that the new immigrants from Eastern Europe would weaken the genetic pool among Americans of

Anglo Saxon descent.[83] Galton's work led to a movement aimed toward advancing eugenics spearheaded by people from the previously referenced professions. They formed organizations and societies that played key roles in shaping education, social, and immigration policies, as well as social and political thinking, in the United States during the first thirty-five years of the twentieth century. In the United States and England, Galton's work led to the publication of journals on heredity as well as the establishment of laboratories and endowed fellowships in recognition of his accomplishments.[84] Although Galton's work reinforced unfounded social-class-biased and racially biased thinking, he was the originator of intellectual tests and statistical methods for handling the measurement of individual differences.[85] Galton's interest in eugenics played a major role in shaping the focus of research in and bringing prestige to the new discipline of psychology during the early years of the twentieth century. Viewing intelligence as the basic index of human worth, psychologists in the United States and Europe displayed considerable interest in the measurement of it.[86]

Although it was during the twentieth century when eugenics emerged as a major force in shaping education, social, economic, and political agendas in the United States, the combined effects of polygenism, social Darwinism, and Galtonian attitudes of contempt toward blacks and other people of so-called inferior racial groups helped to sustain and nurture white supremacy and ideas of racial inferiority. Social Darwinism and Galton's eugenics provided scientific theoretical rationale for racist thinking that opposed policies and programs for the fundamental improvement of the quality of life for black people. From 1860 through the end of the nineteenth century, the scientific theoretical rationales contained in social Darwinism and Galton's work facilitated the crystallization and entrenchment of a racial worldview that depicted people of African descents as inferiors to all other human beings. In so doing, it appears that racial attitudes, which, historically, had been sources of conflict between blacks and whites, may have hardened in ways that would not permit racial equality to become a viable option for blacks until the second half of the next century. The combined effects of polygenism, social Darwinism, and Galton's eugenics may have ensured that freedom from slavery would not end racial oppression.

CITIZENSHIP AND FREEDOM WITHOUT EQUALITY: 1865–1900

During the early years of the 1860s, enslaved Southern blacks exercised more control over their fates than any other time during the nineteenth century. Participation in the Civil War forced many Southern white men to relinquish some of the control they always had exercised over enslaved blacks. Just as the American War of Independence brought freedom for many blacks, the events created by the Civil War suddenly shifted the balance of power in the long-standing power struggle between the enslaved blacks and slaveholders more in the direction of slaves.[87] Recognizing the weakened position of slave owners, slaves demanded significant improvements in living and working conditions as well as an end to the corporal punishment and violence imposed on them.[88]

Although many slaves escaped to freedom, Eugene D. Genovese contends that the vast majority of them did not try to escape during the Civil War.[89] Many slaves believed that the land that they had cultivated belonged to them because it had acquired its value from their labor and suffering.[90] As hope for freedom, social justice, and equality grew, more than 200,000 blacks, including free blacks, ex-slaves, or fugitives, both men and women, played key roles in the Union Army. Although many blacks served in combat roles, Joe William Trotter observes that they also performed nonmilitary and semi-military duties as laborers, spies, scouts, guides, nurses, cooks, carpenters, and general laborers.[91] Working as a spy for the Union, Harriet Tubman was recognized as "the only American woman to lead troops black and white on the field of battle."[92]

While serving in the Union ranks, blacks had many demeaning racially motivated encounters with whites that could have hardened negative attitudes toward whites and reinforced negative associations that they might have had the about the concept of race. Blacks came to recognize that white troops in the Union, and Southern whites, had similar racial attitudes toward them. In addition to receiving unequal pay and unjust treatment by white officers, blacks were assigned the grunt or dirty work, such as digging trenches, hauling logs and cannon, and loading ammunition. Because of slaves' knowledge of the countryside and their willingness to do the dirty work, Union troops provided them the safety of their encampments, but they expressed very little concern about either slavery or the plight of slaves. The maltreatment and abuse of blacks in the Union showed how widespread and deep-seated was the racial worldview of white superiority and black inferiority that white Americans seemed to have shared during the early 1860s. Perhaps the racial stigma associated with blackness had convinced white Union troops that it was acceptable to exploit and abuse blacks since, presumably, blacks were less human than whites. Genovese points out that "Union troops raped black women with an impunity that would have outraged the white South, had it not had so uneasy a conscience on this matter."[93] Because of the slaves' unwavering quest for freedom, it appears that they were determined to endure the abuses and maltreatment as a part of the price for freedom.

As noted earlier, the ruling elites and political leaders in the United States relied on the scientific community for the theoretical and empirical underpinnings to support their racial ideology. During the nineteenth century, political leaders and other influential whites tended to rely more on scientific authority than religious authority for guidance on race issues.[94] The misguided assumption that science was objective and apolitical made appeals to scientific authority a potent weapon for use in influencing social thought and public policy.[95] Presented as scientific theories on race differences, polygenism and social Darwinism helped to perpetuate white supremacy or the conviction of the inherent superiority of people of European descents and sustain beliefs in the subhuman nature of people of African descents. By providing the logic of racial inequality as the natural consequence of the biological inferiority of blacks, polygenism and social Darwinism encouraged people of European descents to preserve the purity and sanctity of the race.[96]

Although polygenism was rejected by many whites for religious reasons, Fredrickson contended that they believed that "the Negro belonged to a separate and inferior species."[97] Similarly, from the early 1860s and well into the twentieth century, social Darwinism increasingly became a major force in shaping social, academic, political, and popular thought on race as well as other policy issues in the United States.[98] Using science to proclaim the racial superiority of Caucasians, proponents of social Darwinism effectively nurtured a social and political climate in the United States from the 1860s through the first quarter of the 1900s that made it relatively easy for white leaders to ignore the concerns and needs of blacks in the United States. Since the belief in the inherent inferiority of blacks had been so widespread among whites long before Darwin's *Origin of Species* was published, Social Darwinism only hardened well-established racist attitudes shared among white Americans. Therefore, it should not be a surprise to note that between 1860 and 1930, no president of the United States championed policies mandating equal rights and social justice for blacks. Although support for the antislavery movement grew steadily among white Americans who resided in the North before and during the Civil War, their racial attitudes and racial practices did not change to an accommodation of African Americans as equal human beings. The following remarks made by future president Abraham Lincoln during a debate in 1858 with Stephen A. Douglas, a congressional leader of the Democratic Party from Illinois, reflect an attitude shared by the vast majority of white Americans who opposed slavery in the nineteenth century:

> I will say then that I am not, nor ever have been in favor of bringing about in any way the social and political equality of the white and black races—that I am not, nor ever have been in favor of making voters or jurors of negroes, nor of qualifying them to hold office, or to intermarry with white people; and I will say in addition to this that there is a physical difference between the white and black races which I believe will forever forbid the two races living together on terms of social and political equality. And inasmuch as they cannot so live, while they do remain together there must be the position of superior and inferior, and I as much as any other man am in favor of having the superior position assigned to the white race.[99]

The attitude expressed by future president Abraham Lincoln shows that the soon to be most powerful leader in the country was not committed to granting to African Americans the individual liberties shared by white Americans. During the first year of the Civil War, Lincoln expressed a desire to emancipate enslaved African Americans and colonize them outside of the United States. He considered colonizing African Americans on a province in Panama, but Central American governments, as well as black leaders in the abolitionist movement, opposed the idea.[100] Fredrick Douglass adamantly opposed the idea of colonizing African Americans outside of the United States. In February 1859, in the essay "African Civilization Society," Douglass made the following observations:

> We object to enrolling ourselves among the friends of that new Colonization scheme, because we believe that our people should be let alone, and given a fair chance to work out their own destiny where they are. We are perpetually kept, with wandering eyes and open mouths, looking out for some mighty revolution in our affairs here, which is to remove us from this country. The consequence is, that we do not take a firm hold upon the advantages and opportunities about us. Permanent location is a mighty element of civilization. In a savage state men roam about, having no continued abiding place. They are *going, going, going*. Towns and cities, houses, and homes are only built up by men who halt long enough to build them. There is a powerful motive for the cultivation of an honorable character, in the fact that we have a country, a neighborhood, and a home. The full effect of this motive has not hitherto been experienced by our people. When in slavery, we were liable to perpetual sales, transfers and removals; and now that we are free, we are doomed to be constantly harassed with schemes to get us out of the country. We are quite tired of all this, and wish no more of it.[101]

In signing the Emancipation Proclamation in 1863, which abolished slavery in the United States, President Lincoln dignified the humanity of African Americans. The Emancipation Proclamation provided a necessary prerequisite for reshaping racial attitudes and racial practices in the United States. Nonetheless, the Emancipation Proclamation did not nor was it intended to change the most salient feature of American slavery, namely, the presumption of the inherent racial inferiority of people of African descents. More than anything else, this assumption was the centerpiece for racism, oppression, and dehumanization, along with other injustices toward African Americans. Although Lincoln viewed blacks as inferior to whites, he supported the Thirteenth Amendment, which outlawed slavery. In January 1865, shortly before the assassination of Lincoln, both houses of Congress voted to send to the states a constitutional amendment that declared slavery as unconstitutional.[102]

THE SIGNIFICANCE OF RACE DURING RECONSTRUCTION

During his tenure as president of the United States, Lincoln set his policy in the direction of granting political rights to African Americans, but he did not demonstrate a commitment to enforce it. Following the Civil War, President Lincoln and his successor, Andrew Johnson, implemented Reconstruction policies that were acceptable to white Southerners, including ex-slaveholders.[103] Except for certain senior-level Confederate military and government officials, President Lincoln pardoned and granted full citizenship rights to white Southerners who took an oath of loyalty to the Union and pledged to support the abolition of slavery. Lincoln suggested that voting rights be granted to the most educated and skilled Southern blacks, but when white Southerners expressed objections to this idea, Lincoln dropped it.

As should have been expected, white Southerners displayed an unwillingness to depart from past racial practices and attitudes. In the fall and winter of 1865 to 1866, the Confederate states enacted "black codes" that denied blacks the right to vote and aided and abetted the activities of terrorist groups like the Ku Klux Klan. Laws were passed that authorized the use of police power to coerce blacks into signing bogus labor contracts.[104] Although strikingly similar to the "slave codes," these "black codes" granted blacks the right to own property, to make contracts, to sue and be sued, to testify in court in cases involving other blacks, and to have legal marriages.[105]

The "black codes" denied African Americans the rights of holding public office, serving as jurors, and testifying against a white person. H. Melville Myers, editor of the *Black Codes of South Carolina*, states in the preface that the Civil War had settled the matter of the abolition of slavery, but this did not mean that Negroes were to be considered citizens.[106] Benjamin G. Humphrey, governor of Mississippi and an ex-Confederate brigadier general, put the belief held by most white Americans in the South in a clear and concise manner: "The Negro is free, whether we like it or not. . . . To be free, however, does not make him a citizen or entitle him to social or political equality with the white man. But the constitution and Justice do entitle him to protection and security in his person and property."[107]

The black codes reinforced blacks distrust of whites and racial awareness among them. Franklin and Moss noted that, in 1865, several black conventions were organized to address racial injustices and racial discriminatory practices in the South.[108] In Nashville, Tennessee, a black convention was held to protest the Tennessee delegation to Congress. Black people contended that the Tennessee legislature failed to display fairness in addressing their concerns. The convention also called on Congress to recognize black citizenship. In Raleigh, North Carolina, a group of 120 African Americans came together and declared that they wanted fair wages, education for their children, and repeal of the discriminatory laws passed by the state legislature. In Mississippi, South Carolina, and Alabama, blacks protested reactionary policies in their states and demanded voting rights as well as the abolition of black codes.

Neither Abraham Lincoln nor Andrew Johnson used the power vested in the Office of the President to promote equal rights for African Americans or grant individual liberties to them. Early in his political career, Andrew Johnson suggested that every white family should have a slave to perform the hard and menial work. After assuming the Office of President of the United States, Andrew Johnson was forthright in proclaiming his support for white supremacy. During the early years of his presidency, Johnson said, "This is a country for white men, and by God, as long as I am president, it shall be government for white men." While addressing the Congress in 1867, he remarked that blacks had "shown less capacity for government than any other race of people."[109] As can be seen from President Johnson's remarks, he was a proponent of white supremacy who had very little or no concern for the hopes and aspirations of the newly freed blacks. Many racist practices and problems that existed in the North and South before the Civil War also existed during and after it. Consequently, racial distrust and racial hostility between white Americans and African Americans worsened, especially in the South.

After the Civil War, the United States government confronted several untested questions that shaped racial attitudes and racial practices into the next century. Many white Americans were asking questions such as: If granted voting rights, would black people vote as a bloc along racial lines? Which political party would they support? If permitted to compete in a free capitalistic economy, whose jobs would they take? If allowed to intermix with white people, what social problems would follow? For African Americans, the concerns about individual liberties, which freemen raised before the Civil War, were the same concerns raised after it. They were concerned about the protection of life, property, the right to make a living, and civil rights for the race. Freemen wanted the same individual liberties that were guaranteed under the United States Constitution to white American citizens. However, after the Civil War, did the newly freed ex-slaves share the same desires and expectations about individual liberties as freedmen?

Unlike the ex-freedmen, who had maintained stable families and hired out their services before the Civil War, many newly freed ex-slaves had been torn away from their spouses, children, and siblings and denied all rights granted under the United States Constitution. Therefore, reuniting with close family members, maintaining family stability, protecting the lives of family members and friends, hiring out their services, and learning to read, write , and count were the highest priorities among newly freed ex-slaves.

On the other hand, before and after the Civil War, freedmen were advocates for equal rights, equal opportunities, voting rights, education, and the same individual liberties for African Americans that white Americans shared. Presentations made by black leaders before, during, and after the Civil War provide support for this assertion. For example, during a presentation delivered before the Military Committee of the Massachusetts legislature, titled "Our Rights as Men," William J. Watkins remarks:

> We have an unrestricted right to the enjoyment of full civil privileges; a right to demand and receive everything which Massachusetts by her Bill Of Rights grants to her citizens, irrespective of any accidental or fortuitous circumstance, the contingency of birth, education fortune or complexion. We are men, and we wish to be treated as men in the Land of the Pilgrims should be treated.[110]

In a speech delivered August 1, 1862, at the West India Emancipation Day Celebration, Dr. John S. Rock noted that free black people wanted the same rights and opportunities that the United States government afforded white Americans. In the speech, Rock states:

When our government shall see the necessity of using the loyal blacks of the free States, I hope it will have the courage to recognize their manhood. It certainly will not mean enough to force us to fight for your liberty. . . and then leave us when we go home to our respective states to be told that we cannot ride in the cars, that our children cannot go to public schools, that we cannot vote; and if we don't like that state of things, there is an appropriation to colonize us. We ask for our rights.[111]

Shortly following the Civil War, ex-freedmen continued their advocacy for equal rights and equal opportunities as American citizens. Addressing the Arkansas Constitutional Convention in 1868, William H. Gray, a black delegate from Phillip County, said:

The Declaration of Independence declared all men born free and equal, and I demand the enforcement of that guarantee made to my forefathers, to every one of each race, who had fought for it. The Constitution which this ordinance would reenact is not satisfactory, as it is blurred all over with the word *white*. Under it one hundred and eleven thousand beings that live in the State have no rights which white men are bound to respect. My people might be ignorant, but I believe with Jefferson that ignorance is no measure of a man's rights.[112]

The following remarks were made before the Louisiana State Senate, July 31, 1868, by Oscar J. Dunn, an ex-freedman and the first lieutenant governor of Louisiana elected under the provisions of the constitution of 1868:

As to me and my people we are not seeking social equality; that is a thing no law can govern. We all have our preferences. We wish to select our associates, and no legislation can select them for us. We ask to be allowed an equal chance in the race of life; and equal opportunity of supporting our children, and of becoming worthy citizens of this government.[113]

Therefore, after the Civil War, the priorities, desires, and expectations of the newly freed ex-slaves were not identical to those shared among the ex-freedmen. Franklin and Moss point out that while newly freed blacks had never experienced freedom, their observations of slaveholders and other free black people shaped their perceptions of its significance.[114] They knew that freedmen owned property, maintained family units, received monetary compensation for their labor services, had freedom of choice to make some decisions, and were able to use the fruits of their labor as they desired. An ex-slave put it this way: "I am now my own mistress, and need not work when I am sick. I can do my own thinking, without having any one to think for me,—to tell me when to come, what to do, and to sell me when they get ready."[115] Her remarks reflected the attitudes of many newly freed ex-slaves. They were primarily concerned with adjusting to an open society with limited rights that they had never experienced. Reuniting with family members who were displaced during slavery was also a priority for them.

As previously noted, the pursuit of individual liberties and full citizenship rights were especially important for ex-freedmen. They desired the same rights that had always been afforded to white Americans. During the Period of Reconstruction, which immediately followed the Civil War, primarily ex-freedmen provided leadership among African Americans. A political priority for these leaders was to obtain full citizenship rights for blacks in America. However, the differences in priorities between the newly freed ex-slaves and their ex-freedmen counterparts made it more problematic for African American leaders to achieve their aims. That is to say, while African American leaders, such as Fredrick Douglass and William J. Watkins, may have been more effective in expressing the concerns and priorities of ex-freedmen than the concerns and priorities of the black masses, namely, the newly freed ex-slaves. Therefore, during Reconstruction, some of the earlier influential black leaders may have been out of touch with concerns that reflected the sentiment that might have existed among many newly freed ex-slaves. This leadership void contributed to the ascendancy of Booker T. Washington, a former slave and college graduate, to a position of influence on behalf of African Americans that was unmatched by any of his contemporaries.

With strong support from whites in the South and North, Booker T. Washington, a former slave, emerged in the early 1880s and assumed a leadership role on behalf of Southern blacks. In his messages to the black masses, Washington urged them to develop vocational skills that would ensure employment, respect the law, and maintain peaceful/cooperative relationships with whites. Although Washington desired equality for blacks, he did not encourage them to vote nor challenge racial discrimination and segregation in the South. Washington's timely advocacy of self-help and economic independence had widespread appeal among the newly freed ex-slaves.

During Reconstruction, blacks experienced great gains in civil rights and civil liberties. Numerous blacks ran for and held political office, built and established public schools, and many voted. This could have only created great psychological stress among whites, generally, but most particularly, in the South. According to Du Bois, to deal with this new fear of job competition from freed blacks and fear of black political power, white people began to form and rely on secret organizations, such as the Ku Klux Klan, to restore the racial and psychological order. To keep blacks from voting and exercising black political power and to keep them from pursuing employment, whites invented the myth of the black male rapist and began to lynch black men and women in extraordinary numbers.[116] This racial terrorism became sanctioned by the state with the Hayes-Tilden compromise of 1876 and the dismantling of the Freedman's Bureau.

Du Bois would articulate the psychological consequences of this relationship of racial terrorism quite clearly, stating that while white workers were poorly compensated economically, they

> were compensated in part by a sort of public and psychological wage. They were given public deference and titles because they were white. They were admitted freely with all classes of white people to public functions, public parks, and the best schools. The police were drawn from their ranks, and the courts, dependent upon their votes, treated them with such leniency as to encourage lawlessness. Their vote selected public officials, and while this had small effect upon the economic situation, it had a great effect upon their personal treatment and the deference shown them.[117]

No less clearly, Du Bois also described the psychological consequences white people's public and psychological wage had upon blacks,

> On the other hand, in the same way, the Negro was subject to public insult; was afraid of mobs; was liable to the jibes of children and the unreasoning fears of white women; and was compelled almost continuously to submit to various badges of inferiority.[118]

When combined with the importance average whites placed on their public and psychological wage, their belief in the inherent cognitive, emotional, and behavioral inferiority of people of African descents clearly illustrates why white Americans were unwilling to change their racial attitudes and practices. Thus, conditions that strained race relations before the Civil War prevailed and often became more intense after it. Most white Americans, especially in the South, vehemently objected to extending to African Americans the same individual liberties that were shared among white Americans. In the North, for example, only six states granted the right to vote to African Americans. African Americans were permitted to vote in Maine, New Hampshire, Vermont, Massachusetts, Rhode Island, and New York. In his writings, Benjamin Quarles pointed out that although African Americans in the North met in convention and published pamphlets and newspapers to attain the right to vote and hold public office, their campaigns fell short of their original aims, with only Iowa, Minnesota, and Wisconsin registering approval before the passage of the Fifteenth Amendment.[119] The passage of the Fifteenth Amendment in March 1870 removed race as a condition for voting and holding public office.

In the North, African Americans were employed primarily in the unskilled trades, domestic work, and menial jobs. In general, they were not admitted into labor unions. Franklin and Moss report that white businesses often employed blacks and paid them low wages to undermine white labor unions.[120] The exploitation of black workers by white businesses not only made it more problematic for them to achieve security and respectability in the workforce, but also it prevented black and white workers from presenting a united front to management. The labor-management practices employed by manufacturers and white business-executives contributed to racial hostility and bitterness among white workers. Moreover, the steady influx of unskilled immigrants from Europe in the North weakened even further the tenuous employment status of black workers. Consequently, black workers were often the last hired and the first fired in the workforce. It seems reasonable to assume that racial discrimination practices in the workforce, as well as the denial of individual liberties in the North, made it impossible for black people to behave, think, and feel like American citizens. The living and working conditions of African Americans in the North served for them as reminders of the psychological and social significance of race.

The Civil War had a devastating impact upon the land, economy, and morale of white Southerners. Reconstruction of the war-torn South and rebuilding its economy without free labor were among numerous problems that Southerners had to confront. Immediately after the war, there was an absence of civil authority in most former slaveholding states. The Union armies had burned and destroyed a great deal of the property, including public buildings and private homes. Many former slaves were left homeless and without jobs. To remedy the numerous problems faced by former slaves and white refugees, the United States Congress established, in 1865, the Freedmen's Bureau. The Freedmen's Bureau provided supplies and medical services, established schools, supervised contracts between ex-slaves and their employers, and managed confiscated or abandoned lands. Out of fear that their dominance over ex-slaves would be jeopardized, white Southerners were embittered by the creation of the Freedmen's Bureau. To ensure the maintenance of the domination over blacks, they used violence as well as political and economic weapons. In *From Slavery to Freedom*, John Hope Franklin and Alfred A. Moss Jr. indicate that before the Congressional Reconstruction Act of 1867, white men in the South conducted violence against blacks, as well as whites who represented the United States federal government.[121] Several coercive organizations comprised of white men who engaged in violence to intimidate blacks and Northern "carpetbaggers" were present throughout the South.

The testimony of Reverend William Thornton, an ex-slave, before the members of the Congressional Joint Committee on Reconstruction during the hearings of February 3, 1866, provides a sample of white Southerners' attitudes toward the Freedmen's Bureau and their racial attitudes after the Civil War. In response to questions raised by Senator Jacob M. Howard of Michigan, Thornton provided the answers that follow:

Question. Were you ever a slave?
Answer. Yes, sir.
Question. When were you made free?
Answer. I was made free under the proclamation.

Question. Where do you reside?

Answer. Hampton, Elizabeth City County, Virginia.

Question. How do the old rebel masters down there feel toward your race?

Answer. The feeling existing there now is quite disagreeable.

Question. Do they not treat the colored race with kindness down there?

Answer. No, sir.

Question. What acts of unkindness can you mention?

Answer. I was asked the other day if I did not know I was violating the law in celebrating marriages. I did not know that was the case, and I went up the clerk's office to inquire; I said nothing out of the way to the clerk of the court; I only asked him if there had been any provision for colored people to be lawfully married. Said he, I do not know whether there is or not, and if they are granting licenses you can't have any; that is my business, not yours. After I found I was violating the law, I went to the Freedmen's Bureau and stated the case. A provision was afterwards made in the bureau granting licenses, and authorizing me to marry. Some days after that an old gentleman named Houghton, a white man living in the neighborhood of my church, was in the church. In my sermon I mentioned the assassination of Mr. Lincoln. Next day I happened to meet Houghton, who said to me, Sir, as soon as we can get these Yankees off the ground and move that bureau, we will put you to rights; we will break up your church, and not one of you shall have a church here. Said I, For what? I think it is for the safety of the country to have religious meetings, and for your safety as well as everybody else's. We will not have it, sir, said he, and then he commenced talking about two classes of people whom they intended to put to rights, the colored people and the loyal white men. I asked him in what respect he was going to put them to rights; said he, that is for me.

Question. Is he a man of standing and condition in the neighborhood?

Answer. He owns property there.

Question. Is he a rebel?

Answer. Oh, yes.

Question. Can you speak of any acts of violence committed by the whites upon the blacks?

Answer. Yes, sir, about three weeks ago a colored man got another one to cut some wood for him, and sent him into the woods adjoining the property of a Mr. Britner, a white man. The colored man, not knowing the line between the two farms, cut down a tree on Britner's land, when Britner went into the woods and deliberately shot him as he would shoot a bird.

Question. Was he not indicted and punished for that?

Answer. They had him in prison.

Question. Is he not in prison now?

Answer. I heard that they had let him out last Sunday morning.

Question. Do you know any other instances of cruelty?

Answer. I have church once a month in Matthews County, Virginia, the other side of the bay. The last time I was over there an intelligent man told me that just below his house a lady and her husband, who had been at the meeting, received thirty-nine lashes for being there, according to the old law of Virginia, as if they had been slaves. This was simply because they were told not to go to hear a Yankee darkey talk. They said he was not a Yankee but was a man born in Virginia, in Hampton.

Question. Why did they not resist being flogged?

Answer. They are that much down.

Question. Did they not know that they had a right to resist?

Answer. They dare not do it.

Question. Why?

Answer. I do not know. On the first of January we had a public meeting there, at which I spoke. The next night when I was coming from the church, which is about a mile and a half from my house, I met a colored man who told me that there was a plot laid for me; I went back to the church and got five of my church members to come with me. I afterwards learned that a fellow named Mahon, a white man, had determined, for my speech that day, to murder me the first chance.

Question. Did that come to you in so authentic a form as to leave no doubt upon your mind?

Answer. I believe he made the threat. The next day he said to me, we hope the time will come that these Yankees will be away from here, and then we will settle with you preachers. That gave me to understand that the threat was made.[122]

Along with white Southerners, many white people in the North expressed strong objection to the Freedmen's Bureau. A common complaint among white Northerners was that it was too costly, and white Southerners complained about federal interference with the relation between worker and employer. Another fear shared by white Southerners was that the bureau had a political agenda for enfranchising blacks and expanding the role of the Republican Party in the South.[123]

Although the economies in the South were in shambles at the end of the Civil War, white Southerners showed more concern about restoring racial practices and policies that were in place before the war than rebuilding war-torn lands and restoring the economies. By putting considerable time and effort into restoring past racial practices, white Southerners permitted the economic gap between the North and the South to significantly increase. They found it very difficult to accept ex-slaves as free people. Many conditions that strained race relations before the Civil War became worse after it. Many racist attitudes and practices remained unchanged. Consequently, the significance of negative experiences and events that might have provided meaning for the concept of race in the psychological makeup of African Americans was continuously reinforced by racism that had become deeply ingrained in American society.

RACISM DURING RECONSTRUCTION

Neither President Lincoln nor his successor Andrew Johnson imposed plans of action to restrict Southern states from adopting "black codes." Over the objections of President Andrew Johnson, the United States Congress instituted the Reconstruction Act of 1867.[124] This act divided the South into five military districts and required Southern states to ratify the Fourteenth Amendment as a condition to be readmitted to the Union. Reversing the United States Supreme Court decision in the Dred Scott case, the Fourteenth Amendment granted citizenship to black Americans. Approved in 1868, the Fourteenth Amendment decreed that:

> No State shall make or enforce any law which shall abridge the privileges or immunities of citizens of the United States; nor shall any State deprive any person of life, liberty, or property, without due process of law; nor deny to any person with its jurisdiction the equal protection of the laws.[125]

The voting rights of white men who supported the Confederacy were suspended, and voting rights were granted to black men in the South. It took the passage of the Fifteenth Amendment, in 1870, before black men nationwide were granted the right to vote. Shortly after the Reconstruction Act of 1867 was instituted, black men were elected to public offices, and they represented a majority of legislators elected in South Carolina. In the South, whites maintained control of the state as well as municipal judiciary and public safety branches of government. The United States Senate also included H. R. Revels and Blanche K. Bruce, two African American senators from Mississippi. The political activity conducted by African Americans showed their desire to be accepted as American citizens.

The effectiveness of black lawmakers was curtailed by the violence and subversive activities carried out by white terrorist groups. The Reconstruction programs orchestrated by the Republican Party, especially black suffrage programs, united white Southerners in their resolve to overthrow Republican rule in the South and restore their control over government affairs as well as black Southerners. They united in efforts to disfranchise black voters and keep the South racially segregated. For approximately ten years after the Reconstruction Act of 1867, there was rapid growth of white terrorist groups, including the Knights of the Ku Klux Klan, the Knights of the White Camellia, the Constitutional Union Guards, the Pale Faces, the White Brotherhood, and the Council of Safety. Members of these organizations were involved in the lynching deaths of many African Americans. These terrorist groups used intimidation, arson, bribery at voting polls, and murder to deprive blacks of political control. They harassed and intimidated black folks indiscriminately. Franklin and Moss report that, in 1871, several black elected officials in South Carolina were given an ultimatum by white Southerners to resign in fifteen days or "retributive justice will as surely be used as night follows day."[126] Many law-enforcement agents and judges were members of the terrorist groups, especially the Ku Klux Klan. Therefore, its members were rarely arrested and convicted for acts of violence toward black people.

In the early 1870s, the Republican Party's advocacy for the protection of the rights and liberties of blacks began to break down. The Republican Party leadership in the North displayed a stronger desire to satisfy the Northern industrialists' efforts to expand their markets in the South. In 1871, the Republican-controlled Congress repealed the law that disqualified many ex-Confederates from voting and holding public office. During the following year, a general amnesty was granted to ex-

Confederates, and with the exception of about 600, they were granted full citizenship rights. Consequently, white Southerners regained political control and enforced many racist policies. They intensified efforts to weaken the political strength of black voters. They passed laws that supported the racial segregation of public and private facilities. New constitutions adopted by Southern state governments firmly established the segregation of races.

Even though remnants of the Reconstruction Act remained in place until 1898, the concessions made by the Republican Party during the 1876 presidential election seriously dampened blacks political hopes and aspirations for full citizenship rights. In a close presidential election in 1876, negotiations on racial and regional issues strongly influenced the outcome of the election. Rutherford B. Hayes assured white Southerners that, if elected, he would adopt a policy of noninterference in Southern race relations.[127] Early in his presidency, Hayes removed federal troops from the South and, thereby, transferred authority from the federal government to Southern state governments in dealing with race relations. In a word, the noninterference policy regarding race relations adopted by President Hayes's administration effectively ended an era of radical or black Reconstruction. In his writings about the demise of the Reconstruction period, Graham Richards puts it this way: "The broad effect of all this on African American morale was extremely negative. . . . The betrayal of the hopes raised by Reconstruction was actually more traumatic than the slavery experience itself—which by 1910 was already history to the under 45s."[128]

With an act of Congress, in 1878, the use of armed troops in elections was forbidden. This congressional act dealt another blow to blacks' participation in the political process. It should be noted that during the 1870s through the first quarter of the twentieth century, social Darwinism was highly popular in the United States and Western Europe. As previously noted, the social Darwinists believed that blacks were descendants of an inferior race and undeserving of humanitarian assistance aimed to put them on equal footing with whites.[129] The combined influence of social Darwinism, eugenics, and the maintenance of white people's public and psychological wage contributed to racial polarization by reinforcing white supremacy and desensitizing whites to the human suffering that was caused by slavery and racism.

In 1883, the United States Supreme Court overruled the Civil Rights Act of 1875. This bill stipulated equal rights for all citizens at hotels, theaters, and other places of public amusement. It permitted blacks to serve on juries in any court case. By the early 1880s, racial segregation in segments of Southern life was complete. In 1896, the United States Supreme Court made segregation the law of the land, and it remained that way for more than a half century. In the 1896 *Plessy v. Ferguson* case, the U.S. Supreme Court upheld a Louisiana law that required separate accommodations for white and black passengers. As a result of this ruling, the separation of races in both public and private facilities was formally institutionalized. As a result of this ruling, the hopes of African Americans to attain equality and participate as equal partners in the American mainstream were given a severe blow. The United States Supreme Court decision in the *Plessy v. Ferguson* case ensured that, at the beginning of the twentieth century, a clear line of demarcation would exist between people with African bloodlines and Caucasians in almost every facet of life in the United States. This decision informed African Americans that there was something so wrong with them that it would be illegal for them to mix with Caucasians from birth to death. The United States Supreme Court ruling in the *Plessy v. Ferguson* case seemed to have been influenced by premises put forth in social Darwinism that suggested that two races could not coexist without amalgamation or extermination of the weaker.[130] The ruling exacerbated disharmony between black and white Americans by providing legal underpinnings for white supremacy and racial oppression. Thus, near the end of the nineteenth century, the social, political, and educational conditions were ripe for race relations in the American society to evolve under the guise of white supremacy.

Significant progress toward community building had occurred among people with African bloodlines in America long before the 1896 U.S. Supreme Court ruling. The activities conducted by white militia organizations served as a wake-up call for many Southern ex-freedmen. Former black slaveholders and other light-skinned Southerners were susceptible also to white racism and violence. Like darker blacks, they also were potential victims of white racial violence. Black Southerners, especially mulattoes, who maintained distance between themselves and the black masses, were forced to establish and/or strengthen ties with the black masses in order to survive and cope effectively in a racially divided society. However, many blacks in the Deep South who had maintained close ties with influential whites during slavery continued to nurture and exploit these relationships for protection against racial hostility and violence visited upon them by white terrorist groups. In his writings about free blacks in the United States, James O. Horton pointed out that, after 1865, wealth and light skin were safeguards against racial violence for many blacks in the Deep South.[131]

Many blacks who had attained career and economic success during slavery retained their positions of leadership and influence in black communities.[132] Some affluent light-skinned Southerners, such as members of the Brown Fellowship Society, continued discriminatory practices against darker African Americans. But, in general, ex-freedmen and newly freed ex-slaves attended the same schools, churches, social gatherings, and so forth and resided in the same neighborhoods. Ex-freedmen often served as teachers and mentors for the newly freed ex-slaves. Notwithstanding the shortcomings of the radical Reconstruction era, the abolition of slavery and the expansion of civil rights led to the steady growth of a black proletariat and yeomanry.[133]

As previously noted, the cultural practices among the newly freed ex-slaves and the ex-freedmen were not identical. In an essay on blacks' roles in shaping American culture, Butcher points out that before the Civil War, free blacks in the South kept their distance from enslaved blacks and displayed outward indifference toward their predicament.[134] Although there were exceptions, in general, they often conformed to European cultural practices and mimicked the conservative, conventional customs of white Southerners. Out of fear, free blacks in the South did not want to appear to in the eyes of white Southerners as a threat to the survival of the institution of slavery.

Since many free blacks in the Upper and Lower South were ex-slaves or descendants of ex-slaves, Butcher's characterization of free blacks may be somewhat exaggerated. Given that they were exposed to the distinctive music, dance, and folklore performed by enslaved blacks, undoubtedly, they incorporated some of it into their lifestyles. Therefore, while European cultural practices were more evident in the lifestyles of many free blacks than enslaved black peasants, rudiments of cultural practices in the slave communities were evident also in the lifestyles of free blacks. Butcher also notes that the distinctiveness in African American cultural practices had its origin in the slave quarters. The distinctiveness in some of these cultural practices reflected an adaptation of African-rooted cultural practices to the burdens of enslavement.

In view of ex-freedmen roles as teachers and mentors for the newly freed ex-slaves in the South during Reconstruction, these practices contributed to expanded opportunities for close psychological and social contact between them. It permitted reciprocal exchanges and the merging of cultural practices and beliefs. It permitted them to share ideas about racial problems and the commonalities in their racial plight. Through these interactions between ex-freedmen and newly freed ex-slaves, they came to recognize each other as members of the same community faced with the same racial problems. As the racial divide became sharper and more intense, the bond between ex-freedmen and newly freed ex-slaves became stronger because white people did not discriminate against any one type of black people. Their psychological wage was gained at the expense of all black people. By the turn of the twentieth century, the cultural transformation culminated and matured into distinct artistic forms and reflected the cultural contributions of both groups. Consequently, the music, dance, and folklore performed by African Americans were distinctive in their own rights and reflected the distinctiveness in the cultural and social experiences of a new people.

THE PSYCHOLOGICAL AND CULTURAL SIGNIFICANCE OF BLACK CHURCHES DURING RECONSTRUCTION

Shortly after the Civil War, black churches entered a period of unprecedented growth. The African Methodist Episcopal Church grew from 20,000 members in 1856 to 75,000 members in 1866. Total membership in the black Baptist organization grew from 150,000 in 1850 to approximately 500,000 in 1870. The Colored Methodist Episcopal Church also emerged with a membership exceeding 103,000 before the turn of the nineteenth century. This growth trend continued into the next century. Black churches played major roles in shaping the distinctiveness in the psychological makeup as well as cultural life of African Americans.

Religion was a mainstay in the lives of African Americans. It shaped their thoughts, feelings, beliefs, and practices about questions dealing with life and death. Religion provided them with direction and hope, with questions concerning death, origin, destiny, suffering, obligations to other humans, and obligations to God. It represented a complex belief system that was shaped early in the lives of ex-slaves during their stay in the slave quarters. Religion played a major role in creating and maintaining the psychological bonds among African Americans. The religion in black churches taught African Americans that they were obligated by God to help each other. Consequently, black churches reinforced the communal orientation in African Americans. Black churches also provided African Americans opportunities to experience freedom of emotions, human dignity, and self-worth. Therefore, the rapid growth of black churches was of major significance in shaping the psyches of African Americans.

Black churches also provided a forum for cultural bonding, refinement, and enrichment between freedmen before the Civil War and ex-slaves who were freed after the Civil War. It is important to note that the cultural practices in these groups were similar but not identical. Freedmen before the Civil War had to blend together cultural practices acquired in slave quarters with European cultural practices in ways that were acceptable to white Americans as well as themselves. These freedmen were not permitted to become immersed in the European cultural practices that dominated American society. In addition, white Americans often expressed disfavor toward freedmen engaging in customs and cultural practices that survived in the slave quarters. The cultural blend that evolved among freedmen contributed to the distinctiveness of African American culture. In her writings, in 1971, on the evolution of African American cultural practices, Margaret Just Butcher provides a rich description of many distinctive features in the expression of the music, religious practices, dance, folklore, and other cultural art forms that evolved in black American society. In writings on blacks' artistic contributions in the shaping of American culture, Butcher observes:

> The Negro has, in fact, many generally recognized qualities of special excellence in the arts. His talents, however, are best understood and interpreted as the cumulative effects of folk tradition and group conditioning.

. . . What might be called . . ."folk virtuosities" must be credited to the special character and circumstances of the Negro group experience. The artistic "virtuosities" have been passed on by way of social heritage; they are just that: a heritage, not an endowment.[135]

Butcher contends that these "artistic virtuosities" included the instrumental versatility in improvisation as well as creative sound and rhythm commonly displayed by black performers. To qualify this observation, she noted that there was an absence of these skills among many blacks in the United States who resided in localities that did not provide adequate support or reinforcement for their survival. That is to say, similarly to the term, or cultural expression, "soul," which was discussed earlier, Margaret Just Butcher describes a new generation's counter-narrative when she asserts that the creative artistic expressions of many black Americans were acquired by way of social heritage or through processes of learning under unique circumstances, and as such, these artistic expressions should not be conceived as by-products of nature.

Black churches provided a forum for newly freed ex-slaves to learn from freedmen cultural practices that complemented the European culture practiced primarily by white Americans as well as the African-rooted slave culture on plantations. In view of the fact that most freedmen had been immersed in the slave culture, especially in religious practices, before their emancipation, many slave cultural practices remained intact in free black communities before the Civil War. These conditions made it easier for freedmen to assist newly freed ex-slaves in their efforts to accommodate to a more open society. Thus, although the freedmen constituted a relatively small segment of the African American population, they may have played a greater role in shaping African American cultural practices than the newly freed ex-slaves. Notable black leaders, such as Bishop Richard Allen, Bishop Daniel Payne, Daniel Coker, Peter Williams, and Thomas Paul, were freedmen who played key roles in shaping the conduct of religious practices in the black church movement during the early and middle years of the nineteenth century. The black church served as the hub for black political thought and black cultural expression from the late eighteenth through the nineteenth centuries. In the book *The Black Church in the African American Experience*, C. Eric Lincoln and Lawrence Mamiya contended that many aspects of black cultural practices evolved in the black church.[136]

THE INTERPLAY BETWEEN RACE, COMMUNALISM, AND INDIVIDUALISM: PSYCHOLOGICAL IMPLICATIONS

For centuries, individualism, or an orientation toward self-interest, has been a mainstay in European American cultural practices. The protection of an individual's pursuit of self-fulfillment and happiness is a centerpiece of the United States Constitution. Since the inception of the United States Constitution, Americans have considered hard work, self-reliance, self-discipline, and self-help as cornerstones for success and happiness. Showered with blessings and funds from white American philanthropists, Booker T. Washington was an outspoken advocate of individualism in African American communities. In *Up from Slavery*, Washington noted that African Americans needed to rely on self-help and hard work to enhance self-worth and achieve happiness in America. With the abolition of slavery and attainment of limited individual rights, a climate arose that permitted a more individualistic orientation to evolve in the larger African American community. The abolition of slavery posed a new challenge for newly freed ex-slaves by providing them with the first opportunity for satisfying self-oriented needs (i.e., individualistic orientation), and, at the same time, they were expected by many African Americans to attend to the group-oriented needs (oppressed communal orientation) of African Americans. The harsh realities of racism in almost every aspect of American life, including racial lynching and other violent activities conducted by white Americans, sustained and strengthened the oppressed communal orientation that already dominated the thinking of African Americans. After the Civil War, the psychological makeup of most African Americans included an oppressed communal orientation as well as an evolving individualistic orientation toward their surroundings. Both the black church and the black press provided forums that reinforced communal and individualistic expressions among African Americans. In response to racism, the black press served as a constant supportive voice for expressing the individualistic and communal concerns of African Americans. Black editors were forthright in stressing racial pride, self-determination, and national identity for blacks. The national identity included the protection of both the individual and the black community against racist behavior, policies, and programs. A national identity also entailed the inclusion in the larger black community with whom individuals shared a common history of racial oppression.[137]

The oppressed communal and individualistic orientations reflect ways of interpreting and responding to conditions or problems in life. These orientations often reflect the underlying motives for a person's actions. Each orientation reflects a different mode of thinking that affects our behavior. The orientation we adopt guides our feelings, judgments, and actions. Individuals who adopt an individualistic orientation in a given situation would be more prone to place the gratification of their wishes and desires above the wishes, desires, and needs of others. Conversely, individuals who adopt a communal orientation would be more prone to place the needs, wishes, and desires of others above their wishes and desires. Since the communal and individualistic orientations are ways of thinking about and responding to problems, they are dynamic mental operations that influence our judgments in most situations. That is to say, communal and individualistic orientations are very active frames of reference in our daily lives. Communalism and individualism are opposite orientations, and, as such, they cannot occupy the same mental space simultaneously in an individual. In other words, while an individual can alternate between a communal orientation or an individualistic orientation in judgment and decision making, that individual cannot fully adopt both orientations simultaneously. Nevertheless, in many situations, people will behave in ways that present one orientation while masking the other. It is generally recognized, for example, that people often perform services to help group members or people in general because of self-interest as well as concern about the well-being of others. In fact, in many situations, people are often uncertain about which orientation was primarily responsible for their actions. For this reason, some people driven by self-serving motives can convince themselves and others that their actions—for better or worse—were performed to help others and/or out of loyalty to their racial or ethnic group.

In decision-making roles, communal and individualistic orientations often require opposite actions. When opposite actions are required and people are driven to fulfill the desires of each orientation, they will experience dilemmas and conflicts. Dilemmas often precipitate contradictory emotions. Let us assume, for example, that an African American has been offered a position by a corporation. The job is desired because it would enable him or her to buy many desired items. Accepting the position would mean a 50 percent increase in pay as well as many opportunities for self-promotion. Yet, the corporation has been criticized by many black people and political leaders concerning its poor affirmative-action record and token hiring practices of blacks. To appease critics and avoid hiring a significant number of black employees, the corporation created a high-profile position with a very attractive salary and benefits for a single black person. The position requires the individual to promote the image of the corporation in black communities and speak out on behalf of its personnel practices. Therefore, the African American is in a situation that requires making a choice between equally undesirable alternatives. Making choices between racial group interests and self-interests has always posed dilemmas for African Americans. These dilemmas can be sources of prolonged emotional distress. Prolonged emotional distress can contribute to psychosomatic diseases, such as high blood pressure, ulcers, and asthma. Psychosomatic diseases are physical illnesses caused in part by emotional distress.

The interplay between communal and individualistic orientations from situation to situation in African Americans made it more problematic for their conflicted motives to be understood, especially by white Americans. In view of their fear of reprisals by whites, it seems reasonable to assume that African Americans were more guarded in expressing individualistic motives in the presence of whites than in the presence of other blacks. Writings in the twentieth century on African American urban youth suggest that, up to the early 1960s, they also were more likely to inhibit violence-prone individualistic behavior in the presence of whites than in the presence of other blacks. In their book *Children of the Dark Ghetto*, Barry Silverstein and Ronald Krate report that, in the early 1960s, African American mothers in Harlem insisted that their children be well behaved and obedient when in the presence of white teachers and white administrators.[138] On the other hand, they urged their children to defend themselves and hold their own in dealings with their African American peers. In the late 1960s and early 1970s, the migration of Southern black children to Northern cities and the civil rights and black power move-ments led to increases in self-assertive and violence-prone aggressive behavior on the part of urban black children and youth toward white teachers. Some black parents encouraged the behavior while others were upset by it. The urban revolts of the mid- and late 1960s in black communities were produced by a culmination of factors, including rac-ism, South-to-North migration, the lack of job opportunities, the lack of police protection, the lack of affordable housing, racial discrimination in the workforce, increasing individualistic aspirations and frustrations, and changing communal racial ideologies. All of these factors, and per-haps even more, contributed to a change in a substantial proportion of African Americans' behavior from deference to whites to confrontation and challenge to white authority. Black-on-black violence also increased in Northern urban areas. During a meeting in the early 1960s with psy-chiatrist Robert Coles, an African American mother, who resided in the South, revealed fears for the well-being of her children in the presence of white people. In his book *Children of Crisis*, Coles reports that because of the danger white people posed for black folks, she insisted that her children be well behaved and obedient in their presence:

> White people are a real danger to us until we learn how to live with them. So if you want your kids to live long, they have to grow up scared of whites; and the way they get scared is through us; and that's why I don't let my kids get fresh about the white man even in their own house. If I do there's liable to be trouble to pay. They'll forget, and they'll say something outside and that'll be it for them, and us too.[139]

African American parents who teach their children to be well behaved and obedient around white people are likely to display the same at-titudes and behaviors around white people. Therefore, they teach their children to be well behaved and obedient around white people through both words and as role models. Children who love their parents and perceive close attachment bonds to them are likely to follow their par-ents' leads, especially when it appears to be effective. Consequently, these children are prone to emulate their parents around white people, especially if the parents have obtained benefits from them.

Although some African Americans may be prone, in the presence of white people, to inhibit expressions driven by individualistic motives—

especially violence-prone behavior—the desire to release these feelings was not reduced. The restraint of these feelings can contribute to emotional distress, including frustration. Frustration has been linked to an increase in the motivation for violence-prone aggressive behavior.[140] If African Americans feel compelled, out of fear of reprisals, to refrain from expressing violence-prone aggressive behavior toward white people, then, does this increase the likelihood that other African Americans will become scapegoats for the expression of their frustration?

As can be seen, the fluidity in the interplay between the oppressed communal orientation and individualistic orientation in African Americans makes it difficult, if not impossible, to know the motivation underlying their actions in many situations. African Americans used oppressed communal and individualistic orientations among themselves, as well as with white people, before and after the Civil War. In other words, African Americans engaged dualistic frames of reference in their daily lives. However, racial group membership influenced the frequency with which African Americans expressed these orientations, the forms they used to express them, as well as the targets they chose for the release of their feelings.

The dualistic orientation in African Americans weakened the trust among them. This conflict between communalism and individualism in African Americans increased the likelihood for African American to pursue self-serving interests at the expense of individual group members, as well as the African American communities at large. The strengthening of the individualistic orientation in African Americans made it easier for white Americans to create and exploit dissension in African American communities. The interplay between race as a psychological construct in combination with the oppressed communal and individualistic orientations in African Americans reflects the complexity and distinctiveness of their psychological makeup. Race, as a psychological construct, almost always intervenes between judgments that involve communal or individual orientations. The concept of race serves as a filter that weighs the impact that orientation choices will have on self and others as a consequence of racial group identification. In its role as a psychological filter, race imposes cost/risk/benefit analyses on ideas generated from the interplay between communal and individualistic orientations in African Americans. Race can compel an African American to consider questions about how other African Americans would be predisposed to perceive and respond to a plan of action intended solely to help them; how his/her plan of action may help and/or hurt self as well as other African Americans; how members of other racial/ethnic groups would be affected by the plan of action if it succeeded or if it failed; and how members of other racial/ethnic groups would be likely to perceive and respond to it. As can be seen here, race serves as a psychological filter in African Americans that assesses the racial implications of their judgments in many decision-making situations. Individuals with relatively high levels of race identification would be more prone to adopt a communal orientation when confronted with a dilemma that requires a choice involving opposite actions. Conversely, individuals who have relatively low levels of racial identification or conflicted racial identification would be predisposed to adopt an individualistic orientation when faced with a dilemma that requires a choice involving undesirable alternatives. While the evidence presented in this work supports the notion of race as being a social and historical construction, it also suggests that, over time, the concept of race eventually became a psychological construct.

The racial attitudes and racial practices of white Americans, especially in the South, sharpened the racial divide that already existed in the larger American society, and it reinforced the psychological significance of race for African Americans. The sharpening of the racial divide also strengthened the oppressed communal orientation among African Americans. In so doing, African Americans were more predisposed than ever before to be influenced by race in their judgments of themselves and others.

5

CHALLENGING CONCEPTIONS OF RACE AT THE TURN OF THE TWENTIETH CENTURY

Shortly after the Reconstruction era ended, the newly freed ex-slaves found that, on the one hand, some things that influenced the quality of their lives had changed radically. However, on the other hand, many things that influenced the quality of their lives had changed only in terms of degree but not in terms of form, structure, or organization. They could legally get married, raise their offspring, hire out their services, manage their personal resources and free time, own property, live on their own in the company of friends and family members, establish organizations, and travel throughout the United States. Perhaps most importantly, the Fourteenth Amendment provided them with recognition as human beings with the rights of United States citizenship rather than the status of property that had been declared by the Supreme Court's ruling in the 1858 Dred Scott case. Although the Fifteenth Amendment provided universal voting rights for black men, laws imposed by local and state governing councils in the South combined with terrorist activities by white Southerners prevented most blacks from voting.[1]

While some things had improved for blacks shortly after the Reconstruction era ended, other things had worsened to such an extent that blacks could not close the social, economic, educational, and political gaps that existed between them and their white counterparts. Commenting on the rise of scientific racism and the inequities of the sharecropping system whites had imposed on black farmers, Graham Richards states, "The broad effect of all this on African Americans' morale was extremely negative . . . the betrayal of the hope raised by Reconstruction was actually more traumatic than the slavery experience itself."[2] Richards's observation suggests that racism and unfulfilled promises during the Reconstruction era cast shadows of doubt on the hopes and aspirations of black Americans. As noted earlier, many white Northerners opposed slavery, but their racial attitudes before and after the Civil War were very similar to those of white Southerners. Like white Southerners, most white Northerners also believed that blacks were inherently inferior to whites and as such, they opposed programs aimed to put blacks on equal footing with them.[3]

The works of leading proponents of social Darwinism and eugenics along with other influential white racial conservatives contributed to the shaping of a social climate that polarized race relations to a point that many, if not most, black Americans in the South faced conditions reminiscent of slavery. Black farmers or sharecroppers, for example, became trapped in a sharecropping system that confined them to permanent economic dependency on white Southern farmers. Poor and consumed with survival considerations, black sharecroppers were forced to borrow money and accept long-term loans from white landowners to cover costs for food, shelter, clothing, land rental, medical care, and other living expenses for their families. After paying off these debts with money derived from the sale of their crops, these sharecroppers rarely, if ever, had enough money left to sustain their families until the next harvesting season. Their indebtedness grew over time because they were compelled to borrow even more money each successive year. Eventually, many black sharecroppers found themselves hopelessly fixated in a quandary that permanently bound them in dependence to white farmers. Expanded modes of industrial production increased competition and hostility between white and black workers for employment opportunities in factories. Often black workers were forced to perform low-paying menial factory jobs where the white workers viewed them with contempt.[4] From the early 1880s through the 1920s, there existed a racially conservative and oppressive climate in the United States that made it very difficult, and often impossible, for blacks to attain substantial wealth, participate in politics, protect and defend their rights, escape poverty and crime, or pursue dreams of greatness.

RACIALLY INSPIRED TERRORISM AND PSYCHOLOGICAL TRANSFORMATIONS IN AFRICAN AMERICANS

Given that the structural paradigm that governed race relations in the United States before the Civil War remained intact after it, the power struggle that seemed to characterize the relationship between blacks and whites continued with intense hostility, bitterness, and distrust, especially in the workforce. The patterns of racially inspired violence-prone actions perpetrated by white Americans against African Americans, which followed the Civil War and continued with increasing intensity into the first quarter of the twentieth century, reflect the complexity of deeply rooted irrational feelings and beliefs white Americans attributed to the significance of race and their desire to protect their public and psychological wage. There were more than 2,500 deaths by racially motivated lynching that occurred during the last two decades of the nineteenth century and 214 deaths by lynching that were perpetrated during the first two years of the twentieth century. Mississippi, Alabama, Georgia, and Louisiana led the United States in lynching during this time.[5]

Even though there was very little empirical evidence to give credence to it, the idea of African American males sexually assaulting white females was a widely held fear among white Americans, especially white males. A close examination of lynching suggests that this idea aroused considerable anxiety and irrational behavior among white Americans. For example, between 1900 and 1914, there were 315 African American lynching victims accused of rape or attempted rape of white women. Castration of lynched victims was a ritual often performed by lynch mobs. While it may be difficult to fathom, no one was ever convicted for these heinous crimes. The criminal justice system did not provide protection for African Americans against white antiblack vigilantes. Undoubtedly, these barbaric practices aroused fear and anger in African Americans as well as exacerbated feelings of despair and hopelessness among them. In his book *Race, Crime, and the Law*, Randall Kennedy, professor of law at Harvard University, argues that the unpunished raping of black women and lynching were viewed by many black Americans as the most vicious and destructive consequence of racially selective under-protection. The refusal to punish white antiblack vigilantes, Kennedy contends, caused many black Americans to lose faith in the criminal justice system. He suggests that they could not adopt a color-blind perspective toward themselves and behave in accordance to it.

During the first quarter of the twentieth century, the color line, which had been mandated by the 1896 decision of the United States Supreme Court, was deeply imbedded in almost all segments of living in the United States. Acts of lawlessness, terror, and violence by white Americans against African Americans were rarely punished. Like their darker-skinned law-abiding counterparts, light-skinned African Americans also lived in fear of being lynched, publicly flogged, or humiliated in other ways by white Americans. In writings on patterns of violence in the United States during the early years of the twentieth century, Franklin and Moss note that, during the first year of the twentieth century, more than 100 black Americans were lynch victims without due legal process, and more than 1,100 African Americans were lynch victims shortly before the outbreak of World War I. While the lynching and race riots precipitated by white Americans reinforced many African Americans' animosity toward and distrust of white Americans, these acts of racial violence also could have reinforced the centrality of race in the psyches of many black Americans.

In August 1904, in Statesboro, Georgia, two African Americans were sentenced to be hanged for the alleged murder of a white farmer and members of his immediate family. After spending two weeks in a Savannah jail, the suspects were brought back to Statesboro for trial. When the sentences were being read to the defendants, a mob of white Americans forced itself into the courtroom and seized the defendants. The defendants were burned alive, and the mob continued to inflict terrorism against law-abiding and innocent African Americans. During the civil disorders that occurred in Statesboro, an African American was severely beaten for riding a bicycle on the sidewalk, and an African American was publicly flogged without cause. An African American mother of a newborn infant was severely beaten and kicked, and her husband was killed by a mob around the same time. There was no punishment of anyone connected to the mob for these heinous crimes. As can be seen, the human rights of African Americans were not protected against acts of violence by racially inspired mobs of white Americans.

Incited by unconfirmed newspaper stories of assaults on white women by black men, John Hope Franklin and Alfred Moss observe:

> The South's most sensational riot occurred in Atlanta in September 1906. For months the city had been lashed into a fury of race hatred by loose talk and by the movement to disfranchise African Americans. . . . On Saturday September 22, newspapers told of four successive assaults on white women by blacks. The country people, in town for the day, joined with the urban element in creating an outraged, panic-stricken mob. Whites began to attack every black person they saw.[6]

The terrorists and police officers made no distinctions between blacks for targets of violence. All blacks, regardless of age, gender, or social economic status, were equally susceptible to becoming victims of enraged mobs of white Americans. In the aftermath, four blacks had been killed, many blacks' property had been damaged or destroyed, and their houses had been looted and burned. Although whites apologized and condemned the white rioters, Franklin and Moss note that the rioters were not punished.

Racial hostility and violence were not limited to Southerners; it was commonplace for gangs of whites to attack blacks in large Northern cities. In Springfield, Ohio, in 1904, a racially motivated riot occurred when an African American male killed a white police officer during a violent confrontation between them. According to Franklin and Moss, a mob of whites broke into the jail where the black man was being held and murdered him in "the doorway of the jail, hung him on a telegraph pole, and riddled his body with bullets. They then proceeded to wreak destruction on the black section of town."[7] In Springfield, Illinois, in August 1908, a racially motivated white mob started a riot that led to the destruction of African American business structures and homes, the death of two black and four white men, and the injury of more than seventy persons. Again, the alleged leaders of the riot went unpunished.[8] As can be seen from these violent, racially motivated confrontations, the social Darwinist and other racial conservative movements heightened and sustained the racist sentiment that already existed in the United States before racial slavery was abolished.

Nothing did more to accentuate the psychological significance of race in African Americans than the epidemic of race riots and lynching that consumed the United States during the early years of the twentieth century. For African Americans, these barbaric terrorist practices were living nightmares. Racially inspired violence reinforced African Americans' distrust of white Americans and reinforced the psychological as well as social significance of race in their daily lives. The persistence of race riots, lynching, racial segregation, and discrimination were constant reminders that in the United States race really mattered for African Americans. Regardless of occupation, education, and skin-color hue, African Americans were expected to accommodate their behaviors, thinking, and feelings in accordance to the United States racial policies and social norms. Accordingly, the significance African Americans attached to social and economic racial lines of demarcation easily overshadowed differences among them resulting from economic factors and skin-color hues.

BLACKS' STRUGGLE FOR CONTROLLING THEIR FATES

By the early 1890s, Southern states had adopted laws that firmly established the color line for a segregated society and ensured that whites would retain power and authority over the governance of almost all institutions in black communities. The United States Supreme Court's 1896 decision in the *Plessy v. Ferguson* case ensured that, at the beginning of the twentieth century, a clear line of demarcation existed between people with African bloodlines and Caucasians in almost every facet of life in the United States. The policies separating the races were implemented with minimal opposition because they always had been commonly practiced. There were constant reminders of the color line in work settings, home settings, schools, churches, social clubs, public facilities, and so forth, and black people, including mulattoes, did not dare challenge its legitimacy. The Supreme Court's 1896 decision sanctioned white Americans to group together all citizens with African bloodlines. More than anything else, the ruling exacerbated racial disharmony by providing the legal underpinnings for white supremacy and racial oppression.

The decisions and practices of some black leaders of independently run black institutions reflected the wishes and expectations expressed by influential whites. Whites often used their influence to affect the conduct of activities by blacks in both the public and private sectors of American society. Unlike in white communities, white lawmakers and other influential whites imposed laws and conditions that curbed the independence, civil rights, and freedom of blacks. Before the turn of the nineteenth century, for many blacks, freedom seemingly was an illusion or a figure of their imagination rather than a reflection of reality in their lives.

At the end of the Reconstruction era, the ruling white elites in the North and South had a monopoly on the political, economic, social, and educational institutions. Thus, they exercised considerable control over the fates of black Americans after the abolition of slavery. Just as during slavery, influential white Americans established or played key roles in shaping the conditions under which blacks worked and lived. Although the driving forces that shaped public policies and public opinion in the United States were heavily weighted against them, the masses of black Americans never conceded the control of their fates and personhood to the ruling white elites. On the other hand, whites never relinquished the power or authority they exercised over the fates and personhood of black Americans. The struggle of black Americans to control their own destiny was pivotal in the relationship between blacks and whites at the close of the nineteenth century. Similar to the relationship between slaves and their masters, the power struggle between blacks and whites never proceeded on the basis of equality and trust.[9] Although whites seemingly almost always held the upper hand in the power struggle with blacks, carefully planned collective efforts on the part of blacks in their dealings with whites usually were effective in helping them to gain more influence over the things or conditions that shaped their fates.

Led by racially conservative notable scholars who operated within the realm of epistemological racism, such as Herbert Spencer and Francis Galton, white lawmakers and other influential whites relied on the academic community for the theoretical and empirical evidence needed to justify keeping blacks in an inferior social and economic position relative to their white counterparts. The research and writings by racially conservative scholars could have removed or significantly reduced feelings of shame, guilt, or remorse when white Americans lynched or engaged in other heinous acts of violence against African Americans.

With the support of progressive white political activists who believed blacks should be treated as equal citizens and assimilated into the American mainstream, during the first quarter of the twentieth century, organizations such as the National Association for the Advancement of Colored People (NAACP) and the National Urban League, along with other social and political organizations committed to racial equality and the expansion of economic opportunities for black Americans, were established. White and black academicians also used the leverage of their scholarship to critically assess the racially conservative arguments put forth by proponents of social Darwinism and eugenics.

Founded in 1910 by a group of distinguished educators, professors, publicists, bishops, judges, and social workers, the NAACP launched programs to expand industrial opportunities for black Americans, to improve police protection for them, and to stop lynching and white terrorist activities against blacks.[10] In 1911, the National Urban League was founded to create more opportunities for blacks in industry and assist Southern black migrants in their adjustments to urban living. It also developed and provided training in social work for young black adults. In sum, the NAACP and the National Urban League, along with leaders of the black churches, assumed leadership roles on many fronts in the struggle of the black masses for survival, control of their destiny, social justice, and racial equality.

Racial segregation and discrimination practices in the United States heightened racial animosity between African Americans and white Americans. It compelled both groups to focus on and justify, in nature and nurture, the things that made them different. White educators, scientists, and social scientists—especially psychologists—published hundreds of papers on racial differences. These publications emphasized the inherent inferiority of black people and, as such, contributed to racial hatred, stereotyping, and racial distrust. Black and white people rarely revealed their true inner feelings about race to members of other racial groups. For many people, from both racial groups, race was an emotionally loaded topic that produced ambivalent emotions and anxiety. On the other hand, there was a dearth of scholarly writings on commonalities in the psychological makeup and cultural practices among African Americans and white Americans. These observations suggest that white Americans were firm in their resolve to protect the white-supremacy doctrine.

THE SIGNIFICANCE OF RACE: POST-RECONSTRUCTION ERA

By the middle years of the last decade of the nineteenth century, nearly two hundred years had passed since the folk idea of race became commonly employed as a way of grouping people into separate and exclusive populations. Nevertheless, the ideological elements noted earlier in the writings of Audrey Smedley, which gave meaning to it, did not change qualitatively.[11] In fact, she concedes that, over the years, these ideological elements of the folk concept of race increasingly became more refined and interconnected. The popularity of the idea that social, political, and economic racial inequality was in keeping with a presumed natural world order was sustained for the duration of the nineteenth century and well into the twentieth century.[12] Consequently, white Americans seemingly became so consumed in race thinking and so conditioned to perceive black Americans as being descendants of an inherently inferior racial group and less human than themselves that they strongly resisted ideas or plans of action that were perceived as threats to their racial perceptions and practices.

As noted in the previously referenced observations, many racially motivated practices that gave meaning to the idea of race for black Americans, while they were in the presence of whites, probably existed at the turn of the nineteenth century. During the first quarter of the twentieth century, white Americans, in general, viewed black Americans with contempt. Protection from lawlessness and social justice were absent in the daily lives of the black masses. Systematically, they were denied economic, political, and education opportunities to improve the quality of their living conditions. As noted earlier, lynching and the destruction of property in black communities by white terrorist groups forced many blacks to live in constant fear of racially motivated violence and aggression. Subordination and resistance to subordination to whites' commands or demands were common experiences for many blacks. These conditions could have hardened preexisting negative perceptions and experiences that gave meaning to the idea of race for black Americans when in the presence of whites. By the same token, concerns about survival among blacks could have compelled them to lean even more on each other for emotional support as well as protection against racially motivated terrorism and humiliation. Under circumstances such as these, racial group identification could have served as a unifying theme for many black Americans and bonded them together to maintain their human dignity and combat racially motivated actions aimed to hurt or destroy them.

The racial segregation and exclusion visited upon black Americans also could have reduced opportunities for blacks to have contact with whites. If there had been more opportunities for positive social contact between blacks and whites, this might have lessened some of the negative associations and feelings about race that blacks could have harbored. Racial segregation and the exclusion of black Americans from the mainstream of society made it easier for them to avoid contact with whites. The absence of social contact with whites may have inadvertently increased the likelihood that blacks maintained preexisting negative attitudes, associations, and feelings that shaped blacks' thinking about race and white people in general. Racial segregation also provided opportunities for black Americans to nurture distinctive cultural practices that, in part, reflected an adaptation to the racially oppressive conditions that influenced their lives. Thus, the cultural gap, which always existed between black and whites, increased.

IN PURSUIT OF A BETTER LIFE: THE GREAT MIGRATION

To escape the hopelessness created by racially motivated lynching, terrorism, humiliation, economic exploitation or poverty, and Jim Crow laws that banned blacks from white facilities during the early years of the twentieth century, Southern blacks began migrating to cities in the Northern and Western regions of the United States. As a leading advocate of black migration and editor of the *Chicago Defender*, a black newspaper, Robert S. Abbott urged blacks to leave the South. In an editorial, he pleads:

> To die from the bite of frost is far more glorious than at the hands of a mob. I beg you, my brother, to leave the benighted land. You are a free man. Show the world that you will not let false leaders lead you. Your neck has been in the yoke. Will you continue to keep it there because some "white folks' nigger" wants you to? Leave for all quarters of the globe. Get out of the South. . . . So much has been said through the white papers in the South about the members of the race freezing to death in the North. They freeze to death down South when they don't take care of themselves. There is no reason for any human being staying in the Southland on this bugaboo handed out by the white press.
>
> If you can freeze to death in the North and be free, why freeze to death in the South and be a slave, where your mother, sister and daughter are raped and burned at the stake; where your father, brother and sons are treated with contempt and hung to a pole, riddled with bullets at the least mention that he does not like the way he is treated. . . . The *Defender* says come.[13]

Pressing blacks to leave the South even if it created a financial burden for them, Abbott states in an editorial, "Every black man for the sake of his wife and daughters especially should leave even at a financial sacrifice every spot in the South where his worth is not appreciated enough to give him the standing of a man and a citizen in the community."[14] Southern blacks from states in the Lower South moved steadily to the North, which the *Chicago Defender* referred to as the "Promised Land" of hope, freedom, and citizenship.[15] The Great Migration, as it had become recognized during World War I, was viewed by black Americans as an "escape from Egypt" and "a journey to the Promised Land."[16]

Black migration to cities in the North and West began during the late nineteenth and early twentieth centuries and turned into the Great Migration during World Wars I and II. Although blacks were encouraged by the white press to remain in the South, Franklin and Moss suggest that, in 1916, the migration movement "spread like wildfire among African Americans."[17] When the United States declared war on Germany in 1917, new employment opportunities were created for black Americans in the country's large industrial cities. A growing demand for American manufactured products during the war forced industrialists to heavily recruit Southern black workers.[18] The federal government supported their recruitment efforts as a wartime emergency measure. An estimated 370,000 black men served in the armed forces during the war, representing nearly 13 percent of all draftees. During World War I, Trotter notes that an estimated 700,000 to 1 million Southern blacks migrated to cities in Northern and Western regions, and an estimated 800,000 to 1 million Southern blacks migrated during the 1920s.[19] As a result of the steady influx of Southern black migrants, approximately 5.1 million blacks lived in industrial cities in the North and West by 1930. However, the South retained the largest population of black Americans throughout the twentieth century.

Southern black migrants were paid significantly more money and had more job opportunities in Northern cities than in the South. In 1902, black farm-workers in South Carolina were receiving an average salary of $10.79 per month compared to an average salary of $26.13 per month for black laborers in New York. Many Southern black farm-laborers were paid at the end of the season, a method to hold workers on the farm until the crop was harvested.[20] During the years of World War I, Trotter observes that wages in Northern industries ranged from $3.00 to $5.00 per eight-hour day compared to $.75 to $1.00 per day in Southern agriculture and $2.50 per nine-hour workday in Southern industries.[21] Though Southern black migrants fared better in the Northern industrial workforce than in the South, they also experienced job discrimination in the North. They were given the tedious grunt work at the lowest level of the industrial ladder. While American-born whites and white immigrants performed the more highly skilled and better paying jobs, blacks performed the most difficult, dangerous, dirty, and low-paying work.[22] Complaints by blacks about the unfairness of working conditions rarely yielded the desired outcome. Consequently, they developed a variety of strategies to cope with racially motivated economic and job discrimination. A popular practice employed by them was "job hopping," or moving frequently from one job to another to improve their wages and working conditions.[23]

Black workers did not only face racial discrimination by their white employers but also by white coworkers. They were denied membership into organized labor unions, and many white workers refused to work alongside black workers.[24] Black workers retaliated against white workers' discriminatory practices by breaking strikes and forming all-black labor unions, such as the National Brotherhood Workers of America and the Brotherhood of Sleeping Car Porters. The National Urban League put forth considerable effort to bring black workers into the organized labor movement on an equal basis.[25]

As the black population grew in the nation's major industrial cities, black Americans were forced to confront more discrimination on social, economic, institutional, cultural, and political fronts.[26] Like the white Southerner, white Northerners maintained distance from blacks and retained impersonal relationships with them in almost every aspect of daily living. Blacks were effectively shut out of the American mainstream and left alone to shape their own social and cultural world. For many newly arrived Southern black migrants, their hopes and dreams of the so-called Promised Land were shattered. Nevertheless, segregation served as an impetus for the creation and expansion of black religious and education institutions, black businesses and professional enterprises, the black middle class or "New Negro," and the culmination and refinement of African American cultural expressions in music, dance, literature, and fine arts.

Joe William Trotter points out that World War I gave rise to the emergence of the "New Negro," portrayed as group of educated and artistically endowed black Americans that sought to build institutions to serve the needs of black Americans and their communities.[27] Trotter notes that their efforts stimulated the grassroots radicalization of the African American population and facilitated the emergence of Marcus Garvey, founder of the Universal Negro Improvement Association (UNIA).[28] After forming the organization in his native Jamaica in 1914, Garvey moved to New York two years later and organized a chapter. Garvey appealed to racial pride at a time when black Americans living in Northern cities were disillusioned with racial inequality in the workplace under conditions characterized by competition with white workers for jobs, which steadily became more intense. In addition, blacks witnessed an increase in negative portrayals of them in popular media coupled with the resurgence of white terrorist organizations. Garvey made his appeal during a period when black Americans in Northern cities were less inhibited in expressing their true feeling about racial conditions in the United States.

In sharp contrast to the negative portrayals of blacks by popular media, Garvey dignified blackness and forcefully promoted the nobility of Africans' past while denouncing racial prejudice. While urging black Americans to take control over their fates, he insisted that the only hope for African Americans was to leave the United States and return to Africa.[29] Garvey's message of racial pride and self-determination appealed to a significant proportion of the urban black migrants in the North. Although Garvey claimed that he had between four million and six million followers during the early 1920s, historians believe his estimation was grossly exaggerated.[30] Nonetheless, Garvey's UNIA became the largest mass organization of blacks in the history of the United States.

Garvey lacked the respect and support of prominent and influential black Americans. He was bitterly denounced as an opportunist, insincere, and a self-imposter by most black American leaders. The highly respected black labor leader A. Philip Randolph coined Garvey "the supreme Negro Jamaican Jackass," and an "unquestioned fool and ignoramus."[31] In making reference to Garvey's organization, Du Bois called it "bombastic and impracticable."[32] Garvey questioned the racial pride of Du Bois and other leaders of the NAACP when he wrote "The N.A.A.C.P. wants us all to become white by amalgamation, but they are not honest enough to come out with the truth."[33] He also referred to the NAACP as the "National Association for the Advancement of Certain People."[34] Unlike Du Bois and other black American leaders, Garvey argued that black and white people had separate destinies and they could not peacefully coexist in the same nation.[35]

Given that Marcus Garvey was a West Indian who spent most of his critical developmental years growing up in a nation that had an overwhelming black population majority, he almost certainly had considerably less direct contact with whites than his black American counterparts. The experiences Garvey had during his youth and young adult years in Jamaica that shaped the meaning of race for him were likely to have been significantly different from the experiences that shaped the meaning of race for black Americans. In contrast to black Americans, most West Indians—especially West Indians with dark complexions—had minimal or no direct contact with white slave-owners. Consequently, there could have been some fundamental differences between Marcus Garvey and black Americans in terms of the significance and meanings they attributed to the idea of race. Although black Americans were well represented among Garvey's followers, his appeal might have maintained their interest because it provided them with temporary therapeutic relief for their negative feelings about their personal or racial identities and a venue to affront white Americans. However, his appeal might have been short lived after their emotions subsided and logical reasoning took over. Garvey might have erroneously equated the circumstances that surrounded the plights of black Americans with other oppressed black people living under European rule. Garvey's background in Jamaica might have imposed limits on his understanding of the black American psyche. The distinctiveness in the psychological makeup of black Americans, as notes W. E. B. Du Bois in *Souls of Black Folk*, reflected an adaptation to unique racially oppressive circumstances that created a unique way of conceptualizing the notion of race. In Garvey's call for blacks to leave the United States and return to Africa, it appears that he had not fully grasped the complexities of the interplay between the circumstances that shaped the psychological distinctiveness of black Americans as described in the writings of Du Bois. He may not have appreciated the extent to which black Americans had become Americans rather than Africans.

CASTING DOUBT ON SOCIAL DARWINISM

During the latter part of the nineteenth century, there was a proliferation of papers published by scientists and other intellectuals to support social Darwinism and white supremacy. The doctrine of biological determinism reflected in social Darwinism purports that social and economic rank order differences observed between and among various classes and racial groups in society were governed by the rules of nature through natural selection. Since the social and economic position of darker races generally were lower than Caucasians, a widely held assumption among Caucasians was that social inequality resulted from biological inequality, proving that they were inherently superior to people of African descents.

Beginning in the last decade of the nineteenth century, some highly regarded social scientists called into question the biological premise of racial hierarchies. In 1894, Franz Boas, a social anthropologist, delivered a paper at a national anthropology conference titled "Human Faculty as Determined by Race." In it, Boas contends that the problem with evolutionary theories is the liability "to interpret as racial characteristics what is only an effect of social surroundings." He suggests that various human populations possessed unique and historically specific cultures that are particular to geographic areas, local histories, and traditions. While making the claim that racial hierarchies are scientifically untenable, he points out that no fact "has been found yet which would prove beyond a doubt that it will be impossible for certain races to attain higher civilization." Noting that, against heavy odds, black Americans had accomplished a great deal in a relatively short period, Boas argues that the primary reason for racial inequality is racism. He concludes that "historical events appear to have been much more potent in leading races to civilization than their faculty, and it follows that achievements of races do not warrant us to assume that one race is more highly gifted than the other."[36]

Although Boas's observations did not gain much recognition in academic circles, by 1910, he had effectively shifted race thinking in the field of anthropology away from theories of biological determinism. Guided by the work of Boas and his students, Lee Baker observes that there was a consensus among anthropologists that black Americans were not inherently inferior to other so-called racial groups and race differences reflected by-products of the unique social environment and historical events that were integral parts of the black Americans' experience.[37]

In a 1907 paper titled "The Mind of Woman and the Lower Races," W. I. Thomas, a prominent sociologist, is highly critical of the social Darwinist views expressed by Herbert Spencer. Thomas argues that "brain efficiency" is approximately the same in all races and in both sexes. Similarly to Franz Boas, he also maintains that psychological differences between racial groups could be accounted for environmentally and historically. Reflecting on Spencer's assertions of "feeble power of inhibitions," "lack of the power of abstractions," and poor mechanical ingenuity in reference to blacks, Thomas declares:

> The extent to which these are manifested is determined entirely by the exigencies of social and cultural life and all races are potentially on a par.

As far as lack of inhibition is concerned primitive life-styles are more hedged with inhibitions than civilized ones, those making the charge mistake differences from European norms in its forms and direction for its absence. Nor do the civilized and "the savages" differ in terms of the "patterns of interest" of everyday life. . . . The fundamental explanation of the difference in the mental life of two groups is not that the capacity of the brain to do work is different, but that the attention is not in the two cases stimulated and engaged along the same lines.[38]

He argued that race differences in mental life were no more than should have been expected in view of the huge education, social, and economic gaps that existed between blacks and whites.

W. E. B. Du Bois, a world-class scholar and a close associate of Franz Boas, was one of the most ardent critics of social Darwinism. Assailing race theories that viewed blacks as inherently inferior to whites, Du Bois asserted that the social and moral problems among blacks stemmed from their social conditions and history in the United States.[39] In observations on the causes of crime and poverty in his classic study of the Philadelphia Negro, Du Bois states:

There are problems which can rightly be called Negro problems: they arise from the peculiar history and condition of the American Negro. The first peculiarity is, of course, the slavery and emancipation of the Negroes. That their emancipation has raised them economically and morally is proven by the increase of wealth and cooperation, and the decrease of poverty and crime between the period before the war and the period since. . . . The second great peculiarity of the situation of the Negroes is the fact of immigration . . . with its increased competition and moral influence.[40]

Du Bois expressed these ideas during a period when most experts viewed blacks as pathological, socially and mentally.[41] Some racially conservative scholars argued that emancipation was the primary cause of the rise in the mental problems among blacks. They contended that black natural traits predisposed them to being incapable of self-governance. On the other hand, Du Bois attributed the mental problems of blacks to the oppression suffered under slavery, segregation, and limitations imposed on blacks' freedom. With the publication of *The Philadelphia Negro*, in 1899, Du Bois provided empirical evidence to support his claim that racial inequality was born from the imposition of the color line, and that imposition created the relationship between "darker to the lighter races of men."[42] As can be seen, he agreed with Boas that racism was the primary reason for racial inequality.

During the early years of the twentieth century, progressive reformers used Du Bois's observations to promote efforts that could improve the psychological well-being of the poor and those individuals who were perceived to have maladjusted personalities.[43] In writings on the role Du Bois played in shaping the damaged image of blacks' psychological makeup, Daryl Scott maintains that Du Bois attempted to elicit sympathy and pity on behalf of blacks from white progressive reformers.[44] They believed that increases in social and mental health problems among poor people were caused primarily by social pathologies in the society. Thus, the maladjusted individuals could and should be treated and reformed rather than ignored.

In the publication *The Souls of Black Folk*, in 1903, Du Bois revealed to whites the inner world of black Americans. In his essay, "Of Our Spiritual Strivings," Du Bois asks the question: "Why did God make me an outcast and a stranger in mine own house?"[45] As he ponders this question, Du Bois reveals psychological characteristics of black Americans that distinguish them from their African-born ancestors. He observes:

> The Negro is a sort of seventh son, born with a veil, and gifted with second-sight in this American world,—a world which yields him no true self-consciousness, but only lets him see himself through the revelation of the other world. It is a peculiar sensation, this double-consciousness, this sense of always looking at one's self through the eyes of others, of measuring one's soul by the tape of a world that looks on in amused contempt and pity. One ever feels his two-ness,—an American, a Negro; two souls, two thoughts, two unreconciled strivings; two warring ideals in one dark body, whose dogged strength alone keeps it from being torn asunder.[46]

Du Bois's revelations indicate that regardless of differences in education, social class, or skin color, black Americans were always getting this message from white Americans: *You are not as good as us. Furthermore, if you want to be accepted by us, you must accept our norms and standards as ways of measuring or judging yourselves. However, no matter what you achieve by our standards, we can never accept you as our equals.* Du Bois's revelations also suggest that black Americans could experience or enjoy sharing a sense of ethnic solidarity and ethnic identity among themselves. Du Bois's reflections on the mental life of black Americans suggest that some aspects of the experiences that gave meaning to the idea of race for black Americans were very similar throughout the United States during the first decade of the twentieth century. Even though black Americans' social environments varied between and within each region of the United States, racial stratification was commonplace in almost every sector of society in every region. Recognizing that the assumption of inequality among racial groups is inherent in a racially stratified society, the idea of race mattered for all black Americans, regardless of their wealth, education, or geographical location.

Before the publication of *The Souls of Black Folk*, most whites treated blacks as though they lacked a soul or an inner world and racial pride. The idea of blacks possessing innate traits that predisposed them to contentment (i.e., carefree darkies singing and dancing down on the levee) was widely held among white Americans, including progressive reformers, at the turn of the nineteenth century.[47] In light of black Americans' longstanding distrust of white Americans and their racial pride, some black intellectuals, including E. Franklin Frazier, the widely acclaimed expert sociologist on black families in the United States, and Horace Mann Bond, a prominent social scientist, challenged Du Bois's revelations. Unlike Du Bois, who characterized the black family as unorganized and dysfunctional, E. Franklin Frazier viewed the ex-slave family as a stable and functional unit after emancipation.[48] In his critique of Du Bois's work, Frazier describes it as "the cry of a sick soul that is divided and is seeking to be made a whole."[49] Horace Mann Bond suggests that the suffering and humiliation endured by blacks did not rob them of their personhood and self-respect.[50]

In light of the fact that Du Bois's description of black Americans' psychological distinctiveness challenged racial conservatives' notion that blacks were content with living in a racially segregated society, as would be expected, they trivialized Du Bois's revelations as expressions of an unhappy educated mulatto who was denied acceptance into the American mainstream. Remarks offered by John M. Mecklin, a professor at the University of Pittsburgh, reflect a point of view that was shared by racial conservatives who commented on Du Bois's work. He states: "It would of course be committing the psychologist's fallacy upon a gigantic scale to read the ideas of *The Souls of Black Folk* into the minds of the masses of the Negroes of the South, and yet it doubtless voices the feelings of a cultured few largely of the mulatto class."[51] Similarly, anthropologist Charles B. Davenport, a major scientific spokesperson in the eugenics movement, put it this way, "One often sees in mulattos an ambition and push combined with intellectual inadequacy which makes the unhappy hybrid dissatisfied with his lot and a nuisance to others."[52] From the turn of the century through the interwar years, many whites, including the educated elites, believed that Du Bois was speaking for the mulatto and not the darker-complexioned blacks.[53]

THE INFLUENCE OF DU BOIS'S WRITINGS ON PERCEPTIONS OF BLACK AMERICANS' PSYCHES

Although W. E. B. Du Bois was criticized sharply by both blacks and whites for his revelations about the unique psychological characteristics that evolved in black Americans in response to racial segregation, inequality, and oppression, his observations were pivotal in shaping the way leading social scientists viewed the thoughts and actions of black Americans. During the first and second decades of the twentieth century, the idea that dark-skinned blacks were content with racial segregation had been tempered among progressive experts, and by the interwar years, they had rejected it.[54] In his presentation on the mental life of black Americans, Du Bois showed how their psychological makeup was shaped by a need to adapt to a unique set of circumstances based on membership in a stigmatized race. African Americans developed psychological coping strategies that enabled them to switch frames of reference or information coding systems with ease when interacting with whites or other black Americans. For many blacks, the psychological dualism Du Bois described could have permitted them to negotiate, cooperate, and collaborate with whites on a variety of issues more effectively.

After rejecting the notion that only mulattoes were unhappy with segregation, social scientists began to view blacks as psychologically damaged victims of social pathologies, such as racial prejudice, racial discrimination, social injustice, and so on. They focused their race research on the social and psychological pathologies that Du Bois alludes to in *The Souls of Black Folk*. In writings on social policy and the characterization of black psychological traits, Daryl Scott argues that social scientists and policymakers exploited the image of the damaged black psyche to gain whites' sympathy and pity for the plights of blacks on humanitarian grounds.[55] They effectively used the argument that racial discrimination caused harm to African American psyche to overturn the United States Supreme Court decision in the 1896 historic case of *Plessy v. Ferguson*, which endorsed racial segregation. They also used it to influence other policies that had an impact on the social, economic, political, and educational status of black Americans.

Led by the sociologist Robert Park, who had previously worked with Booker T. Washington, social scientists of the Chicago school of sociology established themselves as the nations' leading experts in the study of group identity and race relations during the interwar years. Some of the leading black intellectuals of this era were trained at the Chicago school, including sociologists E. Franklin Frazier, Charles S. Johnson, and social anthropologist Allison Davis. The major published studies at the Chicago school during the 1930s and 1940s showed that blacks' self-esteem was damaged from white domination.[56] Drawing from her study of black families in the Mississippi Delta region during the middle years of the1930s, the cultural anthropologist Hortense Powdermaker concedes, "Perhaps the most severe result of denying respect to an individual is the insidious effect of his self-esteem. Few can resist self-doubt in the face of constant belittling and humiliation at the hands of others."[57] These studies also provided a glimpse of the magnitude of the gaps that had evolved between the social and cultural worlds of black Americans and white Americans.

Inspired by the writings of psychologist Kurt Lewin, a Jewish scholar from Nazi Germany who sought to understand the dilemma of assimilated Jews during the interwar years, some social scientists argued that racial prejudice, discrimination, and inequality contributed to self-hatred in black Americans.[58] In writings on self-hatred in Jews, Lewin proposed a self-hate theory that highlighted the interaction between dominant and subordinate groups. He states:

> Accepting the negative stereotypes about his or her own group promoted by the privileged group, the individual develops a "negative chauvinism" toward his or her own and is "ashamed" of belonging. Unable to escape that which they disparage and are ashamed about, marginal individuals discover the hatred turns upon themselves.[59]

Because blacks were rejected and viewed by white Americans with contempt, Lewin believed that black Americans suffered from self-hatred and were ashamed of their racial identity as well as the negative images white people shared about them.

The portrayal of black Americans' psychological dilemma by W. E. B. Du Bois in *The Souls of Black Folk* arguably was significant in the conceptualization of the marginal man theory of personality during the late 1920s by Robert Park, the most influential scholar in the Chicago school on the personality problems of subordinate groups.[60] Like Lewin's self-hatred theory, Park's marginal man theory assumes that social and cultural closeness to the dominant group predisposes members of the subordinated group to psychological injuries. Park notes that the marginal man was an individual torn between two cultural worlds. The process of an individual reconciling the discrepancies between two cultures contributed to personality defects, including "spiritual instability, intensified self-consciousness, restlessness, and malaise."[61] Torn between two cultural worlds in a racially segregated society, Park suggests that black Americans experience internal conflict on cultural and racial grounds. He also maintains that the mulatto experiences the most internal conflict in racially stratified societies.[62]

Elaborating on Park's marginal man theory, Everett Stonequist states, "The individuals of the subordinated or minority group whose social contacts have led them to become partially assimilated and psychologically identified with the dominant group without being fully accepted, are in the marginal situation."[63] In defense of Park's theory, Stonequist suggests that the marginal man suffers from identity insecurity or confusion and feelings of inferiority. In addition, he contends that this individual would be predisposed to perceive malice and discrimination where none existed.

OPPOSITION TO THE PATHOLOGICAL PERSPECTIVE ON BLACK AMERICANS' PSYCHES

Although Park's marginal man theory and Lewin's self-hatred theory influenced the perceptions of black Americans held by many white liberals and sympathizers, there were many black and white social scientists who challenged these theories. In separate studies that tested the marginal man theory in black college students during the 1930s, Francis C. Sumner and Oran W. Eagleson, two black psychologists, report findings that suggest that black college students showed no personality damage from race prejudice. Contrary to Park's contention that the black elite suffered personality damage as a result of marginality, they found that blacks and whites were more similar than different in terms of their neurotic tendencies. Professor Eagleson even argues that his findings suggest that white women have more neurotic tendencies than black women. Challenging Park's position on marginality, the anthropologist Allison Davis suggests that one's racial status was likely to influence an individual's personality if the group was subordinate but, nevertheless, valued the culture of the dominant group.[64] In a study of personality differences between black and white college students published in 1934, James R. Patrick and Verner M. Sims, two white psychologists, argue that race prejudice did not necessarily damage the personalities of blacks.

The writings of sociologists Charles Johnson and E. Franklin Frazier challenged Lewin's position on self-hatred in blacks. On the basis of results derived from a study of blacks in the South, Charles Johnson concludes that blacks do not desire to be white. He maintains that they were evolving as a new people who had light brown skin as their physical ideal appearance. In a later study on skin-color judgments of Negro college students, Eli Marks also found that blacks prefer darker skin color rather than the extremely light end of the color continuum. In a study of black youth in the Border states, E. Franklin Frazier also concludes that black youth do not hate themselves because of their race. Frazier notes that:

> The majority of these youth, so far as the interviews disclosed, appeared to "accept themselves" or thought of themselves in the various roles which they played in their group relations. . . . Only when they felt frustrated in

their wishes and impulses because of their racial identity and imagined themselves carrying out their wishes and desires as white persons and participating in the white world could we legitimately say that they wished that they were white.[65] **[AQ102: Additions to extract OK?]**

William E. Cross and Daryl M. Scott note that even Kenneth and Mamie Clark initially took issue with the notion that blacks had a negative group image.[66] As will be noted later, Kenneth Clark subsequently used the negative group image as evidence against the United States Supreme Court's 1896 historic ruling in the *Plessy v. Ferguson* case.

An American Dilemma, published in 1944 by the Swedish economist K. Gunnar Myrdal, was one of the most comprehensive and influential studies of race relations in the United States. It significantly influenced social science viewpoints on the issue from the 1940s through the early 1960s. Shortly after publication, it became a primary reference source on the discussion of race and culture in the United States. It was a standard text in university curricular and a major guide for shaping social policies on race relations.[67] In 1938, the Carnegie Foundation recruited Myrdal from the University of Stockholm to conduct "a general study of the Negro in the United States." Myrdal hired several scholars, including notable black scholars at Howard University, to prepare reports that were used in the study. According to Graham Richards, the research and report writing were completed in 1940, but editing and other factors delayed the publication of the writings.[68] Myrdal collaborated with Ralph Bunche, a black professor of political science at Howard University, and subsequently an American diplomat, and sociologists Charles S. Johnson and E. Franklin Frazier in the preparation of the study.[69] These black scholars helped shape the tenor and contents of the study.

Myrdal used arguments that reflected the influence of Frazier and the world-renowned anthropologist Frank Boas. Like most graduates of the Chicago school of sociology, Frazier's views on the culture of black Americans were shaped by the teachings of Robert Park, one of the foremost influential scholars on race relations in the United States. Park forcefully asserted that black Americans had no cultural ties to their African past, stating: "The Negro, when he landed in the United States, he left behind him almost everything but his dark complexion and his tropical temperament."[70] On the other hand, Myrdal seemingly ignored the cultural and historical perspectives on blacks contained in the writings of Boas, W. E. B. Du Bois, and Melville Herskovits, a notable anthropologist and student of Boas. In contrast to Park, Boas believed that unique historical and cultural continuities with links to African tradition shaped African American culture. In his writings, Herskovits, a leading anthropologist and a student of Boas, emphasizes the continuities between African and black American cultural practices. Like most of his contemporaries at the Chicago school, E. Franklin Frazier assumed that black Americans' cultural and behavioral practices reflected an "incomplete assimilation of western culture by the Negro masses."[71]

While supporting Frazier's pathological perspective on black American culture, Myrdal argues that:

> In practically all its divergence, American Negro culture is not something independent of general American Culture. The instability of the Negro family, the inadequacy of educational facilities for Negroes, the emotionalism in the Negro church, the insufficiency and unwholesomeness of Negro recreational activity, the plethora of Negro sociable organizations, the narrowness of interests of the average Negro, the provincialism of his political speculation, the high Negro crime rate, the cultivation of the arts to the neglect of other fields, superstition, personality difficulties, and other characteristic traits are mainly forms of social pathology which for the most part, are created by the caste pressure. . . . It is to the advantage of American Negroes as individuals and as a group to become assimilated into American culture.[72]

As can be seen, Myrdal's observations on African American culture were in contrast to the perspectives on it contained in the writings of notable scholars such as Frank Boas, Melville J. Herskovits, W. E. B. Du Bois, Carter G. Woodson, Alain Locke, and Hortense Powdermaker. Myrdal fell short in making positive references to African American culture even though both the folk and formal contributions to American culture were already known. He treated American culture in a manner that suggested it was synonymous to white middle-class cultural practices. However, Myrdal was highly critical of the stereotypes about blacks that were widely held by white Americans. Reflecting on black Americans' social behavior, he notes that "there is a diversity of behavior patterns among Negroes, perhaps as great as in white American society with all its diverse national backgrounds." He concedes that the cackling laugh, appeasing humor, and dumbness expressed by some Negroes developed as an accommodation to caste.[73] Pointing out that blacks seemed no more aggressive than whites, Myrdal also took issue with white Americans' perception of blacks as criminal beasts.[74]

In his writings on the influence of the work of Boas and his students concerning *An American Dilemma* and the United States Supreme Court's 1954 decision in the *Brown v. Board of Education* case, Lee D. Baker notes that Boas and his anthropology team established the only common denominator in studies of race, culture, and society during the 1920s and 1930s.[75] Their writings provided the anchor for the consensus that there was no scientific or irrefutable definitive evidence of any hereditary difference in intelligence or temperament between racial groups. They argue persuasively that historical and environmental factors could account for observed differences between racial groups. Drawing from evidence presented in the writings of Boas and Herskovits, Myrdal contends that there is no objective or scientific basis for making the claim that black people are racially inferior to whites.

By effectively putting the Negro problem into a moral dilemma for white Americans and as a challenge for blacks to work themselves out of poverty, *An American Dilemma* became the foremost authoritative source on race relations in the United States for the next fifteen years.[76] In *An American Dilemma*, Myrdal challenges white Americans to practice what they preach in terms of the "American Creed." He underscores the contradiction between American leaders' appeal for democracy at home and abroad and the absence of equal opportunity for black Americans combined with the unfair treatment of black Americans. Baker sums it up this way:

> Though our study includes economic, social, and political race relations, at the bottom our problem is the moral dilemma of the American—the conflict between his moral valuations on various levels of consciousness and generality. The American Dilemma, . . . is the ever-raging conflict between, on the one hand, the valuations preserved on the general plane which we shall call the "American Creed," . . . and on the other hand, the valuations on specific planes of individual and group living, where personal and local interest; economic, social, and sexual jealousies [exist].[77]

Myrdal maintained that white Americans had to begin working toward the American ideal of equality or be forced to deal with the growing sentiment of racially motivated rebellions. It may be of some interest to note that *An American Dilemma* was cited in the United States Supreme Court's 1954 decision in the *Brown v. Board of Education* case.

Although several notable scholars took issue with the assumption that black Americans had psychological scars that stemmed from segregation, prejudice, and discrimination, this perception of blacks continued to exist deep into the second half of the twentieth century.[78] Focusing on the pathologies of the social environment of black Americans, Abram Kardiner and Lionel Ovesey's publication, *The Mark of Oppression: Explorations in the Personality of the American Negro*, in 1951, strongly reinforces the damaged psychological image of black Americans. While portraying black Americans as being psychologically damaged by matriarchal or female-dominated households and racial oppression, they suggest that black males suffer from anxieties about their masculinity.[79] They argue that matriarchal households cause black males to grow up with ambivalent feelings about females and their manhood. They state: "If the male comes from a female-dominated household, the relation to the mother is generally one of frustrated dependency and hostility. This does not conduce to good relations to the female."[80] Kardiner and Ovesey also suggest that the "Negro" personality and culture reflect an accommodation or adaptation to white racism. However since they only used twenty-five case studies of Harlem residents and no comparable group to support their observations, methodological issues surrounding the research cast serious doubt on their conclusions.[81]

As a part of a strategy of working toward the American ideal of equality, notable white social scientists and social reformers portrayed black Americans as psychologically handicapped or damaged by the social pathology in American society. By the late 1940s and early 1950s, several black scholars, including Kenneth B. Clark, and some civil rights leaders used the same argument as a strategy to get equal rights and social justice, or the same rights and opportunities for black Americans that white Americans received. The strategy was effective in changing or removing many legal, educational, social, economic, and political obstacles that had prevented blacks from participating in the American mainstream on an equal basis with whites.

During the interwar years after World War I, social scientists, social reformers, and leaders brought considerable attention to the negative influence of racial segregation and prejudice on the mental life of black Americans. The perceptions of blacks as being psychologically handicapped or damaged by the social pathology in American society lingered on after the United States Supreme Court overturned the *Plessy v. Ferguson* 1896 decision in 1954. Conceding that the unique social experiences of black Americans had severely scarred them psychologically, leading black and white intellectuals as well as social reformers and civil rights leaders forcefully argued that extensive and prolonged rehabilitation would be needed to remedy this problem.[82] Although the focus on the perceived or alleged psychological damage of blacks caused by racial segregation, prejudice, and discrimination gained widespread sympathy and public support among white liberals, it could have stigmatized the entire black American community.

The stigma of being perceived as psychologically handicapped conveyed a message of racial inferiority to many black Americans. It predisposed some of them to perceive themselves as needy victims or unfit to compete on equal terms on complex mental tasks with their white counterparts. In her book *Beyond the Masks: Race, Gender, and Subjectivity* Mama suggests that it was tantamount to replacing the biological racist image of Negro identity with a damaged Negro psyche image.[83] Being viewed as psychologically damaged, almost certainly reinforced feelings of inferiority for many blacks—especially when they interacted with white Americans. The stigma did very little to improve whites' perceptions of blacks or blacks' perceptions of themselves. During the 1940s and early 1950s, many white Americans living outside of the South supported the desegregation of American public facilities, but they often were resistant to the desegregation and integration of private facilities. This lack of contact between white Americans and black Americans could have reinforced negative feelings and experiences that gave meaning for blacks to the concept of race. Therefore, the black masses most likely retained the attitudes they had acquired about race differences.

In writings on the construction of race during the twentieth century, Lee Baker notes that the idea of racial inferiority helped to define the terms, meaning, and significance of the concept of race for black Americans.[84] The previously referenced observations suggest that during the interwar years of the twentieth century, the concept of race could have become more significant for black Americans than ever before because most of the events and experiences that gave meaning to it still existed and many new negative racial experiences had been added to the old ones over time. The process of integrating new negative racial experiences into existing ones and nurturing or refining connections between existing ones might have contributed to a more complex, coherent, and stable system of associations and ideas that gave meaning to the concept of race for black Americans. For black Americans born during the early through mid-1900s , it appears that the concept of race most likely became a relatively stable primary frame of reference for them that filtered information and guided their thoughts, feelings, and actions.

Given that there were no dramatic shifts in the relationship between blacks and whites during the first half of the twentieth century, the conceptualization of the concept of race for black Americans could have remained relatively stable during this period. On the other hand, during this same period, there was a major scientific transition or paradigm shift in race thinking in academic and learned societies. The early writings of W. E. B. Du Bois and Frank Boas and his graduate students, including notable anthropologists Margaret Mead, Melville Herskovits, and social psychologist Otto Klineberg, exposed flaws in biological determinism as a theoretical explanation for race differences. They effectively argued that there was no scientific evidence to support racial hierarchies. By the 1930s, most notable scientists and scholars agreed that race differences could be explained by the social environment, history, and culture of various groups. In observations on the paradigm shift on race thinking, William Tucker indicates that leading scholars in the sciences and social sciences shared the belief that differences between so-called racial groups, in both mental test scores and cultural achievements, could be accounted for by the history of their cultural experiences rather than by any innate differences in mental abilities.[85] The writings of Robert Park and other members of the Chicago school, social psychologist Otto Klineberg and E. Franklin Frazier, as well as other scholars from the late 1920s through the 1940s, show the powerful influence that the social environment could have on shaping the lifestyles of various groups.

The combined efforts of Boas, Du Bois, Herskovits, Klineberg, Park and other members of the Chicago school, the NAACP, Frazier, and scholars at Howard University ignited a plethora of studies and writings that effectively falsified biological, evolutionary, and innate assumptions about race differences and deconstructed the key elements that sustained the racial worldview. This large body of work provided support for the claim that race differences could be accounted for by the histories, cultural practices, and social environments of various groups. In so doing, it effectively deconstructed the key elements that sustained the racial worldview, such as innateness, permanence, and heritability. In sum, the arguments or explanations put forth to contest innate assumptions about innate race differences tended to be of one or more of the following kinds: "First, that any race differences can be accounted for environmentally. Secondly . . . egalitarianism is a moral imperative unaffected by any empirical evidence. Thirdly . . . innate race differences either have not been, or cannot in principle be, demonstrated. Fourthly, . . . 'race' is an unscientific category, a myth for rationalising oppression and injustice."[86] Forcefully discrediting innate assumptions about race differences in writings about the concept of race, the renowned anthropologist Ashley Montagu contends that race is a nonscientific notion and that it is indefensible to assume that races exist, to recognize them, to describe them, to systematically classify them, or to treat them as objects of objective reality. He observes:

> For two centuries anthropologists have been directing attention towards the task of establishing criteria by whose means races of man may be defined. All have taken for granted the one thing which required to be proven, namely that the concept of race corresponded with a reality which could actually be measured and verified and descriptively set out so that it could be seen to be a fact.[87]

Montagu's observations suggest that the notion of race lacks the core of objective scientific evidence.

Even though the deconstruction of the tenets that sustained the racial worldview made it possible for changes in laws, public policies, and practices that eventually improved the social environment for many black Americans, it did not produce any fundamental change in the social construct of race.[88]

In America, race is the touchstone of all value, the prism through which all else of significance must be refracted before relationships can be defined or relevance ascertained. There is no order of reality large enough to transcend its pervasiveness, small enough to escape its intrusiveness, or independent enough to avoid its imprimatur. . . . Every Black American knows firsthand the slander or invisibility. Anonymity. It comes in a thousand ways: a word, a gesture, a conversation that moves over and around him as though he or she were not present. Invisibility is most painful when it is preclusive—jobs not offered, invitations not issued, opportunities denied. It is a lifelong incubus from which few, if any, African Americans ever escape completely, no matter what their achievements. Racial anonymity derives from the presumption of inconsequence of black persons and of their achievements, actual or potential.[89]

Segregation seemingly had grown into an accepted practice in the lives of white Americans. Thus, there was stiff resistance by many white Americans to change racially motivated habits and attitudes. As black anthropologist Lee Baker notes, many key social and structural components as well as political practices in American society that historically sustained the social construct of race seemingly remained unchanged. He argues:

It is certainly not the same as it was a hundred years ago, but some of the dynamics and relationships still persist. The intersection and convergence of racial politics and discourses produced by the media and social scientists remain integral to the processes that form and reform racial constructs.[90]

Furthermore, since the meaning and psychological significance that black Americans attributed to the idea of race already had been well established and only a few of them would have been aware of the critiques of racist ideology, the paradigm shift on race thinking did not necessarily influence the conceptualization of race among the black masses. As discussed earlier, it also appears that the concept of race already had become a relatively stable primary frame of reference for black Americans through which they filtered information and organized their thoughts, feelings, and actions. Assuming that the concept of race reflected a coherent and meaningful frame of reference for black Americans could have made them more hesitant and cautious in changing the meaning and significance they attributed to it.

PSYCHOLOGY AND RACE: INFLUENCING ATTITUDES AND BEHAVIOR

By 1900, the white-supremacy doctrine was widely accepted by white Americans throughout the country. In keeping with past practices, academicians expended considerable time and resources searching for evidence to support it. In his *The Negro in the Making of America*, Benjamin Quarles notes that during the first and second decades of the twentieth century, the idea that Caucasians were inherently superior to people of African descents became more tenaciously held than ever before.[91] Graham Richards characterizes the period between 1910 and 1940 as peak years for psychological research on race differences in the United States.[92] During this period, W. E. B. Du Bois, Booker T. Washington, and other educated black Americans forcefully debated the nature of the education that should be provided to the black masses. American psychologists involved in the eugenics movement argued that understanding innate racial differences could guide educational policy regarding the curricula and teaching methods appropriate for different racial groups.[93] Infused with the evolutionary thinking underlying scientific racism, the eugenics movement, which included prominent psychologists such as Lewis Terman, Robert M. Yerkes, and Edward L. Thorndike, was a major force in getting American psychologists involved in research on psychological race differences or "race psychology."[94]

During the first quarter of the twentieth century, American psychologists also devoted considerable attention to the United States immigration policies. Proponents of eugenics were concerned about an influx of immigrants from "inferior" European stock. Even though proponents of eugenics and other racial conservatives viewed black Americans as intellectually inferior to white immigrants, they did not view them as a serious threat because blacks were living under segregated conditions. On the other hand, the nation did not have laws that could prevent white immigrants from eventually assimilating into the American mainstream.[95] Therefore, during the years of 1917 through 1926, psychologists involved in the eugenics movement also focused on informing immigration policy by identifying Europeans and nonwhites that should be denied immigration papers to the United States.[96]

With the emergence of mental testing, American psychologists started comparing Negro and white scores among children during the second decade of the twentieth century. The application of psychometric and experimental methods provided psychologists with a central position in shaping the debate on Negro education in the United States. Although the use of these research approaches created the appearance of objectivity, they already had been rooted in the politics of society. Psychologists used subjective evidence that reflected value judgments, while at the same time they attempted to mask their racially conservative social-political agendas. Graham Richards uses the term "empirical racism" to describe the methods used by psychologists to identify race differences.[97] Studies of racial differences in the newly created discipline of psychology seemed destined to prove and give scientific credence to the idea that African Americans were beset with inherent and irreversible cognitive and behavioral defects. According to Frank Margonis, epistemological racism ran so deep that even liberal educators, such as John Dewey, developed educational methods that while appearing race neutral were actually dehumanizing to black students.[98]

The widespread use and abuse of newly developed mental tests by conservative educators, policymakers, and other white professionals reinforced beliefs in white supremacy in the general public. The studies and writings on the psychology of race differences played a central role in shaping local, state, national, and international government policies in the United States concerning racial segregation and discrimination against immigrants from Eastern Europe and nonwhites, especially people with African bloodlines.[99] In his book *Even the Rat Was White*, Robert V. Guthrie documents the widespread existence of civilizational and epistemological racism by noting that early psychologists appeared so blinded by racism that they became consumed with conducting research on those things that divided people and lost sight of those things that united individuals.[100] While this research on race differences might have helped psychologists attain their social-political agendas, it appears that neither science nor society benefited from it.[101] In keeping with the spirit of the times, the results and conclusions reported in these studies provided support for the prevailing assumption of white racial superiority as well as reassurance for the maintenance of racial discriminatory practices. The results of these studies also might have reinforced negative connotations that blacks already associated with the concept of race. These circumstances also could have reinforced the centrality of race as a psychological filter in black Americans.

During the first and second decades of the twentieth century, psychology seemingly contributed more to the misunderstanding of African Americans' behavior, cognition, and feelings than any other field of study. In their writings on race research in psychology, Graham Richards and William H. Tucker review several early psychological studies on race differences that reveal the psychologists' racial biases. A monograph published in 1913 by psychologist Marion J. Mayo investigates school performance of black and white students who were enrolled in integrated schools in New York when the data was collected. Mayo reviewed performance marks on various courses over four years of high school. He reports that white students consistently performed better than black students and attributed the difference to "race heredity." Richards notes that Mayo assumes that white teachers employed impartial grading practices. In light of the racist nature of American society during the second decade of the twentieth century, white teachers might have been predisposed to rate black students below white students. While acknowledging that the hereditary difference might be small, Mayo concludes:

> But in as much as everything in the power of educator, philanthropist, and law giver has been done for the equalization of opportunity, it is hard to escape the conclusion that the fundamental explanation of the difference in scholastic standing is to be found mainly in the factor of race heredity. . . . Not only then does it seem admissible to assume the existence of mental inequality between the races to account for the various facts in our human relationships, but it would seem that a priori considerations, in view of our knowledge of human evolution, would make no other assumption tenable.[102]

Mayo's comments suggest that, similar to proponents of eugenics and social Darwinism, his deep-seated racial prejudices and beliefs preclude him from understanding the influence of black Americans' culture and social environment on their school performance.

Using a 1911 revised version of the mental measurement scales developed in 1905 and revised in 1908 by Alfred Binet and Theodore

Simon, in 1913, psychologist Alice C. Strong published a study on race differences in test performance of black and white schoolchildren who resided in South Carolina. It was the first paper to apply the Binet-Simon scales in a study of race differences. Her samples included 225 white children, with ages ranging from six to twelve years, and 125 black children. She does not specify the age range of the black children, but it is suggested that their ages were similar to the white children, with some older than 12 years. Although her samples pose several methodology issues, that discussion can be explored in a different forum. Strong concludes that black children were mentally younger and "tested more irregularly" than white children of the same age. What should be noted here are some contradictions in her descriptions of the environmental circumstances of the two groups. She states: "The course of study in the colored school is practically the same as that in the white schools. To what extent this difference is due to racial inferiority, to what extent to difference in the home environment, cannot be said. It is certainly not due to difference in school training."[103] Richards points out several inaccuracies in her description. First, there were huge disparities in the expenditures on education in South Carolina between black versus white children during this period. South Carolina expenditure per head on education in 1916 thru 1917 was approximately thirteen times more for white children than for black children; white teachers' salaries were approximately 400 percent higher than black teachers. In 1910, child-staff ratio was 34:1 for white children and 78.5:1 for black children. Strong's description of children's responses to the context of testing environment suggests that the groups might not have perceived it in the same way. She offers the following description of the white children: "There was no difficulty in securing cordial relations with the children. They were always encouraged, and apparently exerted themselves to do their best. They invariably responded with interest, if not with eagerness."[104] On the other hand, she expresses some uncertainty in her description of the black children. She states, "So far as the examiner could judge, the children felt at ease and did their best."[105] It is quite possible, however, that an examiner of their own race might have obtained different results. Richards notes that, although this study was seriously flawed, it came to be identified as a pioneering contribution and the main results were regularly cited.

Under the guise of science, G. O. Ferguson, a prominent psychologist, published in 1916 *The Psychology of the Negro: An Experimental Study*. White Americans in general and white academicians in particular lauded it as a classic psychological study of African Americans. Ferguson reports that the intellectual ability of an African American is related to the amount of white blood the person possesses. He indicates that African Americans possess instability of character, including a lack of foresight, a lack of persistence on tasks, a lack of serious initiative, a tendency to be content with immediate gratification, deficient ambitions, defective morality characteristics, and very limited abstract thinking capacities. Ferguson's observations suggest that he used his personal perceptions as a substitute for objective measurement. Guthrie reports several studies from the archives of psychology that show psychologists provided inaccurate data to support their beliefs.

The introduction of mental tests near the turn of the twentieth century was the most significant development in psychology to reinforce prevailing views and attitudes about the significance of race. Edward L. Thorndike, one of the pioneers of mental testing, proclaims in 1903:

> With sufficient knowledge we could analyze any man's original mental nature into elements. . . . We could determine what innate differences, if any, existed in the intelligence of different races. . . . If differences in innate intelligence could be measured, then a racial scale could eventually be worked out with considerable exactitude.[106]

Thorndike's observations suggest that psychologists were more interested in the study of measurable racial differences in performance on mental tests rather than understanding conditions in living experiences that may account for the differences. Shortly after Thorndike made his remarks, a highly acclaimed psychological test of mental abilities was introduced. Proponents of eugenics and social Darwinism believed that this test could be used to confirm the inherent intellectual inferiority of dark-skinned people. In keeping with well-established practices among white academicians in research on race, psychologists pursued this initiative with a vengeance.

In 1905, Alfred Binet and Theodore Simon devised a series of mental tests to detect different levels of feeblemindedness in children. These tests were deemed effective for identifying and classifying children with special needs in France. In a 1908 revised version of these tests, Binet and Simon define mental age by measuring it in terms of the ability of a child to answer a group of questions that 75 percent of the children of this age group could answer. They point out that the environment and educational opportunities would affect performance on the tests. They also warn that the tests would be appropriate measures of intelligence only of those children who had closely similar environments. In the book *The Mismeasure of Man*, Stephen Jay Gould presents the following three principles that Binet cautions test users and researchers to observe:

1. The scores are a practical device; they do not buttress any theory of intellect. They do not define anything innate or permanent. We may not designate what they measure as "intelligence" or any other reified entity.
2. The scale is a rough, empirical guide for identifying mildly retarded and learning-disabled children who need special help. It is not a device for ranking normal children.
3. Whatever the cause of difficulty in children identified for help, emphasis shall be placed upon improvement through special training. Low scores shall not be used to mark as innately incapable.[107]

After Henry H. Goddard translated the Binet-Simon Scales into English, it was introduced in the United States in 1908 for use at the Vineland Training School in New Jersey. In 1916, Lewis Terman, professor of psychology at Stanford University and later president of the American Psychological Association, published the Stanford-Binet scale of intelligence. Although Binet and Simon had already warned against interpreting tests as measuring hereditary intelligence without taking into account the environment and educational opportunities, Terman proclaimed that his version of the Binet-Simon tests measured hereditary intelligence, contending, "A low level of intelligence is very, very common between Spanish-Indian and Mexican families of the Southwest, and also among Negroes. Their dullness seems to be racial, or at least inherent in the family stocks from which they come." He went on to say that these "differences cannot be wiped out by any scheme of mental culture. No amount of school instruction will ever make them intelligent voters or capable citizens in the true sense of the word."[108] Terman's revised version of the Binet-Simon Scales became the Stanford-Binet intelligence test and the benchmark for objective assessments of intelligence.

The assumption that the Stanford-Binet intelligence test provided a fixed measure of innate intelligence also received the forceful support of Robert M. Yerkes, who was then professor of psychology at Harvard and chairman of the Committee on Inheritance of Mental Traits of the Eugenics Research Association. Commenting on the results derived from tests used to determine the intelligence and aptitudes of men entering the armed services during World War I, Yerkes states:

> "Quite apart from educational status, which is utterly unsatisfactory, the negro soldier is of relatively low grade intelligence." This discovery was "in the nature of a lesson, for it suggests that education alone will not place the negro race on a par with its Caucasian competitors."[109]

The observations of prominent psychologists, such as Yerkes, Terman, and Thorndike, had profound, damaging social consequences.

Results from the Stanford-Binet intelligence test were used to apply apparent objectivity to the debate on the intellectual inferiority of African Americans. Profound variations in the quality of life and educational opportunities between African Americans and white Americans were largely ignored. In touting the Stanford-Binet Scales as measures of hereditary intelligence, psychologists provided racists with a potent tool that was conveniently used to justify racially discriminatory practices, racial oppression, and racially motivated acts of violence against people of African descents. The use of these scales as measures of inherent intellectual dissimilarities between and among members of different racial groups ensured that the racist attitudes, beliefs, and practices would last, as they have, for many generations. In view of the enthusiasm and strong desire expressed by Thorndike and other psychologists during the turn of the century to establish objective tests to measure intellectual dissimilarities, it is understandable that W. E. B. Du Bois would observe in 1903: "The problem of the Twentieth Century is the problem of the color-line."[110]

By 1917, intelligence tests were being used on a mass scale in the United States military services. The impact of intelligence tests was apparent in many aspects of society. The United States Congress established the Immigration Act of 1921 that limited the number of immigrants from Eastern European countries, Asian countries, and African countries.[111] A more stringent immigration act was passed in 1924. Commenting on the Immigration Act of 1924, Senator David A. Reed stated, "The races of men who have been coming to us in recent years are wholly dissimilar to the native-born Americans. . . . They are untrained in self-government—a faculty that it has taken the Northwestern Europeans many centuries to acquire." He went on to suggest that it was best for America "that our incoming immigrants should hereafter be of the same races as those of us who are already here, so that each year's immigration should so far as possible be a miniature America."[112] As can be seen from Reed's remarks, psychological tests of mental abilities provided political ammunition for racist legislation. Results derived from these tests were used quite effectively to justify restrictive immigration policies and racial segregation and racial inequalities in the United States.

The popularity and growth of intelligence tests made it impossible for African Americans to ignore the significance of race in their daily lives. White Americans viewed the 1923 publication of *A Study of American Intelligence* by C. C. Brigham as the leading authoritative source of reference on race differences. Comparing the mental test results from a sample of white and black military draftees, Brigham shows that whites consistently scored higher than blacks. In a seemingly scathing manner, he argues, "The average Negro child can not advance through an educational curriculum adapted to the Anglo-Saxon child in step with that child."[113] Brigham contends that Negro children who achieved a given grade at the same age as the average white child would be the superior ones. On the contrary, white children who achieved the grade at the same age as the average Negro child would be the inferior ones. He also attributed his so-called superior Negro children test performance to a greater amount of "white blood." As a proponent of eugenics who believed in the natural intellectual superiority of Anglo Saxons, Brigham adamantly opposed race mixing, declaring, "We must face a possibility of racial admixture here that is infinitely worse than that faced by any European country today, for we are incorporating the Negro into our racial stock, while all of Europe is comparatively free from this taint."[114] Information and arguments presented in *A Study of American*

Intelligence were used to bolster support for immigration-restriction legislation and national segregation policies.

It should be noted that after critics effectively challenged some of the fundamental premises that had been used by proponents of eugenics and social Darwinism and seven years after the publication of *A Study of American Intelligence*, Brigham recanted the conclusions he had supported earlier. Contrary to a claim made by the British psychologist Charles Spearman, Brigham suggested that the meaning of test scores remained an open question and that test scores might not represent unitary things. Conceding that differences in one's linguistic environment might influence test scores significantly, Brigham notes that it was unacceptable to use mental tests for comparative studies "of individuals brought up in homes where the vernacular is not used, or in which two vernaculars are used."[115]

THE UNDOING OF RACE PSYCHOLOGY IN THE UNITED STATES

Even though Frank Boas repeatedly challenged the scientific basis of early psychologists' contention of the innateness of race differences, he was ignored by them until the 1920s. During the interwar years, the writings of Boas along with his former graduate students, including Margaret Mead, Melville Herskovits, and Otto Klineberg, as well as other notable social scientists, forced psychologists to confront contradictions in their theoretical contention about hereditary race differences. In separate papers on racial testing, social anthropologists Mead and Herskovits argue that no reliable evidence exists to support the claim of innate race differences on measures of intelligence. Mead points out that those results from early psychological studies on race differences in intelligence are inconclusive because they lump together racial and social class factors. Her research reveals that when social class is controlled or held constant, race differences are significantly reduced but not eliminated.

In two papers published in 1928 that were widely read by psychologists, G. H. Estabrooks challenges the methodology used in psychological studies on race differences. Estabrooks concludes, "We cannot measure intelligence under different environmental conditions with any assurance that we are getting comparable results. . . . Practically all work up to present has been done on groups which were by no means physically homogeneous."[116] He argues that a valid comparison would require that the physical criteria by which racial identities have to be defined are themselves normally distributed throughout the population. Estabrooks puts it this way: "All we demand is that the racial criteria have a normal distribution—or a uniform distribution—in each of the groups from a cultural point of view."[117] He also calls into question psychologists' assumptions about the innateness of race difference because their conclusions tend to overlook historical evidence that repeatedly shows an outcast group in one generation "demonstrating it is capable of high culture the next."[118]

Drawing from the teachings of Boas, Otto Klineberg, professor of psychology at Columbia University, studied cultural influences on test performance and learning in Native Americans, African American, and white American children. Klineberg, arguably, was the most ardent and influential critic in the field of psychology of the assumption that race differences were innate.[119] In his 1928 publication *An Experimental Study of Speed and Other Factors in "Racial" Differences*, Klineberg investigates speed and accuracy when taking psychological tests using children with different racial, cultural, and geographic backgrounds. Based on results derived from four tests, he concludes that language, schooling, culture, social and economic status, rapport, motivation, and speed could in different combinations account for group differences in test performance. He reported that whites were not superior in learning ability nor did race mixing with whites increase performance for other races. On the "heredity versus environment" debate, to account for group differences in intelligence test scores or IQ, Klineberg argues that it would be scientifically unsound to use heredity to account for these the differences. In a review of Klineberg's observations, Richards notes that the nature and nurture "cannot be sensibly differentiated at the individual level." Elaborating on this point, he points out that "the gene frequencies in a group may be due to heredity, but differences between groups in gene frequency are not themselves hereditary."[120] Richards suggests that Klineberg's 1928 publication on speed and accuracy in racial differences along with his 1935 publication of *Negro Intelligence*

and Selective Migration and Race Differences effectively silenced notable psychologists, such as Robert M. Yerkes, who had been advocates
of innate racial differences. After 1930, very few psychologists showed
an interest in pursuing research on race psychology until the 1970s.

The intellectual testing movement aroused racial hostilities and accentuated perceived race differences in the psychological makeup of
white Americans and black Americans. It predisposed some members
from both groups to use genetic explanations to account for perceived
racial differences. On one hand, some white Americans maintained that
people of African descents were inherently feebleminded and immoral.
On the other hand and possibly explaining the early appeal of the Nation of Islam,[121] many black Americans believed Caucasians were inherently evil and immoral. Recognizing that white academicians had almost
always conducted research on race differences to obtain evidence to
justify the white-supremacy doctrine, the intellectual testing movement
did not necessarily change most black-American attitudes about themselves. Nevertheless, since black Americans' social environment varied
between and within different geographic locations, it increases the
likelihood that there could have been some unevenness or differences
in terms of how they perceived research on race differences. Earlier
studies and writings on race sensitized African Americans to negative
conclusions about their human attributes. An overwhelming majority of
African Americans did not trust white Americans. Consequently, they
were suspicious of so-called scientific studies about them. Bearing this
in mind, results derived from mental tests that showed black children
consistently scored below white children had very little credence in
African American communities. Many African Americans viewed the
results derived from psychological tests of mental abilities as merely
another effort by white Americans to perpetuate the white-supremacy
doctrine and provide support for racial segregation and discrimination.
Only a very few African Americans possessed the education needed to
present informed rebuttals to studies and writings about race. Nonetheless, African American scholars were adamant in their criticisms of these
works. In his essay titled "Race Intelligence," W. E. B. Du Bois notes:

> For a century or more it has been the dream of those who do not believe
> Negroes are human that their wish should find some scientific basis. . . .

Then came psychology: the children of the public schools were studied and it was discovered that some colored children ranked lower than white children. This gave wide satisfaction even though it was pointed out that the average included most of both races and that considering the educational opportunities and social environment of the races the differences were measurements simply of the ignorance and poverty of the black child's surrounding.[122]

Horace Mann Bond, the first African American president of Lincoln University in Pennsylvania, voiced stern criticisms about the intelligence testing movement and warned African Americans about its dangerous consequences, stating:

The time has passed for opposing these false ideas with science; every university student of Negro blood ought to comprise himself into an agent whose sole purpose is the contravention of such half-truth. . . . There is no longer any justification for the silence of the educated Negro, when confronted with these assertions; and only through his activity and investigation will the truth be disclosed and the ghosts of racial inferiority, mental or physical, set at rest, forever.[123]

Subsequently, Bond conducted a study that demonstrates that black children perform better in the testing situation with black examiners than in testing situations with white examiners.

Given the differences in the social experiences among black American children, undoubtedly, some of them could have suffered psychological damage from the intelligence testing movement. It could have lowered their self-concept, confidence, and achievement motivation. For others, it could have motivated them to work harder to disprove the mythologies of racial differences. On the other hand, the intelligence testing movement could have had no significant effect on the attitudes of some black children about their mental abilities. However, the intelligence testing movement almost certainly reinforced the significance of race as a frame of reference for most black American children during the interwar years.

As noted in the writings of Leon Kamin, shortly after the Stanford-Binet intelligence test was introduced, the use of results derived from it and similar psychological tests became, and remained well into the twentieth century, the most popular evidence employed by white Americans to support racially motivated differential treatment of black Americans, especially in education and work settings. It was more than fifty years after Lewis Terman, Edward Thorndike, and Robert Yerkes pioneered the American mental-testing movement that, in *The Science and Politics of I.Q.*, Kamin observes:

> The I.Q. test in America, and the way in which we think about it, has been fostered by men committed to a particular social view. That view includes the belief that those on the bottom are genetically inferior victims of their own immutable defects. The consequence has been that the I.Q. test has served as an instrument of oppression against the poor—dressed in the trappings of science, rather than politics. The message of science is heard respectfully, particularly when the tidings it carries are soothing to the public conscience. There are few more soothing messages than those historically delivered by the I.Q. testers. The poor, the foreign-born, and racial minorities were shown to be stupid. They were shown to have been born that way. The underprivileged are today demonstrated to be ineducable, a message as soothing to the public purse as to the public conscience.[124]

Notable black American scholars, such as W. E. B. Du Bois and Horace Mann Bond, dispelled the validity of these psychological tests as being measures of hereditary intelligence, but they were ignored in most academic circles. As a result, the intelligence testing movement hardened many black Americans' distrust of white Americans and predisposed many of them to second-guess white Americans' perceptions, judgments, decisions, and actions. The debate surrounding the intelligence of African Americans increased the likelihood that they perceived differences in opinions on a variety of issues with white Americans as expressions of no respect for their judgments concerning the drawbacks of interpreting results from psychological tests as innate differences in the intelligence of different races.

Many black Americans perceived a need to prove their mental capabilities to white Americans. And, when granted the opportunities to do so, they often enthusiastically responded. Believing that to get recognition they must be twice as good as white Americans who performed the same tasks, many African Americans became overachievers and carried out education or job-related assignments beyond the call of duty. On the other hand, many African Americans followed different courses of action in response to white Americans' guarded respect for their intellectual capabilities. For example, they adopted a variety of reactions in work and education settings, such as: curtailing contact and communication with white people, performing job-related tasks at minimal levels of efficiency and effectiveness, following the leads of their white coworkers and doing no more or no less work than them, and sabotaging equipment. Most African Americans did very little, if anything, in response to white Americans' attitudes about their intellectual capabilities. They did not provide enough clues in the workplace or other settings to reveal their feelings and attitudes about it. However, in private gatherings with family members and close friends, these African Americans, in anguish, expressed their daily struggles, disenchantments, disappointments, and hostilities caused by racism. As in the previous century, race was the primary unifying force among African Americans during the first quarter of the twentieth century. Unlike before and during the Civil War years, in which many free blacks in the South maintained distance from other black people, the community bond among black people was more integrated along class and skin-color lines at the turn of the century.

IDENTITY ISSUES AND THE CHANGING DYNAMICS AMONG AFRICAN AMERICANS

The legal separation of races accelerated and solidified the process of community building among African Americans of varying skin colors. Working together to combat racism was a priority for both light-skin and dark-skin African Americans. A sense of two-ness and togetherness developed among them that helped to sustain hope and strengthen the resolve to attain equality and participate as equals in the American mainstream. In 1910, the National Association for the Advancement of Colored People was founded to work for the abolition of racial segregation, equal education for children without regard for race, the complete enfranchisement of African Americans, and the enforcement of the Fourteenth and Fifteenth Amendments.

Marriages and mating between mulattoes and dark-skin African Americans increased steadily. The offspring born from these relationships reflected a rich variety of skin-color shades and physical characteristics. It became commonplace for dark-skinned and light-skinned siblings to appear in the same family. It was not unusual for dark-skinned children with Caucasian physical features and hair textures to have light-skinned brothers and sisters with African physical features and hair textures. It should be noted that Negroid physical features among Africans widely vary from one region to another. The distinctive physical features of most Africans who reside in West African countries make it relatively easy to distinguish them from Africans who reside in East African countries. The physical features vary widely among Africans who reside in the northern and southern regions of Africa. The ancestors of most African Americans came from nations located in West Africa.

The varieties of skin-color shades and mixed-racial physical features among African Americans increased at a steady and rapid rate after the Civil War. This amalgamation coupled with United States racist policies and practices contributed to the disappearance of mulattoes as a distinct group among people of African descents in America. By 1920, the physical features of most African Americans reflected racial bloodline mixes. The realities of racism—such as lynching, underemployment, and rejection, which were fueled by the legalization of racial segregation and discrimination—contributed to racial solidarity in such a manner that it overshadowed the psychological significance attributed to skin color among African Americans. Both light-skinned and dark-skinned African Americans came together to protect each other from terrorism instigated by white Americans. In view of the long-standing psychological and social significance attributed to skin color, along with the wide range of color shades among African Americans, many of them were either unable or unwilling to rid themselves of negative stereotypes associated with blackness.

Because of the control and dominance that white Americans maintained in almost every aspect of living in the United States, white ideal standards were pivotal in constructing the cultural norms used to define human beauty and attractiveness. In a society that denigrates dark skin and other non-Caucasian features, it is inevitable that some individuals with dark skin and distinctive racial features will learn to devalue and have feelings of shame about them. Many African Americans unwittingly adopted some of the prevailing antiblack attitudes and were ashamed of their own pigmentation, hair texture, facial features, and African origins.[125] In European American culture, the physical standards of beauty embody distinctive Caucasian phenotypes, such as hair texture, skin color, nose, and lips. Since the arrival of colonists, whiteness has had positive symbolic connotations in North America. Whiteness implies purity, cleanliness, and beauty in European American culture (e.g., What can make me white as snow? Nothing but the blood of Jesus; Snow White; little white lies). On the other hand, traditionally, blackness has had negative connotations in European American culture. It has been used to imply unattractive characteristics, behaviors, and events (e.g., blackmail; blackball; blacklist; and black sheep).[126]

Considering the dominant position of European American culture from the colonial period through the first half of the twentieth century, it is not surprising that many African Americans adopted white Americans' standards of beauty and had ambivalent feelings about some of their own features. Many African Americans adopted standards of physical beauty that included persons, like themselves, with a mixture of African, Caucasian, and Native American bloodlines rather than white Americans' standards of beauty. Historians, social scientists, and scientists provide a large body of data that shows that bloodlines of most African Americans reflect a blending of African, Caucasian, and Native American heritage.[127] Because of interbreeding, African Americans, like many white Americans, are not members of a pure racial group. It has been reported that the proportion of African Americans with white ancestry is between 20 and 75 percent.[128] Consequently, skin-color shades and facial features vary considerably among African Americans. African Americans' standards of beauty are as varied as skin-color shades, facial features, and other physical features that are among them. Increasingly, most African Americans share features that make it relatively easy to distinguish them from native Africans. It is widely recognized that most African Americans choose spouses and companions from members of their ethnic group. Because of the high degree of variability in skin-color shades and facial features among African Americans, there has been no consensus in standards of human physical beauty adopted by them.

The writings and studies by psychologists during the first half of the twentieth century show the cultural influence of Caucasian standards of human beauty and attractiveness. In an article titled "The Color Question from a Psychoanalytic Standpoint," published in 1924, psychologist O. A. R. Berkeley-Hill provides the following observations about skin color, race, and beauty:

> The strong Feeling-tone that characterizes ideas on the Color question indicates an over determination by unconscious factors. The herd instinct does not account for all the facts. For example, it does not explain why dark-skinned people admire the fair, and why the Australian aborigines believe that a white man is one of them reborn. For an explanation we must turn rather to the relation in the minds of both dark and fair-skinned peoples between blackness, evil and magic. The myths and customs of all races abound in such associations. Blackness is thus associated with a primitive, nonrational fear, in the unconscious of all. In addition to this cause for the dislike of a pigmented skin, there is also another, namely, sexual jealousy, based upon the widespread belief that the Negro is more potent sexually than the white man and therefore sexually attractive to white women.[129]

In an essay titled "Psychological Considerations of Color Conflicts among Negroes," published in 1943, G. B. Bovell contends that black Americans share white-American color standards of human beauty and attractiveness. Bovell concludes that:

> The white race, fearing that it may be inferior to the colored races, bolsters its belief in its own superiority by making whiteness a prestige symbol and by exploiting the colored groups. The Negro has accepted the color standards of the white group and in turn discriminates against its darker members. Color conflicts will continue among Negroes so long as differences in complexion exist among them.[130]

In 1946, M. Seeman conducted a study titled "Skin Color Values in Three All-Negro School Classes." Skin color rating scales were administered to eighty-one children enrolled in grades three through six to measure the significance of skin color in friendship choice and reputation in the group. The results show that lighter color was more frequently associated with greater acceptability and better reputation. The results reported in a study on "Color Names and Color Notions" published in 1946 by Charles H. Parrish also show that many black Americans accepted the color standards of white Americans. Parrish summarizes findings in the following manner:

> Several hundred color names are current among Negroes but only three to five widely recognized color categories have stereotypes attached to them. A light skin and other physical traits approximating the Caucasian are highly regarded in the Negro community. Color, however, has acquired a special significance. Extremely light skin color evokes envy and resentment on the part of darker persons because light skin is identified with conceit and snobbishness. Black Negroes are condemned for being quarrelsome and pitied for feelings of inferiority. Three out of five Negro persons asked, considered black the worst color to be. Favorable attitudes toward persons of medium shades is a compromise between rejection of light and dark. These notions arise because dark skin color is associated with low status.[131]

As evidenced by pictures of black female models and marriage partners often chosen by African American leaders and prominent citizens, many African Americans shared the same conceptions of human beauty that was held by white Americans. For many African Americans, it created a paradox because their perceptions of human beauty were inconsistent with their phenotypes. It follows that they experienced ambivalent feelings about the significance of skin color and other physical traits. Many Garveyites and UNIA sympathizers openly rejected American cultural norms and embraced African phenotypes to define human beauty. However, historical accounts suggest that Garvey's followers were reacting to the hopelessness of their perceived plights. Whether their embracing of African traits was a protest against racism or a true representation of their feelings or a combination of both explanations remains an open question. Thus, it is likely that unresolved conflicts about the significance of skin color were at the core of the belief systems for many African Americans. Consequently, discussions among African Americans about skin color were then and now an unpopular topic.

Racially conservative policies and practices during the early decades of the twentieth century sustained the hostility, distrust, and long-standing power struggle that characterized the relationship between black Americans and white Americans. It also helped to sustain the psychological and behavioral strategies in black Americans that had evolved in response to racially oppressive practices during earlier years. During the first half of the twentieth century, black Americans were more alike in terms of the psychological and social significance they attributed to race than ever before. During the era of legal racial segregation in the United States, an African American could not escape the psychological and social significance of white racial oppression. For African Americans, racial oppression was perceived as a relatively permanent condition for as long as they lived in a society dominated by Caucasians. Therefore, racial oppression was of central importance to the meaning and significance attributed to racial group membership for African Americans.

As previously noted, the preferential treatment by white Americans of both free and enslaved mulattoes over their darker-skinned counterparts almost certainly precluded the former group from developing strong attachment bonds and close identification with the black masses. After the United States government adopted racial policies that legally grouped mulattoes together with other people of African descents, commonalities in the way race was viewed by these groups began to evolve. Mulattoes recognized that their plight for racial equality was intimately linked to the plight of the black masses. Differences in the psychological makeup of light-skinned free blacks—including black slaveholders—and their darker-skinned enslaved counterparts that were likely to have existed before the Civil War were almost certainly replaced by commonalities in their psychological makeup before World War I.

FROM HOPELESSNESS TO HOPE

The United States Supreme Court's decision in the *Plessy v. Ferguson* case chilled the hopes and aspirations of African Americans. Although they were united in their opposition to the 1896 racial segregation decision mandated by the Court, African Americans did not agree on strategies to respond to it. Guided primarily by the leadership of Marcus Garvey and, subsequently, the Honorable Elijah Muhammed, spiritual leader of the Nation of Islam, many African Americans viewed cooperative living and working arrangements with white Americans as hopeless. Accordingly, they were highly critical of white people at home and abroad. They supported racial independence and separation from white Americans.

During the first half of the twentieth century, underemployment and low wages were chronic problems among African Americans. These problems threatened the economic growth and stability in African American communities. In view of the economic problems facing African Americans, the formation of labor unions for black workers was another strategy used by black leaders to fight racial discrimination in the workforce. In 1920, a group of New York activists formed an organization and named it the Friends of Negro Freedom. This organization was established to unionize black migrants, protect black tenants, advance black cooperation, and organize forums through which to educate the black masses.[132] They attempted to fight racial discrimination by the use of the boycott, but it was ineffective. In 1925, A. Philip Randolph led the most significant movement toward the unionization of African Americans. He organized the Brotherhood of Sleeping Car Porters and Maids and secured from the Pullman Company better working conditions and higher wages. By 1937, this union gained full recognition as the bargaining agency for porters and maids employed by the Pullman Company.

In response to the racist direction, practices, and policies adopted by the United States government, some black leaders called for the development of African American businesses to provide jobs and services for African Americans. In 1898, John Hope, president of Atlanta University, said at a conference on the Negro in business:

> Employment must be had, and this employment will have to come to Negroes from Negro sources. . . . Negro capital will have to give an opportunity to Negro workmen who will be crowded out by white competition.[133]

He also said that the policy of avoiding entrance in the world's business would be suicide to the Negro.

Two years after the Atlanta conference, Booker T. Washington took the lead and organized the National Negro Business League. He charged the league to instill in black Americans faith in the business enterprise as the way to economic salvation. Although the organization did not have the impact upon the economic status of black Americans that was hoped for, there were several black businesses that survived and thrived. The overall employment for black workers provided by black businesses was marginal. E. Franklin Frazier, who was department chairman and professor of sociology at Howard University before his death in 1962, provided several explanations to account for the ineffectiveness of many black businesses that grew out of the National Negro Business League. He noted that black businessmen lacked adequate business knowledge and experience. For example, success for some black businessmen was defined often by appearance rather than real profits. Some black businesses that may have looked successful were not operating successfully. Second, white companies found it extremely profitable to employ blacks in advertising products for black consumers, in establishing public relations with the black community, and in sales. The employment of blacks by large white-owned corporations often overshadowed the achievements of black businessmen. Third, black entrepreneurs were unable to obtain financial support from white-owned banks. Fourth, and perhaps most important, black businesses were motivated primarily by the desire for private profits rather than the good of the black community they served. Frazier's analysis suggests that if black businessmen had been guided by a desire to strengthen the economic, social, and educational development of African American communities, more black businesses would have survived.

Targeting the judiciary branches of government at all levels, leaders of the NAACP relentlessly forged a fight for equality in all facets of American living. They were strong advocates for racial integration in schools as well as other institutions. In 1954, the NAACP filed a lawsuit in its efforts to overturn the United States Supreme Court's 1896 decision in the *Plessy v. Ferguson* case. Using empirical evidence derived from Kenneth B. Clark's and Mamie K. Clark's 1939 and 1940 studies on skin color and segregation as factors in racial identification of African American preschool children, Thurgood Marshall, chief counsel for the NAACP and later United States Supreme Court justice, successfully argued, on behalf of the defendant in the *Brown v. Board of Education of Topeka, Kansas* case, that at a very early age African American children were psychologically damaged by attending racially segregated and inferior schools.

Although Cross and Silverstein and Krate summarized thoughtful criticisms of Clark and Clark's studies, these criticisms did not diminish the historical impact that Clark and Clark's research had on shaping public and social policies on race issues in the United States.[134] Kenneth and Mamie Clark conducted studies on the racial attitudes and preferences of samples of African American children, aged three through seven, who resided in the South and North regions of the United States. Each child was asked to choose between two dolls, one with dark brown skin and the other white, in response to the following requests:

1. Give me the doll that you like to play with [or] like best.
2. Give me the doll that is a nice doll.
3. Give me the doll that looks bad.
4. Give me the doll that is a nice color.
5. Give me the doll that looks like a white child.
6. Give me the doll that looks like a colored child.
7. Give me the doll that looks like a Negro child.
8. Give me the doll that looks like you.

According to the Clarks, children's responses to the first four requests would reflect racial preferences; to requests five through seven, awareness of racial differences; and to request eight, self-identification. The results indicated that approximately half of the African American children at every age level preferred the white doll. Awareness of racial differences increased with age: 93 percent of the seven-year-olds and 61 percent of the three-year-olds made correct choices. Light-skinned children showed more white-doll preference than darker-skinned children (70 percent and 59 percent, respectively). Children attending integrated schools in the North expressed greater white-doll preference than did children from segregated Southern schools. Light-skinned children reported the white doll as looking like them more frequently than did medium- or dark-skinned children (80, 26, and 19, respectively).[135] During the 1940s and 1950s, the essential elements of the Clarkses' research were replicated many times, and the results consistently indicated that African American children tended to select white over black dolls.[136]

A popular explanation for results reported in the Clarks' studies was that the majority of African American children had negative feelings about dark skin and preferred white skin. Some psychologists suggested that many black children selected the white doll as looking like them because they themselves may have wished to be white or had a confused sense of racial identity. Some African American children may have reported white-doll preference, not because of negative feelings about dark skin, but rather because of the more privileged social position of white people in general. Some of these children may have believed that by identifying with and establishing closer relationships with white people, they also may become recipients of or vicariously derive the benefits from the more privileged status shared by whites.

Different explanations have been used to interpret results derived from the Clarks' research. Nevertheless, the results clearly showed that for African American children at a very young and tender age and even before they had developed the capacities for logical thought, race had become a central psychological component in self-construction for them. The results showed that these young African American children had become cognizant of the racial inequities in the United States. They also recognized that racial segregation had imposed on them a heavy burden: that of trying to live in two unequal worlds at the same time, one comprised black people with limited rights, opportunities, resources, and authority and the other world composed of white people with many rights, resources, opportunities, and authority. Lawyers representing the plaintiff in the *Brown v. Board of Education* case focused on the psychological damage to African American children caused by segregation:

> Segregation of white and colored children in public schools has a detrimental effect upon the colored children. The impact is greater when it has the sanction of the law; for the policy of separating the races is usually interpreted as denoting the inferiority of the Negro group. A sense of inferiority affects the motivation of a child to learn. Segregation with the sanction of law, therefore, has a tendency to [retard] the educational and mental development of Negro children and to deprive them of some of the benefits they would receive in a racially integrated school system.[137]

Under the leadership of Chief Justice Earl Warren, the Court made the historic ruling that the separate but equal doctrine was unconstitutional. The 1954 *Brown v. Board of Education* decision ruled that segregated schools were a denial of equal protection of the law guaranteed by the Fourteenth Amendment. Chief Justice Earl Warren made the following remarks when he delivered the Court's ruling:

> Today, education is perhaps the most important function of state and local governments. . . . It is the very foundation of good citizenship. It is a principal instrument in awakening the child to cultural values, in preparing him for later professional training, and in helping him to adjust normally to his environment. We come then to the question presented: Does segregation of children in public schools solely on the basis of race, even though the physical facilities and other Tangible factors may be equal, deprive the children of the minority group of equal educational opportunities? We believe that it does. . . . To separate them from others of similar age and qualifications solely because of their race generates a feeling of inferiority as to their status in the community that may affect their hearts and minds in a way unlikely ever to be undone. We conclude that in the field of public education the doctrine of Separate but equal has no place. Separate educational facilities are inherently unequal. Therefore, we hold that the plaintiffs and others similarly situated for whom the actions have been brought are, by reason of the segregation complained of, deprived of the equal protection of the laws guaranteed by the Fourteenth Amendment.[138]

Arguably, this ruling played a greater role in shaping the plights of African Americans for the duration of the twentieth century than anything else that followed it. The United States Supreme Court 1954 decision in the *Brown v. Board of Education* case mandated that African Americans could not be discriminated against because of their racial group. They were entitled to the same rights, protection, justice, and opportunities as other American citizens. The Court's 1954 decision mandated racial desegregation of all public and quasi-public institutions. *Desegregation* refers to the process of eliminating racial discrimination in the operation of these institutions. In view of the large disparities between institutions that provided services for black Americans and white Americans, it is not surprising that black Americans yearned for access to the better facilities and opportunities afforded at white institutions.

While racial segregation could have psychologically damaged many black children, it would be erroneous to assume that racial segregation necessarily caused psychological damage to black children in general. As previously noted, E. Franklin Frazier and Charles Johnson found that most black youth who expressed wishes to be white were not consumed with self-hatred or feelings of racial inferiority but instead envy. They imagined themselves as white in terms of having greater access to wealth, material possessions, and opportunities for personal growth. Moreover, the social environment and socialization practices in black American families varied in different geographical locations and along social class lines. If racial segregation caused self-hatred in black children, family, social class, or geographical factors could have counteracted the psychologically damaging effects of racial segregation. The use of the argument in the late 1940s and early 1950s by social scientists that racial segregation psychologically damaged blacks was an effective strategy to reverse the United States Supreme Court's 1896 ruling in the *Plessy v. Ferguson* case.

Immediately following the Court's 1954 ruling and with persistence, leaders and members of the NAACP, Southern Leadership Conference, Congress of Racial Equality, and National Urban League, as well as many influential white Americans, worked tirelessly for racial integration of public institutions and facilities. *Racial integration* involved increasing the association between members of different racial groups. Supporters of racial integration urged Americans from different racial and ethnic groups to live in the same neighborhoods, attend the same schools, universities, churches, and social gatherings. They urged black and white Americans to put aside long-standing differences and embrace the things they shared together for the common good of the larger society. Equal opportunities and equal rights were among the centerpieces in the racial integration movement.

Many white opponents of racial integration feared that it would lead to racial assimilation and amalgamation. Racial *assimilation* refers here to a process characterized by the fusion of cultures among people of African descents and Caucasians. In this process, distinctive cultural behavior and traditions practiced among African Americans as well as distinctive cultural behavior and traditions practiced among white Americans are merged into a homogeneous unit. *Amalgamation* refers to the fusion of races by interbreeding and intermarriage. In his book *Assimilation in American Life*, Milton M. Gordon provides a thoughtful presentation of the relationship between the two processes. According to Gordon:

> Entrance of the minority group into the social cliques, clubs, and institutions of the core society at the primary group level inevitably will lead to a substantial amount of intermarriage. If children of different ethnic backgrounds belong to the same play-group, later the same adolescent cliques, and at college the same fraternities and sororities; if the parents belong to the same country club and invite each other to their homes for dinner; it is completely unrealistic not to expect these children, now grown, to love and to marry each other.[139]

The idea of amalgamation was a concern shared by many white Americans. Although amalgamation had the potential of eliminating America's race problem because the bloodlines of white Americans and African Americans would be mixed, only a very small minority of white Americans found this choice acceptable. In fact, many white Americans were terrified by the idea of amalgamation.

Black leaders, including Martin Luther King Jr., Adam Clayton Powell Jr., Roy Wilkins, Whitney Young, Bayard Rustin, and A. Philip Randolph, clearly were not championing racial assimilation and amalgamation. They strongly supported the maintenance of African American institutions, traditions, loyalties, and heritage. For them, racial integration did not require African Americans to give up their cultural identity and adopt European American cultural practices. Racial integration allowed for cultural differentiation within a framework of social unity. It recognized the right of groups and individuals to be different so long as the difference did not lead to domination or disunity.[140]

Guided by the leadership of Malcolm X, a minister in the Nation of Islam, many African Americans and self-acclaimed black nationalists supported desegregation but opposed racial integration. Some of them believed that white people were inherently evil and distrustful. Many African Americans also feared that racial integration would endanger the existence of black institutions and cultural heritages. Given the skin color and other physical differences that already existed among African Americans, amalgamation was not a major concern among them.

During the twentieth century, there were no prominent leaders among African Americans speaking out in favor of amalgamation.

Many white people opposed racial integration not only because it was in conflict with their deeply rooted beliefs in the doctrine of biological determinism and white supremacy but also because many white people opposed integration and equal opportunity and equal rights for African Americans as a potential threat to their psychological wage and more privileged positions, especially in educational institutions and the workforce.[141] As institutions moved to comply with the Supreme Court's 1954 ruling, many white people were concerned about being displaced by African Americans in educational institutions and the workforce.

The United States Supreme Court's 1954 decision in the *Brown v. Board of Education* case had a profound impact on all Americans. With the exception of families, it mandated institutions, which represented the principle socialization agents in the United States, to open their doors with equal opportunities and rights for American citizens regardless of their racial origin. The Court's 1954 decision required members of both black and white racial groups to rethink their beliefs, attitudes, thoughts, actions, and feelings about race.

Having been conditioned to keep race in the forefront of their minds throughout their daily lives because of racist practices for several centuries by white Americans, African Americans were confronted with an extraordinary challenge. On the one hand, they desired racial equality, but on the other, they had to work aggressively toward minimizing the significance of race in their daily lives. They had to begin thinking about and taking action to move toward living in an integrated society in which race does not matter. Since race had played a fundamental role in shaping their thoughts, behaviors, and emotions, would it be possible for them to make this psychological transition? For blacks who have lived in a racially oppressive, divided, and polarized society, what effects, if any, would adapting to an integrated and desegregated society have on their self-construction? Would they lose their psychological and cultural distinctiveness? If race became less significant in their psychological makeup, how would it affect their relationships with other people of African descents? Black leaders and scholars expressed concerns about these issues.

After the United States Supreme Court 1954 ruling on desegregation, W. E. B. Du Bois issued a strong warning to African Americans. In 1958, Du Bois published an essay titled "Whither Now and Why," saying that before the year 2000, African Americans must ask themselves: "What will be our aims and ideals?"[142] He believed that an affirmative answer to this question required African Americans to be knowledgeable about who they were as a people and what historical, cultural, and psychological factors serve to distinguish them from other groups, including other people of African descents. Du Bois indicated that if African Americans did not learn about their history and embrace their distinctive cultural characteristics, their future looked bleak. He puts it this way:

> Negroes will simply adopt the ideals of Americans and become what they are or want to be and we will have in this process no ideals of our own. We will take on the culture of white Americans—doing as they do and thinking as they think. Our history and culture will be lost and Negroes will exist only in color.[143]

Have significant changes in the psychological makeup of African Americans occurred since the United States Supreme Court 1954 decision on desegregation? If yes, what changes occurred in the psychological makeup of African Americans? Is race significant in the psychological makeup of African Americans today? These are some of the issues that will be examined in the next chapter.

6

RETHINKING AFRICAN AMERICANS' IDENTITY FROM MID-1900s TO 2010

We are definitely approaching now a time when the American Ne-gro will become in law equal in citizenship to other Americans. . . . When we become equal American citizens, what will be our aims and ideals. Are we to assume that we will simply adopt the ideals of Americans and become what they are or want to be and that we will have in the process no ideals of our own? That would mean that we would cease to be Negroes as such and become white in action if not completely in color.

—W. E. B. Du Bois, 1960, "Wither Now and Why"

FROM NONCITIZEN TO CITIZEN

From 1619 through 1954, black folks in America were compelled to ac-knowledge holidays as well as social traditions and customs established by white European Americans. For example, the national Thanksgiving holiday can be viewed as a celebration of cooperation between early English settlers and Native Americans. Pictures of English settlers shar-ing a bountiful harvest with Native American friends are used to sym-bolize this event. Many African Americans perceive parallels between the experiences of their African ancestors and the plights of Native Americans. They viewed the arrival of English settlers in mainland North America as the beginning of the removal of Native Americans from their ancestral lands as well as criminal behavior and violence directed against them by English settlers. However, African Americans were not permitted to share most social and cultural amenities afforded white people. The United States Supreme Court's 1896 ruling in the *Plessy v. Ferguson* case merely affirmed racist practices that were commonplace and always had existed within the larger American society. The racist policies and practices, in America, caused two separate and unequal but interdependent racial worlds to evolve within the country long before the Court's 1896 ruling. However, given the similarities in the economic interests and religious belief systems of black and white Americans, the well-being of both racial groups was deeply intertwined. Their racial worlds were then and now interdependent.

The racist policies and practices in the United States contributed to the evolving of distinct cultural practices and ways of thinking among black folks, with race serving as the primary force in shaping the distinctiveness. African Americans erected religious and social institutions that accommodated their unique ways of life. They organized fraternal organizations, sororities, and social action groups to bring together men and women of like qualities for concerted efforts on behalf of the larger black community. The body language, speech styles, word usage, music, and various art forms expressed by many African Americans reflected a unique interplay between soul, spirituality, oppressed communalism, and European mores, which served to set most of them apart from other ethnic and racial groups.

Although the media, government, military, contact in the workforce as well as curriculums in education contributed to a great deal of similarities between the social structure, interests, and cultural practices characteristic of both black and white people in America, differences in these areas along racial lines often were apparent between them. Racial oppression compelled black folks in America to develop their own world outside of the mainstream of American life and simultaneously partake of limited participation in the affairs of the larger community. Therefore, in their daily lives, African Americans constantly had to operate psychologically and physically in their own world as well as the world of the larger American community. Reconciling the discrepancies between and accommodating to the two worlds posed a difficult challenge for African Americans, but the vast majority of them learned to master it.

CHANGE AND RESISTANCE

It is widely presumed that the United States Supreme Court's 1954 decision in the *Brown v. Board of Education* case triggered the movement for social justice, racial equality, and the empowerment of minority ethnic groups that extended through more than two decades. But the movement actually began years before. As Michael J. Klarman suggests in a 1994 publication on the *Brown v. Board of Education* decision, the democratic ideology and social movement of World War II and the expansion of economic and political opportunities created by the war heightened a civil rights consciousness in most black Americans.[1] During the war, blacks in Norfolk, Virginia, protested segregation in busing and streetcars, served on war-related boards and councils, joined voter leagues, and successfully lobbied to bring about the appointment of two blacks on the police force. In the North, during the late 1940s and early 1950s, a great deal of antidiscrimination legislation that promoted fair employment practices and open public accommodation was enacted by state and local governments. Klarman argues that since successful civil rights protests occurred during and after World War II, the United States Supreme Court's 1954 ruling in the *Brown v. Board of Education* case was not necessarily the impetus to challenge the racial status quo. He conceded that the 1954 ruling might have helped the civil rights movement indirectly by forcing the civil rights issue onto the national agenda.[2]

The movement can be divided into two phases: a civil rights phase, which spans from the late 1940s through about 1968, and a Black Power phase, which lasted from the mid- to late 1960s through the mid-1970s. Although historians, social scientists, educators, and others continue to debate the social and political impact of the Court's 1954 ruling on the civil rights movement, the ruling contributed to an era characterized by the most significant transformation in the psychological makeup of African Americans since the Civil War.[3] Since 1954, African Americans have been struggling with resolving questions about group identity. The meaning and significance of race in-group identity for African Americans has been in transition since the Court's 1954 decision. Given the centrality of race in the psychological makeup of African Americans, significant changes in the way it is viewed or treated in the larger society are likely to cause some African Americans to experience identity confusion and raise questions about their identities. A logical conclusion that follows from the Supreme Court's 1954 ruling is that, for all Americans, an American nationality must become more important than race or ethnicity in group identification. After more than a half-century since the Court's 1954 ruling, findings reported from several studies conducted in recent years indicate most African Americans still perceive the concept of race to be the most significant defining characteristic for both self and group identification.[4]

Even though affirmative-action policies that began emerging in the 1960s sanctioned preferential treatment for the protected classes, including African Americans, it was intended to provide them with equal opportunities to participate in and partake of the benefits of being an American. It has been almost six decades since this landmark Supreme Court decision, and racial desegregation has occurred in most aspects of American life. However, racial integration has proceeded at a slow pace. With the exception of professional sports and select areas of entertainment, African Americans are either underrepresented in or absent from many aspects of American life. That is to say, they appear to be tokens in many private and public institutions. In what ways have African Americans attitudes about race changed? Is race still the most significant factor in self-identification and group identification for African Americans?

The United States Supreme Court made two separate decisions in the *Brown v. Board of Education* case, one in 1954 and the second in 1955. Ruling that segregated schools were a denial of equal protection of the laws guaranteed by the Fourteenth Amendment, the Court's 1954 decision raised hopes to attain equality and participate as equal partners in the American mainstream for many African Americans. It soon became apparent to both black and white Americans that putting this law into practice would be more difficult than the process of changing the Court's 1896 decision in the *Plessy v. Ferguson* case. Perceiving a need to study alternatives and the effect of its 1954 decision, members of the

United States Supreme Court unanimously agreed to move forward: "with all deliberate speed."[5] In its 1955 decision, the Court outlined general steps for the transition to integrated education. In a book titled *Critical Race Theory* published in 2001, Richard Delgado, professor of law at the University of Colorado, and Jean Stefancic, research associate in law at the University of Colorado, argue that, on several fronts, the implementation of the United States Supreme Court's 1954 decision was slowed down by narrow lower-court interpretations, administrative foot dragging, and delay. In response to slow and often ineffective efforts to remedy racism in American society and led by Derrick Bell, professor of law at New York University, the critical race theory movement was started in the mid-1970s. Consisting of activists and scholars in American law and politics as well as other disciplines, critical race theorists have challenged some basic premises that underlie the process of implementing the Court's 1954 decision. They also have called into question racially motivated practices that serve to maintain and reinforce racial hierarchies that determine who gets privileged opportunities and positions.

The social changes spearheaded by the Court's 1954 racial integration mandate compelled most black Americans to rethink their identity. Cross provides a summary of empirical research from 1939 through the 1980s that shows changes in perceptions of group identity among African Americans.[6] *Group identity* refers to an individual's attitudes about being identified with a particular group—that is, for example, a person's attitude about being an African American. The results from these studies conducted between 1939 and 1960 suggest that most African Americans had negative perceptions about their group identity. That is, most African Americans had negative racial attitudes about their group identity. They showed a preference for European American standards of beauty, social behavior, and cultural practices. Examining 163 studies on black identity conducted between 1968 and 1980, Cross reports that an overwhelming majority of these studies showed a movement toward more positive group identity among African Americans. It cannot be discerned from the results of these studies whether or not the participants had really internalized positive group-identity elements.

The process of identification with a group involves a change in the focus of the sense of self from the individual referent to the group as a whole referent.[7] Identification with a group may lead individuals to behave in ways that are contrary to personal self-interest, even at the cost of personal survival. In 1978, for example, more than 900 members of the Jim Jones People's Temple committed suicide at Jonestown in Guyana. Although individuals' dying on behalf of group goals and group identification rarely occurs in our society, the catastrophe at Jonestown shows that group membership can profoundly influence a person's motives, intentions, judgment, and behavior.

Group membership often influences a person's judgment and behavior when confronted with resolving social dilemmas. Social dilemmas are choice situations in which persons are faced with a conflict between their own individual self-interest and collective interest of the group in which they belong.[8] Summarizing results derived from research on resolving social dilemmas, Brewer and Miller report that when individuals act in their own self-interest, it might lead to collective disaster for members of the group to which they belong. Therefore, when the collective interest of the group is perceived to be in jeopardy, fellow in-group members are under a great deal of pressure to conform their attitudes and behavior in accordance to the interest of the group as a whole.

The positive attitudes about group identity expressed by African American respondents may have been influenced, in part, by the need for group solidarity in response to racism. Black leadership was expounding group solidarity during the civil rights era. When a group perceives a threat to their collective welfare, such as has been the situation often among African Americans, individuals are prone to adopt a cooperative orientation toward fellow in-group members and behave in ways that promote the group's interest rather than self-interest.[9] Thus, when black leadership called for group solidarity and "black pride" among African Americans in response to racially motivated injustice and discrimination perpetrated by white Americans against them, they probably experienced a great deal of inner pressure to conform. Results derived from experimental studies in psychology indicate that shared concerns about the collective welfare of a group may profoundly influence the judgment and behavior of its members.[10] Participants' responses also may have been influenced by "the spirit of the time." During the Black Power phase of the movement, black pride was a popular theme in the larger African American community. Therefore, the measured change from negative to positive attitudes about black group identity among African Americans between 1939 and 1980 probably had more to do with the social climate rather than enhanced knowledge about the distinctiveness of being African American. There is a lack of empirical evidence to support the hypothesis that African Americans' positive attitudes about their group identity was due primarily to a better understanding of their historical and cultural distinctiveness. Very few organizations or institutions, either then or now, provide programs of study for African American youth to learn about the distinctiveness of the African American experience in the United States. More stability in African Americans' group-identity orientation is likely to occur when African Americans gain more knowledge about and understanding of the historical and cultural practices that distinguish them from other ethnic groups.

In the South, there was massive resistance by whites against granting the same citizenship rights afforded them to African Americans. During an official protest against the United States Supreme Court decision in the school desegregation cases, Tom P. Brady, a Mississippi circuit court judge, argued that black people were not capable of becoming equal citizens. Violence was used frequently by Southern whites to deny the rights guaranteed by the United States Constitution to African Americans. During efforts to desegregate public schools in the South, African American children were intimidated and harassed by white students and their parents. As white Americans' resistance to the extension of equal rights to African Americans intensified, African Americans became more determined than ever before to desegregate the society and obtain the citizenship rights guaranteed by the United States Constitution. Chanting and embodying the hymn "We Shall Overcome," African Americans, with support from concerned white Americans, relentlessly pressed for their civil rights. It was a daring challenge that fundamentally changed the psychology of black and white interactions in the United States.

From the mid-1950s through the 1960s, guided by the vision and leadership of Dr. Martin Luther King Jr., the civil rights movement did more to reshape the educational, social, political, employment, and economic opportunities in the United States for African Americans, other nonwhite ethnic groups, and women than anything else during the twentieth century. The collective efforts of the NAACP, Southern Conference Leadership Council (SCLC), National Urban League, Congress of Racial Equality (CORE), and the Student Nonviolent Coordinating Committee (SNCC) galvanized unprecedented political action among African Americans.

In response to civil rights protests, demonstration, agitation, boycotts, and political pressure, civil rights bills were enacted in 1957 and 1960. These bills protected the voting rights of African Americans. Spurred by the March on Washington, the turning point in civil rights legislation occurred in 1964, when Congress enacted a civil rights bill that ensured access to public facilities and denied federal funds to communities that discriminated in federally assisted programs. Nonwhite immigrant groups derived the same benefits as African Americans from the Civil Rights Act of 1964.

The Civil Rights Act of 1968 enabled African Americans to rent or purchase property in all-white communities. The passage of the Civil Rights Act of 1968 capped the twenty-year effort of the civil rights movement to remove the legal barriers that precluded African Americans from the same rights and entitlements afforded white Americans. Summaries of civil rights legislation passed between 1957 and 1968 are highlighted below:

1957—The Civil Rights Act of 1957 (HR 6157-PL 85-315) was the first civil rights legislation passed by Congress since the post–Civil War Reconstruction period. The act prohibited action to prevent persons from voting in federal elections and authorized the attorney general to bring suit when a person was deprived of his voting rights. It also created the Civil Rights Commission and set up the Civil Rights Division in the Department of Justice.

1960—The Civil Rights Act of 1960 (HR 8601-PL 86-449) strengthened provisions of the 1957 act for court enforcement of voting rights and required preservation of voting records. It also contained limited criminal penalty provisions relating to bombing and to obstruction of federal court orders (aimed primarily at school desegregation orders).

1964—The Civil Rights Act of 1964 (HR 7152-PL 88-352) prohibited discrimination in public accommodations and in programs receiving federal assistance. It also prohibited discrimination by employers and unions and set up the Equal Employment Opportunity Commission. Enforcement of voting laws and school and public facilities desegregation was strengthened.

1965—The Voting Rights Act of 1965 (S 1564-PL 89-110) authorized the attorney general to appoint federal examiners to register voters in areas of marked discrimination and strengthened penalties for interference with voter rights.

1968—The Civil Rights Bill (HR 2516-PL 90-284) prohibited discrimination in the sale or rental of about 80 percent of all housing. It also protected persons exercising specified rights such as attending school or working and civil rights workers urging others to exercise their rights. Antiriot provisions also were included.[11]

The civil rights legislation passed by Congress between 1957 and 1968 provides a framework for fundamentally changing, over time, the meaning and significance of race in the psychological functioning of African Americans. In 1960, W. E. B. Du Bois pointed out that African Americans would be forced to reexamine identity issues in response to having the same rights as white American citizens. Thus, it is not surprising that identity development in African Americans has been a topic of keen interest for the Association of Black Psychologists since its inception.[12] In their book, *The Psychology of Blacks: An African-American Perspective*, Joseph L. White, Thomas A. Parham, and Adisa Ajamu discuss contemporary theories about the identity development of African Americans. These theories fail to consider race as a psychological construct that most likely plays a central role in identity development of African Americans. While these identity theories may have heuristic value, there is a paucity of historical information and empirical tests to support them. In the absence of education programs about African American history and cultural practices, changes in the meaning and significance of race for African Americans are likely, over time, to augment debates among African Americans in response to the question: who are African Americans?

Although all nonwhite immigrant groups derived expanded social, education, political, employment, and economic opportunities from civil rights legislation passed in response to the civil rights movement in the 1950s and 1960s, they did not play significant roles in fighting to achieve it.[13] Very few nonwhites joined African Americans in civil rights protest marches and demonstrations against racial inequalities and oppression.

An overwhelming majority of those persons who were arrested, injured, or killed while participating in the civil rights movement were African Americans and concerned white Americans.

THE RELATIONSHIP BETWEEN RACIAL ATTITUDES, RACIAL POLICIES, AND RACIAL INTEGRATION

The implementation of the Court's 1954 decision was the biggest challenge that faced Americans in the twentieth century. Racially motivated violence by white Americans was widespread for many years following the Supreme Court's 1954 decision. When African Americans exercised their constitutional rights granted by the Court's 1954 decision, it was met with stern resistance, and often violence, by Southern whites. Five years following the Court's 1954 decision, white Americans committed 210 acts of racially motivated violence against African Americans. These acts included six murders, twenty-nine assaults with firearms, forty-four beatings, and sixty bombings.[14] Civil rights activists met violent resistance from white Americans, including public safety officers, when they worked to integrate public institutions and facilities. While canvassing and encouraging African Americans to vote, several African American civil rights activists were murdered in Mississippi during the summer of 1955. In spite of these numerous accounts of racially motivated criminal acts, no white American was ever convicted. It was commonplace for white Southerners to impose economic sanctions on black civil rights activists, such as dismissals from jobs, denial of loans, and foreclosures of mortgages.

A vast majority of white Southerners strongly opposed the Supreme Court's 1954 decision and fought, with some success, for several years to forestall its implementation in many aspects of living in the United States. Although results derived from the Gallup polls conducted in December 1955 show that 80 percent of Southern white Americans disapproved of the Court's 1954 decision, it also showed that 55 percent of Southern white Americans believed that the day would come in the South when white Americans and African Americans would be going to the same schools, eating in the same restaurants, and generally sharing the same public accommodations.

Before the 1960s, the implementation of the Court's 1954 ruling was almost in a state of inertia. Only a few black students were enrolled in previously segregated schools in the South, and because of segregated housing patterns, de facto segregation of schools was widespread in the North. In search of employment and a better quality of life with less racism, many African Americans from the South migrated to major cities in the North. As they moved to the major cities, whites moved out of the cities to the suburbs and took with them most of the employment opportunities that the newly arrived African Americans had hoped for. Manufacturing plants were moved to industrial parks in the suburbs to locations that were inaccessible by public transportation. Racial discrimination practices in housing and employment during the 1950s and 1960s precluded African Americans from relocating in suburban communities. Although corporate headquarters usually remained behind in these cities, they offered very limited job opportunities for the unskilled. Corporate centers served primarily as centers for administration and information dissemination.[15] Between 1954 and 1964, the unemployment rates of African Americans was at least double that of white Americans. Underemployment and low salaries were common occurrences among skilled and unskilled black workers. College-trained African Americans had limited professional opportunities in the workforce. More than 80 percent of African Americans who were employed worked at the bottom of the economic ladder. Racial discrimination practices in labor unions reduced opportunities for apprenticeship training and employment for black workers.[16]

Faced with shattered dreams of a better life, African Americans in central cities endured the hardships of living in poverty. Many whites moved to the suburbs but continued to operate small shops and businesses in the cities. These white-owned businesses offered only very limited job opportunities for African Americans. Many whites employed by municipal governments, including policemen, public school teachers, public school administrators, and human service employees, fled to the suburbs to live but continued to maintain their jobs in the cities. Paradoxically, these employees attempted to solve and manage problems in the central cities that they often contributed to by fleeing to the suburbs. Rather than acknowledge the contradictions in their feelings, attitudes, and actions, many of them shifted the blame for the problems in the central cities from themselves to the victims—namely, the newly arrived African Americans. Moreover, many of the whites who worked in the cities but lived in the suburbs did their shopping and spending outside of the cities. While these whites utilized public services provided by municipal governments, they often contributed very little to cover the cost for these services. Bearing this in mind, and at the same time recognizing that the costs for public education and other public services required more and better resources than were available to meet the needs of the newly arrived African Americans, the cities' economic support systems steadily weakened.

The volume and frequency of changes in central cities posed a myriad of unique social, economic, and education problems for both city and public-school officials. With insufficient resources and very little or no experience in remedying the problems they faced, many public servants, school administrators, and teachers were overwhelmed. Increasingly, these problems became more complex and less manageable, and unfortunately, they continue to plague central cities in the United States. After many years of neglect and ineffective management of poverty in the cities, it is very difficult, if not impossible, to distinguish the causes from the effects of poverty.

The depreciation in values of land, houses, and other buildings, combined with the steady growth of unemployment and poverty, accelerated the deterioration of economies in central cities. Hopelessness and despair stemming from poverty and racism in cities predisposed some African American residents to adopt defeatist attitudes. A lowering of self-worth and, sometimes, a lowering of inhibitions to exploit and hurt others characterized their defeatist attitudes. Some of these individuals manifested defeatist attitudes through self-destructive, pleasure-seeking behaviors, including the abuse of alcohol and addictive drugs. They also were prone to use force to both vent their frustrations and achieve their goals against individuals who they perceived to be powerless. Consequently, they often exploited and hurt other African Americans in their immediate surroundings. Their violence-prone behavior may have, in part, stemmed from a need to enhance feelings of self-worth. It follows, then, that the need for police protection against violence-prone aggression and crime for African Americans who resided in poverty-stricken neighborhoods in cities increased steadily as conditions worsened.

The demographics in many central cities changed dramatically between 1954 and 1964, reflecting substantial decreases in white populations and substantial increases in black populations. But an overwhelming majority of the law enforcement officers in central cities were white men. They still constitute an overwhelming majority of law enforcement officers in Northern urban communities. In view of a history of law enforcement authorities' timid protection of blacks from violence and criminality perpetrated by other blacks, very few blacks believed that white law-enforcement officers would provide adequate police protection in predominantly black neighborhoods. Many black residents in central cities did not believe that law enforcement authorities valued their safety and well-being.[17] On the other hand, some blacks denounced police officers for taking forceful action against blacks who engaged in acts of violence against other blacks. They charged the police with being racist and occupiers of their community. To avoid being characterized as racists, some police officers might have viewed it safer to look the other way. Consequently, some of them might have been reluctant to act forcefully against black criminals for fear of being charged with police brutality. Many blacks did not believe that white police officers would put their lives on the line to protect them against violence and criminality perpetrated by other blacks. Therefore, moving from the cities to nearby suburban communities became a dream and goal for many black urban residents.

Recognizing the political, economic, and cultural potential for blacks in central cities of the largest metropolitan areas, a vast majority of the newly arrived African Americans from the South chose to remain in the cities. In concert with African Americans who already had been living there, they enriched the social and cultural life in these cities. They created a climate that enabled a relatively small, but significant, number of black entrepreneurs to prosper. Many of them became "movers and shakers" in central cities and tremendous sources of hope and inspiration for the larger African American community. Through black churches, social organizations, entertainment clubs, fraternities, and sororities, they played central roles in nurturing and preserving the cultural as well as ethnic distinctiveness of African American life. The political activities, especially at the grassroots level, of the newly arrived African Americans helped to increase the representation of African Americans in government at all levels and stimulate national interest in the plight of African Americans. For example, in 1960, the platforms of both the Republican and Democratic parties included support for racial equality and justice. During the 1960 presidential campaign, John F. Kennedy, the Democratic Party nominee, vowed to use the authority vested in the executive office to end discrimination in federally supported housing if elected. President Dwight Eisenhower's administration had been reluctant to use the power vested in the executive branch of the federal government to end racial discrimination and segregation.[18]

African Americans who migrated from the South to central cities in metropolitan areas did not all respond in the same manner to the racism and restricted opportunities they encountered after their arrival. Their reactions to racism reflected a great deal of diversity in this population. Some of them lost hope and the motivation to improve their fates; some of them became self-destructive and addicted to drugs and alcohol; others among them became violence-prone and preyed upon other poor people in their communities. On the other hand, many of the newly arrived African Americans worked hard and saved their funds to seize upon opportunities to move to nearby suburbs. However, the majority of them made a commitment to stay in these cities and develop the political, social, and economic potential in the cities for themselves and other African Americans.

The flight of northern white Americans to the suburbs was accompanied by racial discrimination in housing in these communities. All-white suburban communities were commonplace for many years following the Supreme Court's 1954 ruling in the *Brown v. Board of Education* case. Before the Court's 1954 ruling, discrimination in housing was supported by the federal government. When federal assistance was provided for the construction of new houses, the racial policy adopted by the Federal Housing Administration stated that: "If a neighborhood is to retain stability it is necessary that properties shall be continued to be occupied by the same social and racial classes."[19] In many suburban communities, white homeowners refused to sell their houses to prospective black buyers. With backing from the National Association of Real Estate Boards, many white Americans contended that a property owner had the right to sell her or his property to the person(s) of choice. Therefore, by refusing to sell their properties to nonwhites, they were able to maintain all-white neighborhoods and public schools. According to George Lipsitz, this movement of whites from cities was indicative of what he calls "a possessive investment in whiteness," or a desire to invest and maintain the advantages that come along with the possession of white skin.[20] During the decade following the United States Supreme Court's 1954 desegregation ruling, the unwillingness of many white Americans, including public servants, to comply with the law and end racist practices—especially in housing, education, employment, and public safety—sharply deepened the racial divide, increased racial hostility and tension, as well as crushed hopes of a better life for many African Americans.

In view of the large proportion of white Americans who objected to living in racially integrated communities, it was impossible for African Americans to escape the social and psychological significance of the concept of race even if they strongly desired to do so. As previously noted, the psychological significance attributed to the concept of race by African Americans resulted from the attitudes and behaviors displayed by white Americans toward them and their ancestors over many years. Therefore, when white Americans behaved in a racist manner toward African Americans, it reinforced the significance of race in the psychological functioning of African Americans because the psychological fate of black and white people is tied together in a dialectical relationship. If white folks are actively pursuing a psychological wage that exists relative to the psychological lives of black people, black folks are left with the converse of white advantages to cope with.

The practice of racial discrimination in housing was so deeply entrenched in the suburbs that it persisted in many communities for several decades after it had been declared unconstitutional. The rapid expansion of all-white communities reduced the physical and psychological contact between white Americans and black Americans. Increasingly, the communication gaps and racial tension between members of these racial groups worsened. Consequently, it became easier for members of both racial groups to focus on their differences and assign psychological significance to these differences rather than focus on their human as well as social and cultural commonalities. According to many advocates of critical race theory, these conditions along with long-standing racist practices have served to desensitize many white Americans to racism.

Consequently, racism is so deeply entrenched in their thinking as well as actions that it often is a non-contemplative and ordinary way of being.[21]

THE ROLE OF PSYCHOLOGY IN PERPETUATING RACISM

Since the 1950s, a great deal of empirical research in the field of psychology has been conducted on race differences in cognition, learning, behavior, personality, emotions, and so on. In view of the fact that the leading journals in psychology only publish studies that report statistically significant differences, readers are programmed to focus on racial differences in the psychological profiles of African Americans and white Americans. In interpreting the results from these studies, most white psychologists assumed that African Americans were inferior to whites. Similar to psychologists during the first quarter of the twentieth century, they usually attributed these measured racial differences to innate deficiencies in blacks' cognitive capacities or to cognitive deficiencies caused by environmental deficiencies in the home settings of low-income black children. In writings on the misinterpretation of intelligence tests' results, Silverstein and Krate, as well as Tucker and Richards, summarize and refute these arguments.[22] Silverstein and Krate note that psychologists arguing African American intellectual inferiority rarely attributed results derived from studies of race differences to institutional racism in the larger society. Some psychologists still argued that blacks' low IQ scores relative to their white counterparts were due to hereditary deficiencies.[23]

While noting that low-income black children were handicapped with cognitive deficits, a group of psychologists suggested that these children were victims of cultural deprivation in their home settings. Although the observations of these psychologists helped to spur federally funded early intervention programs, which were needed in low-income, predominantly black communities, they largely ignored the role that institutional racism had played in creating and maintaining the alleged cognitive deficits. Even though questions already had been raised regarding the validity of IQ tests as measures of cognitive abilities, these psychologists never called into question their untested beliefs that low-income black children were riddled with cognitive deficits caused by cultural deprivation. For example, in *An American Dilemma*, Gunnar Myrdal suggested that many of the aspects of black Americans' perceived psychological handicaps were caused by cultural deprivation.[24] Conversely, not only did most white psychologists tend to characterize African Americans as hopeless victims of nature or nurture, they also frequently ignored or distorted the well-documented history of racial oppression and inequities. There were many compelling reasons to assume that these conditions depressed the performance of African American children on IQ and other standardized tests.

Similar to earlier studies on racial differences in intelligence published by white psychologists, there was a proliferation of studies and books in the 1960s and 1970s by behavioral scientists that focused on presumed social and psychological pathologies among African Americans. The development of psychological tests in the United States has been based, largely, on the assumption that there is an ideal or fully developed state. In general, the behavior of middle-class whites has been the standard used for approximating this ideal. Since the founding of psychology, white middle-class behavior has served as the standard against which that of all other groups, especially blacks, has been measured and ranked. When blacks performed below white middle-class norms on so-called intelligence tests, the results were used as scientific proof that they were inherently inferior to whites. In writing about black children's performance on mental tests, Silverstein and Krate make the following observation:

> We now know that the content of such tests largely mirrored white middle-class life experiences. But beyond this cultural bias in test content, a deeper vicious cycle tended to operate: As members of the white middle class, most psychologists regarded white middle-class behavior as normative and desirable; competence in those tasks in which middle-class whites excelled was labeled intelligence; tasks in which other groups excelled were considered of little importance. Intelligence was what middle-class whites said it was and what tests constructed by middle-class white psychologists measured. Once intelligence had been defined in this highly limited fashion, the scores of the tests devised to measure it were used to bolster the argument that the low economic and political status of blacks in America was a result of their genetically determined inability to compete successfully with whites and to adapt to the complexities of the white man's civilization.[25]

As indicated here, the definition used for distinguishing more intelligent from less intelligent people is of central importance in making judgments about the alleged role genetics plays in intelligent behavior. How do psychologists and laypersons conceptualize and define intelligence? There is no consensus about what is meant by *intelligence*. For people living in a drug-ridden, low-income neighborhood, in which people are consumed daily with survival, the way you differentiate between more intelligent and less intelligent people might be very different from the way people living in a wealthy suburban neighborhood would distinguish between more intelligent and less intelligent people. Intelligence can take on different meanings.[26] People's definition of intelligent behavior is influenced by how well people adapt their behavior to the environment in which they live.

Psychologists define *intelligence* as the capacity to learn and profit from one's knowledge of the world, think rationally, and use resources effectively when faced with challenges.[27] Using this definition, it is very difficult to distinguish, with any precision, between more intelligent and less intelligent people. Psychologists purportedly use intelligence tests to remedy this problem. While Alfred Binet devised the intelligence test to identify special needs students in the Paris school system in order to provide them with remedial education, American psychologists used these tests to identify a person's level of intelligence. As previously observed, these tests have been effective in identifying students in need of special education in school settings, in diagnosing cognitive difficulties, and in helping people make optimal education and vocational choices.[28] On the other hand, psychologists strongly disagree about the usefulness of these tests as measures of innate cognitive capacities, especially when used to make comparisons between groups with different cultural and social backgrounds. In search of scientific evidence to support the belief that certain groups or races are inherently superior to others, white psychologists exploited opportunities to use these tests to measure levels of intelligence in African Americans.

The procedure for measuring intelligence employed by modern intelligence tests, including the Stanford-Binet intelligence test and Wechsler Adult Intelligence Scales, have come under scrutiny in recent years. Some psychologists contend that the procedure lacks an underlying conception of what intelligence is. They also have suggested that these tests erroneously conceptualize intelligence as a single unitary general factor.[29] This general factor was thought to underlie performance on every aspect of intelligence, and it was the general factor that was presumably being measured on tests of intelligence. Over the years, the members of the lay community mistakenly have come to believe that IQ tests measure mental ability in a truly general sense. At best, IQ tests measure academic/verbal intelligence. Since the 1980s, the idea that humans have multiple intelligences has received widespread support among psychologists. Some psychologists have suggested that we have *fluid intelligence* and *crystallized intelligence*.[30] Fluid intelligence reflects reasoning, memory, and information-processing capabilities. The information, skills, and strategies that people have learned through experience and that they can apply in problem-solving situations reflect crystallized intelligence. If a person were asked to participate in a discussion that draws largely upon one's own past experience, that person would be likely to rely on crystallized intelligence.

After a study of the talents of well-known people who display unusual ability in certain areas, Howard Gardner, professor of psychology at Harvard University, concluded that humans possess multiple intelligences, with each relatively independent of the others.[31] Gardner suggests that these separate intelligences work together in organizing and guiding our thoughts, feelings, and behavior. Gardner's model of intelligence raises the possibility for test items in which more than one answer can be correct because different kinds of intelligence may produce different—but equally valid—answers to the same question.[32] New approaches in the way intelligence is being conceptualized suggest that using IQ tests to make comparisons between groups of African Americans and whites is an imprecise, potentially misleading, and counterproductive venture.

Although psychologists conducted research on African Americans in a variety of areas from the 1960s through the 1970s, studies of race differences in performance on standardized tests, coined as "measures of intellectual competence," stimulated more interest in the larger public. The results of these studies showed, repeatedly, as mutually exclusive groups, whites performed better than blacks. Recognizing that many white Americans believed IQ scores were valid measures of basic intellectual competence, they displayed high interest in explanations about differences between the scores of African Americans and other racial/

ethnic groups offered by psychologists and other academicians. In the late 1960s, a group of psychologists, led by Arthur Jensen and determined to prove that blacks were inherently inferior to whites, reasserted the notion that the primary cause of racial differences in performance on IQ tests was genetic differences. In his widely read essay "How Much Can We Boost I.Q. and Scholastic Achievement?" Jensen argues that genetic factors can account for more than half of the alleged difference in average IQ between groups of whites and black Americans. Jensen uses test scores derived from intelligence tests that assumed there was a general factor for mental ability. In light of his prominence in the larger academic community, Jensen's essay stimulated many debates among academicians, and it also received considerable media exposure in the general public. While assuaging many white Americans' feelings of guilt and shame for racially oppressive practices imposed on African Americans, Jensen's observations reinforced the psychological significance of race in the lives of African Americans.

Research findings reported later by behavioral geneticists indicate that Jensen's heritability estimate was seriously flawed. In addition, reviews of Jensen's data show that within-group differences in IQ scores among whites were greater than black-white differences in IQ performance. In other words, the genetic variability accounted for significantly more of the total variance in IQ scores of whites than blacks. If genetic variability does not account for the total variance in IQ scores among the black population to the same degree as it does among the white population, then, understanding the distinctiveness in education and socialization experiences of African Americans is absolutely essential for interpreting their test performance.[33] Jensen's analysis includes false data reported in Cyril Burt's earlier studies on heritability and IQ.[34] In Leon Kamin's analysis of Jensen's work, he finds serious distortions or misinterpretations in the presentation of writings published by other researchers.[35]

Unfortunately, scholarly critiques of Jensen's work were published only in academic texts and journals that are rarely read by the public at large. Therefore, criticisms of Jensen's work did not minimize the negative impact it had on public opinion about the intellectual abilities of African Americans. The widespread media attention his work attracted ensured that damage-control observations made by scholars and others would be insufficient to offset the damage it had on public perceptions of African Americans. Even if African Americans desired to minimize the significance of race in their lives, studies on race differences using results derived from standardized IQ tests made it impossible for them to do so. Despite an abundance of evidence to the contrary, the public, at large, views IQ and other standardized tests as unbiased and valid measures of what they purport to measure.

Although Leon Kamin and other critics had already called into question the validity of data used by Jensen and other genetic-determination theorists, in their widely read study, *The Bell Curve*, Richard Herrnstein, a psychologist, and Charles Murray, a sociologist, also made the claim that, although environmental factors played a role, racial differences in performance on IQ tests were largely due to genetically based differences in intelligence between black and white Americans.[36] However, they also admitted that average IQ differences within each racial group were statistically significantly larger than average IQ differences between the racial groups.

There were many criticisms of the arguments put forth in *The Bell Curve*.[37] For example, it was noted that if socioeconomic conditions are held constant, there are still wide variations among individual households, and the living conditions of African Americans and white Americans are not the same even when their socioeconomic status is similar.[38] Even though their socioeconomic status is similar, because of racial discrimination problems, especially in the workforce, African Americans' economic position is likely to be more precarious than is the case for white Americans. Moreover, middle-class African American children are more likely to come from families less affluent or economically stable than middle-class white children to whom they are being compared. Bearing this in mind, the average IQ difference between these two groups may be, in part, due to class differences between them.[39] In his critique of *The Bell Curve*, Carl Jorgenson argues that blatant oversights and misinterpretations in Herrnstein and Murray's analysis suggest that they might have been primarily interested in promoting a social agenda in line with their beliefs.[40] He criticized racially conservative scholars such as Herrnstein, Murray, and Jensen for ignoring or marginalizing arguments put forth by past black intellectuals concerning the social inequities that influenced the test performance of black American children. To provide a more objective analysis and reduce the tendency toward misinterpretation of IQ data, Jorgenson urges researchers who study race differences on intelligence tests to examine critiques of white-supremacy arguments by past black-American intellectuals, most notably W. E. B. Du Bois, Fredrick Douglass, and Benjamin Banneker.

While criticizing the validity of standardized IQ tests, many psychologists have pointed out that traditional IQ and other standardized tests may discriminate against low-income urban African Americans by asking for information drawing from experiences that they are unfamiliar with. People's scores on a standardized test are influenced by their prior exposure to the information requested on it. Therefore, low IQ test scores may not necessarily reflect cognitive deficits; instead, these scores may have been low because test takers were asked about information pertaining to experiences they were unlikely to have had.[41] Findings reported in a study by Sandra Scarr and Richard Weinberg refute the argument of innate inheritability of intelligence.[42] Scarr and Weinberg provide evidence that African Americans who are raised in white middle-class environments do not tend, as a group, to have lower IQ scores than whites raised in similar environments. In the study by Scarr and Weinberg, African American children who were adopted at an early age by white middle-class families were tested. The IQ scores of the children averaged 106—about 15 points above the average of IQ scores of non-adopted African American children reared in their own homes and above the average scores of the general population. In addition, the younger a child's age at the time of adoption, the higher his or her IQ score tended to be. These results also support an earlier observation about the cultural bias in test content. As previously noted, intelligence was what middle-class whites said it was and what tests constructed by middle-class white psychologists measured.[43]

Cultural and socialization practices among African Americans that served to distinguish them from other ethnic groups were almost always ignored by white psychologists who studied them.[44] Failure to consider culture in the analyses and study of an ethnic group predisposes researchers to use their own cultural orientations and biases when they theorize about other cultures. Guided by a misleading belief that African Americans were culturally deprived because, historically, they were denied opportunities to develop a culture, an overwhelming majority of American psychologists assumed that what African Americans mimicked was an aberration of European American culture. They did not bother to study distinctive cultural practices that evolved among African Americans in response to legally sanctioned institutional racism.

In response, in part, to cultural biases underlying the research and misguided assertions about the psychology of African American life advanced by cultural-deprivation and genetic-determination theorists, in 1968, a group of African American psychologists founded the Association of Black Psychologists. An aim of this organization has been to develop psychological paradigms that reflect distinctive cultural and socialization practices among African Americans. Since its inception, the organization's efforts have been directed toward debunking the belief that, psychologically, blacks are inherently inferior to whites.

Undoubtedly, African Americans' distinctive cultural practices influenced their attitudes and behavior toward traditional schooling and test taking. Because the influence of cultural practices and racial oppression on the performance of African Americans on IQ and other standardized tests had been widely ignored, it is not surprising that many African American psychologists raised objections to the writings of Jensen, Herrnstein, and Murray. While the extent of the psychological harm to African Americans caused by these writings remains an open question, clearly these writings contributed to the belief that blacks were victims of nature and genetically inferior to whites.

By the early 1960s, it had become popular in psychology to focus attention on particular background conditions in the lives of urban African American children, such as noise and other distractions from learning in home settings, the absence of books and intellectual games in home settings, overcrowding, lack of parental involvement with children, and limited interactions with positive adult role models. Psychologists attempted to establish connections between such conditions and African American children's, hypothesized, underdeveloped cognitive and learning skills. With very little experimentally tested evidence to support it, several prominent psychologists made far-reaching assertions about the influence of cultural deprivation on the cognitive development of African Americans.[45] These assertions reinforced racial stereotypes and helped to shape public opinions about African Americans' cognitive capacities. Consider the following observations about cognition and learning in urban black children in the writings of Martin Deutsch:

> Visually, the urban slum and its overcrowded apartments offer the child a minimal range of stimuli. There are usually few if any pictures on the wall, and the objects in the household, be they toys, furniture or utensils, tend to be sparse, repetitive and lacking in form and color variations. The sparsity of objects and lack of diversity of home artifacts which are available and meaningful to the child, in addition to the unavailability of individualized training, gives the child few opportunities to manipulate and organize the visual properties of his environment and thus perceptually to organize and discriminate the nuances of that environment. These would include figure-ground relationships and the spatial organization of the visual field. The sparcity of manipulable objects probably also hampers the development of these functions in the tactile area. For example, while these children have broomsticks and usually a ball, possibly a doll or a discarded kitchen pot to play with, they don't have the different shapes and colors and sizes to manipulate which the middle-class has in the form of blocks which are bought just for him, or even in the variety of sizes and shapes of cooking utensils which might be available to him as playthings.[46]

Joseph McVicker Hunt, a leader among psychologists who supported the cultural deprivation theory, argues that if culturally deprived children failed to develop intellectually at a normal speed because of early deficits in neurological or cognitive structures, these early, un-remedied deficits would make it increasingly difficult—perhaps impossible—for the children to meet age-appropriate standards of intellectual behavior as they grew older. Hunt suggests that low-income black children were so handicapped with cognitive deficits by age four that even the Head Start program was too late to prevent the accumulation of intellectual incompetence:

> Head Start may be all too often too little and too late to overcome sufficiently the incompetence inculcated during the first four years to enable from a third to half of these children of the persistently poor to succeed in the public schools and later to enjoy full participation in the mainstream of our technological culture. We need a way to intervene in the lives of families of poverty.[47]

The ideas advanced by cultural-deprivation theorists, such as Hunt and Deutsch, stimulated the creation of many government-sponsored early-childhood-education programs, the view of low-income African American children as riddled with cognitive deficits did not go unchallenged. Sharply criticizing the cognitive-deficits idea asserted by cultural-deprivation theorists, Silverstein and Krate note these theorists convert social injustice into intellectual deficiency (blaming the victim) while failing to recognize the confusion between their own vested interests and the needs and strivings of low-income black people.[48] The term *culturally deprived* has been used rarely since the 1970s in descriptions of low-income African Americans. However, the belief that they are handicapped with cognitive deficits because of low-test scores is still shared by many educators and laypersons.

There is empirical evidence that indicates that tests have less predictive value for individuals who are members of an ethnic group that has been stereotyped about their capacity to succeed. Driven by a concern about the persistence of underperformance—lower standardized-test scores, lower college grades, lower graduation rates—among highly capable African American college students, Claude M. Steele, the Lucie Stern professor in the social sciences at Stanford University, and Joshua Aronson, also a professor of psychology at Stanford University, conducted a series of studies to determine if stereotype threat affects academic performance.[49] They pondered what they believed to be the toughest question: Could something as abstract as stereotype threat really affect something as irrepressible as intelligence? They designed an ingenious experiment to test whether the stereotype threat that African American students might experience when taking a difficult standardized test could depress their performance on the test to a statistically significant degree. After statistically matching the two groups in ability levels, black and white sophomores in college were given a verbal test made up of items from the advanced Graduate Record Examination (GRE). The test was by plan and design particularly hard for them. Steele and Aronson questioned the assumption that when a situation is objectively the same for different groups, each group experiences it in the same way. They argued that for African American students, difficulty with the test makes the negative stereotype relevant as an interpretation of their performance and of them. African American students experience extra pressure and test anxiety because they are concerned about being perceived as having limited ability. Since white students are not stereotyped in this way, they do not experience this extra intimidation.

Steele and Aronson found when the test was presented as a test of ability, African American students performed dramatically less well than white students. When they presented the same test as a laboratory task used to study how certain problems are generally solved, the African American students' performance on the test matched that of white students. Results derived from Steele and Aronson's research show that just sitting down to take a difficult test of ability was enough to make African American students cognizant of their race and stereotypes about it. They also found that the most achievement-oriented, skilled, motivated, and confident students were the most impaired by stereotype threat. Steele and Aronson note that some African American students protect themselves against stereotype threat by ceasing to take the test seriously, and they do not perform well on it. In contrast, some African American students taking the test under stereotype threat tend to try too hard by frequently reading more into a question than is intended. Stressing the distinction between *competence* and *performance*, Silverstein and Krate reviewed a number of studies conducted during the 1960s and early 1970s that demonstrated that varying testing conditions could significantly improve test scores of low-income, African American children on IQ and linguistic measurements.[50] Therefore, interpreting test results as scientific proof that the black population is riddled with cognitive deficits or genetically inferior to the white population is unwarranted. Clearly, it reinforces racism and impedes progress toward racial integration in the larger society.

In summary, the cultural-deprivation and genetic-determination theorists shared the belief that IQ scores are valid measures of basic intellectual competence. They also shared the belief that, in general, white children are more intellectually competent than African American children. The cultural-deprivation theorists attributed the presumed intellectual deficiencies in African American children to environmental factors, and the genetic-determination theorists attributed these presumed deficiencies to hereditary factors. By engaging excessive interest in using results derived from IQ and other standardized tests as scientific proof that African Americans are inferior to whites, American psychologists have contributed more to the misunderstanding of African Americans than any other academic group.

THE ROLE OF THE BLACK CHURCH IN SHAPING AFRICAN AMERICANS' PSYCHOLOGICAL PROFILES

Traditionally, the black church, the independent Christian denominations that have been historically controlled by black Americans, has played a central role in shaping cultural practices and meaning in the lives of African Americans. Founded after the Free African Society of 1787, the black church reflects the deepest values of the African American community and consists of seven major denominations.[51] Over 80 percent of all black Christians are members of one of these seven denominations. Thus, an understanding of the meaning and significance of race in the lives of African Americans require careful consideration of the role that the black church has played in shaping the psyche and behavior of African Americans.

In a study on aggression, findings on church attendance among African American adolescent boys suggest that the black church plays an important role in the functioning of low-income African American families residing in urban communities.[52] Using a sample consisting of 83 African American boys who resided in a low-income section of Paterson, New Jersey, church attendance behavior was studied to assess its usefulness as a predictor of the boys' likelihood of engaging in either socially unacceptable violence-prone behavior or pro-social, cooperative nonaggressive behavior. The boys' self-reported church attendance habits for themselves and their mothers consistently emerged as potent predictors of aggressive behavior. An analysis of the results showed that frequent church attendance (i.e., at least twice a month) was characteristic of boys and their mothers in the nonaggressive group. The relatively high levels of church involvement on the part of nonaggressive boys and their mothers may reflect shared coherent belief systems that are characterized by self-respect and concern for others in these families. The black church provides members with a coherent belief system and stresses the importance of caring about other people. The results in this study suggest that the black church may affect parents' values, and in turn, this may affect parents' disciplinary methods, emotional attitudes toward their children, emotional attitudes toward each other, and their conflict-resolution tactics in the home environment.

Often, Christianity expounded by theologians in the black church is tailored in response to the psychological needs of African Americans. The Christianity that is practiced in the black church reflects a unique synthesis of residual African religious practices and Christianity.[53] In the black church, Christianity is fashioned to fit African Americans' distinctive ways of coping with conditions and problems created by racial oppression. Many African American Christians do not separate secular desires and needs from sacred beliefs in their daily lives. It is a theme that permeates a great deal of the interpretations of black theology and black religion in the black church. For example, a Christian may contend that dancing to nonreligious music is wrong because it is has sexual connotations that would be deemed as a transgression in the eyes of God. In the words of James Cone: "Black music is unity music. It unites the joy and sorrow, the love and the hate, the hope and the despair of Black people."[54] Music in the black church creates a sense of community that reinforces mutual caring and respect among African Americans.

In times of hopelessness and despair, singing black spirituals with handclapping and bodily movements to rhythmic accompaniment serves as a powerful source of hope and inspiration for African Americans. Noting the close connection between the secular desires and sacred beliefs for many African Americans, Charles H. Long asserts that the black church is and has been the locus of the black community.[55] If this is so, then it means that the church is the locus of the expression of black cultural life. Politics, art, business, and all other dimensions of the black community should thus find their expressions as aspects of the religious experience of black folks. As can be seen, the black church frequently adopts a holistic approach in responding to the needs of African Americans.

Many liberal African American Christians make distinctions between their secular desires and sacred beliefs in some situations but not in other situations. In other words, the interplay between the secular and sacred does not follow a fixed pattern for many African Americans. Therefore, there is a complex interplay between these two orientations in the governance of daily activities for many African Americans. This complex interplay makes it very difficult sometimes to understand the feelings, thoughts, and actions of African Americans. Understanding feelings and predicting the behavior of African Americans may require knowledge about their perceptions of the relationship between their nonreligious experiences and sacred beliefs.

Since the antebellum period, the black church has provided blacks in America with a message of hope for freedom in the here and now as well as in the hereafter.[56] The theme of freedom on earth and in the hereafter is linked together in black theology. The emphasis of freedom on earth or in the hereafter tends to vary among black churches. During slavery, the term *freedom* meant release from bondage, and the black church placed a high priority on the survival of blacks in America. From the Reconstruction period through the nineteenth century, freedom referred to the right to be educated, to be employed, and to move about freely from place to place. During this period, a major concern in the black church was helping black people acquire training and skills that could make them more self-sufficient and less dependent on white people. Recognizing that the black church was the only institution African Americans were allowed to operate independently, it provided the backbone for their freedom struggle. With the black church pressing for racial equality, freedom referred to social, political, and economic justice during the twentieth century. Reflecting on the religious significance of freedom for African Americans, C. Eric Lincoln writes: "From the very beginning of the black experience in America, . . . freedom has always meant the absence of any restraint which might compromise one's responsibility to God."[57] Thus, throughout American history, black folks in America have intimately linked their struggle for obtaining first-class citizenship to the will of God.

Through social action from the 1950s to the present, the black church has provided African Americans with a message of freedom from racial oppression and the building of community.[58] In the spirit of liberation and hope, the black church provides African Americans with sacred justification for social actions to eliminate institutional racism and other racially oppressive practices in the United States. There are many observations that provide support for this assertion. Dignifying the humanity of African Americans has been one of the most significant contributions of the black church. It has provided a place where the status and dignity of even the lowliest and most rejected persons can be affirmed. Persons who are illiterate, unskilled, and poor can be deacons, trustees, ushers, and Sunday School superintendents in church congregations comprised largely of professionals with wealth. In these Christian leadership roles, they provide African American youth with role models of character. In this mode, they encourage African American youth to define self-worth in terms of the quality of one's character rather than one's wealth and professional status.

In his assessment of the black church, C. Eric Lincoln notes that the black church was clearly the most significant institution in shaping African American cultural practices.[59] It always has served as a cradle for candid expressions of the African American experience. Many aspects of African American cultural traditions and expressions are deeply rooted in the black church. Religious tradition in the black church influenced African Americans' music, drama, literature, art, public speaking, and humor.

It was pointed out earlier that, often, African Americans are faced with a dilemma when they have to reconcile discrepancies between individualistic and communal orientations. An individualistic orientation involves interpreting and responding to situations in a person's life in a self-serving manner. It compels an individual to place self-serving interests and the gratification of one's desires above the desires and needs of others. On the other hand, a communal orientation involves giving primary consideration to the wishes and needs of others while giving secondary consideration to one's self-serving interests. The black church provides a forum that allows for individualistic and communal orientations to complement each other in a manner that reinforces a sense of family and community among its worshipers. Black churches usually provide a support system for worshipers to become totally immersed in the religious experience. This immersion of the self in the religious experience is almost always supported and encouraged by other worshipers. During this religious experience, the individual expresses genuine emotions of affection and caring for the well-being of others. It is an emotionally moving experience that often becomes contagious and incites similar reactions from other worshipers who witness it.

The black church's ageless commitment to relieving suffering from racial oppression in black communities serves as a potent indicator of the significance of race in African Americans' daily experiences. Its unwavering message of freedom from the burdens of racial oppression has been one of the most powerful sources for reinforcement of the possible centrality of race in the psychological functioning of African Americans. Thus, the black church has been a major contributor to the evolution of African Americans as a new people. Since its inception, the black church has been the most significant institution in shaping and nurturing distinctive cultural practices in the personal and collective lives of African Americans.[60]

Given the pivotal position of the black church in shaping, preserving, and reinforcing African American cultural practices, if the black church sustains its influence among the masses of African Americans, then, racial integration should not pose a serious threat to the cultural identity of African Americans. Although there are many African Americans who do not attend church consistently, the vast majority of the "movers and shakers" who reside in predominantly black neighborhoods attend black churches regularly. These community leaders play key roles in establishing cultural expressions and norms of conduct in their local communities. They often assume leadership roles in spreading messages from their churches to their respective communities.

Leading theologians and religious scholars tend to agree that, excluding the family, the black church plays a greater role in shaping the beliefs, emotions, behavior, and worldviews among the masses of African Americans than any other institution. Yet explanations provided by psychologists for results derived from studies comparing African Americans with other groups rarely reflect consideration of the possible influences from the Christianity expounded in the black church. Bearing this in mind, it follows that interpreting results from studies in psychology, which compare African Americans with other groups, runs the risk of being biased by the researchers' cultural orientation. When psychologists and other social scientists conduct studies on African Americans and ignore the possible influence of the black church or the African American cultural experiences, they are prone to provide theoretical explanations that may be seriously flawed. Additional information on issues concerning psychological studies on blacks can be found in the reference section.[61]

AFRICAN AMERICAN FAMILY LIFE: THEN AND NOW

Because of the unique historical path that African Americans have taken, many African Americans do not share the same meaning of *family* held by the larger American population. The United States Bureau of the Census defines a family as two or more individuals related to each other by ancestry, marriage, or adoption living together in the same household.[62] The roles played by the family are germane for the maintenance of our society. The family ensures that the society's population will be maintained; the society's values, beliefs, attitudes, knowledge, skills, and techniques will be transmitted to its members; the family's identity will be shared among its members; and economic production and consumption will be divided among family members. Although the meaning and roles of the family for African Americans and other American ethnic groups are similar, African American families often adopt practices that are not commonplace in other American ethnic groups.

In the larger African American community, family can mean people who are related to each other through blood linkage, people who feel they belong to each other, people who live together in the same house, and people who feel among themselves to be closely related but who live in different houses and often different locations altogether. However, for the duration of black folks' existence in America, the concept of family always has meant very strong bonds of kinship.[63] The concept of family also includes church members, an especially important group for African American single mothers.

The convening of annual family-reunion meetings is a tradition among African Americans, and many of them use vacation days to attend these gatherings. Usually during the summer, several hundred kinfolks in a black family come together for several days to renew bonds of kinship, reflect on their family history and heritage, celebrate and rejoice family achievements, and educate young family members about values, beliefs, and attitudes that constitute the strength of the family. During black family reunions, older family members are dignified with special recognition for their wisdom and contributions to the family. Frequently, they share stories that capture significant historical events in the family as well as highlight distinctive family cultural practices. The convening of family reunions is an important indicator of the bonds of kinship and significance African Americans attribute to family life. The kinship network represents the centerpiece in defining African American families. In many African American families, the kinship network includes both blood kin and non-blood kin.

In addition to immediate family members, first cousins, second cousins, third cousins, and sometimes fourth cousins are considered blood kin in African American families. Therefore, sexual contact between them is considered taboo. If it occurs, members of that family are likely to be stigmatized within the African American community. With a few exceptions, there is strict adherence to this unwritten code of ethics in African American families.

In writings about the historical paths of black family life in America, Franklin and Moss and Andrew Billingsley note that, from the period of enslavement of black people in America to the present, the extended kinship network provides the only safety net available for many black families.[64] The safety net services include borrowing and lending money, moving in with kinfolk during times of crisis, taking care of older relatives and friends, and providing childcare while parents are working and during times of crises.

The extended kinship network is deeply rooted in the African American experience. During blacks' enslavement in America, black mothers relied on older friends and relatives in slave quarters to oversee the children while they worked in the fields. During illness, injury, and death, they took care of each other because there was no one else. When death or sale took the parents of young children, the children were raised and cared for by other enslaved black people, irrespective of blood linkage. Thus, bonds of kinship were established among them without blood linkage.

The family and the church were the only institutions to which enslaved blacks and free blacks could be openly committed. American black families and black churches always have been inseparable institutions in black communities. Black families have served as the building blocks for the black church, and through its ministry and service roles, the black church has provided an anchorage for stability and unity in African American families. The black church relied on active involvement of black families in its ministry for fulfilling its mission. Black families rely on the black church for hope, meaning, direction, and human dignity.

Family members receive moral and social guidance, spiritual uplift, and a coherent belief system through the black church. Recognizing that most African Americans could not afford insurance coverage for private, professional counseling services, black clergy frequently provide family and individual counseling services at no charge for parishioners as well as other local residents. Black families also use black churches as forums for networking with each other. It is important to note that findings reported in the previously referenced study, "Aggression in African-American Boys," show that black adolescents who attended church on a regular basis were more cooperative, supportive, and sensitive to the needs of others than their counterparts who rarely attended church. These adolescent boys also indicated that their mothers attended church and displayed sensitivity toward them on a consistent basis. These findings support the belief that many African American families are intimately connected to the black church because of the shared commitment on the part of these institutions to the socialization of young blacks.

Prominent scholars such as Andrew Billingsley and Herbert G. Gutman, who have for many years studied the history of African American family life, contend that African American families are among the strongest and most resilient institutions in the United States. They point out that although the American slavery system was designed to destroy family life among the enslaved population, it had the opposite effect. The oppressive and dehumanizing intent of enslavement forged bonds and kinships among the enslaved population to strengthen their resolve to survive. Describing family life in slave quarters, Franklin notes that the close emotional bonds of family life helped many slaves endure the inhumane and abusive conditions of slavery hardships.[65] The very strong kinship bonds in black families were confirmed by observations shortly after the Civil War. Following emancipation, it was commonplace for ex-slaves to search for family members separated by the American slavery system. In many cases, they were seeking to make their marriages legal and declare themselves as legal guardians of their offspring.

During the Reconstruction period through the end of the nineteenth century, black families were stable with both parents present in almost all households. Long marriages and close attachment bonds between family members characterized the families. Because of remnants of racial oppression along with restrictive economic and employment opportunities, it was commonplace for two or more black families to share the same living quarters.

During the first half of the twentieth century, black families in the United States collectively represented a viable and stable institution. In *Black Family in Slavery and Freedom*, Gutman reports that, in 1925, six out of seven black families had either a husband or father.[66] In *The Truly Disadvantaged*, William Julius Wilson reports that, before 1954, more than 80 percent of black families in the United States had both parents in households.[67] Thus, the family tradition among African Americans survived the American slavery system, Reconstruction, legal racial segregation, discrimination, racial injustice, and enforced poverty. It survived racially hostile policies and practices in both the public and private sectors in the United States.

Although a variety of extended family structures existed among black folks before and after the Civil War, in *The Black Family in Slavery and Freedom*, Gutman reports that the two-parent, nuclear family structure was the predominant form in black families during the last quarter of the nineteenth and twentieth centuries. Using data on black family patterns in urban areas of New York, Alabama, Virginia, and South Carolina, Gutman observed that between 70 percent and 90 percent of black households included both parents, and a majority of these households consisted of nuclear families. In addition, widowhood accounted for many female-headed households in black communities. Moreover, in search of employment opportunities, black men sometimes were compelled to be away from their families.

From the early 1950s through the twentieth century, there were dramatic shifts in family patterns among low-income African American families. An alarming steady increase of female-headed families evolved among African Americans residing in low-income communities. Female-headed black families increased from 17.6 percent in 1950 to 21.7 percent in 1960 and to 41.9 percent in 1983.[68] Increases in the proportions of births out of marriage to teenage and young adult mothers were a significant contributor to the growth of female-headed black families. In 1980, 68 percent of births to black women between fifteen and twenty-four years of age were out of wedlock, compared to 41 percent in 1955. In 1995, 70 percent of black births to young mothers were outside of marriage.[69]

Inspired by Daniel Patrick Moynihan's report *The Negro Family: The Case for National Action*, several social scientists and public officials asserted that African American families in low-income neighborhoods were highly unstable, with female-headed households caused by marital instability and births outside of marriage. The relatively high percentage of teenage mothers created a perception of "babies raising babies" in these families. The poverty rate of female-headed households among African Americans also was very high. William Julius Wilson notes that 71 percent of all poor black families were female-headed in 1982.[70] Maintaining stable and organized families under these circumstances posed major challenges for them. They relied a great deal on family members, friends, and social service agencies for support to manage problems involved in parenting and running households. Many younger, black single mothers live in another family group where someone else is considered the head of household. In a paper on black single-parent families, Michelene R. Malson points out that in this type of family configuration, black single mothers are often part of an extended support system and often receive help with their children from other family members.[71] The following expression has been widely used by African American single mothers in low-income communities to describe supportive social ties: "I talk to my mom a lot and she gives me encouragement. Family support to me is real important."[72] It has been a common practice among African American single mothers to form subfamilies in extended family structures, often with their child's grandmother.[73]

By 1984, 50.2 percent of black children under eighteen years of age lived in a one-parent family headed by their mothers. It was common for teenage and other young, unmarried mothers frequently to disrupt their formal education, become breadwinners, or accept public welfare assistance. Contrary to popular opinion, in 1984, most black single mothers, including teenage mothers, were in the labor force. In a study of stresses and strengths in black single-parent families, Malson indicates that 54 percent of black, unwed mothers with children less than eighteen years of age were in the labor force.[74] Given the more stringent federal regulations enacted by the United States Congress during the 1990s, the percent of black single mothers in the labor force has grown during the past decade. A large proportion of these women still live in poverty because they are employed in low-paying jobs.

Overwhelmed by a combination of inadequate resources, poor financial-management skills, racism, and the lack of effective planning skills and resources to fulfill their wishes and expectations, some black female-headed families are too unstable and overburdened with problems to instill in children the knowledge and skills needed for effective participation in the American mainstream. In these families, mothers struggle with managing the dual responsibilities of functioning as breadwinners and parents. The growth of female-headed, black families contributed to a belief that the traditional nuclear family consisting of mother, father, and children existed more in imagination than in reality in low-income black families. Consequently, there was a growing concern among educators, social service providers, and public officials, as well as others, that the black family in low-income communities was headed for extinction and lacked the capabilities to socialize children into the traditional American European culture.

With less than 18 percent of black children living in single-parent households in 1950, it is reasonable to conclude that, collectively, African American families constituted a stable and cohesive institution. It was after the middle of the twentieth century that noticeable signs of family instability and disorganization were emerging in predominantly low-income African American communities. This trend was not a heritage of slavery. On one hand, there are many black female-headed families in poverty-stricken communities that are dysfunctional; on the other hand, there are many black single mothers living in poverty with several well-adjusted and well-behaved children under eighteen years of age. In a study of fifty low-income, urban African American women, including forty-five single mothers, Janet Todd and Judith Worell finds that these mothers showed resilience and determination to survive or prevail. Unlike black female-headed dysfunctional families, black female-headed functional families rarely receive the attention of journalists, academicians, and newsmakers. Black female-headed functional as well as dysfunctional families are, too often, erroneously lumped together. For this reason, misconceptions and stereotypes about African American families are perpetuated. Findings reported in the study titled "Aggression in African-American Boys" indicate that significant differences in socialization practices exist between functional and dysfunctional black female-headed families in low-income urban communities.[75] Results from this study show that nonaggressive boys reported that their mothers were prone to express love toward them through emotional and psychological support. On the other hand, boys in the aggressive groups tended to define their mothers' expressions of love to them in terms of the material goods provided. The following explanations were frequently used by the former group to describe the love of their mothers: "I know my mother loves me because she punishes me when I do something bad and she praises me when I do something good"; "She plays and talks to me"; "She tells me right from wrong." As can be seen from these quotations, nonaggressive boys interpreted the power-assertive disciplinary methods used by their mothers as expressions of love and caring. Boys in the aggressive groups frequently used the following explanations to define their mothers' love: "My mother loves me because she gives me money to have fun"; "She buys me clothes"; "She gives me money when I ask her"; "She bought me a bicycle." Data derived from the aggressive groups suggest that these boys received less love and emotional support from their mother than the nonaggressive boys. Unlike the aggressive boys, the nonaggressive boys reported that their mothers punished them consistently when they disobeyed.

Both groups of aggressive boys reported relatively high levels of aggression directed toward their mothers and siblings. The high levels of intra-family aggression reported by aggressive boys suggest that their households were likely to be dysfunctional and plagued by persistent conflicts and strained communication among family members. The absence of persistent conflicts among family members in the nonaggressive group suggests that their households were likely to be functional. The results of this study suggest that the norms for the expression and tolerance of intra-family aggression are likely to be very different in functional and dysfunctional black female-headed households in low-income communities.

The steady increase in the percent of unwed black mothers is one of the most dramatic changes in African American family life in the twentieth century. It is logical to assert that young unwed mothers exacerbated problems that already existed in many low-income black families. The steady rise in the number of out-of-wedlock births, broken marriages, and female-headed households among African Americans raises the following question: What factors have contributed to structural changes in African American families in the United States?

It should be noted that the growth in black female-headed families reflects a trend in some Western countries for women to form independent households. Female-headed families have become increasingly more common and socially accepted in the United States and other Western societies. The rise in the proportion of unmarried mothers has occurred in Canada, England, France, Denmark, and Sweden, where approximately one-third of out-of-wedlock births are to teenage mothers. Many single-parent families are headed by black women who are either separated or divorced from the fathers of their offspring.[76] However, females who never married head an overwhelming majority of black single-parent families.

Focusing on poverty and changes in the family structure in low-income black families, William Julius Wilson contends that high unemployment among black males is one of the most significant factors related to the rise in black female-headed families.[77] Wilson points out that beginning in the early 1950s and ending in the late 1960s, there was a steady flow of black migrants from the South to central cities in the Northeast, Northwest, and West regions in the United States. The majority of these black Southern migrants possessed limited skills or education and were from rural areas in the South. As previously noted, structural economic changes in the workforce also were in progress during this period. The structural economic changes included the shifts from goods-producing to service-producing industries, the increasing polarization of the labor market into low-wage and high-wage sectors, technological innovations, and the relocation of manufacturing industries out of the central cities to areas inaccessible by public transportation.

In light of the steady flow of these black migrants, it is unlikely that they were aware of the economic transformations that were in progress before they arrived. The urban centers were undergoing an economic transformation from "centers of production and distribution of material goods to centers of administration, information exchange, and higher-order service provision."[78] In a paper titled "Urban Change and Minority Opportunities," John Kasarda notes that the greatest job losses in industries located in the central cities were among unskilled employees, and job-growth opportunities were available primarily in positions that required higher levels of education. Many blacks who were eligible to enter the labor force were unable to because of the changing education requirements in high-growth industries. Kasarda's analysis suggests that blacks' educational backgrounds did not match the jobs available in the growth industries. Describing the bleak economic picture that black residents in urban centers faced, Kasarda states, "Essentially all of the national growth in entry-level and other low education requisite jobs have accrued in the suburbs, exurbs, and nonmetropolitan areas far removed from growing concentrations of poorly educated urban minorities."[79] When racial job discrimination is considered in combination with Kasarda's analysis, then high unemployment and underemployment rates among African Americans are inevitable. Unemployment and underemployment among black males has made marriage less attractive to them. It also has been a major contributor to breakups in legal as well as common-law marriages in African American families.

Motherhood receives strong positive reinforcement in the larger American society. For some women, giving birth is perceived as a duty when they reach the childbearing age. They view giving birth as the most significant measure of their womanhood and self-worth. From the early childhood years, females learn through dolls, parents, television, schoolteachers, and so on to aspire for motherhood. Given limited options for marriage in low-income communities, some black females may be less inhibited about becoming pregnant because of strong desires to enhance their feelings of self-worth and fulfill their childhood dreams of being a mother.

While on the one hand, humans learn a great deal through direct experience, on the other hand, they also learn from what they observe other humans doing and saying. Many sex-role-type behaviors are learned by children at early ages by observing and mimicking the behaviors of their primary caregivers and significant others. Children learn effective and ineffective strategies for resolving conflicts by observing their parents. It is not uncommon in African American families for children to observe their parents debate, quarrel, and compromise on many issues. Bearing in mind that black male and female children reared in mother-headed households usually do not get exposure to conflict-resolution activities that are common occurrences in a marriage, many of them may experience a great deal of inner insecurities about the prospect of being married, and marriage may become a less attractive option for them. In addition, the lack of exposure to marital-conflict-resolution strategies could make children from single-parent families, when they reach adulthood, less effective in resolving disagreements in a constructive manner with their marital partners. That is to say, adults who were reared in functional and dysfunctional single-parent families are predisposed to be more insecure in a marriage than their counterparts reared in two-parent functional families.

It has been a long-standing practice in traditional black churches to impose stern moral sanctions against worshipers who give birth out of wedlock, the density combined with impersonal interpersonal interactions in central cities makes it relatively easy for unwed mothers to maintain anonymity without fear of moral and social sanctions. Moreover, in most Western societies, church attendance among teenagers and young adults between ages sixteen and thirty years of age tends to be low. Bearing this in mind, many young unwed mothers are less likely to experience the shame and guilt that often results from the moral constraints imposed by black churches.

It is important also to note that many church worshipers in low-income urban areas, including never-married mothers, attend smaller "storefront" churches rather than traditional black churches. There is considerable variation in the teachings and practices in smaller "storefront" churches. These churches do not necessarily impose the same social and moral constraints on their worshipers commonly imposed in traditional black churches.

Most worshipers in traditional black churches are members of closely knit functional single-parent and two-parent families. Although teenagers and young adults in these families may not attend church on a regular basis, they often curb their behavior to moral, social, and religious teachings in home, school, and community settings. It is not a common practice for unmarried females from families involved in traditional black churches to give birth out of wedlock. Thus, given the shortage of educationally and occupationally compatible African American male partners, many black females from functional closely knit black families are not likely to have the option of marriage to an African American soul mate. Therefore, it is likely that as these females evolve into maturity, they may be compelled to seek non–African American husbands or male partners. Bearing this in mind, black females from single-parent and two-parent intact families are more likely as adults than their counterparts from dysfunctional families to become leaders and adopt influential roles in the African American community. If they marry partners outside of their racial or ethnic group, over time, their families could significantly change the dynamics and cultural practices in African American communities.

If a significant proportion of educated, upwardly mobile, and influential African American females, select marital partners other than African American males, what effect, if any, would it have on the meaning and significance of race for African Americans? Consideration of the variation in gender-related roles in parenting might shed some light on this issue. As primary caregivers during early childhood, mothers function as principal socialization-agents for their offspring. "Socialization refers to those processes whereby the standards," values, and beliefs "of any given society are transmitted from one generation to the next."[80] Mothers play central roles in children's acquisition of the standards, values, and beliefs that children come to conform to and eventually adopt as their own. There is a large body of research in psychology that indicates that early childhood is a period characterized by the most rapid psychological and social development in children. The behavior and attitudes of mothers, as primary caregivers, toward their offspring are of paramount importance in how they become socialized. The socialization of children is influenced by mothers' affection ties and emotional attitudes, their rewards and punishment, and their ways of habit training.[81]

In his frequently referenced work on attachment formation, John Bowlby asserts that the young child is "pre-wired" to develop attachment to its primary caregiver by virtue of its genetic endowment.[82] Therefore, mothers are predisposed to be the first human love objects of their offspring. Once an enduring attachment bond between the primary caregiver and child has been established, the child tends to behave in accordance to the wishes and expectations of the primary caregiver to maintain it. Alternative theoretical explanations, which focus on environmental rather than genetic factors to account for early bonding between the primary caregiver and child, have been posited by other prominent scholars. For example, B. F. Skinner asserts that when mothers attend to the primary needs of their developing children, the attention and things the mothers do serve as positive reinforcement. The child becomes attached to the mother because she provides reinforcement for certain behaviors they do. Although different theoretical explanations have been posed to explain the attachment bonds between mothers and their young offspring, both Bowlby's and Skinner's theories share the assumption that the attachment bonds between parents and children are pivotal to the socialization process and that primary caregivers serve as principal socialization agents for their offspring.

Recognizing that in Western societies, mothers serve as primary caregivers more frequently than fathers, they are the principal socialization agents. Therefore, African American females who marry non–African American males but retain their African American identities are likely to transmit the same beliefs and cultural practices to their offspring. Biracial children reared by an African American female with relatively strong ethnic ties and a white American male are likely to perceive themselves as African Americans and may not necessarily experience any ethnic identity confusion.

In 1967, the United States Supreme Court ruled in the *Loving v. Commonwealth of Virginia* case that antimiscegenation legislation was unconstitutional. Since the Court's ruling, interracial marriages between black and white partners have increased steadily.[83] Biracial births have grown twenty-six times faster than all United States births.[84] Although "mixed race" births involving black and white partners have been common occurrences throughout American history, before the 1960s, these mixed race offspring were rarely by-products of mutual consent between adult partners involved in it, and marriage almost never preceded nor followed the period of conception.

Most interracial marriages in the United States involve professional African American males rather than African American females. It is beyond the purview of this work to examine factors that may contribute to this trend. Nonetheless biracial children reared by white mothers may experience ethnic/cultural identity confusion if these mothers deemphasize the significance of race in the socialization process. These biracial children may grow up viewing themselves as marginal people. That is, people who stand on the margins of two cultural worlds, namely, black and white, but are not fully members of either group.[85]

In a study of the changing dialectic between society and the racial identity of biracial individuals, Korgen found that racial appearance is a very important determinant of how African Americans and white Americans react to a biracial person.[86] Korgen indicated that biracial persons who appear neither black nor white expressed fewer problems than biracial persons who appear either black or white about being supported as racially mixed by African Americans and white Americans. For example, John, a biracial participant in this study who appeared mixed, made the following remarks about his identity:

> Because there is such ambiguity in how I look, I have a lot of freedom to create my own self-perception. If I was darker, then it would be set. I would have felt more inclined to toe the line and define as black. Similarly, if I looked white, I'd probably be more inclined to define as white.[87]

Korgen reports that marginality was especially evident among biracial Americans perceived as black and raised in upper-middle-class, predominantly white neighborhoods. They often indicated that they shared little in common with African Americans they meet who live in different areas and on a lower socioeconomic level. While comparing themselves to "aliens," several biracial respondents perceived as black indicated that they felt different from those around them because of their biracial background, and they yearned for a community that shared their racial background. These biracial individuals display attitudes about race that are similar to the attitudes of African Americans in the pre-encounter stage described by Cross in his theory on black identity.[88] Cross characterized African Americans in the pre-encounter stage as persons with attitudes toward race that range from low salience to race neutrality to antiblack. He indicated that they place value in things other than their race, such as their religion, lifestyle, social status, profession, and so on. They seldom use race in self-identification, and when pressed to give self-referents, they may say that they are "human beings who happen to be black." African Americans with low-salience attitudes toward race view it as a problem or social stigma. Accordingly, they may engage in collective action to eliminate the social stigma with their racial group membership without sharing feelings of allegiance for other collective concerns shared among African Americans. Cross maintains that as long as these African Americans' pre-encounter attitudes bring them a sense of fulfillment, a meaningful existence, and an internal sense of stability, order, and harmony, race is likely to remain a secondary consideration in their daily lives.

The similarities in attitudes about race between African Americans with pre-encounter attitudes and biracial persons are illustrated in the following remarks made by Rasheed, an eighteen-year-old, biracial college participant in Korgen's study who is perceived by most people as an African American. His white mother and his black father—who were never married, though Rasheed's father still played an active role in his life—raised him in a middle-class household along with siblings.

> When I was five, my neighborhood was more racially even, but I think it's a little bit more white now. . . . But my closest friends are white or Hispanic, pretty much. I have just more in common with them really.
>
> It's really weird, I don't think about stuff like this until people ask questions. I just don't think about race. I just like people by their interests. . . .
>
> At home we never really talked much about the fact that my father is black and my mother is white. . . . The fact that my father's black and my mother's white was never an issue with anyone when I was growing up. They never voiced it if it was, and I never felt anything from anybody. . . .
>
> It's weird. I don't really think about race. When I'm describing somebody to somebody, I really seldom say that.[89]

Korgen points out that in dating, Rasheed was attracted to women with Caucasian features. He indicated that his girlfriends had been white but race would not matter to him when it comes to whom he might eventually marry. Commenting on the advantageous status of his mixed identity, Rasheed offered the following observation:

> Honestly speaking, I put down black for the SATs and college applications because I knew some colleges would have liked affirmative action, or whatever. Although I knew I could get in on my grades, every little bit helps. . . . I'm not good at taking timed tests, so there's nothing I could really do about that. So I wrote down that I was black.[90]

As can be seen here, in a racially stratified society, persons perceived as African Americans who also attribute very little significance to race, display no shame in reaping benefits from affirmative-action programs. These individuals often may convince themselves that race had nothing to do with their achievements. Conversely, they attribute their achievements to individual initiative. The lack of clarity about who are African Americans makes it relatively easy for other nonwhites who can pass for African Americans to exploit affirmative-action programs intended for African Americans when it serves their self-interest to do so.

The privileged status of white Americans, coupled with the negative stereotypes that have been expressed about black people, increases the likelihood that biracial children will adopt European American cultural practices. Therefore, biracial children reared by mothers who deemphasize the significance of race in the socialization process are more likely to experience a greater sense of connectedness to white Americans than African Americans. Growing up as biracial is pivotal in the psychological makeup of biracial Americans and poses an identity dilemma for them.

The recognition of the distinctiveness in a person's or group's background does not mean that they are a distinct ethnic group. There is nothing cultural or ethnic that distinguishes biracial Americans from Americans in general. Although biracial Americans are not an ethnic group, they may share distinctive psychological characteristics that may preclude them from being grouped together with either African Americans or white Americans. For example, unlike African Americans, race may not be a central frame of reference for biracial persons who were reared in families that deemphasized the significance of race in self-identification. Under these conditions, biracial individuals are not likely to internalize race as a source of self-identification.

Even though biracial children may be socialized to ignore race in judging themselves and others, racially motivated social and cultural practices by both African Americans and white Americans make it almost impossible for them to escape the significance of race in their daily lives. Thus, while biracial Americans and African Americans may differ in terms of the meaning and significance each group attributes to race, it most likely influences the behavior, emotions, and thinking in both groups. While race is likely to be a primary factor in making judgments for most African Americans, it is likely to be a secondary consideration for many biracial persons who were born after the civil rights era. If strong racial identification pressures are imposed on biracial people who prefer to not be identified by one of the United States' traditional racial categories, then they are likely to feel imprisoned by race.

As African Americans increase their knowledge about and understanding of themselves, they are likely to feel better about being themselves and embrace their distinctive ethnic characteristics. As a result, biracial Americans and African Americans may be forced to reexamine the perceptions they share about each other. For example, will African Americans focus more on differences between themselves and biracial Americans or vice versa? Will the uneasiness created by marginalization in a racially stratified society compel biracial Americans to use their unique perspective to bridge communication gaps between African Americans and white Americans?

Guided by the assumption that the significance and meanings African Americans associate with the idea of race reflects an adaptation to the unique circumstances in a racially stratified society, it seems reasonable to suggest that the attitudes and behavior of white Americans toward African Americans had a marked influence on the connotations of race for African Americans in the presence of white Americans. Though white Americans exerted control over many of the reinforcement contingencies involved in the learning processes that helped to shape African American attitudes about race, the experiences African Americans shared with each other also were of central importance in shaping the meanings and significance of it for them. Therefore, in some situations, the idea of race may have negative or unfavorable connotations for many blacks in the presence of whites and positive or favorable connotations for them when in the company of other blacks. African Americans' responses to, as well as knowledge and understanding of, racially motivated experiences also help shape the meanings and significance they associated with the idea of race.

Perhaps the most important factor that could influence the meaning and significance that African Americans attribute to race is knowledge about themselves. In reflections on his experiences in concentration camps in Germany, Viktor E. Frankl notes that there were different reactions among the imprisoned Jews to the brutality, humiliation, and inhumane treatment they endured.[91] Jews who could find something in their Jewish identity that could give meaning to their suffering were more likely to cope and retain a coherent sense of self under extreme brutality and deprivation. Describing psychological adjustments to confinement in the concentration camps, Frankl provides these impressions:

We who lived in concentration camps can remember the men who walked through the huts comforting others, giving away their last piece of bread. They may have been few in number, but they offer sufficient proof that everything can be taken from a man but one thing: the last of the human freedom—to choose one's own way. And there were always choices to make. Every day, every hour, offered the opportunity to make a decision, a decision which determined whether you would or would not submit to those powers which threatened to rob you of your very self, your inner freedom; which determined whether or not you would become the plaything of circumstance, renouncing freedom and dignity to become molded into the form of the typical inmate.[92]

A logical inference from Frankl's observations is that humans can maintain independence of mind in extreme conditions of psychic and physical stress. Knowledge about and understanding of one's self helps a member of a subordinate group to retain independence of mind when confronted with racist and abusive behavior by members of a majority group.

In keeping with Frankl's observations as well as W. E. B. Du Bois's reflections in "Whither Now and Why," changes in the significance and meanings African Americans attribute to race are likely to be strongly influenced by their knowledge about and understanding of themselves. Reflecting on the value of African American history and cultural practices, Du Bois states, "Negro history must be taught for many critical years by parents, in clubs by lecture courses, by a new Negro literature which Negroes must write and buy. This must be done systematically for the whole Negro race in the United States."[93] Even though Du Bois's observations were made almost fifty years ago, they still are relevant for African American families today. Regardless of the configuration of African American families, it is of central importance that African American children develop independence. Independence of mind could help a child from a subordinate group maintain a coherent sense of self in a changing society that is racially polarized and comprised of many different racial and ethnic groups. Therefore, it is important for parents and guardians to ensure that African American children acquire knowledge about and understanding of themselves. In so doing, African Americans would be better equipped to define themselves rather than have members from other ethnic groups define them. Knowledge about the events that shaped African American thought, history, and cultural practices also could help to buffer or temper negative experiences that African Americans may tend to associate with the notion of race.

WHAT HAPPENS WHEN BLACK SOUTHERN MIGRANTS MEET BLACK WEST INDIAN IMMIGRANTS?

When African Americans from the South arrived in the central cities of large metropolitan areas, for the first time, most of them met black residents who were either immigrants or the first-generation offspring of immigrants from the West Indies. Many of these immigrants had spent their childhood and adolescence outside of the United States. Like Ghanaians, they spent their most critical years of socialization in societies comprised of an overwhelming majority of people with African bloodlines. Like African Americans, their ancestors were enslaved by European colonists, but unlike enslaved blacks in America, enslaved West Indians outnumbered the colonists. For example, during the nineteenth century in Jamaica, there were over thirteen enslaved Africans to every white person, and in Barbados, there were approximately four enslaved Africans to every white person.[94] On the other hand, with the exception of South Carolina and Mississippi, the white population outnumbered the enslaved population in the North American South.

During slavery in West Indian societies, European colonists imposed a social hierarchy structure that allowed for preferential treatment of black folks according to degrees of intermixture of African and European blood.[95] It was socially acceptable in the Caribbean Islands for white men to impregnate African females. There was no social stigma attached to miscegenation in the islands. During the period of slavery in the Caribbean Islands, Antigua was the only colony to legislate against miscegenation.[96] Even in Antigua, however, white men openly ignored these codes and engaged in extramarital liaisons with black mistresses. Since many Caucasian slaveholders, merchants, managers, and overseers in the Caribbean Islands were young bachelors or married men who had left their children and wives in England, they did not restrain their sexual appetites and behaviors toward mulattoes and black West Indian females. Many white planters whose wives and children lived with them in the islands openly kept black concubines. Viewed as chattel property with no rights that a white person was either required or expected to respect and faced with the possibility of a public flogging or even death if they refused to acknowledge, with approval, sexual advances by white men, mulattoes and black West Indian females were open game as sexual objects to fulfill the sexual cravings of white male predators. Poor and powerless, these females were unable to fend off white men's sexual gestures. There was a visible mulatto population on these islands, and they were treated more humanely by whites than other people with African bloodlines. In his essay on mulattoes or racially mixed offspring in the British colonies, Winthrop D. Jordan notes that it was considered improper to work mulattoes in the field.[97] It was a common practice to use them as tradesmen, house servants, and the women as concubines. Describing the social accommodation for the practice of white men sexually exploiting black women in the islands, Jordan observed that the practice of having concubines was such an integral part of island life that to legislate against it would have been tantamount to abolishing sugar cane on the islands. The acceptability of miscegenation gave rise to the preferential treatment of mulattoes in the Caribbean Islands. For example, in the 1730s, the Jamaican legislature passed numerous private acts providing mulattoes the rights and privileges of white persons, including the right to inherit the planter's estate. A Jamaican slaveholder named William Bonner, having fathered four mulatto children, freed their mother when he died and bequeathed the children with one hundred acres of his best land together with twenty of his enslaved Africans. It is safe to conclude that, in general, the quality of life for mulattoes was considerably better than it was for their darker counterparts.

Most white planters and merchants in these islands maintained close ties with their English roots and did not view the islands as their homes. They viewed the Caribbean Islands primarily as a business with a focus on the production of agricultural staples. In a word, most whites in the Caribbean Islands were there to make money, gratify their sexual cravings, and enjoy extravagant lifestyles by exploiting powerless and poor people with African bloodlines. To ensure that their English culture would not accommodate to cultural practices of the enslaved Africans, white people in these islands held steadfast to their British cultural practices. Unlike American colonists, they frequently visited England to reinforce their British connections and reassure themselves that they were maintaining cultural practices in keeping with British standards.[98] In light of the white islanders low regard for African cultural practices along with their need for reassurance of their English backgrounds, they tended to exaggerate British formalities and mannerisms in the West Indies. Given the dominant position of European colonists in these islands, black West Indians were predisposed to adopt many aspects of European culture. The size and isolation of the islands also made it easier for European cultural and socialization practices to be imparted among the people in these societies.

Mulattoes in British colonies in the Caribbean Islands embraced British customs and cultural practices and, simultaneously, rejected and denigrated cultural practices associated with the lower and darker caste. Light skin-color shades, Caucasian physical features, and British cultural practices and mannerisms were symbols of beauty, power, and social status. Consequently, mulattoes maintained as much distance as possible between themselves and the enslaved darker blacks. The social significance attributed to skin color and European cultural practices heightened feelings of hostility between light- and dark-complexion West Indians in the Caribbean Islands. Mulattoes in the Caribbean Islands were envied and resented by the dark-complexion peasantry. In his book titled *Ethnic America*, Thomas Sowell makes reference to the significance that West Indians attributed to skin color. Sowell points out that gradations of color fragmented the West Indian black population down through history significantly more than it did the black population in the United States.[99] The social significance black West Indians attributed to skin color may have been viewed primarily as a social-class difference rather than racial snobbery. Recognizing that the West Indian population in the Caribbean Islands was, then and now, overwhelmingly black, it is unlikely that racial group membership played the same role in self-identification and group identification for them as it played for black folks in the United States.

In 1838, slavery was abolished in British colonies in the Caribbean Islands. After abolishing slavery, the British government maintained colonial rule in the Caribbean Islands. While the British government set forth governance policies, former slave masters retained domination over local politics and economies in the Caribbean Islands through the nineteenth century. Descendants of slave masters and white merchants maintained control over local politics and economies in the Caribbean Islands through approximately three-quarters of the twentieth century. After emancipation, people with African bloodlines, especially mulattoes, increasingly assumed positions in the administration and management of local government and community services in the islands. Black West Indians in these positions usually had more direct contact with the black population in the islands than their Caucasian counterparts. From 1838 through more than three-quarters of the twentieth century, British rule on the Caribbean Islands was more indirect than direct, with native West Indians overseeing and managing a great deal of the day-to-day government and community service affairs. A logical conclusion is that to obtain local services, the black masses had more direct contact with native black West Indians and very limited or no contact with Caucasians in the Caribbean Islands.

Before emancipation in the Caribbean Islands, the economies had weakened. This downward trend continued after emancipation in these islands. Employment options for the previously enslaved blacks were very limited. The plantation system continued in a modified form after emancipation. In his book *Sugar and Slaves*, Richard S. Dunn observes a relationship between low economic productivity and class consciousness in these islands. The privileged white minorities who possessed wealth indulged in extravagant, conspicuous consumption and waste, while the underprivileged black masses struggled to survive. In view of the power and authority that the white minorities exercised over the economies, politics, and social interactions, their lavish indulgence in luxuries almost certainly enhanced the darker underprivileged West Indians' sensitivities to and awareness of the significance attributed to social class. It also seems reasonable to assume that the lifestyles of the privileged minorities in the islands increased black Caribbeans' desire for a better life. Without glimmers of hope for a better life, undoubtedly, emigration became an attractive option for many native islanders. Many previously enslaved blacks' only options were emigration, return to work on the plantations, or face the likelihood of starvation.

In response to the prolonged duration of economic stagnation in the Caribbean Islands, many descendants of ex-enslaved blacks immigrated to the United States and settled in New York early in the twentieth century. In view of the high visibility and accessibility of black West Indians in government positions, it is very likely that they were perceived by many black peasants as contributors to the economic hardships in the islands. Under these oppressive economic conditions, black West Indians employed as overseers and managers were more likely than white Caribbean to be targets of anger, hostility, resentment, and aggression for many black natives in the Caribbean. In contrast to the experiences of African Americans, many native black West Indians may not have made a direct association between white racial oppression and racial group membership. In other words, rather than link their oppressive economic conditions and limited resources to British economic policies, they linked it to black West Indians' mismanagement and ineffective administration of resources. In so doing, many black peasants' animosity was directed more toward other black West Indians rather than white government officials in the islands. Therefore, the attitudes of black West Indians toward race and racism were likely to be different from African American attitudes toward the same.

During the first quarter of the twentieth century, approximately 130,000 West Indians immigrated to the United States and settled in New York City. They were relatively young with more than half under thirty years of age.[100] The positions they assumed in the workforce were similar to the positions assumed by Southern black migrants who arrived in central cities in the Northeast at about the same time. Consequently, the two groups vied for jobs. In view of the cultural differences along with differences attributed to the meaning and significance of race between black West Indian immigrants and African American migrants from the South, the conditions were ripe for tension, hostility, and conflict between them. Because of the centrality of race in the psychological functioning of African Americans, many Southern migrants most likely assumed that black West Indians shared their perceptions about race and racism. As previously noted, many West Indian immigrants did not share African Americans' perceptions about the meaning and significance of race. This misunderstanding contributed to conflicts, hostility, and tension between these two black groups during the first half of the twentieth century, especially from 1900 through the 1930s.

Hostility, conflict, and tension have long characterized the relationship between black West Indian immigrants and African Americans.[101] However, overt violence-prone actions have rarely occurred in response to conflicts between these groups. The two groups have maintained, as much as possible, social distance between each other. It was during the first quarter of the twentieth century when tension peaked between African Americans and the newly arrived black West Indians.[102] It was during this period when the largest number of West Indians from the British-controlled islands arrived in the United States and sizable proportion of African Americans migrated from the South to the North.[103] The West Indian Committee, the Foreign Born Citizen's Alliance, and the West Indian Reform Association were established to resolve conflicts and reduce tension between the two ethnic groups.

The psychological profiles of American-born offspring of black West Indian immigrants were different from their parents. Although they adopted some of the distinctive West Indian cultural practices, they shared the perceptions of other African Americans about race and racism. The social and psychological significance attributed to race in the United States makes it impossible to ignore for any child with African bloodlines who is born and reared here. In general, American-born offspring of black West Indian immigrants defined themselves as a part of the larger African American community. It appears reasonable to assume that they played a pivotal role in reducing tension between the West Indian and African American communities during the 1940s and 1950s. When African Americans migrated from the South to the North during the 1950s, a great deal of the tension between these communities had subsided.

During the 1960s and 1970s, approximately 90,000 West Indians immigrated to the United States in each decade. In general, black West Indians who immigrated to the United States after 1954 were more skilled, more ethnically diverse, and better educated than their predecessors. Many of these immigrants came to the United States using a student visa and shared strong identification with their native countries and ethnic groups. Racial group membership was, at best, a secondary consideration for most of them. Consequently, many black student immigrants from the Caribbean Islands viewed their stay abroad as short-lived and did not bother to change their cultural practices and attitudes nor establish close friendship ties with African Americans. They established student Caribbean organizations on university campuses throughout the United States. Through these organizations, Caribbean students were able to embrace cultural traditions and serve as support groups for each other. They seldom interacted with African American students outside of the classroom. The lack of personal and social contact between African Americans and black West Indian immigrants reduced opportunities for them to have cultural exchanges and develop mutual respect for each other. Consequently, bridges of trust between these groups often failed to evolve.

Recognizing that race served as a unifying theme for many African Americans, but not necessarily for black West Indian students, differences in the meaning and significance attributed to race contributed to tension and a lack of harmony between the two black groups. Black West Indian students were viewed often by some African American students as arrogant traitors consumed with a desire for the approval, acceptance, and companionship of white people. These perceptions of African American students are likely to reflect the social and psychological significance they attribute to race in combination with their direct experiences with racism in the United States. Direct experiences with racism serves to reinforce the idea shared among some African Americans that many Caucasians are predisposed to exploit and oppress people with African bloodlines. Consequently, these African American students believe that people with African bloodlines should unite against it. Therefore, when black student immigrants appear to spend more time with Caucasians than African American students, African American students may view them suspiciously.

African Americans were easily offended and outraged when some black West Indian immigrants would exalt their status and blamed African Americans, rather than racism, for problems such as high unemployment and underemployment rates in some African American communities. Although unnervingly insulted and outraged by such comments, African Americans do not discriminate against them nor criticize them for the opportunities they also may derive from the sacrifices of African Americans. Does the distinctiveness in the meaning and significance of race for African Americans make them share feelings of duty and obligation to be supportive of other black ethnic groups?

The issues previously posed between African Americans and black West Indian immigrants are still sources of tension and hostility between them. As American public interest in affirmative-action programs increases, some African Americans publicly are expressing strong displeasure about black and other nonwhite immigrants unjustly criticizing them while deriving better career opportunities and other benefits created by the struggles, sacrifices, and political activities of African Americans. The term *affirmative action*, which first appeared in an executive order issued in 1963 by President John F. Kennedy, called for positive initiatives to recruit nonwhites and women for jobs, promotions, and educational opportunities. Although, affirmative action has been sharply criticized by a few blacks, an overwhelming majority of African Americans view affirmative action as the most important mechanism now operating in the fight against institutional racism and discrimination in the United States. While they may vehemently deny it, many staunch black and nonwhite critics of affirmative action have derived successful career opportunities primarily through affirmative-action programs.

Some African Americans contend that many employment, educational, housing, and economic opportunities in the United States enjoyed by other nonwhite groups are primarily by-products of the civil rights and human rights struggles as well as political activities of African Americans. Moreover, they believe that for non–African American blacks and other nonwhite immigrants to blame African Americans for many problems that beset them while prospering from opportunities in the United States brought about through the sacrifices of African Americans are unconscionable. Exemplary of this attitude is the response of Jean Barby to a letter written by an Asian Indian that criticized the conduct of an African American. Barby's retort was published in a local newspaper in the central region of New Jersey in a note to the editor titled "Blacks Paid Dues for Other Minorities" and makes the following observations:

> Immigrants who, in appearance, cannot be mistaken for Caucasian have benefited from the struggles and initiatives of African-Americans in this country. The benefits come among fair housing, no discrimination in employment and equal opportunity in education. Yet, because of the detrimental impact of the negative image of black African-Americans portrayed via movies, television and other means of communications throughout the world, these and other immigrants who have contributed

nothing to this country enter the United States with the smug, superior attitude of Sekhar.

Until immigrants, particularly non-Caucasian immigrants such as Sekhar, have sacrificed their lives voluntarily or involuntarily, have expended their physical energy, have expended their intellectual energy and have sacrificed their opportunity for financial gain for the civil and other rights that increase the quality of living of others in America besides their own ethnic group, no immigrant and certainly not Sekhar should advise Cosby to grow up.[104]

Affirmative-action programs were created primarily for African Americans to remedy educational, social, and economic adversities caused by racial injustices against them. Yet they have rarely condemned black or other nonwhite immigrants who have derived benefits from such programs. Racial oppression has predisposed many African Americans to empathize with immigrants, especially black people, from poor and underdeveloped countries. Therefore, in general, African Americans are prone to support, show compassion for, and establish cooperative relationships with nonwhite immigrants. Strong racial identification among African Americans often leads them to render help to other people with African bloodlines without requirements or expectations of reciprocity. Although this expression is in keeping with practices among African Americans, a lack of reciprocity should invite a call for greater appreciation of the African American tradition of struggle for equality, greater sensitivity to the plight of African Americans, and mutuality of effort in their struggle for expansion of opportunities that also benefit other nonwhites. This raises the question of whether a lack of reciprocity should preclude the welcoming extension when the struggle and responsibility are not shared.

AFRICAN AMERICANS' ATTITUDES TOWARD RACIAL INTEGRATION

As would be expected, African Americans strongly supported the desegregation of public accommodations and public transportation. During interviews for a Gallup poll conducted in December 1955, Southern blacks were asked to respond to the following question: "The

Interstate Commerce Commission has ruled that racial segregation on trains, buses, and in public waiting rooms must end. Do you approve or disapprove of this ruling?" The results show that 82 percent of them approved of this ruling, and 70 percent believed that the day would come in the South when whites and blacks would be going to the same schools, eating in the same restaurants, and generally sharing the same public accommodations.[105]

Many African Americans' hopes for expanded opportunities in education and the workforce were uplifted by the Supreme Court's 1954 decision in the *Brown v. Board of Education* case. But they were sharply divided in their views on whether or not racial integration was a viable way of remedying the race problem. Results derived from the Gallup polls conducted in November 1955 indicate that while 53 percent of Southern blacks favored school integration, 36 percent of them did not. Southern blacks who disapproved of racial integration in public schools were largely those individuals with grade-school education, those living on farms, and those fifty years of age and over. It is likely that the distrust and resentment of Southern whites was so strong that many blacks may have preferred to remain in all-black schools rather than put their children at risk as tokens in predominantly white schools. Clearly, African Americans recognized that racial integration in all segments of the larger American society would require them to make radical changes in their daily lives. In view of the centrality of race in self-construction for African Americans, many of them perceived racial integration as a threat to their personal and ethnic identity. They feared that they would have to extinguish their social and cultural practices and replace them with European American cultural practices to be accepted by white Americans and enter the American mainstream.

In his book *Race and Social Justice*, Howard McGary, professor of philosophy at Rutgers University, provides a critical review of the debate among black leaders on the question of the integration of the black race with the white race. McGary notes that some black leaders believed that the cultural roots of African Americans would be lost through racial integration. These leaders purported that racial integration would force African Americans to reject their black identity and lead lives without a sense of meaning and purpose. Many African Americans believed that white Americans could not be trusted to make the commitments necessary for eliminating racism and ensuring equal opportunity for them. Many African Americans desired equal opportunity and access to previously segregated facilities, but they did not desire to be in the company of white Americans. On the other hand, many African Americans believed that the similarities between the black race and white race in America outweighed the differences between them. They contended that the racial differences were created by racist policies and practices, and as such, American institutions should eliminate racial barriers so that African Americans could be partners with white Americans for the betterment of the larger society.

Results derived from a Gallup poll conducted in 1955 show that a majority of white Americans supported the United States Supreme Court's decision in the *Brown v. Board of Education* case. Nevertheless, racial integration in most aspects of the American society has not happened in a manner that reflected a strong desire among Americans to close the racial divide. Many white Americans and black Americans have been reluctant to be in the company of each other whenever possible. On the one hand, they may often display tolerance and friendliness toward each other in public and private settings that require them to do so. On the other hand, these same individuals may rarely mingle in home, community, and social settings that would provide more and better opportunities for them to get to know, respect, and care for each other. They are likely to avoid, whenever possible, participation in emotionally loaded discussions about race in racially mixed audiences, especially if only a few members of their racial group are present. Under these circumstances, racist beliefs and attitudes held by individuals present are likely to go unchallenged. Under these circumstances, feelings of racial distrust and resentment are not likely to get better.

CONDITIONS UNDERLYING PSYCHOLOGICAL TRANSFORMATION IN AFRICAN AMERICANS

Processes and activities involved in implementing the United States Supreme Court's 1954 decision in the *Brown v. Board of Education* case triggered psychological transformations in African Americans that are still in progress. Because these transformations are being driven primarily by African Americans' interactions with white Americans and other ethnic groups in America as well as their reactions to both racist practices and plans of action to remedy racism, African Americans most likely will continue to undergo significant transformations in their psychological makeup through the first quarter of the twenty-first century. The most salient factors contributing to the psychological transformations in African Americans include changes in their relationships with other ethnic groups in the United States, especially white Americans; changes in the psychological interplay between their individualistic and communal orientations; changes in the meaning and significance of race; and maintaining cultural distinctiveness while accommodating and assimilating into a more integrated society.

RELATIONSHIPS BETWEEN AFRICAN AMERICANS AND WHITE AMERICANS

When considering conditions that have contributed to psychological transformations in African Americans, their interactions with and attitudes toward white Americans cannot be ignored. The Court's ruling in the case of *Brown v. Board of Education* challenged African Americans to forgive white Americans for racist misdeeds and learn to trust and accept them as equal humans without regards for race, creed, or skin color. Undoubtedly, African Americans who have confronted this challenge with a willingness to change have had to make significant psychological adjustments in their perceptions of themselves as well as white Americans.

In *The Nature of Prejudice*, Gordon Allport eloquently illustrates how ignorance or the lack of knowledge about an individual or group of individuals can lead to hostility and contempt toward them. The hostility and tension between African Americans and white Americans have been well documented.[106] Hostile groups tend to maintain relatively high social distance from each other and avoid situations that bring them together.[107] By avoiding contact, the groups become fixated on their differences and miss out on opportunities that would allow them to explore their commonalities. Mutual avoidance perpetuates stereotyping, hostility, and contempt between hostile groups. Therefore, the removal of all barriers that preclude contact between African Americans and white Americans is a necessary prerequisite to breakdown stereotypes and reduce the hostility and contempt between these groups. Although many African Americans, especially urban residents, have minimal contact with white Americans, increasingly, a growing number of African Americans experience contact with white Americans in workplaces, academic settings, community settings, and social gatherings on a regular basis.

In a classic experiment in intergroup relations, Muzafer Sherif and associates observed that effective integration initiatives required contact between hostile groups over an extended period of time or multiple cooperative interactions.[108] They found that if hostile groups worked together in order to achieve important needs shared by members of both groups, it improved intergroup relations and reduced intergroup hostility. Since the United States Supreme Court's 1954 ruling in the *Brown v. Board of Education* case, contact experiences in a variety of situations between African Americans and white Americans have increased steadily at a rapid pace. Despite numerous interracial conflicts, results derived from public-opinion polls indicate that communication between these groups has improved a great deal since the civil rights era ended. Findings reported from several studies in psychology show multiple intergroup contact experiences between different members of hostile groups help to improve communication and break down stereotypes.[109] It also produces more generalized change in intergroup attitudes than experiences that are limited to a few group members or a single interaction.[110] Thus, if opportunities are created that significantly increase the quantity and quality of contact between African Americans residing in urban areas and white Americans, then the pace of integrating the United States and improving relations between African Americans and white Americans inevitably will be accelerated. Opportunities to recognize the important needs shared by members of both groups that can be best achieved by mutual cooperation will increase.

Improved understanding of and knowledge about the African American experience among African Americans also should improve the quality and quantity of their interactions with white Americans. With a better understanding of their distinctive cultural practices, psychological characteristics, and historical experiences, African Americans would be more likely to embrace their ethnicity and reduce their dependency

on racial group membership identity. Race would more likely be perceived in terms of its psychological significance in African Americans.
The significance of its connection for them to other people of African
descents is likely to diminish. Moreover, African Americans would be
predisposed to perceive their distinct ethnic characteristics more favor-
ably. This psychological shift would enable them to exercise more control over defining their group identity. If these events come to fruition,
African Americans are likely to give greater recognition to similarities in
interests, attitudes, values, and goals they share with white Americans.
In general, people are likely to be attracted to other individuals that they
are similar to in preferences, attitudes, and values.[111]

On the other hand, if African Americans embrace their ethnicity, it
could contribute to increased social distance between them and other
American nonwhite ethnic groups that they perceive themselves to be in
competition with for limited economic or social resources. Some African
Americans believe that many nonwhite ethnic minorities enjoy economic and social benefits derived from the sufferings, sacrifices, and political activities of African Americans as well as some white Americans.
This observation raises the following questions: Will African Americans
permit, in a cooperative manner, this perceived pattern to continue? Or,
will they view it as an unfair intrusion of other groups on resources and
opportunities African Americans struggled to obtain?

CHANGES IN COMMUNAL AND INDIVIDUALISTIC ORIENTATIONS

Another factor contributing to psychological transformations in many
African Americans has been expanded opportunities for them to pursue personal goals and to satisfy self-oriented desires and needs. With
the cooperation of the federal judiciary, legislative, and executive
branches of government, polices and practices have been instituted
that expand career, education, employment, and social opportunities for African Americans. In view of expanded opportunities to
become successful capitalists and participate in America's economic
mainstream, more African Americans than ever before are challenged
frequently to resolve conflicts between their oppressed communal and

individualistic frames of reference. In a variety of situations, African Americans often are confronted with making tough choices between self-oriented desires or needs and their sense of duty to attend to group-oriented needs of African Americans. Making choices between self-oriented desires or needs versus the group-oriented needs of African Americans may be especially problematic when group unity and collective actions are needed to achieve racial equality and social justice. Many African Americans have been driven to rethink their personal priorities and commitment to the well-being of other African Americans. This process of self-assessment usually takes more than minutes, hours, or a few days and almost always leads to significant psychological adjustments.

THE MEANING AND SIGNIFICANCE OF RACE

Drawing from the history of African Americans, race has always played a critical role in their psychological functioning. For African Americans, race serves as a psychological frame of reference. The assumption that race serves as a frame of reference is not a new idea. As noted earlier, in his writings in *The Souls of Black Folk*, W. E. B. Du Bois notes in 1903 that the meaning of race for African Americans was intimately linked to their psychological makeup in a unique manner when he described the problem of double consciousness.

Du Bois suggests that racial oppression changed the psychological makeup of African Americans in a unique manner. Du Bois's observation suggests that the meaning of race for African Americans played a central role in shaping their thoughts, feelings, and behavior. If Du Bois's observations are valid, then race is of paramount importance in self-construction and identity formation for African Americans. Therefore, changes in the meaning and significance of race for African Americans will contribute to psychological transformations in them.

As previously observed, Du Bois believed that the problem of double consciousness in African Americans evolved in response to racial oppression. Unlike the indigenous people in Ghana as well as in other former African colonies, African Americans have experienced direct racial oppression in a variety of forms. While African Americans have always lived and worked among white people, most native Africans who reside in Africans' nation-states have not. Therefore, African Americans have many opportunities in a variety of situations to experience firsthand the humiliation of racism. They learned to employ a variety of creative coping strategies to respond to racist practices.

Since the 1800s, black people who reside in countries located in West Africa have been economically exploited and deprived of benefits derived from the natural resources in their countries by Caucasians from Europe. The masses of native Africans had no direct contact with Caucasians. Europeans' rule over blacks in these countries was indirect rather than direct, as it was for white people over black people in the United States. Before these African nations gained independence from European domination, blacks chosen by Europeans administered the day-to-day affairs and local ordinances. This practice created the appearance to the indigenous population that blacks were in control. For this reason, many indigenous people believed that other blacks, rather than Europeans, were responsible for their economic exploitation. Native Africans did not necessarily perceive their economic exploitation by Europeans as a form of racial oppression visited upon them. It follows then that the problem of double consciousness most likely did not evolve in them. The lack of contact with Caucasians suggests that race may not play a significant role in the psychological functioning in blacks that reside in countries in West Africa. Given the differences in relationships with Caucasians, most Africans may not share the same attitudes and feelings toward Caucasians that have been observed among many African Americans.

The lack of uniformity in the ways that African Americans experience racism in their daily lives often makes it very difficult, if not impossible, to determine the unique roles race plays in shaping their thinking, feelings, and actions. While the meaning and significance of race are not the same for all African Americans, it is reasonable to conclude that race is a central component in their psychological makeup, especially among those individuals who have already reached young adulthood. Because of the centrality of race in the psychological functioning of African Americans, minimizing its significance in them will profoundly affect their ways of interpreting and responding to events in life; interactions with and perceptions of members of other racial and ethnic groups;

interactions with and perceptions of members of their racial group who are not African Americans; interactions with other African Americans as well as perceptions of themselves both as individuals and as members of an ethnic group.

MEASURING THE PSYCHOLOGICAL SIGNIFICANCE OF RACE IN AFRICAN AMERICANS AND LOOKING AHEAD

People are speculating—why am I as I am? To understand that of any person, his whole life, from birth, must be reviewed. All our experiences fuse into our personality. Everything that ever happened to us is ingredient. . . .

An objective reader may see how in the society to which I was exposed as a black youth here in America, for me to wind up in a prison was really just about inevitable.

—Malcolm X, *The Autobiography of Malcolm X* (1965)

Racial segregation, integration, assimilation, accommodation, and acculturation are experiences in American life that have profoundly influenced the attitudes, beliefs, actions, and emotions of African Americans. The research reported in this book underscores the distinctive experience of African Americans in the United States. Although remnants of their African ancestry may be apparent in African American cultural expressions, the meanings African Americans attribute to them are not the same as the meanings native Africans attributed to similar cultural expressions. The environment surrounding cultural expressions for African Americans differs fundamentally from the contexts for Africans in Africa. These observations invite the question: did the distinctive racially categorized experiences of African Americans in American life transform them into a group that can no longer be viewed in the same light as other people of African descents?

In his work published in 1690, *An Essay Concerning Human Understanding*, John Locke put forth a doctrine about the role of experience in shaping the mind that has played a central role in cultural and socialization practices in American life. John Locke's philosophical writings have been so influential that he is frequently called the "philosopher king" of the American Revolution. Arguing that the mind is like a blank slate at birth, Locke contended that all knowledge is learned through experience. He believed that certain ideas might seem to be innate to humans because these ideas have been taught to us constantly from early childhood through adulthood. Thus, as humans evolve into maturity, they come to believe that these ideas are innate. Reflecting on the role of experience in shaping the psychological makeup of humans, Locke wrote:

> Let us then suppose the mind to be, as we say, white paper void of all characters, without any ideas: —How comes it to be furnished? Whence comes it by that vast store which the busy and boundless fancy of man has painted on it with an almost endless variety? Whence has it all the materials of reason and knowledge? To this I answer, in one word, from Experience. In that all our knowledge is founded; and from that it ultimately derives itself.[1]

Consistent with Locke's argument, cultural practices and beliefs that can be traced to early historical records provide evidence that humans always shared the belief that experience is pivotal in shaping our actions, attitudes, beliefs, and emotions. Similarities in experience make people more alike in their psychological makeup, while differences in experience contribute to distinctiveness in the psychological makeup of human beings. Although fallacies in Locke's philosophical position have been well documented, from the beginning of the twentieth century through present times, psychologists have provided a plethora of research findings that show experience is of paramount importance in shaping the psychological makeup and functioning of human beings. During moments of introspection, often a person carefully looks inward and reflects on questions such as: Who am I? Why do I behave one way in some situations and a different way in other situations? Why do I feel a certain way toward some groups in a given situation and different toward other groups in the same situation? How did I become the person that I am? While reflecting, it is common for an individual to carefully examine significant life experiences during early childhood, middle childhood, adolescence, and adulthood. During each of these developmental stages, the person is likely to reflect on her or his behavior, thinking, and feelings in home, school, and community settings as well as work, religious, and other settings. Socialization practices and experiences in home settings during early and middle childhood are primary determinants in the formation of an individual's beliefs, values, and attitudes toward self and others.

As early as the seventeenth century, childhood was regarded by some philosophers as a unique stage of life and crucial to a person's behavior, beliefs, and attitudes in later years. John Locke, for example, urged parents to be patient with their children and show affection toward them. He also emphasized parental instruction to shape children's character. Jean-Jacques Rousseau, in some ways Locke's French counterpart, was an advocate of close bonding between mothers and their offspring. He urged parents to give children the freedom to develop their innate abilities but regulate their experiences. Early in the twentieth century, psychologists pointed out that socialization practices and other experiences in childhood might permanently influence a person's behavior and personality.

In his popular theory of personality, Sigmund Freud, one of the most influential psychologists of the twentieth century, suggests that childhood is a sensitive period in the formation of an individual's personality. The idea of a *sensitive period* refers to a time that is optimal for certain capacities to emerge and in which an individual is most susceptible to being influenced by things that are experienced. Often, psychological changes that occur during a sensitive period are relatively stable over time.[2] Thus, Freud's theory suggests that early childhood experiences, particularly with respect to a mother's socialization practices, are likely to be most influential in shaping social behavior and personality.

According to Freud's theory, children begin internalizing the beliefs and values of parents before school age. Influenced by the work of Freud, Erik Erikson, a prominent psychoanalyst in the latter part of the twentieth century, proposed a theory of development that supports the belief that experiences in childhood are likely to influence an individual's personality and social behavior through adulthood. Erikson noted that early childhood experiences are critically important in the formation of a person's conception of self as well as the establishment of relationships with other people. Erikson's theory suggests that the duration and consistency of parenting practices play significant roles in shaping a person's personality. In his seminal watershed book *Childhood and Society*, Erikson maintained that consistency in meeting children's needs from birth through two years of age is essential for the development of trust in others. Parenting practices that persist over time are likely to have a relatively permanent influence on an individual's personality. In other words, experiences that occur repeatedly during childhood are more likely to have a longer lasting influence on social behavior and personality development than experiences that rarely occur in a person's life. Findings derived from numerous studies in psychology suggest that children's behavior patterns, beliefs, and attitudes develop early. Moreover, many distinctive behavior patterns and personality traits associated with parenting practices and other childhood experiences tend to be relatively stable over time.[3] Therefore, it is not surprising that events in home settings are likely to receive a great deal of attention during personal reflections on one's life experiences.

Before reaching school age, many African American children are exposed repeatedly to racist behavior and racial inequities. The assumptions posited in Freud's and Erikson's theories suggest that race might be a relatively stable psychological construct in African Americans before they reach middle childhood. During sensitive periods in personality development, many African American children must deal with the significance of racial group membership on a daily basis. As noted earlier, findings reported in research on race awareness in young children indicate that African American children attribute significance to race before they enter kindergarten. Given the early emergence of race awareness in African American children, many African American parents are compelled to discuss racial issues with their young children and construct parenting practices in response to racial oppression. When African American children inquire about discrepancies between racial inequities and racial cooperation, parents are faced frequently with a dilemma that raises even more complex questions from children. The search for answers to such questions about race reinforces its significance for African American children.

Recognizing the criticality of early childhood experiences in the formation of personality, race most likely serves as a frame of reference for many African American children before they reach school age. Frames of reference are enduring dimensions of thinking that help people organize and interpret experiences. Because of the significance attributed to race in the United States, it probably becomes a more fixed and stable frame of reference for them as they grow older. As race becomes more fixed as a frame of reference in African American children, it exerts more influence on how they perceive themselves as well as other people.

On the other hand, native African and black Caribbean children grow up in societies in which they have minimal or no contact with people from other racial groups. Home, community, school, and other settings afford very few opportunities for black children in African and Caribbean societies to interact with people from other racial groups. While these children are likely to have knowledge about other racial groups through television, parents, and other people, it is unlikely that they attribute psychological significance to differences observed among racial groups. For these reasons, black parents in African as well as Caribbean societies are less likely than African American parents to face questions from their children concerning racial issues. In contrast to parenting practices in many African American households, it is unlikely that parenting practices in native African and Caribbean families are influenced by race. Therefore, native African and black Caribbean children receive fewer opportunities during early childhood than African American children for race to evolve as a frame of reference. Although transformations in thinking may occur at a later stage in a person's personality development, since early theories of personality suggest that the core of identity is formed during early childhood, it is unlikely that this transformation in thinking will change core identity structure at a later stage of personality development. If race evolves as a frame of reference after childhood in individuals, it is likely to be unstable. Consequently, these individual may be prone to use race as a frame of reference primarily in situations that are self-serving.

As can be seen here, while growing up in the United States at a very young age, black children are exposed to racial practices that might predispose them to attribute meanings and significance to race that are not shared by the vast majority of their counterparts with African bloodlines. Empirical studies have not provided evidence to support or refute this idea. Results from empirical studies that compare and contrast the different roles that race might play in the psychological functioning among people with African bloodlines have not been published. Conclusions drawn about race are derived often from anecdotal observations. It is important to note that anecdotal observations provide nonempirical evidence that can and often does perpetuate ignorance.

With an aim of providing a better understanding of the social and psychological significance of race among people with African bloodlines, I conducted studies to assess the significance of race in self-construction among the indigenous people in Ghana, African Americans, and people of African descents who live in the United States but were born in other countries. These studies investigated the changing meaning and significance of race, ethnicity, nationality, and religion among members of these groups. Several questions designed to shed light on the significance of race in the psychological makeup of persons in these groups guided the studies. For example, the following questions were of interest in this work: Do African Americans perceive race to be of paramount importance in self-construction? Do they perceive their ethnic group membership with other African Americans to be more important than either their religious, social class, or racial group membership with other people of African descents? Do African Americans feel greater allegiance to other African Americans than Americans in general? Is the changing significance of race likely to augment their relationship with other people of African descents?

In order to determine whether race might play a different role in the psychological functioning of African Americans in comparison to other members of their racial group, similar questions about Ghanaians also were of interest in this work. Do most Ghanaians perceive race as significant in self-identification? Do most Ghanaians perceive their ethnic identification to be more important than either their nationality, religious, class, or racial grouping?

As previously indicated, there is a paucity of empirical evidence that sheds light on the questions raised here. Empirical studies are guided by evidence obtained through direct observations in a systematic and objective manner. For most people, powerful belief systems guide their behavior rather than empirical evidence. As we know, belief systems can, either consciously or unconsciously, bias a person's judgments. Empirical evidence helps to keep in check our belief systems and predispositions to make assertions that may or may not be true.[4] To enhance empirical knowledge about the questions raised in this work, studies were conducted independently in both Ghana and the United States. Using two questionnaires to measure the significance of race, face-to-face interviews with participants were conducted. Participants and interviewers in these studies were unaware of the research questions that were being investigated. Study 1 denotes the research conducted in Ghana, and study 2 denotes the research conducted in the United States. Both studies required participants in the study to answer a series of questions asked by an interviewer. Participants were asked to provide explanations for their answers to the questions asked. The explanations provided were used in the interpretation of findings. Undergraduate students attending the University of Ghana, including one male and two females, served as interviewers and administered the questionnaires in study 1. Four male and eight female African American undergraduate students attending William Paterson University in New Jersey conducted interviews in study 2. Interviewers received training and instruction in research sampling procedures and interviewing before and during data gathering.

RESEARCH APPROACH IN STUDY I

In view of the fact that West Africa consists of many countries and within each country there are many different ethnic groups, it was beyond the scope of this research to focus on the entire region. Ghana, which is a country located in West Africa with a population of approximately sixteen million people, including approximately sixty-one different ethnic groups, was chosen to conduct the study presented here. Ghana was chosen for several reasons. First, inspired by the leadership of Nkrumah, race was used as a unifying theme to resist the British colonial rule in that region. Second, most ancestors of African Americans were transported across the Atlantic Ocean from Ghana. Third, Ghana has been a major center for Pan-African activities, and it has maintained friendly ties with other black nations in Africa. Fourth, unlike many other former colonies, there has not been a significant violent confrontation as a result of ethnic differences in Ghana. Fifth, the geography of Ghana made it more cost-efficient to travel and select participants in the study from each region in the country. Finally, because of the size of Ghana's population, it was possible to select a sample that was more representative of the population than it would have been in a larger West African country, such as Nigeria. Because of Ghana's distinctive history, some of the findings reported in this study may not be applicable to other countries in West Africa.

Participants in the study conducted in Ghana consisted of 366 Ghanaians, including 196 males and 170 females, randomly selected from 39 tribes. The average age for all participants was 35.6 years, with no significant difference between males and females. Using geographical location, tribe, occupation, and gender as strata, a stratified random sample was selected from the northern, middle, and southern regions of Ghana, with no less than 110 respondents chosen from each region. A stratified random sample was chosen by separating the population into nonoverlapping groups and then, randomly selecting participants within each group. In order to make the sample representative, respondents were selected from several villages in each region. Random sampling was evident in the diversity of each subgroup. For example, each subgroup consisted of members from different tribes and villages. There were no cases reported in which more than one member of the same immediate family was interviewed.

Participants reported sixty-seven different occupational positions. These positions were reclassified with the following membership representation in each subgroup: 80 unskilled workers, 52 skilled workers, 106 professional workers, 21 chiefs, 13 queen mothers, 52 college students, and 42 precollege students. A total of 200 participants indicated they have traveled to other countries, and 166 participants indicated they have not traveled outside of Ghana. The examiners introduced themselves as college students conducting research to assess Ghanaians knowledge about themselves and people living in other countries. To facilitate their cooperation and openness, participants were informed that their identities would not be disclosed. There were no reported cases in which a Ghanaian refused to cooperate.

An adaptation of a scale measuring closeness and social distance developed by Emory S. Bogardus was used to assess participants' reported closeness to people from different racial groups and nationalities.[5] The scale consisted of the following groups: Japanese, Jamaicans, Germans, white French, Arabs, black South Africans, Chinese, Nigerians, African Americans, white South Africans, Bahamians, white Americans, Liberians, black Brazilians, Barbadians, Russians, white English British, black Canadians, and Trinidadians. Factors reported to be of primary importance in self-identification were measured by a self-identification questionnaire developed by the principle investigator. The Bogardus scale employs a Likert-type, seven-choice response format. Participants were asked to indicate the number that best expressed their desired closeness to each group along with explanations. Using a range from (1) to (7), participants were presented with the following choices: (1) close enough for kinship by marriage; (2) close enough to be members of my association as personal friends; (3) close enough to live on my street as neighbors; (4) close enough for members of that group to be coworkers on my job; (5) close enough for citizenship in my country; (6) close enough as visitors only to my country; (7) would exclude from my country.

Factors reported to be of primary importance in self-identification were measured by a self-identification questionnaire developed by the principle investigator. Using a scale from (1) to (5), with (1) representing most important in defining self and (5) representing least important in defining self, the questionnaire was administered orally to each participant. Participants were asked to indicate the importance of the following groups in defining self (i.e., self-identification, self-construction) and to assign the appropriate numerical value: Africans in Africa; Ghanaians; tribe; my occupational group; my religious group; people of African descents around the world; and people residing in my community. Thus, the rating system employed here permitted respondents to assign the same numerical values to different groups. It should be noted that "people of African descents around the world" was used as an index for reference to race. Questions were presented in appropriate tribal language and responses were recorded in English. Following an analysis of the data, interviews were conducted with individuals who were members of the groups represented in the study. These individuals were not interviewed in the survey. They were asked to provide explanations for findings reported in the study. Their comments enriched the interpretation of the findings.

DETERMINANTS OF SELF-IDENTIFICATION AMONG GHANAIANS: FINDINGS AND CONCLUSIONS

In general, Ghanaians perceived nationality to be of greater importance in self-identification than any other self-identification factor used in the study. Among participants in this study, 61 percent ranked being Ghanaian to be of primary importance in self-identification. Using occupation as the criterion for classification, participants were divided into groups. For each group, the percent that ranked "being Ghanaian" to be of primary importance in self-identification is as follows: unskilled workers, 65 percent; skilled workers (tradesmen), 60 percent; professionals, 60 percent; undergraduate college students, 67.4 percent; students attending secondary schools, 59 percent; queen mothers, 55 percent; and tribal chiefs, 47 percent.

With approximately 54 percent of participants in the study reporting the tribe to be of primary importance in self-identification, it was second overall in importance when compared with other factors in this study. Tribal identification was reported to be of primary importance by 58 percent of unskilled workers, 48 percent of skilled workers, 52 percent of professionals, 49 percent of college students, and 47 percent of students attending secondary schools. The maintenance of stable family systems and long-standing traditions within the tribe may account for the strong tribal identifications reported among participants. The tribe plays an important role in shaping the values and beliefs of its members, especially among unskilled members. The relatively large number of unskilled Ghanaians reporting the tribe to be of primary importance in self-identification may reflect their dependency on its members and leaders in meeting needs that may not be met otherwise due to their limited resources and social status.

Tribal chiefs and queen mothers often exercise a great deal of local influence, especially among members of their tribes. As expected, the tribe was reported to be of primary importance in self-identification by more tribal chiefs (68 percent) and queen mothers (69 percent) than other self-identification factors in the study. However, approximately thirty percent (30 percent) of the chiefs and queen mothers did not report the tribe to be of importance in self-identification. This observation might reflect a declining significance of tribes in the governance of community life in Ghana. In an effort to enhance understanding of tribal chiefs' and queen mothers' perceptions about the importance of nationality and tribal affiliation in self-identification among Ghanaians, representatives from these groups were asked to provide explanations to account for the findings reported here. Excerpts from these interviews shed light on the complex interplay between nationality and ethnicity in self-identification for some Ghanaians.

Interviewer: What is important to Ghanaians when it comes to answering the question "Who am I?" I am interested in what is of primary importance for Ghanaians in terms of self-identification. What we found is that Ghanaians reported being Ghanaian was more important in defining themselves than all other things such as tribe, religion, occupation, and race. Why do you think we found what we found and what do you think it means?

Queen mother: When I talk to you, I will take myself first as a Ghanaian because if I see myself as a Ghanaian, I'm able to work and communicate with other Ghanaians from other parts of the country for the betterment of the entire country. If you put your tribe first, it changes your outlook completely. Especially when dealing with people from other ethnic groups you become prejudiced because every ethnic group has reservations about others. So you can't trust the person you are working with and so you're not able to share everything totally with the person whereas if you were working with someone from your ethnic group, you could trust that person with a number of things. So I feel that to be able to work and uplift our country, we should see ourselves as Ghanaians and not as tribal entities. We can then work well with each other in every field.

Interviewer: What is a queen mother? What is her role in this society? How long have you been a queen mother? How did you become a queen mother?

Queen mother: I'm a Queen mother in Otublohum. I was made the Queen mother in 1974. My role is to involve all the women in the family in our traditional celebrations. When they have problems, they come to me—both old and young. They talk to me about it and I accompany them to the Chief to sit and discuss until a solution is found. Then when there is a funeral for instance, the Chief and myself are informed. We visit the funeral house and also select elderly women to go and perform the necessary rites for the dead person in him or her house. We join the celebrations too. In actual fact the family bears part of the cost of the funeral. The family puts its contribution down first. A Queen mother is more or less the mother of family so everyone comes to you with their problems and you don't have to tell them you are busy and so can't be of help. I could for instance have said I'm busy and so can't receive you but I must not do that. I should be able to receive them anytime they come to me and discuss their problems and help find solutions.

Once you are a Queen mother, you're a Queen mother wherever you go. So in this neighborhood, anyone who is in difficulty comes to me.

Interviewer: So you play a very prominent role in the life of the larger family. You use the word family a lot. Could you tell what you mean when you use that word?

Queen mother: The Nii Kofi Appenteng family is the descendants of Nii Kofi Appenteng. He had four daughters. One had no offspring but the three had offspring. The descendants of these three form the family. I happen to be the Great grand daughter of a female descendant. I was made the Queen mother in Otublohum because I'm a descendant. In our system the Chief is in charge of decision-making. The Queen mother gives advice but the Chief may take it or not. He consults me when he is doing things and I give him my advice but he may choose to take it or not.

The responses of the queen mother reflect a communal orientation toward others. She views helping others, regardless of their ethnic background, as her duty. While noting on her duty to help others, the queen mother remarked, "It doesn't matter which tribe you're in. There was a time when an Akan woman came to tell me about problems she was having with her landlady. Someone told her there was a Queen mother in the area. So she came to see me and I went with her to see the landlady. I spoke on her behalf and she was allowed to stay in her room for three months more until she found another place and moved. You are not just for your people. You are for the community in which you live. If they have a problem, they will come to you. People even bring the children to stay with me. I have had three of such girls who stayed with me until they got married."

In reflecting on the importance of nationality and tribal affiliation in self-identification among Ghanaians, a chief also provided observations that reveal the complex relationship between these factors:

> **Chief:** From historical point of view, we could say that the Ghanaian was identified through the tribal line. So one considered himself a member of his tribe, then to a larger extent the country and then of the African continent as a whole. Now with development and civilization, the Ghanaian realizes that to be able to rub shoulders with his counterparts elsewhere, he must be identified first and foremost as a Ghanaian and an African. So I would say, in the larger context, from a world point of view, to be a Ghanaian is most important because we now have a feeling that tribalism tends to divide rather than build. So when we consider ourselves as Ghanaian and then as Africans, we work from our basic Ghana towards Africa and extend to the world. So I personally would like to be a Ghanaian first and foremost and then work towards the larger community outside of Ghana.

Identification with other native Africans was third in overall importance when compared to other self-identification factors in this study. Among participants in the study, approximately 47 percent reported Africans residing in Africa to be of primary importance in defining themselves. It was reported to be of primary importance by 49 percent of unskilled workers, 41 percent of skilled workers, 45 percent of professionals, 53 percent of college students, 49 percent of students attending secondary schools, 44 percent of tribal chiefs, and 57 percent of queen mothers.

There are several reasons that may account for Ghanaians perception of Africans residing in Africa to be of primary importance for self-identification. International trade and travel between countries in West Africa are steady and have a long history. Consequently, it affords many opportunities for lasting friendships to be established among West Africans. In addition, Ghana has served as a refuge for many Africans in exile from bordering countries. Therefore, many opportunities for bonding between Ghanaians and other Africans exist in Ghana. In view of the fact that countries in close proximity to Ghana were also former British colonies, their common oppression under British rule might have fostered bonding among many West Africans. Perhaps many Ghanaians remain committed to the notion of Pan-Africanism and feel a special bond to neighboring countries that have reciprocated cooperative and friendly engagements, especially in dealings with Western nations and other non-African nations.

Among participants in this study, 43 percent reported religion, 42 percent reported occupation, and 35 percent reported the community they reside in to be of primary importance in defining themselves. With a few exceptions, the ratings of these self-identification factors were relatively evenly distributed among the previously referenced groups. More unskilled workers (52 percent) and queen mothers (50 percent) reported religion to be of primary importance in defining themselves than other groups. They were followed by students attending secondary schools (47 percent), college students (46 percent), skilled workers (44 percent), professionals (34 percent), and tribal chiefs (31 percent). Religion appears to be a strong force in shaping the lives of many Ghanaians. It may serve to unite them in ways that overshadow tribal and class differences.

Results from groups reporting occupation to be of primary importance in defining themselves were as follows: 48 percent of students attending secondary schools, 46 percent of unskilled workers, 45 percent of chiefs, 43 percent of college students, 40 percent of queen mothers, 39 percent of skilled workers, and 39 percent of professionals. The opportunities for making changes in vocation and career occupations in Ghana are limited. Therefore, many Ghanaians remain in the same occupations throughout their employment histories.

Approximately 35 percent of the participants in this study reported the community they reside in to be of primary importance in defining themselves. More unskilled workers (39 percent) reported it to be of primary importance in defining themselves than members of other groups. The results from other groups were as follows: students attending secondary schools, 44 percent; queen mothers, 39 percent; chiefs, 35 percent; college students, 29 percent; skilled workers, 27 percent; and professionals, 24 percent. Many Ghanaians reside in communities with strong tribal ties. Thus, the interplay between tribe and community affiliations may account for some Ghanaians reporting the community they reside in to be of primary importance in defining themselves.

More unskilled workers (49 percent) and students attending secondary schools reported the community they reside in to be of primary importance than other groups. Given that unemployment rates were above 20 percent when participants were interviewed, unskilled workers and high school students were more likely to have greater economic dependency on local resources. Therefore, members of these groups would have a greater need to be connected to other community members.

MEASURING THE SIGNIFICANCE OF RACE IN GHANAIANS

As noted earlier, a major area of interest in this study is the significance of race in the psychological makeup of Ghanaians. Do they perceive race as a significant factor in the social and psychological descriptions of themselves? An analysis of results derived from the self-identification questionnaire suggests that most Ghanaians do not consider race as a primary factor in defining themselves. To measure the significance of race in self-identification, participants were asked to rate the importance of "people of African descents around the world." Only 30 percent of them reported "people of African descents around the world" to be an important factor in defining themselves. More queen mothers (55 percent) reported it to be of primary importance in self-identification than other participants in this study. Given the humanist persona of some queen mothers as well as the communal orientation vested in their roles, they are more likely than other groups in this study to identify with people outside of their primary reference groups. Therefore, some queen mothers' responses may have been guided primarily by humans in general rather than race.

Only 21 percent of professionals reported "people of African descents around the world" to be of primary importance in defining themselves. Results of the percent from the remaining groups that rated "people of African descents around the world" as a primary factor in defining themselves are as follows: 39 percent of skilled workers, 35 percent of unskilled workers, 29 percent of students attending secondary schools, 30 percent of college students, and 27 percent of the tribal chiefs. It should be noted that many Ghanaians do not consider people of African descents who were forcefully displaced outside of Africa to be African. For example, most native Ghanaians refer to African Americans residents in Ghana as *obruni*, which means "white" or "foreigner."

Recognizing that Ghanaians live in a society with very few Caucasians or foreigners from other continents, race is less likely to be needed in self-identification. It is more likely to be a secondary consideration in self-identification. In contrast to the experiences of African Americans, a minority group in a racially stratified society, the concept of race for many native Ghanaians may lack cultural content. Cultural resources are at the inner core of group identities in Ghana as well as other African nations. Many Ghanaians may not perceive special bonds with displaced people of African descents because of race.

Analyses of results derived from the Bogardus scale, which was used to measure desired or perceived closeness to people from various racial groups and nationalities, provide clues about Ghanaians' attitudes toward African Americans as well as the significance they attribute to the concept of race. Similarly to results derived from the self-identification questionnaire, participants reported desired closeness to Ghanaians was statistically significantly higher than to other groups in this study. This finding suggests that Ghanaians have made considerable progress toward bridging gaps of communication between different tribes in Ghana. Results concerning the desired or perceived closeness toward other groups reported by Ghanaians in this study do not show a consistent pattern in their attitudes toward race.

Ghanaians reported desired closeness to African Americans and black South Africans was statistically significantly higher than to other groups in this study. Their higher expressed closeness to African Americans and black South Africans may be due, in part, to the high level of media exposure and world attention given to racial problems confronted by these groups over many decades. Heightened awareness of the racial problems confronted by African Americans and black South Africans may have generated and sustained a great deal of empathy and sympathy among Ghanaians. Because of racial discord in the United States and South Africa, race may operate as a unifying theme in Ghana. Many black people in Ghana may be predisposed to make links between their racial problems and problems facing other people of African descents in the diaspora. For several decades, African Americans have been advocates for improving the conditions of people of African descents around the world. They have assumed the role as their "brothers' keepers." Moreover, improvements in the conditions of African Americans that have almost always resulted from protests and revolts have been accompanied often by revolts against racial oppression and exploitation in nations comprised of people of African descents. Do African Americans inspire other Africans to follow their lead? Do they look to African Americans for leadership and direction?

In recent years, many African Americans have traveled to Ghana seeking to establish business, cultural, and educational ties. Pan-African conferences reflecting collaborative efforts between African Americans and Ghanaians have been held in Ghana. Therefore, bridges for communication between African Americans and Ghanaians have been established and nurtured by representatives from both groups with support provided also by the government in Ghana. These activities have provided opportunities for friendship, partnerships, and other cultural exchanges to occur. It allows Ghanaians to interact with African Americans who have excelled in many professions. Given the profiles of African Americans who visit Ghana, it should increase the likelihood that Ghanaians would desire to be close to them—especially Ghanaians who have not traveled abroad.

Many Ghanaians view the United States as the richest and most powerful nation in the world. Because of effective political and economic activities in the United States, many Ghanaians perceive African Americans as the best-educated, economically affluent, and politically effective people of African descents in the world. Therefore, Ghanaians may desire the closeness of African Americans because of their political and economic effectiveness as well as the benefits they may derive from a relatively close relationship between themselves and African Americans. Excerpts from an interview with a tribal chief provide support for this hypothesis:

> **Interviewer:** During my previous interviews some respondents indicated that they viewed African-Americans in an eye of importance to a greater degree than they viewed other groups. Would you please comment on this observation?

> **Tribal Chief:** I think it's mainly because of their economic power. I read somewhere—I think it was in *Ebony*—that the African-American

economy is the fifth in terms of rank. I think we associate economic power with eminence. So we tend to value the whole United States. Until recently, Japan was insignificant on the political scene. But as they gained economic power, people see them as being on par with the United States and countries like Germany. So I think it is mainly an economic factor. Consider a country like Jamaica. It is a developing country. We are all members of African-Caribbean-Pacific Economic Association. Because we are equals, we are striving for development and so we have no reason to admire them. Jamaicans can't contribute to our developmental efforts, but African Americans can.

The chief's remarks indicate that Ghanaians desired closeness to African Americans is driven primarily by economic rather than racial considerations. A few Ghanaians expressed concern about Africans' role in the slave trade. Excerpts from an interview with a female Ghanaian college student indicate this issue may be significant to some Ghanaians:

Interviewer: The results from our study indicated that Ghanaians had a strong desire for closeness to African-Americans. I would like for you to share what you think might be reasons for this finding?

Female college student: Well, I think that somehow they feel some sense of guilt towards them that they sold them out into slavery and so at the very least, have an obligation towards them to make them feel wanted back. So basically I think that's the reason why.

An essay by G. Paschal Zachary published March 14, 2001, in the *Wall Street Journal* indicated that Ghanaians do not feel indebted to African Americans because of the slavery legacy of African ancestors.[6] Audrey Gadzekpo, a newspaper columnist in Ghana, put it this way "The African role in the slave trade is not an issue in Ghana. People here are totally detached from any guilt or responsibility for their ancestors selling other Africans into slavery. It's like there's some collective amnesia."[7] In spite of efforts to obtain citizenship by African Americans who live in Ghana, government officials in Ghana have shown very little interest in granting it to them. "We feel very betrayed," said Victoria Cooper, who heads the African American Association of Ghana. "It's like we've been hoodwinked. Ghanaians want our money, but they don't want us."[8]

African American music is very popular in Ghana. The accomplishments in music and athletics elevate the status of African Americans in Ghana. They have become idols and trendsetters for many Ghanaians. The accomplishments of many African Americans are on display in the museum at the Cape Coast in Ghana. School-age Ghanaian children are exposed to the museum on a regular basis. Several Ghanaians indicated that African Americans' accomplishments in music and athletics increase attractiveness of closeness to them. In response to a question about the desire for closeness to African Americans, a Ghanaian remarked, "I think in America itself, the dominant culture is African American culture. If you look at music and sports, they tend to be dominant and culture in America tends to dominate cultures throughout the world. So people tend to see more black Americans in Africa and they want to identify with them. . . . American culture is more appealing and extends further than that of smaller countries like Jamaica. I think this is an important reason because if you take Jamaica for example, their music is particularly important to Africa, but it is not as popular as African American music."[9]

Ghanaians that have not traveled abroad express a higher desire for closeness to African Americans than Ghanaians that have traveled abroad. In contrast to Ghanaians who have traveled abroad, Ghanaians who have not traveled abroad may have had contact with a very limited proportion of African Americans. African Americans who travel to Ghana are likely to be highly educated professionals who project a very favorable image of their ethnic group. On the other hand, Ghanaians who have traveled to the United States have had opportunities to have both pleasant and unpleasant interactions with African Americans across the socioeconomic spectrum. Moreover, they may have been in competition with African Americans for jobs and other resources. Therefore, many Ghanaians who have been to the United States may be less inclined to desire closeness to African Americans. Other Ghanaians who traveled abroad, but not to the United States, may also have a more objective perception of other nationalities than their Ghanaian counterparts who have not traveled abroad. They may be more knowledgeable of cultural differences and problems it may pose when diverse groups are brought together under conditions that foster permanent accommodation and assimilation on the part of the hosting group. Thus, Ghanaians who have traveled abroad may be more cautious about and less receptive to becoming permanent hosts for groups from other nations.

It is important to note that a careful review of Ghanaian responses in this study failed to reveal any reference to race as an explanation for their desired closeness to African Americans. Moreover, participants in this study reported higher desired closeness to white Americans, white British, and Japanese than to other groups comprised of African people. They expressed favorable views toward white Americans because of their work in the Peace Corps in Ghana. Several Ghanaians pointed out that Ghana needs the economic and technology assistance provided by the public and private sectors in the United States and Great Britain.

The results presented in this study strongly suggest that, for most native Ghanaians, race does not play a primary role in shaping their priorities. It does not seem to be of primary importance for them in establishing and maintaining close psychological bonds with other people of African descents around the world. On the other hand, the results suggest that Ghanaians may be more focused on the political and economic expediency of using race in establishing and maintaining relationships with African Americans.

RESEARCH APPROACH IN STUDY 2

This study included 147 native African Americans and 21 West African immigrants who resided in urban and suburban communities in the northeast region of New Jersey. The ages of participants in this study ranged from 13 to 48 years, with an average age of 22 years. African American and Caribbean American college students served as examiners and administered the questionnaires used in this study. Adaptations of the questionnaires used in study 1 were used also in study 2. It should be noted that in study 2, "being American" denoted nationality and "being African American" denoted an ethnic group. *Ethnic group* refers to a group set apart from others because of its national origin or distinctive cultural patterns.[10] Unlike study 1, study 2 included "cultural group" as a measure of self-identification.

In light of the racial and ethnic diversity in the United States, the Bogardus scale was expanded to include the following groups: Trinidadians, Filipinos, Puerto Ricans, Dominicans, Colombians, Mexicans, Cubans, Haitians, and Ghanaians. The procedures used in studies 1 and 2 were similar. The examiners introduced themselves as college students conducting research in partial fulfillment of course requirements. Each participant was told that answers to questions were confidential and names of participants were not recorded.

DETERMINANTS OF SELF-IDENTIFICATION AMONG AFRICAN AMERICANS: FINDINGS AND CONCLUSIONS

Recognizing that African Americans' interactions with other racial and ethnic groups vary within as well as between each state in the United States, it important to proceed with caution in generalizing the findings presented here to African Americans residing in other regions of the country. Thus, any conclusions derived from these finding should be viewed as tentative. Nevertheless, findings reported in this study should provide useful insights for understanding the psychological distinctiveness of African Americans.

Results derived from the self-identification questionnaire and Bogardus scale indicate race plays an important role in the psychological functioning of African Americans. Using procedures similar to those in study 1, participants in study 2 were asked to indicate the importance of different groups in defining self. They were asked to assign the appropriate numerical value, with (1) denoting most a part of and (5) denoting least a part of. An analysis of data derived from the self-identification questionnaire showed that, with few exceptions, participants in this study reported that "Africans in Africa," "African American," "cultural group," and "people of African descents around the world" were ranked significantly higher than other groups, such as "Americans," "my religious group," "people residing in my community," and " my occupational group." Thus, race and ethnic group membership were perceived as more important than nationality and religious group membership in self-identification among African Americans in this study. This finding indicates that the significance attributed to the concept of race in self-identification by African American participants in this study is different from the significance attributed to race by Ghanaian participants in study 1.

African American participants reported a higher preference for "closeness" to other people of African descents than to Caucasians in general. Commenting on the importance of perceived relationship with other people of African descents, approximately 54 percent of the respondents stated, "We are all alike or bonded in some way." However, African Americans reported a higher preference for "closeness" to white Americans than to other Caucasian groups in this study. African Americans also reported the same degree of preference for "closeness" to white Americans, West Indians, and Africans. For the duration of African Americans' existence, they have had firsthand contact in a variety of settings with white Americans. Results reported in June 2001 from a study conducted by the Joint Center for Political and Economic Studies shows that African Americans between ages eighteen and twenty-five lived more integrated lives and were more hopeful about race relationships in the United States than older African Americans. Approximately 87 percent among respondents in this group indicated that they interact on a regular basis with people from other ethnic and racial groups in the work settings. Approximately 85 percent of these respondents reported that the situation of black people in the United States was either better or about the same. Many younger, more formally educated African Americans are more similar in their psychological makeup and cultural practices to white Americans than to older, less school-educated other members of their racial group. These observations may account, in part, for the findings reported here.

Conversely, African American participants reported a higher preference for "closeness" to Latino Americans than white Americans and Africans. Latino Americans and African Americans are highly integrated in community, school, and work settings in the northeast region of New Jersey. Bearing this in mind, there is a great deal of social and cultural interactions between African Americans and Latino Americans who reside in this area. The absence of a major conflict between these groups suggests that they maintain mutual respect and cooperative relations. Anecdotal observations from schoolteachers and other educators suggest that, in some schools, African American and Latino groups often keep apart when not forced to interact in school activities. Therefore, opportunities for conflicts and confrontations between them may be reduced.

African Americans in this study reported a higher preference for "closeness" to other African Americans than to other groups. In response to a question concerning the importance of identification with African Americans, approximately 64 percent of the respondents said, "I am Americanized. It's who I am." On the other hand, approximately 31 percent of the respondents said, "I am very different from Americans." These observations suggest that African Americans may perceive cultural practices that serve to distinguish them from other members of their racial group. In addition, it also supports the hypothesis that African Americans perceive characteristics in their psychological makeup that distinguish them from other members of their racial group. African Americans also reported a higher preference for "closeness" to black West Indians than Africans. Historically, African Americans have had considerably more contact with West Indians than Africans. Moreover, intermarriages between African Americans and West Indians are more commonplace in the United States than intermarriages between African Americans and Africans. Several generations of African Americans are the offspring of West Indian immigrants, and therefore, it is not surprising that African Americans expressed a higher preference for closeness to West Indians.

DETERMINANTS OF SELF-IDENTIFICATION IN WEST AFRICAN IMMIGRANTS: FINDINGS AND CONCLUSIONS

African immigrant participants in this study included twenty-one Africans residing in urban communities in the northeast region of New Jersey. In light of the limited number of participants in this group, findings as well as conclusions reported here are tentative and should be considered with caution. The findings should raise questions that stimulate more research on determinants of self-identification among nonwhite immigrants in the United States.

African immigrants reported race, tribal group membership, and nationality as important determinants of self-identification. This finding suggests that the meaning and significance of race for African immigrants may change when they adapt to living in the United States. As previously reported, native Ghanaians did not perceive race as important in self-identification. An analysis of data derived from the Bogadus scale shows that African immigrants reported a higher desired "closeness" to African Americans than Caucasian groups as a whole in this study. They expressed no difference in preference of "closeness" between other groups in this study. That is to say, African immigrants made no distinction in preference of "closeness" on the basis of ethnic group membership and nationality. Furthermore, when white Americans were considered independent of other Caucasians in the data analysis, African immigrants made no distinctions in preference of "closeness" on the basis of race.

The significance attributed to racial group membership in the United States precludes African immigrants from escaping it in self-identification. Living in a racially stratified society forces people to become more sensitive to the role race plays in shaping attitudes and behavior. Although African immigrants may have been socialized in societies that did not attribute social and psychological significance to race, they become sensitive to racism and the plight of blacks in America shortly after they arrive. Consequently, the behavior of African immigrants might change in accordance to racial protocol in the United States. While African immigrants' attitudes about racism also might change, they may not change their original ways of thinking about the meaning and significance of race in self-construction. Given that African immigrants made no distinctions in preference of "closeness" to Caucasian groups and nonwhite groups in this study, it appears that race may not carry the same psychological and social significance for them as it does for African Americans.

CONCLUSIONS FROM AND IMPLICATIONS OF RESEARCH DATA

The data and other observations presented in this work indicate that racial practices in the United States contributed to transformations in the overall psychological makeup of African Americans. The concept of race is of paramount importance in the psychological functioning of African Americans. It has played a major role in the transformation of African Americans into an ethnic group with distinctive cultural practices and psychological characteristics. The centrality of race in the psychological functioning of African Americans predisposes them to focus on cultural similarities between themselves and other black people who have different histories. The meanings and significance African Americans attribute to race predispose them to define themselves in terms of a racial group rather than an ethnic group. Thus, they are prone to search for and embrace things that foster a sense of "we-ness" and bring them closer to other people of African descents globally. When racial tension increases in the United States, African Americans gravitate for support toward each other as well as other members of their racial group. In so doing, many African Americans tend to give less attention to their unique heritage and unique cultural practices. For this reason, they fail to embrace the unique features of African American culture that evolved from the unique experiences in their history in the United States.

Ghanaians as well as African immigrant participants in these studies defined themselves primarily in terms of nationality and tribal group affiliation. Race was, at best, a secondary consideration in self-identification for most members of these groups. In contrast to African Americans, members of these groups are not prone to attribute cultural content to the concept of race. Therefore, they are less likely than their African American counterparts to search for and embrace things that foster a sense of "we-ness" on the basis of race.

The role that the concept of race plays in the psychological functioning of African Americans predisposes them to feel obligated to shoulder responsibility for problems confronted by other people of African descents globally. The behavior and attitudes of many African Americans suggest that the meaning of race for them includes a collective conscience. This collective conscience is characterized by African Americans displaying empathy and sympathy for other black people they perceive are being exploited or mistreated by members of other racial groups. In keeping with commitments to racial solidarity, many African Americans believe it is their duty to help other blacks overcome racial oppression. For example, African Americans effectively used political and economic clout as well as moral persuasion in the United States to help dismantle apartheid in South Africa. They protested and conducted similar activities that helped restore the legitimate government leadership in Haiti. The Black Congressional Caucus and Trans-Africa have worked to ensure that the United States government adopts policies and practices that contribute to the economic development of African countries as well as other predominantly black countries.

While African American leaders have been consistently outspoken against racial oppression directed toward all people of African descents, the relative silence among them concerning ethnic genocide, atrocities, and oppression that occurred in African countries such as Rwanda, Liberia, Nigeria, Uganda, and Sierra Leone as well as slavery in Sudan poses several issues. Did African American leaders feel they could not influence the outcomes of these conflicts? Did lack of knowledge among African Americans about causes of these ethnic conflicts preclude them from intervening? Did African American leaders fear that by intervening, whites would exploit intra-racial group conflict (i.e., "divide and conquer") to justify unfavorable social and public policies toward people of African descents? Were African American leaders too embarrassed to speak out against such inhumane practices by members of their racial group? Unlike racial oppression, African American leaders may not have perceived ethnic nonracial conflicts in African countries as relevant to national or political interest of African Americans. Hence, they did not adopt an active role in settling these disputes.

African Americans have supported affirmative action as a policy for all people of African descents in the United States. Strong racial group identification has led African Americans to render help to other black people without expectations for reciprocity or accountability. African Americans' relentless struggle against racial oppression has helped to attract global attention and constructive action to remedy racism both nationally and internationally. In the absence of African Americans' protests against racism and advocacy for racial equality globally, the plights of all people of African descents would be in jeopardy.

Differences associated with the roles that race play in the psychological functioning of African Americans and other black people may contribute to conflicts and misunderstandings between them. It may preclude, for example, bridges of trust to emerge between African Americans and other blacks. It also may lead to miscommunication or breakdowns in communication between African Americans and other blacks, foster stereotyping behavior between them, and create and harden barriers that interfere with social and cultural exchanges that serve to enhance the well-being of each group.

8

TOWARD DEFINING
THE AFRICAN AMERICAN

In this long battle . . . the unforeseeable effects of which will be felt by many future generations, . . . the black man was motivated by the need to establish an identity. And despite the terrorization which the Negro in America endured and endures sporadically until today, despite the cruel and totally inescapable ambivalence of his status in his country, the battle for his identity has long ago been won. He is not a visitor to the West, but a citizen there, an American; as American as the Americans who despise him, the Americans who fear him, the Americans who love him—the Americans who became less than themselves . . . by the virtue of the fact that the challenge he represented was inescapable. He is perhaps the only black man in the world whose relationship to white men is more terrible, more subtle, and more meaningful than the relationship of bitter possessed to uncertain possessor.

—James Baldwin, *A Stranger in the Village,* 1953

WHO ARE AFRICAN AMERICANS? MAJOR INFLUENCES ON THE EVOLUTION OF AFRICAN AMERICANS

The psychological and cultural transformations that have led to the evolution of African Americans reflect more than 400 years of struggle driven by desires to survive, strive, and thrive in a society dominated by many Caucasians viewing them with contempt. The long history of racial oppression, racist behavior, and social rejection visited upon African Americans forced them to develop novel strategies to survive. African Americans were compelled to adapt to dehumanizing conditions in a racially divided society with cultural and social practices that were radically different from those in African societies. Under these conditions, the emergence of distinct behavioral patterns, ways of thinking, and counter-narratives among African Americans was inevitable.

The process of adapting to conditions in the United States made the psychological makeup and cultural practices of American-born blacks and native Africans noticeably different. Commenting on early artistic and psychological characteristics that distinguished blacks in America from native Africans, Margaret Just Butcher, in her popular book *The Negro in America Culture*, indicates that in contrast to the Africans' predominant concern for the arts of decoration and design, blacks in America focused on the arts of music, dance, and folklore. As early as the first generation of American-born blacks, Butcher suggests that the process of adapting to racial oppression and enslavement in a new society made blacks in America less similar to native Africans in terms of their attitudes and emotional demeanor.

Describing differences in emotional reactions and attitudes between blacks in America and native Africans, Butcher remarks:

> When the African was transplanted to America, more than a change of art forms and cultural patterns resulted. There was a reversal of emotional temper and attitude. The spirit of African expression, by and large, is disciplined, sophisticated, laconic, and fatalistic. The emotional temper of the American Negro has been exactly the opposite. What has often been thought of as primitive in the American Negro—his naiveté, sentimentalism, his exuberance, and his improvising spontaneity—is not characteristically African. Nor can these qualities be explained as an ancestral heritage. They are the result of the African Negro's peculiar experience in America, with its emotional upheavals, ordeals, and sufferings.[1]

Throughout the twentieth century, descendants of European American colonists maintained many racist policies and practices established by colonists. Thus, the process of adapting to a racist society necessitates changes in the psychological makeup of American-born blacks that also would enhance the distinctiveness of their behavior, attitudes, beliefs, and emotional expressions.

The climate and geographic conditions of the country in which people reside also influence cultural practices adopted by them. In comparing and contrasting cultural practices between native Africans and African Americans, Thomas Sowell, in his book *Ethnic America*, provides a thoughtful analysis of how the climate and geography in Africa shaped the distinctive cultural practices among Native Africans. Therefore, changes in the psychological makeup of blacks in America as well as the process of adopting practices needed for survival in their new physical environment necessitated changes in cultural practices among them.

AFRICAN AMERICAN CULTURAL PRACTICES

Shunned and denigrated from participating in the mainstream of American cultural life by white Americans, African Americans devised distinctive ways of expression that helped them to sustain and maintain their human dignity. W. E. B. Du Bois notes that African Americans aspired for recognition and acceptance of their own cultural and psychological distinctiveness. Du Bois believed that, in this way, African American's ethnic distinctiveness could be preserved and play a larger role in shaping American life. The process of adapting to racial oppression and racism along with racially motivated social rejection contributed to a sense of alienation among African Americans, especially young African Americans, toward many social, behavioral, and cultural practices in the United States.[2] Thus, rather than adopt standards of conduct set forth primarily by the dominant culture, African Americans commonly improvise or even radically change such practices in ways that reflect their own distinctive modes of expression.

My research findings presented in the previous chapter show that African Americans report "being African" as more important than "being American" in self-identification. A review of comments provided by forty-three respondents suggests they mean that race (i.e., being of "African descents") comes first in self-identification and being American comes second in self-identification. In response to a question concerning the importance of "being African" in defining self, 43 percent of respondents indicated that they either "did not know about them" or "did not relate to them at all." Respondents who ranked "being African" to be of primary importance in defining self, provided the following explanations: "I was born in Africa but I live in America," "My parents are Africans," or "My ancestors are African." Commenting on the primary importance of "people of African descents around the world" in defining self, 59 percent of the respondents reported, "We are all alike or bonded in some way, so we feel close." However, analyses of respondents' comments concerning the primary importance of "being African-American" in defining self suggest that they may construe "being African" in terms of their African American ethnic group membership rather than a connection to other people of African descents. For example, commenting on the primary importance of "being African-American," 74 percent of the respondents made one or more of the following remarks: "I am Americanized. It's who I am," "I live with them in my country and I identify with them," "We seem and relate as the same." Approximately 17 percent of respondents' comments show that they assigned the highest numerical ranking to "being American" in defining self.

It has been suggested that rejection and hostility by white Americans forced African Americans to view themselves as estranged from feeling American. Although African Americans have experienced racial hostility and discrimination, Howard McGary notes, "They have been able to construct and draw upon institutions like the family, church, and community to foster and maintain a healthy sense of self in spite of the obstacles that they have faced."[3] Alienation among African Americans has compelled many of them to draw from their strengths and devise creative means of expressions. Today, young African Americans adopt distinctive styles of dress (i.e., baggy pants, sleeveless shirts), verbal expressions (i.e., chill out, that's cool, I feel you, He/She dissed me, He/She sonned you), nonverbal expressions (i.e., handshakes, body gestures), and dancing that other racial and ethnic groups subsequently adopt.

DANCING

Dancing always has been a popular mode of artistic expression among African Americans. African Americans create new dances at such rapid pace that records of them are not well maintained. While dancing, spontaneity and freedom of expression are common among African Americans. They improvise and display graceful body and creative foot movements in both solo and group dancing. While dancing, many African Americans display rhythm that begins within as a body vibration, and as dancing progresses, they often become more engrossed in it. African American dancers often display unrivaled skills to elaborate upon a basic rhythm by changing, doubling, and skipping beats.[4] The large repertoire of dancing styles crafted by African Americans mirrors a sophisticated blending of African-rooted rhythm and African American soul. This soul reflects creative emotional expressions that are by-products of African Americans' adaptation to racial oppression and racism in American society. The creative and colorful qualities in modes of expression that characterize young African Americans have helped to make them popular trendsetters among people of African descents throughout the diaspora.

LITERATURE

The writings of prominent African American literary scholars, such as Langston Hughes, James Weldon Johnson, Paul Laurence Dunbar, Zora Neale Hurston, Claude McKay, Countee Cullen, James Baldwin, Ralph Ellison, Amiri Baraka, Richard Wright, Niki Giovanni, Sonia Sanchez, Alice Walker, Gwendolyn Brooks, Henry Louis Gates Jr., Maya Angelou, and Toni Morrison, provide a growing body of universally acclaimed literary materials that depict the greatness and distinctive characteristics of African American literature. These writings capture the distinctive and complex emotions that often are hidden in the African American experience. *The Norton Anthology of African American Literature*, edited by Henry Louis Gates Jr. and Nellie Y. McKay, provides an excellent comprehensive presentation of major works by literary scholars who have pioneered the distinctiveness and defined the tradition of African American literature. Since 1990, numerous books authored by African Americans have won literary prizes and appeared on the best seller list of the *New York Times*. In 1993, Toni Morrison, won the Nobel Prize for literature, and for writings on the life of W. E.

B. Du Bois, David Levering Lewis was awarded a Pulitzer Prize in 2001.

Although literary critics question the literary merits of it, African American literature of the 1920s and 1930s was unquestionably original and American in the truest sense. The literary movement during this period expressed African American resolve to maintain human dignity in spite of white American determination to deny them of it. The following poem, "The White House," by Claude McKay offers a vivid testimony that supports this observation:

> Your door is shut against my tightened face,
> And I am sharp as steel with discontent;
> But I possess the courage and the grace
> To bear my anger proudly and unbent,
> The pavement slabs burn loose beneath my feet,
> A chafing savage, down the decent street;
> And passion rends my vitals as I pass,
> Where boldly shines your shuttered door of glass.
> Oh, I must search for wisdom every hour,
> Deep in my wrathful bosom sore and raw,
> And find in it the superhuman power
> To hold me to the letter of your law!
> Oh, I must keep my heart inviolate
> Against the potent poison of your hate[5]

Sylvestre C. Watkins observes that illiteracy and racism stifled the development of African American literature.[6] In writings about the limited universal literary merits accorded earlier African American literature, Gates and McKay note that as a result of racially motivated practices and policies which denied blacks access to formal education, African American literature did not begin to flourish until well into the 1900s.[7] During the past decade, African American literature has made tremendous progress toward attaining universal recognition. African American literature has grown steadily as an academic field of study in higher education institutions in the United States. However, reliance for exposure and judgment of African American literary scholarship on the larger American literary community imposes limits on the rate of growth and cultural influence of African American literature.

MUSIC

Music always has been of central importance in African American culture. From the beginning of United States history to the present, the distinctive cultural qualities in the musical expressions by blacks in America have been apparent. Both spiritual and secular music created by African Americans have achieved eminent respectability and universal meaningfulness, especially the blues and jazz. The distinctive originality of the melodies and harmonic styles of African American music has achieved recognition as the most original and valuable musical strain in America. Since 1894, spirituals, American black's most serious religious emotional creation, have been considered the main strand in American folk song. Antonín Dvořák used spirituals to represent American atmosphere in his symphony *From the New World*.

Sentimental expressions of grief, hard luck, and disillusionment are frequent motifs in the blues. During the early 1900s, jazz rhythm, harmony, and creative improvisation evolved from the blues. With the creation of jazz music, African American musicians devised new techniques of playing wind and brass instruments, including saxophones, trumpets, trombones, and clarinets. Jazz music has been foremost in shaping the universal distinctiveness of American music. Influenced by the creative vocal sounds, such as voice slurs, changes of harmony, and quavers, that often characterize African American singing, jazz musicians use instruments to simulate these vocal sounds. The freestyle improvisation and interpolation employed by jazz musicians played a tremendous role in shaping the distinctiveness of the American music culture.

Traditionally, music served as a popular, and often the only, venue blacks used to express their sufferings, needs, desires, hopes, and dreams. Music is a cultural expression that allows for the masses to collectively engage their feelings and talents. Jazz, spirituals, and the blues not only express the deep complex emotional experiences of African Americans, but also they touch the human spirit of people in general across the world.

Similarly to the blues, the themes contained in popular contemporary secular music developed by African American artists in this era, such as hip-hop and rap music, also depict tragedies, irony, and disillusionment in the lives of young African Americans residing in poor urban communities. Unlike the lyrics of blues that focused often on the joys and sorrows of sex and love affairs between a man and woman, lyrics used in rap music reflect alienation between the sexes and the defiant voices of youth who perceive themselves as powerless, rebelling outcasts in the larger main society. Anger, bitterness, frustration, and aggression often characterize lyrics in rap music. As can be seen in excerpts from lyrics from of a popular hip-hop song, "Rock N Roll," young African American youth perceive themselves as outcasts and are pleading for help.

> (Huh) My grandmomma was raised on a reservation
> (Huh) My great-grandmomma was, from a plantation
> They sang—songs for inspiration
> They sang—songs for relaxation
> They sang—songs, to take their minds up off that fucked up situation
> I am . . . yes I am . . . the descendant (yes yes)
> Of those folks whose, backs got broke
> Who, fell down inside the gunsmoke
> (Black people!) Chains on they ankles and feet
> I am descendants, of the builders of your street
> (Black people!) Tenders to your cotton money
> I am . . . hip-hop[8]

Although both hip-hop and rap music are folk in character, these musical forms have gained universal appeal among youth in their relatively brief history. The universal appeal of hip-hop and rap music may indicate commonalities in the frustrations shared among youth, adolescents, and young adults living in societies that are strongly influenced by Western values and practices.

ARE AFRICAN AMERICANS A "NEW PEOPLE"?

Historical and empirical observations presented in this work provide support for the claim that no other factor has been more potent in shaping the psychological distinctiveness in African Americans than the meanings and significance attributed to the concept of race by white Americans. In response to social peculiarities inherent in a racially stratified society, the concept of race acquired psychological properties and emerged as a unifying theme for blacks in the United States. In light of the dominant social, political, and economic position of white Americans in the society, African Americans were compelled to give psychological significance to the concept of race because white people have also done so. For most of their existence, African Americans were forced to use race as a primary factor in shaping their hopes, career aspirations, dreams, and so on. Race conveyed meanings beneath the skin for them. Race served as a benchmark for governing the social and cultural practices they adopted. Race continues to play a key role in structuring many aspects of their daily activities.

The intimate relationship between people's psychological makeup and cultural practices is widely recognized. The cultural practices adopted by members of a group almost always reflect attitudes, beliefs, ways of thinking, and emotional attitudes shared among them. Thus, meanings and significance attributed to the concept of race have been major forces in shaping the distinctiveness in the psychological makeup and cultural practices among African Americans.

Characterized by a strong sense of duty to be loyal, caring, protective, and committed to the well-being of members of their racial group, oppressed communal orientations among African Americans have been maintained primarily by racial oppression and racism. On the other hand, the attainment of individual rights and liberties guaranteed by the United States Constitution also allowed African Americans to adopt individualistic orientations. The interactions between these different orientations illuminate dualism in frames of reference that African Americans employ to interpret and respond to situations they encounter. The oppressed communal and individualistic orientations operate in combination with race as frames of reference in African Americans. This complex interplay in ways of thinking denotes distinctiveness in the psychological makeup of African Americans.

Through the process of adapting to the European American cultural and social practices in a racially stratified society, African Americans have evolved into a "new people" or a relatively new ethnic group. African Americans display behavior characteristics, as well as ways of thinking, that distinguish them from other members of their racial group. Even when African Americans display cultural expressions that appear similar to cultural expressions by other people of African descents, such as singing, dancing, and shouting, the historical context and meanings of these expressions are likely to be different.

Social and psychological factors associated with the meaning of race change a great deal from one decade to another, especially in the United States. Racial meanings among African Americans are strongly influenced by their knowledge about and understanding of themselves as well as by the way white Americans treat them. Conditions that influence the meaning and significance attributed to race frequently change over time. Reflecting on the changing meaning of race, Michael A. Omi points out that the meaning of race in the United States changes constantly.[9] The concept of race derives its meaning in a society structured by forms of inequality that are organized along racial lines. Therefore, as long as interactions between African Americans and white Americans are organized along racial lines, race will play a significant role in the psychological functioning of African Americans. Given the fluidity of racial meanings, the psychological makeup among African Americans could change a great deal from one generation to the next. Thus, if social and psychological meanings attributed to race significantly change in the United States, fundamental differences in the psychological makeup between African Americans born during the second quarter of the twenty-first century and their predecessors should follow.

LOOKING AHEAD: IS RACISM DYING? IMPLICATIONS FOR THE PSYCHOLOGICAL SIGNIFICANCE OF RACE

Taking into account that racial policies and practices in the United States have changed considerably since 1954, the social significance and psychological significance of race have fluctuated considerably among African Americans. Although racism is still a major concern among African Americans, many legal barriers that impeded their progress toward racial equality have been removed. In general, younger generations of African Americans are likely to be less dependent upon race as a frame of reference than older African Americans. The concept of race might operate already as a secondary consideration for making judgments among African American children that consistently have favorable social contact with white American children.

In his writings about *The Nature of Prejudice*, Gordon W. Allport points out that social contact that promotes true acquaintance between opposing groups reduces hostile attitudes they hold toward each other. He maintains that both knowledge about and acquaintance with members of opposing groups lessens hostility toward them. Allport also indicates that casual contacts characterized by a lack of openness in communication between opposing groups makes matters worse than before.

In a review of studies on the effectiveness of personal contact as a method of reducing intergroup hostility, Cook reports that it can produce favorable attitudes when:

1. the situation promotes equal status interactions between members of the opposing groups;
2. the contact encourages behavior and dialogues that breakdown stereotypes that the groups hold of each other;
3. cooperative behaviors are required to achieve goals shared among members of both groups;
4. the situation must have high "acquaintance potential" of promoting intimate contact between participants;
5. the social norms in the situation must be perceived as favoring intergroup acceptance.[10]

As previously noted, results from national public opinion polls show steady improvements in white Americans' attitudes toward racial integration, but results from several social surveys also indicate that they hold negative racial stereotypes about black people. *Stereotypes* refer to widely held beliefs that people have certain characteristics because of their membership in a particular group.[11] *Racial stereotypes* and *ethnic stereotypes* refer to widely shared beliefs about members of particular racial or ethnic groups. Stereotypes reflect unreliable generalizations about members of a group that fail to take into account individual differences.[12] Racial and ethnic stereotypes can affect people's perceptions about, behavior toward, and interactions with members of the stereotyped group.[13] Furthermore, members of a stereotyped group almost always are cognizant of the racial or ethnic stereotypes other groups share about them. Unpleasant defensive reactions as well as accusations of racism by African Americans commonly follow when white Americans display behaviors or express ideas that reflect racial stereotyping toward them in their presence.

Racial stereotyping of African Americans reinforces the significance of race in their psychological functioning as well as sharpens the racial divide between white Americans and African Americans. Results reported from several studies show that negative stereotyping of African Americans is a widespread practice among white Americans. In *The Scar of Race*, Paul M. Sniderman and Thomas Piazza indicate: "Whites will not openly endorse negative racial stereotypes for fear of appearing to be racist, large numbers of them—rarely less than one in every five and sometimes as many as one out of every two—agree with frankly negative characterizations of blacks."[14] Characterizations of African Americans as being "not too bright," lazy, happy-go-lucky, irresponsible, lacking in motivations to help themselves, and violence prone are widely shared among white Americans.[15] Most white Americans attribute these negative characterizations of blacks to environmental defects and group cultural traditions rather than innate predispositions. During the early and mid-twentieth century, these negative characterizations were more likely to be construed by white Americans as the products of natural endowment.[16] But regardless of the explanations employed by white Americans to account for negative racial stereotyping, the implications of it are rooted in the assumption that the stereotyped group is inferior to them. Explanations given to account for negative racial stereotyping do very little to reduce the pain and suffering of the stereotyped group.

A danger in negative racial stereotyping is the self-fulfilling prophecy potential. A self-fulfilling prophecy is an incorrect assumption about a situation that comes to pass because people accept the incorrect assumption and act on it to make it become true.[17] That is to say, if select members of a group hold negative racial stereotypes about members of another racial group, either consciously or unconsciously, they could arrange conditions in a manner that leads to behavior by members of the stereotyped group that supports their negative racial stereotypes. For example, believing that blacks are ignorant, lazy, and irresponsible, white managers in a large corporation assign black employees less challenging and significant tasks than other employees. Black employees are promoted less frequently than their white, Latino, and Asian coworkers.

In response to managers' contempt, the black employees reduce their performance levels and use more personal and sick days during the year than other employees. In this example, the white managers confirm the negative racial stereotypes in the process performed by the self-fulfilling prophecy. Furthermore, this example illustrates how negative racial stereotypes can be maintained and used by whites to justify racial discriminatory behavior.

The interplay between negative racial stereotyping and the self-fulfilling prophecy also may occur in academic settings. Consider, for example, that a white professor believes that African Americans are more limited in their abstract reasoning abilities than other racial and ethnic groups. While teaching a class comprised of African American students, the professor "dumbs down" the instructional material. To "dumb down" instructions involves spending too much time dwelling on concepts that are relatively easy to grasp and giving very little or no attention to concepts and topics that require higher reasoning skills. Bored, disappointed, and insulted, the students may display openly a disinterest in the class. They may be inattentive and talk among themselves during class meetings. They may arrive late and leave early or sporadically show up for classes. They also may exert minimal effort to prepare for examinations in the course. Consequently, their overall class performance on examinations is poor. The professor would perceive the students' attitudes and poor test performance as confirmation of her/his beliefs about their cognitive abilities. As can be seen here, the professor confirmed the process of the self-fulfilling prophecy and reinforced the negative racial stereotype. Furthermore, the professor's behavior shows how stereotyping helps to confirm that members of a stereotyped group should be treated as unequal humans and denied the same benefits afforded members of the dominant group.

Because of the close relationship between a person's attitudes and actions, white Americans who share negative racial stereotype beliefs about African Americans could display racial insensitivity unintentionally. In an article published November 19, 1996, in the *New York Times* about complaints of racial discrimination at Texaco Inc., the following experience reported by an African American employee vividly shows the damaging effect of negative racial stereotyping:

It had started as one of the happiest birthdays in Sheryl Joseph's life. The day before, Ms. Joseph, a secretary at Texaco's office in Harvey, Louisiana, had learned she was pregnant with her second child. She had shared the good news that day in 1988 with her Texaco colleagues, who at the time were preparing a little office party. Ms. Joseph's boss walked forward with a birthday cake. But her smile fell as she looked at the cake. On the top was drawn a black woman, obviously far along in a pregnancy. The dark skin and huge Afro on the woman offended Ms. Joseph, for she never had an Afro and was light skinned. But it was the words on the cake that took her breath away. "Happy birthday, Sheryl," the cake read. "It must have been all those watermelon seeds." "When I saw the inscription" she said, I just kind of stared at it and said, Oh, thank you. "I didn't feel I could get angry. I had just found out I was pregnant. I needed my job."[18]

Racist insults help to maintain and strengthen the significance of race as a primary frame of reference in African Americans. Reflecting on her experience at Texaco, Joseph remarked, "I hate to say I was discriminated against, because I have always been a black person who hates to use that. But that is what it was." While it appears that Joseph's boss did not intend to insult her, racial sensitivity was overshadowed by her boss's racist beliefs.

The examples presented here show how micro-aggressions and individual and institutional racism can persist even after legal barriers that perpetuate racism have been removed. Reductions in racial stereotyping between white Americans and African Americans could contribute to fundamental changes in the role that race plays in the psychological functioning of African Americans. Substantial improvement in the quantity and quality of contact between these groups is likely to reduce racial stereotyping and enhance communication between them.

Even though contact between African Americans and white Americans has increased steadily since 1954, racism has sharply curtailed progress toward reducing racial tension and hostility. When members of one racial group exercise power (i.e., political, economic, social, military, etc.) intended to devalue the humanity of members of another racial group, this practice denotes racism. Racism is a belief system that involves the denial of equal treatment of members of a racial group by contending that they are either genetically or culturally inferior.[19] Racism can reflect conscious and deliberately harmful intentions toward a person or group, or it can involve harmful consequences toward individuals without those who harm them intending to harm them on racial grounds or without any intent to harm them.[20] Actions defined as racism range from racial slurs, insults based on race, day-to-day socioeconomic discrimination, education discrimination, and job discrimination to national rules of exclusion from all social, civil, or political rights. Racism can be viewed from both individual and institutional perspectives. *Individual racism* involves an action performed by one person or a group that produces racial abuse, such as verbal or physical mistreatment. *Institutional racism* refers to discriminatory racial practices and policies built into prominent structures such as the political, economic, and education systems. It involves a discriminatory legacy of past racist behavioral patterns maintained from eras when racist actions were widely accepted.[21]

Many African Americans are forced to deal with individual racism routinely or daily. Combating institutional racism poses a more formidable challenge for the larger African American community. In writing about the significance of race and racism, Charles Bates Doob, professor of sociology, contends "institutional racism is the prime factor in maintaining racism."[22] Studies show that while institutional racism is not as blatant as it was before 1954, it still persists on a wide scale in the United States. Because institutional racism is impersonal and often not immediately apparent, it can be refuted more easily than individual racism. People in general are more predisposed to deny the existence of institutional racism or adopt the attitude of "out of sight, out of mind." Institutional racism can spread unnoticed from one institution to another. For example, public funding levels for urban school districts often lag behind public funding levels in affluent suburban school districts. High property tax rates in affluent suburban communities contribute to differences in school funding levels. Many poor urban school districts consist of a relatively high percentage of African American children, and the vast majority of children enrolled in suburban school districts are Caucasians. Parental involvement with education visually is higher in suburban than in poor urban school districts. Thus, better education resources are available to children attending suburban schools than their counterparts in poor urban school districts. Given that formal education background is a minimal prerequisite for high-skill positions in the United States, most African American children attending poor urban schools are denied systematically an equal opportunity to the economic benefits afforded white children attending suburban schools.

Some observers contend that, frequently, African American children in poor urban school districts do not take advantage of the educational opportunities the schools provide. Many children effectively change the school environment in a manner that is more congruent with their "street world." Fearful of being labeled as "nerds" or desire to be accepted as members of the "in crowd," scholarship and academic achievement are devalued by many students in urban schools. In schools dominated by students with negative attitudes toward scholarship, it is relatively easy for teachers to lose sight of their professed aim to foster students' thinking, learning, and achieving.[23] Under these circumstances, a decline in teachers' and students' morale is inevitable. Thus, *while institutional racism* contributes to underachievement in poor urban school districts, students, teachers, and parents also share the blame. Without sufficient parental involvement to counteract anti-school peer-group influence, the peer group often wins and can destroy the learning atmosphere as well as teacher morale in school settings.

Although legal as well as legislative actions are taken frequently to remedy the racial inequities, many white Americans express objections and engage in actions to resist such changes. In general, African Americans perceive these actions of white Americans as racist. For this reason, in part, white Americans' efforts to dismantle affirmative action programs are viewed as institutional racism by many African Americans. Critics of affirmative action programs argue that the most advantaged reap more than the truly disadvantaged African Americans from these programs. They also assert that employing lower standards for African Americans is racist because it suggests that they cannot meet the same standards that whites can. Accordingly, a poor white boy is less "protected" (i.e., he cannot get affirmative action benefits) compared with children of affluent, educated African American families. This situation represents unjust reverse discrimination from their vantage point.

President Lyndon B. Johnson supported affirmative action to rectify racial inequities caused by racial discrimination. Although laws were passed that prohibited racial discrimination in housing, employment, and academic settings, past racist practices restricted opportunities for many African Americans to acquire qualifications commensurate with white Americans. While the validity of qualifications required to fill positions is rarely tested, to justify giving preference to white over black applicants, critics of affirmative action argue that it is not racism but rather differences in their qualifications. Traditionally, the lack of qualifications has been a popular explanation used to support racial discrimination.

Virginia Held, a highly acclaimed philosopher and supporter of affirmative action, asserted that to make reasonable progress in achieving social justice for women and racial minorities, affirmative action would be necessary.[24] Anything less, she maintained, would constitute an affront to the self-respect of members of these groups. Bernard Boxill, professor of philosophy at the University of North Carolina in Chapel Hill, and McGary contend that "since women and racial minorities were discriminated against and excluded because of their race and sex, they now deserve to have their race or sex taken into account because it is the only reasonable way to compensate them for the disadvantage they now experience."[25] They also argue that even if African Americans of middle and upper income families benefit more from affirmative action programs than poor African Americans, it does not necessarily follow that they are not entitled to it. These philosophers point out that it is unreasonable to assume that educated and economically affluent African Americans experience less racial discrimination than poor African Americans. Recognizing that African Americans of middle and upper income families are likely to have more opportunities to have contact with white Americans in work, academic, and community settings, it seems logical to conclude that they experience more racial discrimination than their disadvantaged counterparts. Conversely, it could be argued that discrimination directed at poor African Americans might be greater because they are less able to fight it effectively.[26] Debates surrounding the fairness of affirmative action often arouse strong negative emotions of supporters and non-supporters of it, especially when discussants consist of members from different racial groups. However, these discussions are needed because they can serve to enhance African Americans' and white Americans' understanding of each other. If these discussions are guided by careful thought and reasoning, they can serve as important prerequisites for closing the racial divide in the United States.

Notable scholars, such as William Julius Wilson, have deemphasized the significance of racism in accounting for the economic and social disparities between African Americans and white Americans.[27] However, results derived from several studies indicate that while racism may be subtler than in the past, it remains widespread in the United States, especially institutional racism. In his book, *Disintegration: The Splintering of Black America*, Eugene Robinson describes events during the past decade that show patterns of institutional racial discrimination affecting African Americans in all income levels. There is a large body of evidence in work settings, criminal-justice systems, and housing that shows widespread racism in both institutional and individual forms.

The widely published racial discrimination lawsuit settlements at Texaco, Inc. in 1997 and Coca-Cola in 2000 indicate the depth and breadth of institutional racism in work settings in the United States. Texaco, Inc. paid out $176 million and Coca-Cola paid out $192.5 million to settle racial discrimination lawsuits brought by African American employees in these respective corporations. The lawsuits claimed that these corporations discriminated against black salaried employees in pay, promotions, and evaluations. Evidence derived from an investigation reported in the *New York Times* in 1996 revealed numerous examples of blatant racism that were standard operating practices at Texaco. The following excerpt from an incident report illustrates an example of racism at Texaco that is not unique in white-dominated industries in the United States:

> Michael Moccio, a manager in the oil giant's Denver office, had read the company's equal-opportunity policies and guidelines on proper conduct toward other employees. So when Mary Devorce, a black accountant in that office, filed a complaint with the government in 1991, contending she had been subjected to racism at Texaco, Moccio was ready. First, he assured Ms. Devorce that, Texaco would treat her fairly. To demonstrate the company's concern, Moccio even offered her new duties that would remove her from the situation she found discriminatory. It was all going exactly as it should. Then Moccio, who is white, called his supervisor, Jim Woolly, a white assistant controller in Houston. He filled in his boss on the complaint and described how he had handled it. Woolly was not impressed, according to a sworn affidavit by Moccio. "I'd fire her black ass," Woolly responded. When Moccio protested that Texaco could not dismiss someone for contending she was a victim of discrimination—a

move that saved Ms. Devorce—Woolly shrugged it off. "I guess we treat niggers differently down here," he replied according to the affidavit, filed in a federal discrimination suit.[28]

Although antidiscrimination and equal-opportunity policies are in place at larger corporations, such as Texaco and Coca-Cola, they are often ineffective. With minimal oversight by top executives, midlevel or senior managers in large American corporations often operate by their own rules. An overwhelming majority of these executives are Caucasians. There is only "token" representation of African Americans in midlevel and senior level executive positions in many corporations. Evidence presented in the *New York Times* article indicated that of the 873 executives at Texaco who were receiving more than $106,000 annually, slightly more than 6 percent were black. The article also revealed that while the number of executives in the highest pay grade had grown 44 percent over a span of four years, to 49, not a single black person held such a job. The *New York Times*'s revelations about racism in corporate America suggest that many white managers' decisions in the workplace are influenced by negative racial stereotypes. Midlevel and senior-level managers play central roles in defining the norms that guide employees' behavior and attitudes. By condoning norms that promote institutional racism, employees help in perpetuating racist practices in the workplace.

An overwhelming majority of complaints of racial discrimination in the workforce are never mentioned in popular news media. Consequently, the larger public may be poorly informed about the depth and breadth of institutional racism in the workforce. In July 2001, the United States Equal Employment Commission reported a $635,000 settlement of a racial discrimination lawsuit filed against Salomon Smith Barney, the nation's second largest retail brokerage firm. The thirteen plaintiffs reported that they were subjected to disparate treatment and harassment based on their race and/or national origin. Table 2 provides data on the total number of charge receipts filed and resolved under Title VII of the Civil Rights Act of 1964 compiled by the Office of Research, Information, and Planning from the U.S. Equal Employment Opportunity Commission. As can be seen, more than 55,385 complaints have been filed each year since 1992, with no significant decline in recent years. These statistics are disturbing because they show that racially motivated tension in the workplace may be widespread in the United States. Furthermore, policies and practices aimed to remedy institutional racism in the workplace may not be as effective as needed. As long as African Americans perceive or experience racism in the workplace, race most likely will play a central role in the psychological functioning of African Americans.

As noted earlier in chapter 4, most African Americans do not believe that they receive the same treatment as white Americans in the criminal justice system at the municipal, state, and federal levels of government. Many African Americans do not believe that white law-enforcement agents are sincerely concerned about protecting their property, human rights, and civil rights. They believe that individual racism, as well as institutional racism, is pervasive in the criminal justice system.[29] Many African Americans believe that being an African American makes you a suspect in the eyes of white law-enforcement agents. African Americans are more likely than white Americans to be stopped, searched, arrested, and imprisoned. Results derived from a national survey conducted by the Gallup Poll in 1999 showed that 36 percent of African Americans had unfavorable opinions of their local police, and 26 percent had unfavorable opinions of state police. There was no noticeable difference in the responses among blacks based on education and income levels.

In recent years, "racial profiling" has become recognized as the criminal justice system's most blatant display of racial oppression and institutional racism. Racial oppression involves the unjust exercise of authority or power by representatives of a dominant group over members of a subordinate group based upon race. Racial profiling occurs when the police target individuals for investigation on the basis of race, national origin, or ethnicity.[30] However, it is widely held that white law-enforcement officers use race as a primary criterion for selecting candidates to stop for questioning on possible minor driver violations. Thus, racial profiling involves the use of race to determine which drivers to stop for minor traffic violations and the use of race to determine which motorists or pedestrians to search for contraband. Racial profiling shows how negative racial stereotyping can trigger racist behavior in white law-enforcement officers.

Gallup Poll analyses in December 1999 revealed that racial profiling was perceived as widespread, especially among young black men. Respondents were asked to respond to the following question: "It has been reported that some police officers stop motorists of certain racial or ethnic groups because the officers believe that these groups are more likely than others to commit certain types of crimes. Do you believe that this practice, known as 'racial profiling,' is widespread or not?" The results indicate 77 percent of blacks said that racial profiling was widespread compared to 56 percent of whites. Approximately four out of ten African Americans reported that they had been victims of racial profiling. Results derived from a survey conducted in 2001 by the Gallup Poll indicated that approximately nine out of ten whites feel that they are treated fairly by state or local police, compared to barely half of blacks. As can be seen here, the gap between blacks and whites in perceived treatment by law enforcement agents is larger than the gap reported in 1999. Undoubtedly, racial profiling has strengthened many African Americans' perceptions that there is a systematic bias based upon race in the United States criminal justice system. On the other hand, considerably fewer whites than African Americans share the belief that the criminal justice system is racially biased.

The discrepancies in perceptions about racial profiling and social injustices between African Americans and white Americans can precipitate frustration and exacerbate feelings of hopelessness among African Americans. In his essay entitled "Racism, Social Justice, and Interracial Coalitions," Howard McGary contends that African Americans' lack of confidence in the criminal justice system produces frustration, especially in young African Americans. Many African American children are taught that all men are created equal and they live in a just society. But as they mature, their lived experiences with racial profiling and other social injustices reveal the fallacies in previously learned assumptions about racial equality and social justice. They begin to realize that the idea that racism is a thing of the past in American society is a myth. It is a dream that may not come to fruition in their lifetime. Thus, racial profiling frustrates young African Americans' dreams about a just society by showing them that Jim Crow justice is alive and well in the United States. Clearly, racial profiling experiences enhance the meaning and psychological significance African Americans attribute to the concept of race. Racial profiling may increase African Americans' hostility toward and distrust of white Americans.

Although racial discrimination in housing is illegal under the 1968 federal Fair Housing Act, it has been a consistent complaint among African Americans. To remedy racial discrimination in housing, in 1998, the U.S. Department of Housing and Urban Development (HUD) conducted a massive housing discrimination audit and expanded fair housing enforcement activities. In announcing the audit, Andrew Cuomo, secretary of HUD, remarked, "It is disturbing that after 30 years of fair housing enforcement, we still need to fight this fight, but report after report, complaint after complaint, only confirms the need for this audit.[31]

Despite massive efforts to combat it, racism in housing is alive and well in the United States. In an August 5, 2001, article on racial discrimination in housing, the *Washington Post* reported that housing discrimination is a problem in the Washington, D.C., area, including surrounding communities in Virginia and Maryland. Commenting on results from a study on housing discrimination conducted by Gregory Squires and Samantha Friedman, professors of sociology at George Washington University, Squires states, "Black home-seekers simply do not enjoy the same opportunities as whites in the Washington area. Blacks . . . are about half as likely to obtain their first choice of housing unit, even after controlling for differences in income, education, housing tenure, and their place of residence."[32] They found that 33 percent of blacks surveyed said that they "were not able to move into their first choice of housing, as compared to 20 percent of their white counterparts." According to the researchers, money or credit worthiness was not a factor.

Given the long history of racism in the United States, it stands to reason that African Americans should be quite sensitive to it. As noted earlier in chapter 1, from early ages through adulthood, many African Americans witness or directly experience racism in their daily lives. African Americans' attitudes toward racism reflect many years of conditioning, and as such, the extinction of these attitudes also may take many years. In keeping with principles in classical conditioning theory, the removal of racism from our society is a prerequisite for eliminating social ills caused by it. Therefore, as long as racism exists in the United States, the concept of race almost certainly will convey meanings beneath the skin for African Americans and serve as a unifying theme among them.

VISIONS OF HOPE

Historically, African Americans and white Americans have had more contact with each other than with other ethnic or racial groups. The cultural influence that each group has had on the other has been well documented throughout history. Describing the role of blacks in shaping American society, Margaret Just Butcher contends that the lives of black Americans and white Americans were interlocked through successive generations. Butcher states, "Together, and only together, they have interwoven the vital, sturdy patterns of American society. Together they have been responsible for both the basic characteristic structure of American society and the dynamic social changes that distinguish a democratic society from others."[33] While African Americans and white Americans may be more similar to each other in their psychological makeup and cultural practices than to most other ethnic or racial groups, racial hostility and distrust often preclude them from focusing on things they share in common. With a decline of racial hostility, African Americans and white Americans would be more inclined to explore and embrace shared beliefs, opinions, social interests, and so on. Therefore, if opportunities for personal contact between African Americans and white Americans are expanded and encouraged, then racism is likely to decline at a more rapid pace than in the past.

Favorable changes in racial attitudes between African Americans and white Americans since the Supreme Court ruling in the 1954 case of *Brown v. Board of Education* support the theory that an effective way to change people's attitudes is to first change their behavior.[34] The Court's ruling that segregation was unconstitutional forced African Americans and white Americans to have more contact in social, educational, community, and work settings. It also forced white Americans to be more tolerant, humane, and civil toward African Americans. If individuals with racist attitudes are compelled to be in situations in which they must engage in positive social interactions with members of the despised group, this inconsistency or dissonance in their behavior and attitudes will result in changes of attitudes to justify the new behavior.[35] Accordingly, dissonance creates an unpleasant state of tension that motivates people to reduce it by changing their attitudes.

Racism is driven by a variety of factors, including irrational fears, fantasies, and personal as well as economic insecurities. Commenting on economic insecurity and self-esteem, Gordon W. Allport writes:

> The apprehensive and marginal man is vaguely terrified at any signs of ambition or progress on the part of any member of the out-group, whether or not it may constitute a realistic danger. . . . Economic worries have their origins in hunger and the need to survive. But they continue to exist long after this rational function has been fulfilled. They ramify into the need for status, prestige, and self-esteem. Food is no longer the issue, nor is money—excepting so far as it can buy that one thing in life that is always short in supply: *differential status*.[36]

Allport also notes that while it is widely assumed that not everyone could be "on top" in any society, most people want to be higher on the status ladder than they are. Personal and economic insecurities may exacerbate racist feelings when members of a racial group are forced to acknowledge, with equal status, people from other racial or ethnic groups that they deem inferior to them. However, if individuals with racist attitudes are forced repeatedly to engage nonracist behavior, then these racist feelings could be short-lived. Dissonance theory suggests that the inconsistency in people's behaviors and attitudes propel them in the direction of attitude change. Therefore, individuals may be predisposed to change their racist attitudes to accommodate nonracist behavior.

Racial hostility in the United States stems largely from a long-standing racial conflict, namely: the desire of many white Americans to maintain superordinate-subordinate relationships that were established with African Americans approximately four hundred years ago—their public and psychological wage—and the desire of African Americans to change these relationships. Undoubtedly, this superordinate-subordinate paradigm is inherently racist, and as such, it promotes hostility and tension between these groups. The complete extinction of the superordinate-subordinate relationships between white Americans and African Americans is necessary to eliminate racism and defuse racial hostility between them. The elimination of racism would bring about dramatic transformations in the psychological makeup of African Americans and white Americans alike. For example, the significance of race in making judgments about themselves and others would diminish. Thus, race would no longer be pivotal in the psychological functioning of most African Americans and white Americans. Consequently, communication between African Americans and white Americans would improve, and expanded opportunities for bridges of trust should almost certainly evolve between them. If racism continues to decline in a slow "snail-like" manner, then long-lasting partnerships and cooperative ventures between African Americans and white Americans could be forestalled indefinitely.

According to the United States census report of 2000, the population in the United States is more racially and ethnically diverse than ever before. Moreover, the growth rate in the nonwhite population is proceeding at a faster rate than the Caucasian population. The American Spanish-speaking population, which consists of a large variety of ethnic groups, is the fastest growing population in the United States. The growth of ethnic groups could give rise to ethnocentrism in the United States. *Ethnocentrism* involves an ethnic group putting its interest and well-being ahead of other groups. When an ethnic group believes that its mode of living, values, and patterns of adaptation are superior to those of other groups, this refers to ethnocentrism. Henry Louis Gates Jr., director of the W. E. B. Du Bois Institute and professor at Harvard University, contends that ethnocentrism will be the problem of the twenty-first century. If ethnocentrism becomes a major problem in the United States, African Americans will be forced to rethink the nature of their racial group membership identity. They also will be forced to reconsider how they should relate to members of their own racial group, Caucasians, Latinos, and other nonwhite groups.

African Americans are approaching a "crossroads" with respect to their relationships to other groups. As noted earlier, since the seventeenth century, race has served as a unifying theme among them. They consistently have displayed an interest in native Africans and other African descendants in the diaspora. Traditionally, African American leaders have denounced racial oppression and racially motivated exploitation of African descents globally. Reciprocity has not played a role in African Americans' initiatives on behalf of other black people. Symbolic gestures of gratitude are rarely extended to African Americans for the advocacy role they play.

During the coming years, African Americans are likely to learn more about the distinctiveness of their history, cultural practices, and psychological makeup. With growth in knowledge about and understanding of themselves, fewer African Americans are likely to perceive the concept of race in terms of cultural and psychological connections to other people of African descents. They would be predisposed to focus primarily on commonalities among members of their ethnic group. The relationship between African Americans and other people of African descents could change. African American leaders may explore partnerships with other people of African descents as well as other ethnic groups and nations from the standpoint of collective self-interest. The feasibility of partnerships with other groups would be more carefully examined.

Recognizing that African American participants in the study reported here expressed a stronger desire for closeness to each other followed by Latino Americans than to other members of their racial group, the significance of race globally for African Americans already may be declining. Therefore, if African Americans increasingly embrace their group distinctiveness, they may become more selective in rendering support on behalf of other nonwhite groups or nations. In a word, African American leaders may be more inclined to raise questions concerning the benefits and costs for African Americans that may result from helping other groups.

As can be seen, African Americans could be faced with making decisions concerning the path they will follow in shaping relationships with other racial and ethnic groups. They could choose to maintain strong racial group membership ties and provide unconditional support for black people in general, regardless of differences in nationality or ethnicity. They also could choose to establish partnerships and cooperative ventures with other African descendants, Caucasians, or other nonwhite ethnic groups that would be mutually beneficial to all parties involved. In pursuing this option, African Americans could be at risk of becoming involved in interethnic or interracial disputes that may lead to undesirable consequences. This option also could increase the risk of African Americans perpetuating ethnocentrism.

Embracing and extolling their American nationality is a viable option for African Americans to pursue. African Americans are Americans in the truest sense. Denied freedom to partake of native African cultural practices as well as European American cultural practices, blacks in America were forced to develop novel cultural practices to facilitate their adaptation to a new world. Conversely, early British settlers adopted cultural practices acquired in Europe. The conduct and organization of early American institutions were guided by British colonial rule. Therefore, early American culture reflected replications of British cultural practices. Over time, many cultural practices developed by blacks in America were infused into the dominant European American culture.[37] This infusion process enriched and contributed to the distinctiveness of many American cultural practices.

Writings about early black American heroes and heroines, such as Benjamin Bannaker, George Washington Carver, David Walker, Fredrick Douglass, Phyllis Wheatley, Sojourner Truth, and Harriet Tubman, show that they yearned to be recognized as Americans, but racism denied them that opportunity. Writings and speeches by African American heroes and heroines of the twentieth century, such as James Weldon Johnson, Alain Locke, Carter G. Woodson, W. E. B. Du Bois, A. Philip Randolph, Adam Clayton Powell Jr., Charles Drew, Martin Luther King Jr., Ida B. Wells, and Mary McLeod Bethune, indicate that they also yearned to be recognized as Americans, but racism denied them that opportunity. Blacks in America have fought and died in all American wars as well as made substantial contributions in all areas that have elevated the United States to the level of greatness it has achieved. Undoubtedly, African Americans have irrefutable reasons to extol their pride in being American.

In writings about "the problem of double consciousness," Du Bois eloquently pointed out that African Americans could champion and embrace both African American ethnicity and American nationality without a contradiction. He noted that the peculiar racial experiences of blacks in America equipped them with abilities to maintain coherence and a sense of pride in their ethnic as well as nationality identities. Traditionally, African Americans' pride in "being American" has been influenced by white Americans' attitudes and behaviors toward them. Both individual racism and institutional racism have been and remain major obstacles that frustrate and preclude many African Americans from taking pride in "being American."

The changing dynamics of America's "race problems" demonstrate humans' enormous capacity to change long-standing attitudes, beliefs, and behavior as well as the capacity to resist change in the same, even when faced with contradictive evidence. For example, blacks in America witnessed their legal status change from being subhuman with no rights to citizens with the same rights guaranteed by the United States Constitution to any American citizen. During their struggle for legal recognition as citizens with the same entitlements afforded other Americans, African Americans were able to cling to their human dignity while adapting to conditions that threatened their existence as members of the human family. Throughout blacks' struggle, white academicians presented evidence to justify racial discrimination and racial inequities. White theologians used the pulpit to do the same. White legislators introduced bills that helped to maintain racial inequities. The capacity to sustain and maintain human dignity for any subordinate group against the overwhelming odds that faced blacks in the United States is a testimony that humans can make fundamental changes in their attitudes and beliefs if they strongly desire to do so. Thus, white Americans can rid themselves of racism if they strongly desire to do it.

The elimination of racism would change the course of American history, and race problems eventually would become extinct in the United States. If a substantial majority of Americans expressed a strong desire to eliminate racism, especially institutional racism, race problems could be sharply reduced during this decade in the United States. However, the concept of race is still likely to carry significant meanings beneath the skin for African Americans long after the social healing process from racial turmoil has ended. The ugliness of racial supremacy always should be remembered to ensure that it does not play a major role in shaping the direction our society takes as it moves ahead. African Americans should never forget that racial oppression, racism, and racially motivated social rejection transformed them from people of African descents living in America into African Americans, a "new people."

NOTES

INTRODUCTION

1. Joseph L. Graves, *The Emperor's New Clothes: Biological Theories of Race at the Millennium* (New Brunswick, NJ: Rutgers University Press, 2005), 193–96.

2. Michael Omi and Howard Winant, *Racial Formation in the United States: From the 1960s to the 1990s*, 2nd ed. (New York: Routledge, 1994), 53–77, 95–118. See also ibid.

3. Howard Dodson, "'What's at Stake?' Re-defining African-American" (keynote address, conference at Hunter College of the City University of New York, organized by the Global Afro Latino and Caribbean Initiative (GALCI), March 27, 2007).

4. Thomas A. Parham, Joseph L. White, and Adisa Ajamu, *The Psychology of Blacks: An African-Centered Perspective* (Upper Saddle River, NJ: Prentice Hall, 1999).

5. Faye Belgrave and Kevin W. Allison, *African American Psychology: From Africa to America* (Thousand Oaks, CA: Sage, 2006).

6. Ibid., 36–42. See also Janet Helms, *Black and White Racial Identity: Theory, Research, and Practice* (New York: Greenwood, 1990).

7. Sherle L. Boone and Steve Buyske, "A Test of Racial Conceptualization between African Americans and Indigenous Africans," *Social Identities* 14, no. 3 (2008): 313–31.

8. W. E. B. Du Bois, *Black Reconstruction in America: 1860–1880* (New York: Free Press, 1965), 700.

CHAPTER I

1. Ivan Hannaford, *Race: The History of an Idea in the West* (Washington DC: Woodrow Wilson Center, 1996), 187–207.

2. Ira Berlin, *Many Thousands Gone: The First Two Centuries of Slavery in North America* (Cambridge, MA: Belknap Press of Harvard University Press, 1998).

3. Audrey Smedley, *Race in North America: Origin and Evolution of a Worldview* (Boulder, CO: Westview, 1993), 171–77; Edmund S. Morgan, chapters 15–18 in *American Slavery, American Freedom: The Ordeal of Colonial Virginia* (New York: Norton, 1975), 295–388; Theodore W. Allen, chapter 13 in *The Invention of the White Race: The Origin of Racial Oppression in Anglo-America* (London: Verso, 1997), 203–22.

4. Theodore W. Allen, *The Invention of the White Race: The Origin of Racial Oppression in Anglo-America* (London: Verso, 1997), 203–4.

5. Smedley, *Race in North America*, 174.

6. Allen, *The Invention of the White Race*, 212–22.

7. Ibid., 239–44.

8. Ibid., 177–80.

9. Gary B. Nash, *Red, White, and Black: The Peoples of Early America* (Englewood Cliffs, NJ: Prentice-Hall, 1982), 283.

10. W. E. B. Du Bois, *Black Reconstruction in America* (New York: Free Press, 1992), 10.

11. Cheryl L. Harris, "Whiteness as Property," *Harvard Law Review* 106, no. 8 (1993): 1709–91, 1718.

12. Thomas R. R. Cobb, *An Inquiry into the Law of Negro Slavery in the United States* (Philadelphia: Johnson; Savannah: Williams, 1858), 66–69; Harris, "Whiteness as Property," 1720.

13. David Roediger, *Wages of Whiteness: Race and the Making of the American Working Class* (New York: Verso, 1991).

14. Noel Ignatiev, *How the Irish Became White* (New York: Verso, 1996).

15. Du Bois, *Black Reconstruction*, 27.

16. Smedley, *Race in North America*, 41–70; Audrey Smedley, "Social Origins of the Idea of Race," in *Race in 21st Century America*, ed. Curtis Stokes, Theresa Meléndez, and Genice Rhodes-Reed (East Lansing: Michigan State University Press, 2001), 1–24.

17. Smedley, *Race in North America*, 52–61; Leonard P. Liggio, "English Origins of Early American Racism," *Radical History Review* 3, no. 1 (1976): 1–36.

18. Smedley, *Race in North America*, 60.

19. John C. Greene, *Science, Ideology, and Worldview: Essays in the History of Evolutionary Ideas* (Berkeley: University of California Press, 1981).

20. Smedley, *Race in North America*, 171–73.

21. Ibid., 27–28.

22. Ibid., 28.

23. Kwame A. Appiah, *In My Father's House: Africa in the Philosophy of Culture* (New York: Oxford University Press, 1991), 28–46; Naomi Zack, *Thinking about Race* (Belmont, CA: Wadsworth, 1998), 1–7; Stephen Jay Gould, *The Mismeasure of Man* (New York: Norton, 1981); Ashley Montagu, *Statement on Race* (New York: Oxford University Press, 1972), 40.

24. Montagu, *Statement on Race*, 40.

25. William I. Thomas and Dorothy Swaine Thomas, *The Child in America: Behavior Problems and Programs* (New York: Knopf, 1928), 572.

26. Howard Winant, "The Theoretical Status of the Concept of Race," in *Theories of Race and Racism: A Reader*, ed. Les Back and John Solomos (London: Routledge, 2000), 181–88.

27. Joyce E. King, "Dysconscious Racism: Ideology, Identity, and the Miseducation of Teachers," *Journal of Negro Education* 60, no. 2 (1991): 133–46, 135.

28. Ibid., 135.

29. Jean Barby, "Blacks Paid Dues for Other Minorities," *Home News Tribune*, June 21, 2009.

30. Irving Leonard Markovitz, *Leopold Senghor and the Politics of Negritude* (New York: Atheneum, 1969).

31. Joshua A. Fishman, "Language and Ethnicity" (unpublished paper presented at a conference on ethnicity in Eastern Europe, University of Washington, Seattle, 1976), quoted in *Ethnic Groups in Conflict*, ed. Donald L. Horowitz (Berkeley: University of California Press, 1985), 59–60.

32. A. Adu Boahan, *Topics in West African History* (London: Logman Group Limited, 1966), 110.

33. W. E. B. Du Bois, "The Conservation of Races," in *Negro Social and Political Thought, 1850–1920*, ed. Howard Brotz (New York: Basic Books, 1966), 489.

34. David Levering Lewis, *W. E. B. Du Bois: Biography of a Race, 1868–1919* (New York: Holt, 2000).

35. Appiah, *In My Father's House*, 28–46.

36. Paul T. Zeleza, *Rethinking Africa's Globilization*, vol. 1, *The Intellectual Challenges* (Trenton, NJ: Africa World, 2003).

37. Frank Tannenbaum, "Slavery, the Negro, and Racial Prejudice," in *The United States and Latin America*, ed. Herbert L. Matthews (Englewood Cliff, NJ: Prentice-Hall, 1947), 46–52.

38. Stanley M. Elkins, *Slavery: A Problem in American Institutional and Intellectual Life* (Chicago: University of Chicago Press, 1968), 74.

39. Tannenbaum, "Slavery, the Negro, and Racial Prejudice," 46–52.

40. Orlando Patterson, *Rituals of Blood: Consequences of Slavery in Two American Centuries* (Washington, DC: Civitas/CounterPoint, 1998), 1–67.

CHAPTER 2

1. Smedley, *Race in North America*, 171.

2. Berlin, *Many Thousands Gone*, 20–23.

3. Ibid., 1–14.

4. Thomas Gossett, *Race: The History of an Idea in America* (Dallas, TX: Southern University Press, 1975), 28–31.

5. Allen, *The Invention of the White Race*, 240–51.

6. Ibid., 52–61, 85–90.

7. Berlin, *Many Thousands Gone*, 102–5.

8. Ibid., 95–108.

9. Berlin, *Many Thousands Gone*.

10. Ibid., 97.

11. Ibid., 121.

12. Ibid., 100.

13. Winthrop D. Jordan, *White over Black: American Attitudes toward the Negro, 1550–1812* (New York: Norton, 1968), 28.

14. Virginia General Assembly, *Virginia Slavery Act*, state law, 1705. Reprinted in *Statutes at Large: Being a Collection of All the Laws of Virginia*, vol. 2, ed. Williams Waller Hening (Richmond, VA: Samuel Pleasant, 1809–23), 270.

15. Jeremy Bentham, *The Theory of Legislation 69* (New York: Oceana, 1975), 1690, quoted in Harris, "Whiteness as Property," 1729.

16. Georg Lukacs, *History and Class Consciousness*, trans. Rodney Livingstone (1971), 83, quoted in Harris, "Whiteness as Property," 1730.

17. Hannaford, *Race: The History of an Idea in the West*, 187.

18. Eugene D. Genovese, *Roll, Jordan, Roll: The World the Slaves Made* (New York: Vintage Books, 1974), 54–59.

19. Berlin, *Many Thousands Gone*, 2–3.

20. Ibid., 3.

21. Smedley, *Race in North America*, 51–52; Allen, *The Invention of the White Race*, 17–24.

22. Richard Delgado and Jean Stefancic, *Critical Race Theory: An Introduction* (New York: New York University Press, 2001), 6–9.

23. Genovese, *Roll, Jordan, Roll*, 432.

24. Berlin, *Many Thousands Gone*, 120.

25. John W. Blassingame, *The Slave Community: Plantation Life in the Antebellum South* (New York: Oxford University Press, 1979), 20–24; Genovese, *Roll, Jordan, Roll*, 394–98.

26. Sterling Stuckey, *Slave Culture: Nationalist Theory and the Foundations of Black America* (New York: Oxford University Press, 1987), 8–17.

27. Du Bois, *Black Reconstruction*, 3.

28. Berlin, *Many Thousands Gone*, 251–69.

29. Ibid., 95–108.

30. Daniel C. Littlefield, *Rice and Slaves: Ethnicity and the Slave Trade in Colonial South Carolina* (Urbana: University of Illinois Press, 1991), 2.

31. Peter H. Wood, *Black Majority: Negroes in Colonial South Carolina from 1670 through the Stono Rebellion* (New York: Knopf, 1974), 34–62.

32. Littlefield, *Rice and Slaves*, 81.

33. Berlin, *Many Thousands Gone*, 152–53; Berlin, *Generations of Captivity: A History of African-American Slaves* (Cambridge, MA: Belknap Press of Harvard University Press, 2003), 77–81.

34. Thomas Jefferson Wertenbaker, "Patrician and Plebian" (doctoral dissertation, University of Virginia, Charlottesville: Michie, 1910), 212.

35. Berlin, *Generations of Captivity*, 67–81.

36. Berlin, *Many Thousands Gone*, 198.

37. Berlin, *Generations of Captivity*, 58–59.

38. Gary B. Nash and Jean R. Soderlund, *Freedom by Degrees: Emancipation in Pennsylvania and Its Aftermath* (New York: Oxford University Press, 1991), 55.

39. William H. Tucker, *The Science and Politics of Racial Research* (Urbana: University of Illinois Press, 1994), 9–12.

40. Smedley, *Race in North America*, 184.

41. Joseph L. Austerwell and Thomas L. Griffiths, "Seeking Confirmation is Rational for Deterministic Hypotheses," *Cognitive Science* 35, no. 3 (2011): 499–526; Nancy E. Furlong, Eugene A. Lovelace, and Kristin L. Lovelace, *Research Methods and Statistics: An Integrated Approach* (Stamford, CT: Cengage Learning, 2000), 13.

42. David Hume, *Essays: Moral, Political, and Literary*, ed. T. H. Green and T. H. Grose, 2 vols. (London, 1875), 1:252. From a footnote added in the 1753–54 edition of his essay "Of National Characters," first published in 1748.

43. Smedley, *Race in North America*, 184.

44. Jordan, *White over Black*, 123.

45. Smedley, *Race in North America*, 13–36.

46. Jordan, *White over Black*, 137.

47. Ibid., 110–15.

48. Ibid., 112.

49. Georgia State Legislature, "An Account of the Negroe Insurrection in South Carolina (1739)," *The Colonial Records of the State of Georgia, 1737–40* (New York: AMS, 1970), 22:232–36.

50. Jordan, *White over Black*, 212–14; Berlin, *Many Thousands Gone*, 138–39.

51. George Whitefield, *Three Letters from the Reverend Mr. G. Whitefield . . . Letter III. To the Inhabitants of Maryland, Virginia, North and South Carolina, Concerning Their Negroes* (Philadelphia, 1740), 15; also printed in *New England Weekly Journal*, April 29, 1740; also printed in L. Tyerman, *The Life and Times of the Rev. John Wesley, M.A., Founder of the Methodists*, 3 vols. (London,1870–71), 2:132; quoted in Jordan, *White over Black*, 214.

52. John Woolman, *Consideration in Keeping Negroes; Recommended to the Professor of Christianity, of Every Denomination. Part Second* (Philadelphia, 1762), reprinted in *Journal and Essays of Woolman*, ed. Gummere, 353, 363, 366–68, 380.

53. Jordan, *White over Black*, 310.

54. Ibid., 281.

55. Anthony Benezet, *Short Observations of Slavery, Introductory to Some Extracts from the Writing of the Abbe Raynal, on that Important Subject* (Philadelphia, 1781), 11–12; Hewat, *Account of S.C. and Ga.*, 2: 101; Wesley, *Thoughts upon Slavery*, 47; Hopkins, *Dialogue Concerning Slavery*, 44; Rush, *Address upon Slave-Keeping*, 2.

56. Ibid.

57. Quoted in James Oliver Horton, *Free People of Color: Inside the African American Community* (Washington, DC: Smithsonian Institution Press, 1993), 148. Lyman H. Butterfield, Wendell D. Garrett, and Marjourie Spraque, eds. *Adams Family Correspondence*, vol. 1 (Cambridge, MA: Harvard University Press, 1963), 369.

58. Ibid., 150.

59. Quoted in Jordan, *White over Black*, 290. David Cooper, "Serious Address on Slavery," 12–13, *Boston Massachusetts Spy*, January 28, 1773.

60. Berlin, *Generations of Captivity*, 103.

61. Thomas Paine, *The Complete Writings of Thomas Paine*, ed. Philip Foner, 2 vols. (New York: Citadel Press, 1945), 2:15–19; quoted in Jordan, *White over Black*, 291–94; quoted in Berlin, *Many Thousands Gone*, 220; quoted in Berlin, *Generations of Captivity*, 100.

62. Berlin, *Generations of Captivity*, 100.

63. From the Methodist Resolution of 1784, quoted in Lucius C. Matlock, *The History of American Slavery and Methodism from 1780 to 1849* . . . . (New York: Matlock, 1849), 15–16.

64. Berlin, *Many Thousands Gone*, 223.

65. Benjamin Quarles, *The Negro in the Making of America* (New York: Collier Books, 1987), 56–57.

66. Berlin, *Generations of Captivity*, 104.

67. Quoted in Quarles, *The Negro in the Making of America*, 59. "Yorktown and Slavery: 1788 Act of Manumission." http://www.yorktownhistory.org/homepages/February01.htm.

68. Horton, *Free People of Color*, 156.

69. Berlin, *Generations of Captivity*, 107.

70. Berlin, *Many Thousands Gone*, 223.

71. Ibid., 265.

72. Allan Kulikoff, *Tobacco and Slaves: The Development of Southern Cultures in the Chesapeake, 1680–1800* (Chapel Hill: University of North Carolina Press, 1986), 337–43, 394–406.

73. Berlin, *Many Thousands Gone*, 267.

74. Berlin, *Generations of Captivity*, 119.

75. Berlin, *Many Thousands Gone*, 282–83, 288–89.

76. Jordan, *White over Black*, 408.

77. Berlin, *Generations of Captivity*, 118.

78. Ibid., 127.

79. Smedley, *Race in North America*, 192–202.

80. Berlin, *Many Thousands Gone*, 305.

81. Whittington B. Johnson, *Black Savannah: 1788–1864* (Fayetteville: University of Arkansas Press, 1996), 7–9, 113.

82. Ulrich Bonnell Phillips, "Racial Problems, Adjustments and Disturbances," in *Slave Economy of the Old South: Selected Essays in Economic and Social History by Ulrich Bonnell Phillips*, ed. Eugene D. Genovese (Baton Rouge: Louisiana State University Press, 1968), 60–61.

83. Ibid., 61.

84. Johnson, *Black Savannah*, 111.

85. Jordan, *White over Black*, 429.

86. Thomas Jefferson, *Notes on the State of Virginia*, ed. Peden, 162–63; quoted in Jordon, *White over Black*, 434.

87. Jefferson, *Notes on the State of Virginia*, 138–40.

88. Smedley, *Race in North America*, 171–253.

89. Berlin, *Many Thousands Gone*, 372–78.

90. Ibid., 333–34.

91. Ibid., 334.

92. Berlin, *Generations of Captivity*, 143–54.

93. *Minutes of the Proceedings of the National Negro Conventions, 1830–1864*, ed. Howard Holman Bell (New York: Arno, 1969); quoted in Berlin, *Generations of Captivity*, 156.

94. Smedley, *Race in North America*, 177–92.

95. James Madison in *The Federalist*, ed. Jacob E. Cooke (Middletown, CT: Wesleyan University Press, 1961), 367–68; quoted in Jordan, *White over Black*, 323.

96. Smedley, *Race in North America*, 192–202.

97. Graham Richards, *'Race,' Racism and Psychology: Towards a Reflexive History* (London: Routledge, 1997), 7.

98. Quoted in Jordan, *White over Black*, 438–39. See also Jefferson, *Notes on the State of Virginia*, 140–43.

99. Tucker, *The Science and Politics of Racial Research*, 5–8.

100. Ibid.

101. Dreama Moon, "White Enculturation and Bourgeois Ideology," in *Whiteness: The Communication of Social Identity*, ed. Thomas Nakayama and Judith Martin (Thousand Oaks, CA: Sage, 1999), 177–98.

102. James Scheurich and Michelle Young, "Coloring Epistemologies: Are Our Research Epistemologies Racially Biased?" *Educational Researcher* 26, no. 4 (May 1997), 4–16, 8.

CHAPTER 3

1. Margaret Just Butcher, *The Negro in American Culture, Based on Materials Left by Alain Locke* (New York: Knopf, 1972), 49.

2. Blassingame, *The Slave Community*, 145–48; Berlin, *Generations of Captivity*, 195–96.

3. Blassingame, *The Slave Community*, 147–48.

4. Ibid., 191.

5. bell hooks, *Yearning: Race, Gender, and Cultural Politics* (Boston: South End, 1990), 149.

6. Theodore Raph, *The American Song Treasury: 100 Favorites* (Mineola, New York: Dover Publications, 1986), 353.

7. Blassingame, *The Slave Community*, 184–91.

8. Lunsford Lane, *The Narrative of Lunsford Lane*, Electronic Edition, University of North Carolina, Chapel Hill, NC, 1999, 6.

9. Ibid., 186.

10. Ibid., 186.

11. Ibid., 187.

12. Austin Steward, *Twenty-Two Years a Slave, and Forty Years a Freeman* (Oxford, UK: Blackwell Publishing Ltd., 1861), 97.

13. "Narrative of James Curry," reprinted in John W. Blassingame, *Slave Testimony: Two Centuries of Letters, Speeches, Interviews, and Autobiographies* (Baton Rouge: Louisiana State University Press, 1977), 128–33.

14. Smedley, *Race in North America*, 224.

15. Ibid., 206.

16. B. R. Hergenhahn and Matthew H. Olson, *An Introduction to Theories of Learning* (Englewood Cliffs, NJ: Prentice Hall, 1993), 34.

17. Stuckey, *Slave Culture*, 199, 208–9.

18. *Minutes of the Proceedings of the National Negro Conventions*, 14–15, quoted in Stuckey, *Slave Culture*, 204.

19. Horton, *Free People of Color*, 122–44.

20. Smedley, *Race in North America*, 221–23.

21. Gossett, *Race*, 173, 244, 364.

22. Lee D. Baker, *From Savage to Negro: Anthropology and the Construction of Race, 1896–1954* (Berkeley: University of California Press, 1998), 13.

23. Smedley, *Race in North America*, 171.

24. Leslie H. Fishel Jr. and Benjamin Quarles, *The Negro American; A Documentary History* (Glenview, IL: Scott, Foresman, 1967), 138.

25. Smedley, *Race in North America*, 191, 198–99.

26. Ibid., 211.

27. Tucker, *The Science and Politics of Racial Research*, 10.

28. Ibid., 10.

29. Charles White, *An Account of the Regular Gradation in Man, and in Different Animals and Vegetables; and From the Former to the Latter* (London: printed for C. Dilly, 1799), 94–95.

30. Ibid., 39.

31. White, *An Account of the Regular Gradation in Man*, 134–35.

32. Jordan, *White over Black*, 501.

33. Smedley, *Race in North America*, 233.

34. Richards, *'Race,' Racism and Psychology*, 7.

35. Ibid.

36. Samuel George Morton, *Crania Americana* (Philadelphia: Dobson, 1839), 5–7, 54, 65, 93, quoted in Tucker, *The Science and Politics of Racial Research*, 18.

37. Gould, *The Mismeasure of Man*, 45.

38. Quoted in ibid.

39. Richards, *'Race,' Racism and Psychology*, 7–9.

40. Gossett, *Race*, 65–66.

41. Fishel and Quarles, *The Negro American*, 204.

42. A. M. French, *Slavery in South Carolina and the Ex-Slaves* (Charleston, SC: BiblioBazaar, 2009), 61–62.

43. Berlin, *Generations of Captivity*, 160–63.

44. Horton, *Free People of Color*, 139–40; Joel Williamson, *New People: Miscegenation and Mulattoes in the United States* (New York: Free Press, 1980), 16–18.

45. Horton, *Free People of Color*, 140.

46. Larry Koger, *Black Slaveowners: Free Black Slave Masters in South Carolina, 1790–1860* (Jefferson, NC: McFarland, 1985), 18–23.

47. Berlin, *Generations of Captivity*, 144–45.

48. Ibid., 177–81.

49. Johnson, *Black Savannah*, 4.

50. Ibid., 2–3.

51. Ibid., 39.

52. Ibid., 85–86.

53. Ibid., 85–86, 131.

54. Horton, *Free People of Color*, 56–74.

55. Genovese, *Roll, Jordan, Roll*, 399.

56. Ibid., 648.

57. Horton, *Free People of Color*, 3.

58. Berlin, *Many Thousands Gone*, 7.

59. Peter Williams Jr., "Abolition of the Slave Trade" (an oration delivered in the African Church, New York, January 1, 1808), quoted in Philip S. Foner, ed., *The Voice of Black America: Major Speeches of Negroes in the United States, 1797–1971* (New York: Simon & Schuster, 1972), 20–25.

60. Viktor E. Frankl, *Man's Search for Meaning: An Introduction to Logotherapy* (New York: Washington Square, 1984), 22.

61. Joe William Trotter Jr., *The African American Experience* (Boston: Houghton Mifflin, 2001), 150–54.

62. Ibid., 152.

63. Berlin, *Generations of Captivity*, 168.

64. Trotter, *The African American Experience*, 152.

65. Berlin, *Generations of Captivity*, 167.

66. Horton, *Free People of Color*, 15–16.

67. "Duties of Overseers," in *Cotton Plantation Record and Account Book No. 3 Suitable for a Force of 120 Hands, or Under*, 7th ed. (New Orleans: Norman, 1857).

68. Berlin, *Generations of Captivity*, 165.

69. Trotter, *The African American Experience*, 161–63.

70. Ibid., 163.

71. Berlin, *Generations of Captivity*, 191.

72. Genovese, *Roll, Jordan, Roll*, 338–41.

73. Michael A. Gomez, *Exchanging Our Country Marks: The Transformation of African Identities in the Colonial and Antebellum South* (Chapel Hill: University of North Carolina Press, 1998), 1–4, 291.

74. Ibid.

75. Robert S. Starobin, ed., *Denmark Vesey: The Slave Conspiracy of 1822* (Englewood Cliffs, NJ: Prentice Hall, 1970), 24; also quoted in Koger, *Black Slaveowners*, 161–62.

76. *Journal of the Senate of South Carolina* (1835), 43; Koger, *Black Slaveowners*, 174–78.

77. Trotter, *The African American Experience*, 165.

78. Berlin, *Generations of Captivity*, 178.

79. Trotter, *The African American Experience*, 165.

80. Berlin, *Generations of Captivity*, 175, 178.

81. David Holmes to James Wilkinson, July 22, 1812, in Clarence E. Carter, ed., *Territorial Papers of the United States* (Washington, DC: Government Printing Office, 1937), 6:299, quoted in David J. Libby, *Slavery and Frontier Mississippi, 1720–1835* (Jackson: University of Mississippi Press, 2004), 56; also quoted in Berlin, *Generations of Captivity*, 175.

82. Population statistics in Berlin, *Generations of Captivity*, 272–80.

83. 1820–60 populations are drawn from *Population of the United States in 1860* (Washington, DC: GPO, 1864), 598–604.

84. Koger, *Black Slaveowners*, 19.

85. Genovese, *Roll, Jordan, Roll*, 404.

86. Ibid., 399.

87. Koger, *Black Slaveowners*, 19–20.

88. Stuckey, *Slave Culture*, 126–28.

89. Jordan, *White over Black*, 4–11; Hannaford, *Race*, 166–68; Smedley, *Race in North America*, 167.

90. Jordan, *White over Black*, 7.

91. Ibid., 7.

92. Ibid., 11.

93. Hannaford, *Race*, 199.

94. Ira Berlin, *Slaves without Masters: The Free Negro in the Antebellum South* (New York: New Press, 1974), 58; Stuckey, *Slave Culture*, 199; Horton, *Free People of Color*, 125–26.

95. Robert L. Harris Jr., "Charleston's Free Afro-American Elite: The Brown Fellowship Society and the Humane Brotherhood," *South Carolina Historical Magazine* 82, no. 4(1981): 289–310.

96. Horton, *Free People of Color*, 125–26.

97. Ibid., 125.

98. Koger, *Black Slaveowners*, 31.

99. Berlin, *Generations of* Captivity, 182–83; Genovese, *Roll, Jordan*, Roll, 408–9; Koger, *Black Slaveowners*, 19.

100. Alfred Huger to Henry D. Lesesne, December 8, 1858, Alferd Huger Letter books, 1853–1863. Cited in Michael Johnson and James L. Roark, *Black Masters: A Free Family of Color in the Old South* (New York: W.W. Norton & Company), 192.

101. Quoted in E. Horace Fitchett, "The Status of the Free Negro in Charleston, South Carolina, and His Descendants in Modern Society," *Journal of Negro History* 32 (1947): 439–46; also quoted in Berlin, *Slaves without Masters*, 389.

102. Horton, *Free People of Color*, 122.

103. Berlin, *Generations of Captivity*, 153–55.

104. Quoted in Theodore D. Jervey, *The Slave Trade: Slavery and Color* (Whitefish, MT: Kessinger, 2007), 223–25.

CHAPTER 4

1. Edmund L. Drago, *Charleston's Avery Center: From Education and Civil Rights to Preserving the African American Experience* (Charleston, SC: History Press, 2006), 21–49.

2. Koger, *Black Slaveowners*, 1.

3. Genovese, *Roll, Jordan, Roll*, 407.

4. Koger, *Black Slaveowners*, 85.

5. Genovese, *Roll, Jordan, Roll*, 399.

6. Ibid., 406–7.

7. U.S. Bureau of the Census, *Sixth Census of the United States, 1840: Schedule I, Charleston Neck, Charleston County, South Carolina*, 115; Henri-

etta P. Jervey, ed., "The Private Register of Rev. Paul Trapier," *South Carolina Historical Magazine* 58 (1957): 177; Bills of Sale vol. B 1846–1849 (Secretary of State), 186; Record of Wills vol. 49 1856–1862 (Charleston County), 868; Guardian/Trustee/Returns: Probate Records vol. M 1858–1864 (Charleston County), 352–53; also quoted in Koger, *Black Slaveowners*, 177–78.

8. Berlin, *Slaves without Masters*, 273–78.

9. Ibid., 275.

10. Koger, *Black Slaveowners*, 29.

11. Koger, *Black Slaveowners*, 107.

12. Milton M. Gordon, *Assimilation in American Life: The Role of Race, Religion, and National Origins* (New York: Oxford University Press, 1964), 56.

13. Barry Silverstein and Ronald Krate, *Children of the Dark Ghetto: A Developmental Psychology* (New York: Praeger, 1975), 61–85, 241–64.

14. Berlin, *Generations of Captivity*, 211.

15. Ibid., 212.

16. Ibid., 212–14.

17. Ibid., 214.

18. Josiah Henson, *The Life of Josiah Henson Narrated by Himself to Samuel Eliot* (1849), reprinted in Fishel and Quarles, *The Negro American*, 86–87; also see Josiah Henson, *Father Henson's Story of His Own Life*, ed. Walter Fisher (New York: Corinth, 1962).

19. Berlin, *Generations of Captivity*, 217; Trotter, *The African American Experience*, 156.

20. Frederick Douglass, *Narrative of the Life of Frederick Douglass: An American Slave*, ed. Houston A. Baker (New York: Penguin, 1982), quoted in Trotter, *The African American Experience*, 156.

21. Berlin, *Generations of Captivity*, 227.

22. Trotter, *The African American Experience*, 203.

23. Genovese, *Roll, Jordan, Roll*, 624.

24. Berlin, *Generations of Captivity*, 216.

25. Ibid., 221; Trotter, *The African American Experience*, 166–68.

26. Ibid., 223; Johnson, *Black Savannah*, 92–94.

27. Clement Eaton, "Slave-Hiring in the Upper South: A Step toward Freedom," *MVHR 46* (1960): 663–67.

28. Genovese, *Roll, Jordan, Roll*, 406; Berlin, *Generations of Captivity*, 225.

29. Genovese, *Roll, Jordan, Roll*, 648–57.

30. Berlin, *Generations of Captivity*, 223.

31. Genovese, *Roll, Jordan, Roll*, 404–5.

32. Berlin, *Generations of Captivity*, 226.

33. Genovese, *Roll, Jordan, Roll*, 410.

34. Horton, *Free People of Color*, 170–71; Trotter, *The African American Experience*, 214–15.

35. Berlin, *Generations of Captivity*, 231.

36. Quarles, *The Negro in the Making of America*, 92–93.

37. John Hope Franklin and Alfred A. Moss Jr., *From Slavery to Freedom: A History of African Americans* (New York: McGraw-Hill, 1994), 183–88.

38. Berlin, *Generations of Captivity*, 234.

39. Horton, *Free People of Color*, 58.

40. Quarles, *The Negro in the Making of America*, 92.

41. Ibid.

42. Smedley, *Race in North America*, 209.

43. Ibid., 188.

44. Theodore S. Wright "Prejudice against the Colored Many," *Liberator*, October 2, 1837, quoted in Foner, *The Voice of Black America*, 63–72.

45. John S. Rock, "I Will Sink or Swim with My Race," *Liberator*, March 12, 1858, quoted in Foner, *The Voice of Black America*, 203–8.

46. Trotter, *The African American Experience*, 147.

47. Berlin, *Generations of Captivity*, 141–44.

48. Robert Brent Toplin, "Between Black and White," *Journal of Southern History* 45 (1979): 185–200.

49. Horton, *Free People of Color*, 126–30.

50. Tucker, *The Science and Politics of Racial Research*, 30. "Last Words on Douglas," *New York Times*, February 27, 1895.

51. Horton, *Free People of Color*, 128–34.

52. Ibid., 127–28.

53. Ibid., 137–38.

54. Joanna C. Colcord, *Roll and Go: Songs of American Sailormen* (Indianapolis, IN: Bobbs-Merrill, 1924), 17.

55. Berlin, *Generations of Captivity*, 238–39; Trotter, *The African American Experience*, 147.

56. Stuckey, *Slave Culture*, 199–215.

57. Patrick Rael, *Black Identity and Black Protest in the Antebellum North* (Chapel Hill: University of North Carolina Press, 2002), 27–29.

58. Trotter, *The American Experience*, 2001, 260–68, 368–72. Franklin and Moss, *From Slavery to Freedom*, 1994, 317–22.

59. Smedley, *Race in North America*, 249.

60. Ibid.

61. E. Barker, *The Politics of Aristotle* (New York: Oxford University Press, 1950), 16–17.

62. Richards, *'Race,' Racism and Psychology*, 7.

63. Smedley, *Race in North America*, 243.

64. Richards, *'Race,' Racism and Psychology*, 7; Smedley, *Race in North America*, 244.

65. Gould, *The Mismeasure of Man*, 45; Baker, *From Savage to Negro*, 15.

66. Smedley, *Race in North America*, 233–44.

67. Ibid., 242.

68. Tucker, *The Science and Politics of Racial Research*, 25–26.

69. Ibid., 28; Baker, *From Savage to Negro*, 84–87.

70. Richard Hofstadter, *Social Darwinism in American Thought* (Boston: Beacon Press, 1992), 45.

71. Richards, *'Race,' Racism and Psychology*, 21.

72. Herbert Spencer, "The Comparative Psychology of Man," *Popular Science Monthly* 8 (1876): 257–59.

73. Tucker, *The Science and Politics of Racial Research*, 30–31.

74. Ibid.

75. Ibid., 27.

76. Richards, *'Race,' Racism and Psychology*, 17–20.

77. Ibid., 17.

78. Tucker, *The Science and Politics of Racial Research*, 43–44.

79. Ibid., 39.

80. Galton, *Hereditary Genius: An Inquiry into Its Laws and Consequences* (London: Macmillan, 1869), 24, 38–39, 41.

81. Gossett, *Race*, 155–56.

82. Tucker, *The Science and Politics of Racial Research*, 45–49.

83. Ibid., 59–62.

84. Baker, *From Savage to Negro*, 92.

85. Edwin G. Boring, *A History of Experimental Psychology*, 2nd ed. (New York: Appleton-Century-Crofts, 1950), 270.

86. Tucker, *The Science and Politics of Racial Research*, 72.

87. Berlin, *Generations of Captivity*, 246.

88. Ibid., 246–47.

89. Genovese, *Roll, Jordan, Roll*, 149–50.

90. Trotter, *The African American Experience*, 265.

91. Ibid., 245.

92. Ibid., 254.

93. Genovese, *Roll, Jordan, Roll*, 153.

94. Baker, *From Savage to Negro*, 12.

95. Tucker, *The Science and Politics of Racial Research*, 6.

96. Smedley, *Race in North America*, 251.

97. George M. Fredrickson, *The Black Image in the White Mind: The Debate on Afro-American Character and Destiny, 1817–1914* (Middletown, CT: Wesleyan University Press, 1987), 90.

98. Tucker, *The Science and Politics of Racial Research*, 27; Foner, *The Voice of Black America*, 276–83.

99. Abraham Lincoln, "Fourth Lincoln-Douglas Debate," Charleston, Illinois, September 18, 1858, New York: Library of America, *Speeches and Writings 1832–1858*, 1989, 636.

100. Quarles, *The Negro in the Making of America*, 113–15.

101. Frederick Douglass, "African Civilization Society" (originally published as a pamphlet, New Haven, CT, 1861), quoted in Howard Brotz, ed., *Negro Social and Political Thought, 1850–1920; Representative Texts* (New York: Basic Books, 1966), 262–66.

102. Quarles, *The Negro in the Making of America*, 124; Horton, *Free People of Color*, 161–64.

103. Trotter, *The African American Experience*, 271.

104. Ibid., 272.

105. Quarles, *The Negro in the Making of America*, 130.

106. H. Melville Myers, comp., preface to *Stay Law and . . . Freedmen's Code* (Charleston, 1866), quoted in Gossett, *Race: The History of an Idea in America*, 256; also see *Acts of the General Assembly of the State of South Carolina, 1864–1865*, 291–304.

107. Quoted in Hodding Carter, *The Angry Scar: The Story of Reconstruction* (Westport, CT: Greenwood Publishing Group, 1959), 52.

108. Franklin and Moss, *From Slavery to Freedom*, 227–28.

109. Quoted in Trotter, *The African American Experience*, 271. See also "The State of the Union Address: Andrew Johnson," December 3, 1867. U.S. Historical Documents.

110. William J. Watkins, "Our Rights as Men," in *The Voice of Black America; Major Speeches of Negroes in the United States, 1797–1971*, ed. Philip S. Foner (New York: Simon & Schuster, 1972), 130–44.

111. John S. Rock, "I Will Sink or Swim with My Race," in *The Voice of Black America; Major Speeches of Negroes in the United States, 1797–1971*, ed. Philip S. Foner (New York: Simon & Schuster, 1972), 257–58.

112. William H. Gray, "Justice Should Recognize No Color," in *American Cyclopedia* (1869), 8:33–35.

113. Oscar J. Dunn, "We Ask an Equal Chance in the Race of Life," in *The Voice of Black America; Major Speeches of Negroes in the United States, 1797–1971*, ed. Philip S. Foner (New York: Simon & Schuster, 1972), 353–55.

114. Franklin and Moss, *From Slavery to Freedom*, 227–37.

115. Benjamin Drew, *The Refugee: or the Narratives of Fugitive Slaves in Canada* (Boston: Jewett, 1856), 77, quoted in Kenneth M. Stamp, *The Peculiar Institution: Slavery in the Ante-Bellum South* (New York: Vintage Books, 1989), 89.

116. Angela Y. Davis, *Women, Race and Class* (New York: Vintage Books, 1983), 172–201.

117. Du Bois, *Black Reconstruction*, 700–701.

118. Ibid., 701.

119. Quarles, *The Negro in the Making of America*, 102–4.

120. Franklin and Moss, *From Slavery to Freedom*, 235–36.

121. Ibid., 247–59.

122. Congressional Joint Committee on Reconstruction, *Testimony of William Thornton*, hearings, February 3, 1866.

123. W. E. B. DuBois, *Black Reconstruction in America: 1860–1880* (Harcourt, Brace, 1935), 220–30, 310–11; Franklin and Moss, *From Slavery to Freedom*, 228–59.

124. Trotter, *The African American Experience*, 275.

125. Raoul Berger, *The Fourteenth Amendment and the Bill of Rights* (Norman: University of Oklahoma Press, 1989).

126. Franklin and Moss, *From Slavery to Freedom*, 250.

127. Trotter, *The African American Experience*, 285.

128. Richards, '*Race,*' *Racism and Psychology*, 66.

129. Tucker, *The Science and Politics of Racial Research*, 27.

130. Ibid., 30–31.

131. Horton, *Free People of Color*, 161.

132. Berlin, *Generations of Captivity*, 268.

133. Trotter, *The African American Experience*, 264–68.

134. Butcher, *The Negro in American Culture*, 20.

135. Ibid., 28.

136. C. Eric Lincoln and Lawrence H. Mamiya, *The Black Church in the African-American Experience* (Durham, NC: Duke University Press, 1990), 7.

137. Martin E. Dann, ed., *The Black Press, 1827–1890; The Quest for National Identity* (New York: Putnam, 1971), 1–14.

138. Silverstein and Krate, *Children of the Dark Ghetto*, 61–66.

139. Robert Coles, *Children of Crisis: A Study of Courage and Fear* (Boston: Little, Brown, 1967), 66.

140. John Dollard, Neal E. Miller, Leonard W. Doob, O. H. Mowrer, and Robert R. Sears, *Frustration and Aggression* (New Haven, CT: Yale University Press, 1939), 7.

CHAPTER 5

1. Trotter, *The African American Experience*, 282–83.

2. Richards, *'Race,' Racism and Psychology*, 66.

3. Fredrickson, *The Black Image in the White Mind*, 90.

4. Richards, *'Race,' Racism and Psychology*, 66.

5. Franklin and Moss, *From Slavery to Freedom*, 277–85, 314–17.

6. "Atlanta Swept By Raging Mob," *Atlanta Constitution*, September 23, 1906, quoted in Franklin and Moss, *From Slavery to Freedom*, 314.

7. Roberta Senechal, *The Sociogenesis of a Race Riot: Springfield, Illinois, in 1908* (Urbana: University of Illinois Press, 1990), quoted in Franklin and Moss, *From Slavery to Freedom*, 315–16.

8. Ibid., 316–17.

9. Berlin, *Many Thousands Gone*, 2–5; Berlin, *Generations of Captivity*, 4–5.

10. Franklin and Moss, *From Slavery to Freedom*, 319.

11. Smedley, *Race in North America*, 167–68.

12. Richards, *'Race,' Racism and Psychology*, 68.

13. Robert S. Abbott, editorial, *Chicago Defender*, May 13, 1917, quoted in Emmett J. Scott, *Negro Migration during the War* (New York: Arno, 1969), 31; also quoted in Trotter, *The African American Experience*, 380.

14. Robert S. Abbott, editorial, *Chicago Defender*, May 13, 1917, quoted in Trotter, *The African American Experience*, 380.

15. Robert S. Abbott, editorial, *Chicago Defender*, May 13, 1917, quoted in Trotter, *The African American Experience*, 380.

16. Robert S. Abbott, editorial, *Chicago Defender*, May 13, 1917, quoted in Trotter, *The African American Experience*, 374.

17. Franklin and Moss, *From Slavery to Freedom*, 340.

18. Trotter, *The African American Experience*, 374.

19. Ibid., 378–80.

20. Franklin and Moss, *From Slavery to Freedom*, 277.

21. Trotter, *The African American Experience*, 381–86.

22. Ibid., 389.

23. Ibid., 392–96.

24. Franklin and Moss, *From Slavery to Freedom*, 281.

25. Trotter, *The African American Experience*, 395–96.

26. Ibid., 398–401; Franklin and Moss, *From Slavery to Freedom*, 308–12.

27. Trotter, *The African American Experience*, 402.

28. Ibid., 402–15.

29. Darlene Clark Hine, William C. Hine, and Stanley Harrold, *The African American Odyssey* (Upper Saddle River, NJ: Prentice Hall, 2000), 399–402.

30. Franklin and Moss, *From Slavery to Freedom*, 357–60.

31. *Messenger*, 1922/1923, quoted in Jeff Henderson, "A. Philip Randolph and the Dilemmas of Socialism and Black Nationalism in the United States: 1917–1941," *Race and Class* 20, no. 2 (1978): 149; also quoted in Hine, Hine, and Harrold, *The African American Odyssey*, 402.

32. Franklin and Moss, *From Slavery to Freedom*, 358. See also *Messenger*, January 1923.

33. Ibid., 358. See also *Messenger*, January 1923.

34. Marcus Garvey, *The Marcus Garvey and Universal Negro Improvement Association Papers*, vol. 9, *Africa for Africans*, ed. Robert A. Hill (Berkeley: University of California Press, 1995).

35. Ibid., quoted in Hine, Hine, and Harrold, *The African American Odyssey*, 402.

36. Franz Boas, "Human Faculty as Determined by Race," *Proceedings of the American Association for the Advancement of Science* 43 (1895): 326, quoted in Baker, *From Savage to Negro*, 104–5.

37. Baker, *From Savage to Negro*, 99–126.

38. William I. Thomas, "The Mind of Woman and the Lower Races," *American Journal of Sociology* 12 (1907): 435–69, quoted in Richards, *'Race,' Racism and Psychology*, 27–30.

39. Daryl Michael Scott, *Contempt and Pity: Social Policy and the Image of the Damaged Black Psyche, 1880–1996* (Chapel Hill: University of North Carolina Press, 1997), 3.

40. W. E. B. Du Bois, *The Philadelphia Negro: A Social Study* (New York: Schocken Books, 1967; 1st ed., 1899), 283–84.

41. Scott, *Contempt and Pity*, 12.

42. W. E. B. DuBois, *The Philadelphia Negro: A Social Study* (New York: Schocken Books, 1899), summarized in Baker, *From Savage to Negro*, 112.

43. Scott, *Contempt and Pity*, 10–11.

44. Ibid., 2–11.

45. W. E. B. Du Bois, *The Souls of Black Folk* (New York: Bantam Books, 1989; 1st ed., 1903), 2.

46. Du Bois, *The Souls of Black Folk*, 364–65.

47. Scott, *Contempt and Pity*, 14.

48. E. Franklin Frazier, *Negro Family in the United States* (Chicago: University of Chicago Press, 1939), 481–82.

49. E. Franklin Frazier, "The Negro's Struggle to Find His Soul" (unpublished paper, E. Franklin Frazier Paper Collection, Howard University, Washington, DC), quoted in Scott, *Contempt and Pity*, 65.

50. Horace Mann Bond, "Intelligence Tests and Propaganda," *Crisis* 28, no. 2 (1928): 24–25.

51. John M. Mecklin, *Democracy and Race Friction* (New York: Macmillan, 1914), 154–55.

52. American Philosophical Society, *Proceedings* (1917), 364–68, quoted in Gossett, *Race*, 379.

53. Scott, *Contempt and Pity*, 15–17.

54. Ibid., 19–40.

55. Ibid., 17.

56. Ibid., 55.

57. Hortense Powdermaker, *After Freedom: A Cultural Study in the Deep South* (New York: Atheneum, 1968), 369.

58. Scott, *Contempt and Pity*, 27.

59. Kurt Lewin and Gertrud Weiss Lewin, ed., *Resolving Social Conflicts, Selected Papers on Group Dynamics* (New York: Harper, 1948), 192, 197–98.

60. Scott, *Contempt and Pity*, 19–28.

61. Robert E. Park, "Mentality of Racial Hybrids," *American Journal of Sociology* 36 (1931): 545, 548.

62. Ibid., 534.

63. Everett Stonequist, *The Marginal Man: A Study in Personality and Culture Conflict* (New York: C. Scribner's Sons, 1937), 121.

64. Scott, *Contempt and Pity*, 29.

65. E. Franklin Frazier, *Negro Youth at the Crossways, Their Personality Development in the Middle States* (Washington, DC: American Council on Education, 1940), 180–81.

66. William E. Cross Jr., *Shades of Black: Diversity in African-American Identity* (Philadelphia: Temple University Press, 1991), 20–22; Scott, *Contempt and Pity*, 32.

67. Baker, *From Savage to Negro*, 194–95.

68. Richards, *'Race,' Racism and Psychology*, 149.

69. Baker, *From Savage to Negro*, 180–82.

70. Robert Park, "The Conflict and Fusion of Cultures with Special Reference to the Negro," *Journal of Negro Education* 4, no. 2 (1919): 116.

71. E. Franklin Frazier, "Is the Negro Family a Unique Sociological Unit?" *Opportunity* 5 (June 1927): 155–68.

72. Gunner Myrdal, *An American Dilemma: The Negro Problem and Modern Democracy* (New York: Harper Row, 1969; 1st ed., 1944), 928–29.

73. Ibid., 956.

74. Ibid., 957–61.

75. Baker, *From Savage to Negro*, 181.

76. Ibid., 194–95.

77. Ibid., 194.

78. Scott, *Contempt and Pity*, 137–60.

79. Abram Kardiner and Lionel Ovesey, *The Mark of Oppression: Explorations in the Personality of the American Negro* (New York: Norton, 1951), 68–69.

80. Ibid., 70.

81. Richards, *'Race,' Racism and Psychology*, 239–40.

82. Scott, *Contempt and Pity*, 137–44.

83. Amina Mama, *Beyond the Masks: Race, Gender, and Subjectivity* (London: Routledge, 1995), 162–65.

84. Baker, *From Savage to Negro*, 25.

85. Tucker, *The Science and Politics of Racial Research*, 138–41.

86. Richards, *'Race,' Racism and Psychology*, 71.

87. Ashley Montagu, *Race, Science, and Humanity* (Princeton, NJ: Van Nostrand, 1962), 6, quoted in Hannaford, *Race*, 391.

88. Baker, *From Savage to Negro*, 17, 208–28.

89. C. Eric Lincoln, *Race, Religion, and the Continuing American Dilemma* (New York: Hill and Wang, 1984), 45–46, 94.

90. Quoted in Baker, *From Savage to Negro*, 208.

91. Quarles, *The Negro in the Making of America*, 148–49.

92. Richards, *'Race,' Racism and Psychology*, 65–92.

93. Ibid., 70.

94. Ibid., 68, 88–91; Tucker, *The Science and Politics of Racial Research*, 71–74; Gossett, *Race*, 364–69, 376.

95. Tucker, *The Science and Politics of Racial Research*, 77.

96. Leon Kamin, *The Science and Politics of I.Q.* (Potomac, MD: Lawrence Erlbaum, 1974), 15–33.

97. Richards, *'Race,' Racism and Psychology*, 67.

98. Frank Margonis, "John Dewey's Racialized Visions of the Student and Classroom Community," *Educational Theory* 59, no. 1 (2009): 17–39.

99. Tucker, *The Science and Politics of Racial Research*, 53–61; Gossett, *Race*, 370–408.

100. Robert V. Guthrie, chapters 1, 2, and 3, in *Even the Rat Was White: A Historical View of Psychology* (Boston: Allyn and Bacon, 1998), 3–83.

101. Richards, *'Race,' Racism and Psychology*, 16.

102. Marion J. Mayo, "The Mental Capacity of the American Negro," *Archives of General Psychiatry* 28 (1913): 67, quoted in Richards, *'Race,' Racism, and Psychology*, 81–82.

103. Alice C. Strong, "Three Hundred Fifty White and Colored Children Measured by the Binet-Simon Measuring Scale," *Pedagogical Seminary* 20 (1913): 501.

104. Ibid., 487.

105. Ibid., 500.

106. Edward L. Thorndike, "Eugenics: With Special Reference to Intellect and Character," *Popular Science Monthly* 83 (1913), 125–38.

107. Gould, *The Mismeasure of Man*, 46–52.

108. The preceding quotes are found in Lewis Madison Terman, *The Measurement of Intelligence* (Boston: Houghton Mifflin, 1916), 91–92.

109. Robert M. Yerkes, "Psychological Examining in the United States Army," National Academy of Sciences, *Memoir* 15 (1921): 790 ff, quoted in Gossett, *Race*, 368–69.

110. W. E. B. DuBois, "The Forethought" in *The Souls of Black Folk* (New York: Bantam Dell, 1903), xxx.

111. Gossett, *Race*, 369.

112. Reed's remarks taken from: David A. Reed, "Comments on American Immigration Policy," in "The Constitution of the United States," in *Documents of American History*, ed. Henry Steele Commager (New York: Appleton-Century-Crofts, 1963), 372–74.

113. Carl C. Brigham, *A Study of American Intelligence* (Princeton, NJ: Princeton University Press, 1923), 209.

114. Ibid., quoted in Richards, *'Race,' Racism and Psychology*, 90–91.

115. Carl C. Brigham, "Intelligence Tests of Immigrant Groups," *Psychological Review* 37, no. 2 (1930): 165, quoted in Kamin, *The Science and Politics of I.Q.*, 22.

116. G. H. Estabrooks, "The Enigma of Racial Intelligence," *Journal of Genetic Psychology* 35 (1928): 137.

117. Ibid., 138.

118. G. H. Estabrooks, "The Question of Racial Inferiority," *American Anthropologist* 30, no. 3 (1928): 474.

119. Richards, *'Race,' Racism and Psychology*, 127.

120. Ibid., 129.

121. James Baldwin, *The Fire Next Time* (New York: Vintage, 1963).

122. W. E. B. Du Bois, "Race Intelligence," in Race Intelligence, The Crisis, Vol. 20, No. 3, July 1920.

123. Horace Mann Bond (1924 or 1927?).

124. Kamin, *The Science and Politics of I.Q.*, 1–2.

125. James A. Banks and Jean Dresden Grambs, ed., *Black Self-Concept; Implications for Education and Social Science* (New York: McGraw-Hill, 1972), 141–7.

126. Silverstein and Krate, *Children of the Dark Ghetto*, 62.

127. Gossett, *Race*, 409–30.

128. Meleville J. Herskovitz, *The Anthropometry of the American Negro* (New York: Columbia University Press, 1930), 15.

129. O. A. R. Berkley-Hill, "The Color Question from a Psychoanalytic Standpoint," *Psychoanalytic Review* 11 (1924): 246–53.

130. Gilbert Balfour Bovell, "Psychological Considerations of Color Conflicts among Negroes," *Psychoanalytic Review* 30 (1943): 447–59.

131. Charles H. Parrish, "Color Names and Color Notions," *Journal of Negro Education* 15, no. 1 (1946): 13–20.

132. Franklin and Moss, *From Slavery to Freedom*, 382.

133. John Hope, "Negro Business," in *Proceedings of Fourth Atlanta University Conference on The Negro in Business* (Atlanta, GA: Atlanta University, May 30–31, 1899), 56–60.

134. Silverstein and Krate, *Children of the Dark Ghetto*, 61–88.

135. All preceding information concerning the Clark and Clark studies is found in Kenneth B. Clark and Mamie K. Clark, "The Development of Consciousness of Self and the Emergence of Racial Identification in Negro Preschool Children," *Journal of Social Psychology* 10, no. 4 (1939): 591–99; Kenneth B. Clark and Mamie K. Clark, "Segregation as a Factor in the Racial Identification of Negro Pre-School Children: A Preliminary Report," *Journal of Experimental Education* 8, no. 2 (1939): 161–63; Kenneth B. Clark and Mamie K. Clark, "Skin Color as a Factor in the Racial Identification in Negro Preschool Children," *Journal of Social Psychology* 11, no. 1 (1940): 159–69.

136. Silverstein and Krate, *Children of the Dark Ghetto*, 61–66.

137. Henry Steele Commager, ed., "The Constitution of the United States," in *Documents of American History* (New York: Appleton-Century-Crofts, 1963), 330. *Brown v Board of Education*, Chief Justice Earl Warren, 1954.

138. Leon Friedman, *Argument: The Oral Argument before the Supreme Court in* Brown v. Board of Education of Topeka, *1952–1955* (New York: Chelsea House, 1969), 329–30. Brown v Board of Education, Chief Justice Earl Warren, 1954.

139. Gordon, *Assimilation in American Life*, 68.

140. Ibid.

141. David T. Wellman, *Portraits of White Racism*, 2nd ed. (Cambridge: Cambridge University Press, 1993).

142. W. E. B. DuBois, "Whither Now and Why" in *The Education of Black People: Ten Critiques, 1906–1960*, ed. Herbert Aptheker, 149–158.

143. Ibid., 149.

CHAPTER 6

1. Michael J. Klarman, "How *Brown* Changed Race Relations: The Back-lash Thesis," *Journal of American History* 81, no. 10 (1994): 81–118.

2. Ibid., 85–86.

3. A summary of the short-term effect of the Court's 1954 ruling on politics and education in the South can be found in Klarman, "How *Brown* Changed Race Relations," 85–88.

4. Oyeshiku C. Smith, Douglas W. Levine, Emile P. Smith, Jean Dumas, and Ron J. Prinz, "A Developmental Perspective of the Relationship of Racial-Ethnic Identity to Self-Construct, Achievement, and Behavior in African American Children," *Cultural Diversity and Minority Psychology* 15, no. 2 (2009): 145–57; Howard. C. Stevenson and Edith G. Arrington, "Racial/Ethnic Socialization Mediates Perceived Racism and the Racial Identity of African-American Adolescents," *Cultural Diversity and Ethnic Minority Psychology* 15, no. 2 (2009): 125–36; Boone and Buyske, "A Test of Racial Conceptualization between African Americans and Indigenous Africans," 313–31; Shawn O. Utsey, Mark H. Chae, Christina F. Brown, and Deborah Kelly, "Effect of Ethnic Group Membership on Ethnic Identity, Race-Related Stress and Quality of Life," *Cultural Diversity and Ethnic Minority Psychology* 8 (2002): 366–77; Rosemary E. Phelps, Sarah Tranakos-Howe, John C. Dagley, and Michelle K. Lyn, "Encouragement and Ethnicity in African American College Students," *Journal of Counseling and Development* 79, no. 1 (2001): 90–97; Stephanie J. Rowley, Robert M. Sellers, Jabbye M. Chavous, and A. Mia, "The Relationship between Racial Identity and Self-Esteem in African American College and High School Students," *Journal of Personality and Social Psychology* 74, no. 3 (1998): 715–24.

5. *Brown v. Board of Education of Topeka*, 347 U.S. 483 (1954).

6. Cross, *Shades of Black*, 16–38.

7. Marilynn B. Brewer, "The Social Self: On Being the Same and Different at the Same Time," *Personality and Social Psychology Bulletin* 17 (1991): 475–82.

8. Marilynn B. Brewer and Norman Miller, *Intergroup Relations* (Pacific Grove, CA: Brooks/Cole, 1996), 34–35.

9. Ibid., 107.

10. Marilynn B. Brewer and Roderick M. Kramer, "Choice Behavior in Social Dilemmas: Effects of Social Identity, Group Size, and Decision Framing," *Journal of Personality and Social Psychology* 50 (1986): 543–49.

11. "Civil Rights Legislation," *Congress and the Nation*, vol. 11, *Civil Rights Legislation 1957–1968* (Washington, DC: Congressional Quarterly).

12. Parham, White, and Ajamu, *The Psychology of Blacks*.

13. *Congress and the Nation*, vol. 2, *1965–1968* (Washington DC: Congressional Quarterly, 1969).

14. Randall Kennedy, "History: Unequal Protection," in *Race, Crime, and the Law* (New York: Vintage Books, 1998), 29–75.

15. William Julius Wilson, *The Truly Disadvantaged: The Inner-City, the Underclass, and Public Policy* (Chicago: University of Chicago Press, 1988), 20–62.

16. Franklin and Moss, *From Slavery to Freedom*, 513.

17. Kennedy, "History: Unequal Protection," 71.

18. Franklin and Moss, *From Slavery to Freedom*, 494, 498.

19. Federal Housing Administration, *Underwriting Manuel: Underwriting and Valuation Procedure under Title 11 of the Housing Act with Revisions to April 1, 1936* (Washington, DC), part II, section 2, quoted in Franklin and Moss, *From Slavery to Freedom*, 512.

20. George Lipsitz, *The Possessive Investment in Whiteness: How White People Benefit from Identity Politics* (Philadelphia: Temple University Press, 1998).

21. Delgado and Stefancic, *Critical Race Theory*, 3–6.

22. Silverstein and Krate, *Children of the Dark Ghetto*, 123–170; Tucker, *The Science and Politics of Racial Research*, 213–39; Richards, *'Race,' Racism and Psychology*, 261–86.

23. Arthur R. Jensen, "How Much Can We Boost IQ and Scholastic Achievement?" *Harvard Educational Review* 39 (1969): 1–123.

24. Myrdal, *An American Dilemma*, 928–29.

25. Silverstein and Krate, *Children of the Dark Ghetto*, 123–24.

26. David Lohman, "Complex Information Processing and Intelligence," in *Handbook of Intelligence*, ed. Robert J. Sternberg (New York: Cambridge University Press, 2000), 285–340; Janet E. Davidson, "The Suddenness of Insight," in *The Nature of Insight*, ed. Robert J. Sternberg and Janet E. Davidson (Cambridge, MA: MIT Press, 1995), 125–55; Howard Gardner, "Are There Additional Intelligences? The Case for Naturalist, Spiritual, and Existential Intelligences," in *Education, Information, and Transformation: Essays on Learning and Thinking*, ed. Jeffrey Kane (Upper Saddle River, NJ: Prentice-Hall, 1999), 111–31; Robert J. Sternberg, "Toward a Triarchi Theory of Intelligence," *Behavioral and Brain Science* 7 (1984): 269–315.

27. Robert J. Sternberg and James C. Kaufman, "Human Abilities," *Annual Review of Psychology* 49 (1998): 479–502.

28. David Henry Feldman, "The Development of Creativity," in *Handbook of Creativity*, ed. Robert J. Sternberg (New York: Cambridge University Press, 1999), 169–86.

29. Robert J. Sternberg, *Wisdom: Its Nature, Origins, and Development* (New York: Cambridge University Press, 1990); Robert J. Sternberg, "Human Intelligence: Its Nature, Use, and Interaction with Context," in *Current Topics in Human Intelligence*, vol. 4, *Theories in Intelligence*, ed. Douglas K. Detterman (Norwood, NJ: Ablex, 1994).

30. John L. Horn and Raymond J. Cattell, "Refinement and Test of the Theory of Fluid and Crystallized General Intelligences," *Journal of Educational Psychology* 57, no. 5 (1966): 253–70; K. Warner Schaie, "The Course of Adult Intellectual Development," *American Psychologist* 49, no. 4 (1994): 304–13.

31. Howard Gardner, *Frames of Mind: The Theory of Multiple Intelligences* (New York: Basic Books, 1983); Howard Gardner, Mindy L. Kornhaber, Warren K. Wako, *Intelligence: Multiple Perspectives* (Orlando, FL: Harcourt Brace, 1995).

32. Feldman, "The Development of Creativity," 169–86.

33. Silverstein and Krate, *Children of the Dark Ghetto*, 122.

34. Cyril Burt, "The Genetic Determination of Differences in Intelligence: The Study of Monozygotic Twins Reared Apart and Together," *British Journal of Psychology* 57 (1966): 137–53; Cyril Burt, "Intelligence and Social Mobility," *British Journal of Statistics* 14 (1961): 3–24.

35. Tucker, *The Science and Politics of Racial Research*, 265–66.

36. Richard J. Herrnstein and Charles Murray, *The Bell Curve: Intelligence and Class Structure in American Life* (New York: The Free Press, 1994).

37. Such studies include Claude S. Fischer et al., *Inequality by Design: Cracking the Bell Curve Myth* (Princeton: Princeton University Press, 1996); Steven Fraser, ed., *The Bell Curve Wars: Race, Intelligence, and the Future of America* (New York: Basic Books, 1995); Jack Block, "A Contrarian View of the Five-Factor Approach to Personality Description," *Psychology Bulletin* 117 (1995): 187–215.

38. Feldman, "The Development of Creativity," 169–86.

39. Silverstein and Krate, *Children of the Dark Ghetto*, 130.

40. Carl Jorgenson, "The African American Critique of White Supremacist Science," *Journal of Negro Education* 64 (1995): 232–42.

41. Silverstein and Krate, *Children of the Dark Ghetto*, 138–39.

42. Sandra Scarr and Richard A. Weinberg, "IQ Test Performance of Black Children Adopted by White Families," *American Psychologist* 31, no. 10 (1976): 726–39.

43. Silverstein and Krate, *Children of the Dark Ghetto*, 123.

44. Parham, White, and Ajamu, *The Psychology of Blacks*, 2–23. This point is also emphasized in Wade Nobles, *Africanity and the Black Family* (Oakland,

CA: Black Family Institute, 1985), and Joseph L. White, "Toward a Black Psychology," in *Black Psychology*, ed. R. L. Jones (New York: Harper and Row, 1972).

45. Martin P. Deutsch, "The Disadvantaged Child and the Learning Process," in *Education in Depressed Areas*, ed. A. Harry Passow (New York: Teachers College Press, 1965). This error can also be observed in studies by J. McVicker Hunt, "The Psychological Basis for Preschool Enrichment as an Antidote for Cultural Deprivation," *Merrill-Palmer Quarterly* 10 (1964): 236, 211–50 and Jerome Kagan, "On Cultural Deprivation," in *Environmental Influences: Biology and Behavior*, ed. David C. Glass (1968), 211–50.

46. Deutsch, "The Disadvantaged Child and the Learning Process," 170.

47. Joseph McVicker Hunt, "Parents and Child Centers: Their Basis in the Behavioral and Educational Sciences," *American Journal of Orthro-psychiatry* 41, no. 1 (1971): 28–29.

48. Silverstein and Krate, *Children of the Dark Ghetto*, 129.

49. Claude M. Steele and Joshua Aronson, "Stereotype Threat and the Intellectual Test Performance of African Americans," *Journal of Personality and Social Psychology* 69, no. 5 (1995): 797–811.

50. Silverstein and Krate, *Children of the Dark Ghetto*, 122–69.

51. Lincoln and Mamiya, *The Black Church in the African-American Experience*, 1–19.

52. Sherle L. Boone, "Aggression in African American Boys: A Discriminant Analysis," *Genetic, Social, and General Psychology Monographs* 117, no. 2 (1991): 205–28.

53. Charles Joyner, "'Believer I Know': The Emergence of African-American Christianity," in *African-American Christianity: Essays in History*, ed. Paul E. Johnson (Berkeley: University of California Press, 1994), 18–46.

54. James H. Cone, *The Spirituals and the Blues* (New York: Seabury, 1972), 5.

55. Charles H. Long, "Assessment and New Departures for a Study of Black Religion in the United States," in *African American Religious Studies: An Interdisciplinary Anthology*, ed. Gayraud S. Wilmore (Durham, NC: Duke University Press, 1989), 34–49.

56. Robert A. Bennett, "Black Experience and Black Bible," in *African American Religious Studies: An Interdisciplinary Anthology*, ed. Gayraud S. Wilmore (Durham, NC: Duke University Press, 1989), 129–30; Lincoln and Mamiya, *The Black Church in the African-American Experience* (Durham, NC: Duke University Press, 1968), 168–94.

57. Lincoln and Mamiya, *The Black Church in the African-American Experience*, 4.

58. Ibid., 129–30.

59. Ibid., 7–10.

60. Ibid., 105–16.

61. Jelani Mandara, Fatma Varner, and Scott Richman, "Do African American Mothers Really 'Love' Their Sons and 'Raise' Their Daughters?" *Journal of Family Psychology* 24, no. 1 (2010): 41–50; Ronald D. Taylor, "Risk and Resilience in Low-Income African American Families: Moderating Effects of Kinship Social Support," *Cultural Diversity and Ethnic Minority Psychology* 16, no. 3 (2010): 344–51; Marybeth Gasman, "A Growing Tradition? Examining the African American Family Foundation," *Nonprofit Management and Leadership* 21, no. 2 (2010): 121–38.

62. United States Bureau of the Census, https//askcensusgov/app/answers/list, 2005.

63. Andrew Billingsley, *Black Families in White America* (Englewood Cliffs, NJ: Prentice-Hall, 1968), 97–101; Herbert G. Gutman, *The Black Family in Slavery and Freedom: 1750–1925* (New York: Vintage Books, 1976), 3–45; Franklin and Moss, *From Slavery to Freedom*, 117.

64. Billingsley, *Black Families in White America*, 19–31.

65. Franklin and Moss, *From Slavery to Freedom*, 137–40.

66. Herbert G. Gutman, *The Black Family in Slavery and Freedom, 1750–1925* (New York: Pantheon, 1976), 515.

67. Wilson, *The Truly Disadvantaged*, 63–66.

68. U.S. Bureau of the Census, *Current Population Reports, 1965, 1970–1984* (Washington, DC: GPO, Series P-23). See also Greg J. Duncan and Willard Rogers, "Single-Parent Families: Are Their Economic Problems Transitory or Persistent?," *Family Planning Perspective*, Vol. 19, No. 4, 1987, 171–76.

69. Jane E. Costello, and others, "The Prevalence of Serious Emotional Disturbance: A Re-analysis of Community Studies," *Journal of Child and Family Studies* 7, no. 4 (1998): 411–32.

70. Wilson, *The Truly Disadvantaged*, 69.

71. Micheline R. Malson, "The Black Working Mother as Role Model," *Radcliffe Quarterly* 72 (1986): 24–25.

72. Janet L. Todd and Judith Worell, "Resilience in Low-Income, Employed, African American Women," *Psychology of Women Quarterly* 24, no. 2 (2000): 119–28.

73. Jane L. Pearson, Andrea G. Hunter, Margaret E. Ensminger, and Sheppard Kellan, "Black Grandmothers in Multigenrational Households: Diversity in Family Structure and Parenting Involvement in the Woodlawn Community," *Child Development* 61, no. 12 (1990): 434–42.

74. Malson, "The Black Working Mother as Role Model," 24–25.

75. Boone, "Aggression in African American Boys," 203–28.

76. Costello and others, "The Prevalence of Serious Emotional Disturbance," 411–32.

77. Wilson, *The Truly Disadvantaged*, 20–62.

78. John Kasarda, "Urban Change and Minority Opportunities," in *The New Urban Reality*, ed. Paul E. Peterson (Washington, DC: Brookings Institute, 1985), 33.

79. Ibid.

80. H. Rudolph Schaffer, *Social Development* (Cambridge, MA: Blackwell, 1996), 213–31.

81. Ibid.

82. John Bowlby, *Attachment*, 2nd ed. (New York: Basic Books, 1969), 211–34.

83. Aaron Gullickson, "Black/White Interracial Marriage Trends," *Journal of Family History* 31, no. 3 (2006): 289–312.

84. Candy Mills, Editorial, *Interrace*, December 1994/January 1995, 2.

85. Gordon, *Assimilation in American Life*, 56–57.

86. Kathleen O. Korgen, *From Black to Biracial: Transforming Racial Identity among Americans* (Westport, CT: Praeger, 1998), 25–37.

87. Ibid., 72.

88. Cross, *Shades of Black*, 39–74.

89. Korgen, *From Black to Biracial*, 34–35.

90. Ibid., 36.

91. Frankl, *Man's Search for Meaning*, 17–100.

92. Ibid., 104.

93. Du Bois, "Whither Now and Why," 149.

94. Orlando Patterson, *The Sociology of Slavery: An Analysis of the Origins, Structure, and Development of Negro Slave Society in Jamaica* (London: McGibbon and Kee, 1967), 145–81.

95. Winthrop D. Jordan, "American Chiaroscuro: The Status and Definition of Mulattoes in the British Colonies," *William and Mary Quarterly* 19, no. 2 (1962): 183–200.

96. Richard S. Dunn, *Sugar and Slaves: The Rise of the Planter Class in English West Indies, 1624–1743* (New York: Norton, 1972), 228.

97. Jordan, "American Chiaroscuro," 183–200.

98. Ibid.

99. Thomas Sowell, "West Indians," in *Ethnic America: A History* (New York: Basic Books, 1981), 216–20.

100. Ibid.

101. Ibid.

102. Nancy Foner, "West Indian Identity in the Diaspora: Comparative and Historical Perspectives," *Latin American Perspectives* 25 (1998): 173–88; Revel

Rogers, "'Black Like Who?' Afro-Caribbean Immigration, African-Americans and the Politics of Group Identity," in *Islands in the City: West Indian Migration to New York*, ed. Nancy Foner (Berkeley: University of California Press, 2001), 169–92; Mary C. Walters, "Growing up West Indian and African-American: Gender and Class Differences in the Second Generation," in *Islands in the City: West Indian Migration to New York*, ed. Nancy Foner (Berkeley: University of California Press, 2001), 193–215; R. Ueda, "West Indians," in *Harvard Encyclopedia of American Ethnic Groups*, ed. Stephan Thernstrom (Cambridge, MA: Harvard University Press, 1980), 1024.

103. Nathan Glazer and Daniel Patrick Moynihan, *Beyond the Melting Pot*, 2nd ed. (Cambridge, MA: MIT Press, 1970), 24–44, 91–122; Florette Henri, *Black Migration: Movement North, 1900–1920* (Garden City, NY: Anchor, 1979), 89–90.

104. Barby, "Blacks Paid Dues for Other Minorities."

105. Howard McGary, *Race and Social Justice* (Malden, MA: Blackwell, 1999), 43–59.

106. Gordon W. Allport, *The Nature of Prejudice* (Reading, MA: Addison-Wesley, 1981), 48–63, 189–204.

107. Brewer and Miller, *Intergroup Relations*, 107.

108. Muzafer Sherif et al., *Intergroup Conflict and Cooperation: The Robbers Cave Experiment* (Middletown, CT: Wesleyan University Press, 1988), 171–76.

109. Studies include: Renee Weber and Jennifer Crocker, "Cognitive Processes in the Revision of Stereotypic Beliefs," *Journal of Personality and Social Psychology* 45, no. 5 (1983): 961–77; Stuart W. Cook, "Experimenting on Social Issues: The Case of School Desegregation," *American Psychologist* 40, no. 4 (1985): 452–60; Patricia W. Linville, Gregory W. Fischer, and Peter Salovey, "Perceived Distributions of the Characteristics of In-Group and Out-Group Members: Empirical Evidence and a Computer Simulation," *Journal of Personality and Social Psychology* 57, no. 2 (1989): 165–88; Mir R. Islam and Miles Hewstone, "Dimensions of Contact as Predictors of Intergroup Anxiety, Perceived Out-Group Variabilty, and Out-Group Attitude: Intergrative Model," *Journal of Personality and Social Psychology* 19, no. 6 (1993): 700–10.

110. Brewer and Miller, *Intergroup Relations*, 107.

111. Ibid., 28–31.

CHAPTER 7

1. John Locke, *An Essay Concerning Human Understanding* (London: Eliz. Holt for Thomas Bassett, 1690), Book 2, Chapter 1.

2. Laura Berk, *Child Development* (New York: Allyn and Bacon, 1994), 25.

3. Dan Olweus, "Familial and Temperamental Determinants of Aggressive Behavior in Adolescent Boys: A Causal Analysis," *Developmental Psychology* 16, no. 6 (1980): 644–60; Dan Olweus, "Aggression and Peer Acceptance in Adolescent Boys: Two Short-Term Longitudinal Studies of Ratings," *Child Development* 48 (1977): 1301–13; Dan Olweus, "Stability of Aggressive Reaction Patterns in Males: A Review," *Psychological Bulletin*, 86 (1979), 852–75; Diana Baumrind, "Child Care Practices Anteceding Three Patterns of Preschool Behavior," *Genetic Psychology Monographs* 76 (1967): 43–83; William McCord, Joan McCord, and Alan Howard, "Famial Correlates of Aggression in Nondelinquent Male Children," *Journal of Abnormal and Social Psychology* 62 (1961): 79–93; R. R. Sears, Eleanor E. Maccoby, and H. Levin, *Patterns of Childrearing* (Evanson, IL: Row, Peterson, 1957).

4. Fred N. Kerlinger, *Behavioral Research: A Conceptual Approach* (New York: Holt, Rinehart, and Winston, 1979), 3–15.

5. Emory S. Bogardus, "Social Distance in the City," *Proceedings and Publications of the American Sociological Society* 20 (1926): 40–46.

6. G. Paschal Zachary, "Tangled Roots: For African Americans the Grass Isn't Always Greener—Seeking the 'Motherland,' They Find Echoes of History and a Chilly Welcome," *Wall Street Journal*, March 14, 2001.

7. Ibid.

8. Ibid.

9. Interview with Indigenous Ghanaian, July 1996.

10. Schaffer, *Social Development*, 213–31.

CHAPTER 8

1. Butcher, *The Negro in American Culture*, 44–45.

2. Howard McGary, *Race and Social Justice* (Malden, MA: Blackwell, 1999), 19–24; June Jordan, *On Call: Political Essays* (Boston: South End, 1985).

3. McGary, *Race and Social Justice*, 20.

4. Butcher, *The Negro in American Culture*, 44–45.

5. Claude McKay, "The White House," in *The Norton Anthology of African American Literature*, ed. Henry Louis Gates Jr. and Nellie Y. McKay (New York: Norton, 1997), 986.

6. Sylvestre C. Watkins, "Anthology of American Negro Literature," in *The Norton Anthology of African American Literature*, ed. Henry Louis Gates Jr. and Nellie Y. McKay (New York: Norton, 1997), xxxv.

7. Henry Louis Gates Jr. and Nellie Y. McKay, eds., *The Norton Anthology of African American Literature* (New York: Norton, 1997), 1–3, 2612–23.

8. Mos Def (artist), "Rock N Roll" (New York: Rawkus Records), released October 1999.

9. Michael A. Omi, "The Changing Meaning of Race," in *America Becoming: Racial Trends and Their Consequences*, ed. Neil J. Smelser, William Julius Wilson, and Faith Mitchell (Washington, DC: National Academy, 2001), 243–63.

10. Stuart W. Cook, "Experimenting on Social Issues: The Case of School Desegregation," *American Psychologist* 40, no. 4 (1985): 452–60.

11. Wayne Weiten, *Psychology: Themes and Variations* (Pacific Grove, CA: Brooks/Cole, 1998), 643–44.

12. Lawrence O. Bobo, "Racial Attitudes and Relations at the Close of the Twentieth Century," in *America Becoming: Racial Trends and Their Consequences*, ed. J. Smelser, William Julius Wilson, and Faith Mitchell (Washington, DC: National Academy Press, 2001), 264–301; Patricia G. Devine, "Stereotypes and Prejudice: Their Automatic and Controlled Components," *Journal of Personality and Social Psychology* 56 (1989), 5–18; Patricia G. Devine and Andrew J. Elliot, "Are Racial Stereotypes Really Fading? The Princeton Trilogy Revisited," *Personality and Social Psychology Bulletin* 21 (1995): 1139–50.

13. Lawrence Bobo and Camille L. Zubrinsky, "Attitudes on Residential Integration: Perceived Status Differences, Mere In-Group Preference, or Racial Prejudice?" *Social Forces* 74, no. 3 (1996): 883–909; Elijah Anderson, *Streetwise: Race, Class, and Change in an Urban Community* (Chicago: University of Chicago Press, 1990); Joe R. Feagin and Melvin P. Sikes, *Living with Racism: The Black Middle Class Experience* (Boston: Beacon).

14. Paul M. Sniderman and Thomas Leonard Piazza, *The Scar of Race* (Cambridge, MA: Harvard University Press, 1993), 12.

15. Paul M. Sniderman and Edward G. Carmines, *Reaching beyond Race* (Cambridge, MA: Harvard University Press, 1997), 59–97; Mary R. Jackman and Mary Scheuer Senter, "Images of Social Groups: Categorical or Qualified?" *Public Opinion Quarterly* 44 (1980): 341–61; Mary R. Jackman and Mary Scheuer Senter, "Different, Therefore Unequal: Beliefs about Trait Differences between Groups of Unequal Status," *Research in Social Stratification and Mobility* 2 (1983): 309–35; Tom W. Smith, *Ethnic Images: General Social Survey, Technical Report, No. 19* (Chicago: National Opinion Research Center, University of Chicago, 1990); Lawrence D. Bobo and James R. Kluegel, "Opposition to Race-Targeting: Self-Interest, Stratification Ideology, or Racial Attitudes?" *American Sociological Review* 58 (1993): 443–64; Lawrence D. Bobo and James R. Kluegel, "Laissez-Faire Racism: The Crystallization of a Kinder,

Gentler, Anti-Black Ideology," in *Racial Attitudes in the 1990s: Continuity and Change*, ed. Steven A. Tuch and Jack Martin (Westport, CT: Praeger, 1997), 5–42.

16. Bobo, "Racial Attitudes and Relations at the Close of the Twentieth Century," 264–301.

17. Christopher B. Doob, *Racism: An American Cauldron* (New York: HarperCollins, 1996), 7–8.

18. "Texaco: Case Study of Corporate Racism," *New York Times*, November 19, 1996.

19. Wilson, *The Truly Disadvantaged*, 12; McGary, *Race and Social Justice*, 17–18.

20. Zack, *Thinking about Race*, 38–45; Omi and Winant, *Racial Formation in the United States*, 69–78.

21. Doob, *Racism*, 7–8.

22. Ibid.

23. Silverstein and Krate, *Children of the Dark Ghetto*, 202–27.

24. Virginia Held, "Reasonable Progress and Self-Respect," *Monist* 57, no. 1 (1973): 1.

25. McGary, *Race and Social Justice*, 130.

26. McGary, *Race and Social Justice*, 19–24.

27. Ibid., 67–78.

28. Ibid., 137–38.

29. Kennedy, *Race, Crime, and the Law*, 29–74.

30. American Civil Liberties Union, "Sanctioned Bias: Racial Profiling Since 9/11," February 26, 2004, 1–16, www.aclu.org; Gene Callahan and William Anderson, "The Roots of Racial Profiling," *Reason* 4 (2001): 36.

31. Ted Sickinger, "American Dream Denied," *Kansas City Star*, February 28, 1999.

32. Gregory Squires, quoted in "Myths and Facts about Affirmative Action," *Washington Post*, August 5, 2001.

33. Butcher, *The Negro in American Culture*, 3.

34. Leon Festinger and James M. Carlsmith, "Cognitive Consequences of Forced Compliance," *Journal of Abnormal and Social Psychology* 58, no. 2 (1959): 203–10.

35. Michael R. Leippe and Donna Eisenstadt, "Generalization of Dissonance Reduction: Decreasing Prejudice through Induced Compliance," *Journal of Personality and Social Psychology* 67, no. 3 (1994): 395–413.

36. Gordon W. Allport, *The Nature of Prejudice*, 142.

37. Butcher, *The Negro in American Culture*, 3.

INDEX

Abbott, Robert S., 183

abolitionist movement, 3, 49–50,
51–53, 55, 105, 126, 127–28, 135,
146

Adams, Abigail, 52

affirmative action, 236, 277–78, 288,
289, 324, 340–41

Africa: African American activism in,
xii, 323–24, 349–50; colonialism
in, 2, 17; ethnic identification in,
14–15, 28, 77, 82; postcolonial
racial politics in, 17; precolonial,
14–15; racial atrocities in, 324;
slaves' cultural foundations in, 38,
40, 42; traditional religions in, 15,
260. *See also* Africans; West Africa

African American Association of
Ghana, 316

African Americans: American
nationality and, 351–52; ancestors
of, 306; artistic expression of,
326, 328–32; associative value of

race for, 83–84, 88–89, 92, 107,
110, 123, 137, 144, 182, 201, 206,
279; in business, 185, 223–24,
245; class differences among,
228, 341; common identity of,
65, 66, 76–78, 85, 92, 94, 97, 98,
100, 102, 105, 107, 119, 123, 127,
129, 130, 137, 167, 178, 182,
186, 191, 217, 218, 222, 236,
237–39, 290; community-building
among, 161, 162, 163, 164, 217;
counter-narratives of, 37, 76,
78, 165, 326; cultural evolution
of, 39–40, 75–86, 99–100, 102,
162–63, 164–66, 185, 245, 262,
274, 325–34; cultural practices of,
327–32; cultural theories about,
196–97; cultural uniqueness of,
xiii, 14, 38, 78, 79, 163, 164, 182,
229, 231, 234, 239, 245, 254–55,
260, 263, 290, 293, 299–300, 317,
322, 323, 326, 327, 333, 350;

Berlin, Ira, 4, 24, 28, 31, 35, 58, 59, 63, 67, 94, 99, 106, 118, 121, 122

Bethune, Mary McCloud, 351

Billingsley, Andrew, 265, 266

Binet, Alfred, 206, 208–9, 250

biology, racial research in, 12

biracial Americans, 275, 276–79

black church, 259–63; in black family life, 264, 265–66, 273; in civil rights movement, 180, 261; development of, 62, 63–64; expansion of, 185; leadership in, 262, 263; practices in, 260; during Reconstruction, 163–66; theology of, 260, 261; traditional values in, 273; *The Black Church in the African American Experience* (Lincoln and Mamiya), 165–66

black codes, 148–49, 158

Black Codes of South Carolina (Myers), 148

black conventions, 149

Black Family in Slavery and Freedom (Gutman), 267

Black Power movement, 169, 235, 238–39

black press, 166–67, 182–83

Black Slave Owners (Koger), 116

Blassingame, John W., 77, 80, 83

Blumenbach, Johann Friedrich, 45, 109

Blyden, Edward W., 14, 107

Boahen, Adu, 15

Boas, Franz, 188, 196, 197, 198, 201, 202, 212

Bogardus, Emory S., 307

Bond, Horace Mann, 191, 215, 216

Bonner, William, 282

Bovell, G. B., 220

Bowlby, John, 274, 275

Boxill, Bernard, 341

Brady, Tom P., 239

Brewer, Marilynn B., 238

Brigham, C. C., 211–12

British colonies: class system in, 3–4, 5, 7, 8, 26, 281, 283, 284; cultural practices in, 282–83; early labor force in, 25, 29–30; emancipation in, 283–84; ethnocentrism in, 26–27, 45–46; interracial relationships in, 47, 281–82; plantations in, 27, 29, 31, 34, 38, 40, 41–42; racial classification in, 2, 3–8, 10, 30, 31–32, 33–34, 35, 36; slavery in, 3–8, 24–50; in West Africa, 305, 311–12. *See also* Chesapeake region; North; South

Brooks, Gwendolyn, 329

Brotherhood of Sleeping Car Porters and Maids, 185, 223

Brown Fellowship Society, 84, 110–11, 131

Brown v. Board of Education (1954), xv, 198, 199, 224–25, 226–27, 230, 235–37, 290, 291, 347

Bruce, Blanche K., 159

Bryan, Andrew, 63

Buffon, Comte de, 109

Bunche, Ralph, 196

Burt, Cyril, 252

Butcher, Margaret Just, 162, 163, 164, 326, 347

Caribbean. *See* West Indians

Carnegie, Andrew, 140

Carnegie Foundation, 196

Carver, George Washington, 351

Census Bureau, U.S., 264

Census of 2000, 349

ABOUT THE AUTHOR

Sherle L. Boone is a professor of psychology in the College of Humanities and Social Sciences at William Paterson University of New Jersey. He has published papers in the areas of human aggression, identity formation in people of African descent, and parenting strategies in African American families. Boone is the founder and president of the W. E. B. Du Bois Scholars Institute, Inc., housed on the campus of Princeton University. He has served on the Mellon Mays University Fellows Dissertation Grants Selection Panel sponsored by The Woodrow Wilson National Fellowship Foundation.